THE AUSTERITY STATE

The fall-out from the economic and financial crisis of 2008 had profound implications for countries across the world, leading different states to determine the best approach to mitigating its effects. In *The Austerity State*, a group of established and emerging scholars tackles the question of why states continue to rely on policies that, on many levels, have failed.

After 2008, austerity policies were implemented in various countries, a fact the contributors link to the persistence of neoliberalism and its accepted wisdoms about crisis management. In the immediate aftermath of the 2008 collapse, governments and central banks appeared to adopt a Keynesian approach to salvaging the global economy. This perception is mistaken, the authors argue. The "austerian" analysis of the crisis is ahistorical and shifts the blame from the under-regulated private sector to public or sovereign debt, for which public authorities are responsible.

The Austerity State provides a critical examination of the accepted discourse around austerity measures and explores the reasons behind its continued prevalence in the world.

STEPHEN MCBRIDE is a professor and Canada Research Chair in Public Policy and Globalization in the Department of Political Science at McMaster University.

BRYAN M. EVANS is a professor in the Department of Politics and Public Administration at Ryerson University.

The Austerity State

EDITED BY STEPHEN MCBRIDE
AND BRYAN M. EVANS

UNIVERSITY OF TORONTO PRESS
Toronto Buffalo London

ISBN 978-1-4875-0236-2 (cloth)   ISBN 978-1-4875-2195-0 (paper)

∞ Printed on acid-free, 100% post-consumer recycled paper with vegetable-based inks.

_____

Library and Archives Canada Cataloguing in Publication

The austerity state / edited by Stephen McBride and Bryan M. Evans.

Includes bibliographical references.
ISBN 978-1-4875-0236-2 (cloth). – ISBN 978-1-4875-2195-0 (paper)

1. Global Financial Crisis, 2008–2009.   2. Neoliberalism.   3. Economic
policy.   I. McBride, Stephen, editor   II. Evans, Bryan M., 1960–, editor

HB3717.2008A97 2017   338.5′42   C2017-903203-8

_____

This book has been published with the help of a grant from the Federation
for the Humanities and Social Sciences, through the Awards to Scholarly
Publications Program, using funds provided by the Social Sciences and
Humanities Research Council of Canada.

University of Toronto Press acknowledges the financial assistance to its
publishing program of the Canada Council for the Arts and the Ontario
Arts Council, an agency of the Government of Ontario.

Canada Council   Conseil des Arts
for the Arts   du Canada

ONTARIO ARTS COUNCIL
CONSEIL DES ARTS DE L'ONTARIO
an Ontario government agency
un organisme du gouvernement de l'Ontario

Funded by the   Financé par le
Government   gouvernement
of Canada   du Canada

Contents

Acknowledgments

The editors gratefully acknowledge funding from the SSHRC Connections Grants program, and the McMaster University Institute for Globalization and the Human Condition (Austerity Research Group), which made it possible to hold a workshop at McMaster University in October 2014. At the workshop, draft versions of these chapters were presented and intensively discussed by workshop participants. Sorin Mitrea and Jacob Muirhead provided invaluable assistance in organizing the workshop. We would like to thank the anonymous reviewers who provided very detailed and helpful comments on the manuscript. We also wish to sincerely thank Daniel Quinlan of the University of Toronto Press for his wise counsel and leadership in guiding this manuscript to publication.

Stephen McBride and Bryan M. Evans

THE AUSTERITY STATE

1 The Austerity State: An Introduction

BRYAN M. EVANS AND STEPHEN MCBRIDE

Neoliberalism remains an apparently intractable part of the political economy of most "mature" capitalist industrial countries, and policies of austerity reflect neoliberal conventional wisdom of how to deal with the economic and financial crisis that began in 2007–8. There was a brief moment, roughly from 2008 to 2010, when governments and central banks appeared to be retrieving the lessons of Keynes to save the global economy from collapse. The contributions to this book, however, take the view that although some economic stimulus was a feature of the early reaction to the crisis, to see those as "Keynesian" was a misinterpretation of events.

In the aftermath of the crisis, some policies were applied that did involve economic stimulus. Whether this adds up to any deviation from neoliberalism in the direction of Keynesianism is much more problematic. The position taken here is that stimulus is not coterminous with Keynesianism (nor, for that matter, is austerity necessarily coterminous with neoliberalism, though in the current context we would argue that it is). So we need to be clear about how we are using these terms.

Elaborating upon the various elements that make up a policy paradigm like Keynesianism or neoliberalism may be helpful, in particular the distinctions made by Hall (1993) between goals, instruments, and settings. The goal of the Keynesian paradigm was for the state to engage in counter-cyclical state action to maintain the economy at full-employment levels. It was a response to events, not an autonomous political decision made by states independent of the times or corporate (and labour) demands.

It could achieve its goal (full employment) by using a variety or a combination of policy instruments. These could include fiscal policy (spending levels, tax levels); monetary policy (interest rates, affecting the price of money; quantitative easing, affecting the quantity of money); and other measures like labour market policy. Depending on the business cycle, the settings of the policies could be expansionary or stimulative to create growth and employment; or restrictive, to rein in growth, inflation, and employment as the economy "overheated." In the latter conditions, austerity measures might be applied. So austerity itself is not outside the Keynesian repertoire.

Neoliberalism's economic policy goal is control of inflation, control of government spending and debt, and reduction in the role of the state, especially its social dimensions. The paradigm might similarly employ a range of instruments. Like Keynesianism, it needs to be located in the particularities of the crisis it responded to and to the configuration of social forces, in which labour's influence progressively weakened. Full employment is not a goal. Rather, unemployment should be allowed to gravitate to its natural level, or to the "non-accelerating rate of unemployment" (NAIRU), i.e., the level of unemployment consistent with stable rates of inflation. Settings on fiscal and monetary policy may often be restrictive to ensure that inflation does not develop beyond the target range. However, if there is a *deflationary* threat, the settings may be adjusted to provide stimulus. So stimulus does not equal Keynesianism and can, in fact, be part of the neoliberal repertoire, as it was in the immediate post-crisis period.

Notwithstanding some ongoing debates about the appropriate degree of stimulus or contraction to be delivered to the economy, as well as some elite attachment to the view that there is no need to choose, since austerity itself could be expansionary (Giavazzi and Pagano 1990), the neoliberal project and its preference for austerity was recast and reinforced. The role of the state in designing and implementing neoliberalism is obvious, given the foregoing. Andrew Gamble was among the first to note the paradox at the heart of what, in the 1970s and into the 1980s, was then called monetarism, and later Thatcherism, was the political construction of the "free economy and the strong state" (Gamble 1979). In other words, it took the authority and power of the state to create the conditions – political, policy, and regulatory – to enable the rollout of free market fundamentalism. In this volume, we refer throughout to the austerity state and neoliberalism in varying contexts, whether together in some manner or as stand-alone terms, which always imply the political and ideological relationship of neoliberalism to the state. And in particular and with concern for some greater specificity, we characterize the state in the wake of the Great Financial Crisis as an austerity state, given that austerity was, and continues in some greater or lesser degree to be, the overarching policy theme focus of governments of the centre-right and centre-left. Austerity policies have simply deepened the objectives of neoliberalism, as defined as a political economic paradigm that favours the market as the most effective means to regulate production and distribution. While it may appear "counter-intuitive" (Konings 2012) to suggest that neoliberalism has resulted in significant concentration of political control within the state to drive regime-change forward, this is precisely the case of neoliberalism currently. Paradoxically it entails simultaneously hollowing out the state (as far as its redistributive and corporatist functions are concerned) and concentration of political power (Bakker 1996; Jessop 2004; Albo 2002). As Albo succinctly puts it, neoliberalism has become "a far broader project of regulating social life through market imperatives, and incorporated within it the Third Way strategies of 'progressive competitiveness' that accepted the parameters imposed by the current distribution of income and assets, and by world markets" (Albo 2008, 356). At its core, neoliberalism is based on principles of competition, laissez-faire, efficiency, productivity, profitability, and individual autonomy (Larner 2000), and most often manifests itself in policy forms such as liberalization, deregulation, and privatization. The state's sole role is concerned primarily with facilitating "conditions for profitable capital accumulation on the part of both domestic and foreign capital" (Harvey 2005, 7). In this sense, the austerity state continues with the policy prescriptions that have characterized government action since the 1980s but importantly, post-2007, have been more aggressively pursued. Neoliberalism and austerity are integrated both theoretically and in political terms.

In this volume, Marjorie Cohen (chapter 4) explores claims of expansionary austerity, with specific reference to expenditures on social reproduction, and Simon Lee (chapter 6) provides a detailed critique of the expansionary fiscal consolidation hypothesis in the UK case. He concludes that far from being expansionary, fiscal consolidation was contractionary. These accounts tend to support Colin Crouch's answer to a question he posed: "What remains of neoliberalism after the financial crisis?" In response to his own question he wrote, "Virtually everything" (Crouch 2011, 179).

However, it will be useful to briefly outline the case that a Keynesian moment existed in 2008–10 and continues to the present in the form of monetary policies known as "quantitative easing," which have a stimulus effect on the economy. Those committed to the idea that economic stimulus represents a Keynesian moment can certainly point to some orthodox examples involving spending, or the electorates' desire for it.

On the latter point, Canadian political parties offering greater spending and less concern with budget deficits won provincial elections in Alberta (2015) and Ontario (2014), and in the federal election of 2015. Anti-austerity parties have experienced unprecedented support electorally, allowing several anti-austerity parties to hold the balance of power in some European parliaments. However, it may be doubted whether electoral preferences have significantly shifted elites' preference for austerity.

Gerard Boychuk (2015) pointed to considerable fiscal stimulus in the United States at the federal level and argued that this continued by stealth after the initial program terminated. Whether this type of stimulus was sufficient to offset the drive to fiscal orthodoxy at the state government level is unclear (Kregel 2011). In the view of Federal Reserve Chair Janet Yellen, "At the federal level, the fiscal stimulus of 2008 and 2009 supported economic output, but the effects of that stimulus faded ... By 2011, federal fiscal policy actions became a drag on output growth when the recovery was still weak" (quoted in Davis 2016). On balance, therefore, there seems little to suggest that the United States was an exception to the prevailing pattern of fiscal austerity in the Western world.

Another argument in favour of the view that Keynesianism has revived might be that monetary policy in the guise of quantitative easing (QE) has been the policy of choice in some countries (the United Kingdom and United States being prime examples) and that this has had major stimulative effects. QE is a form of money creation that consists of the central bank acquiring liabilities (debts) from private banks that then receive equivalent amounts of new money, which, it is assumed, they will lend to investors and thus stimulate the economy. It has attracted support from some Keynesian analysts on the basis that anything that adds to aggregate demand would be beneficial in the current context. Other Keynesians (e.g., Palley 2011) point to QE being based on bidding up asset prices, to the immediate benefit of financial institutions, in the hope that this will "trickle down" to the real economy and stimulate demand. The fact that some countries have relied on monetary stimulus by means of QE, and others have not, does point to a certain variety in crisis responses, just as there were varieties of

Keynesianism (see Esping-Andersen 1990), varieties of capitalism (Hall and Soskice 2003), and varieties of neoliberalism (Macartney 2011).

In the context of QE, Benford et al. (2009, 90) note, with respect to QE in the United Kingdom, that the Bank of England's Monetary Policy Committee "is injecting money into the economy to provide an additional stimulus to nominal spending *in order to meet the inflation target. The conventional way for the MPC to conduct monetary policy is by setting Bank Rate. The introduction of asset purchases has shifted the focus of monetary policy, but the objectives have not changed. The MPC's remit is still to maintain price stability* – defined as an inflation rate of 2% on the CPI measure – and, *subject to that,* to support the Government's economic policy, including its objectives for growth and employment" (emphases added). The article continues: "The inflation target is symmetric. If inflation looks set to rise above target, then the MPC tightens monetary policy to slow spending and reduce inflation. Similarly, if inflation looks set to fall below 2%, the Bank loosens monetary policy to boost spending and inflation." In this case, stimulus is entirely consistent with neoliberal goals. It is not applied to achieve full employment, as would be the case with Keynesian stimulus, but rather to obtain a level of inflation at which unemployment will stabilize at its natural (and non-inflationary) level.

In any case, the stimulative effects may have been exaggerated. In this volume Gary Teeple (chapter 2) contends that QE has functioned to redistribute value to the corporate sector and the rich without producing much stimulus, because there is little incentive for investment in the real economy when demand is sluggish. That situation is exacerbated by austerity policies designed to ensure that state debts are paid for by transfers from working-class people, pensioners, and recipients of social programs who must make do with less. Similarly, John Peters's discussion (chapter 3) makes it clear that monetary measures supporting the financial sector far outweighed stimulative spending on social programs in many countries. But, acting on the supply side, these are hardly Keynesian measures designed to bring about full employment, especially when delivered in a context where any "trickle down" effects are moderated by fiscal restraint and labour market flexibilization.

Arguably, however, the launch of Neoliberalism 2.0 after 2010 ushered in a distinct variant from the neoliberalism of the mid-1970s to 2008, which had begun to demonstrate signs of its unsustainability. The 2008 Great Financial Crisis re-energized the project in providing an unprecedented economic and ideological platform from which to renew the assault on the remaining pillars of the welfare state and further pursue the freedom of capital.

The contemporary expression of austerity is broadly defined as (1) comprising fiscal consolidation, (2) structural reforms of the public sector, and (3) flexibilization of labour markets. This is the default policy response for most states and international organizations. Fiscal consolidation means giving priority to achieving state budget balance within a reasonable period and reducing public debt as a percentage of GDP. The favoured instrument for this is reduced spending by the state, a vehicle that in practice targets social assistance and is consistent with austerity's underlying goal of reducing or eliminating the socially progressive redistributive role the state had assumed in the post-war period. Structural reforms include further flexibilization of the labour force and public sector restructuring to achieve "efficiency" as defined in New Public Management doctrines, through such instruments as privatizing public services, reducing public subsidies, reforming disability and illness insurance, extending the period of working life before pensions can be accessed, reducing employment benefits, and ending short-work-time programs.

The contributions presented in this volume take the political and policy response to the 2008 Great Financial Crisis as their point of departure. What has been observed since 2008 is the launch of a new austerity phase in the history of the neoliberal project. The new austerity builds upon deep roots within neoliberalism and earlier phases of liberalism, and a number of contributions emphasize that the current turn to austerity can be understood only in historical perspective.

Most contributions address the ideational rationale for austerity measures but, finding it unconvincing as an overarching explanation, also attempt to identify the particular alignment of class and other political forces enabling austerity, and the role that these measures play in the evolution of the neoliberal global economy. Despite the still common framing of neoliberalism as anti-state fundamentalism, what is made evident through this collection is the central role of the state in constructing austerity. This represents a critical paradox within the neoliberal project, both ideologically and in policy terms. While neoliberalism often is cast as a project concerned with shrinking the role of the state, this requires greater nuance. Indeed the authority and capacity of the state in particular spheres is central to the design, implementation, and reproduction of neoliberalism with (as several contributions note) profoundly undemocratic implications. However, the state retains its liberal democratic shell, and this requires the ability to construct viable electoral coalitions to win elections, and may constrain how far and fast the project proceeds. It is reminiscent of Gramsci's oft-quoted characterization of the rise of fascism, where "the crisis consists precisely in the fact that the old is dying and the new cannot be born; in this interregnum a great variety of morbid symptoms appear." In this context, the state is a critical site of contestation for political and economic power; this is true of state power at the national level and in its emerging supranational forms as, for example, with the European Union. Contributions here are concerned specifically with the role of the state as a site not only of struggle in the liberal democratic context, but also of challenges of a more radical nature.

Within this context, three related themes weave through the contributions presented in this volume.

First, the structural roots of austerity – in the political demands of capital and business for a strong but limited state – centred upon dismantling the post-war labour-capital compromises. Strategies and tactics are rolled out to achieve this goal, including fiscal rules giving priority to constraining public expenditures through balanced budget orthodoxy, by lowering the acceptable level of public debt, and – in a strategy to "starve the beast" and eviscerate the state's fiscal capacity to improve or establish new public services – by reducing state revenues by cutting taxes and eliminating progressivity. Beyond fiscal conservatism, other interventions seek to lower the cost of labour both in the private and public sectors through policies that flexibilize the labour force by disempowering unions (unions being cast as "labour market rigidities") and deregulating the labour market. This, in essence, translates into reducing labour standards, health and safety protections, and business liability for environmental damage and consumer protection. The dominant defence is that the level of public debt, excessive expenditures, and uncompetitive domestic economies (in other words, labour is too expensive) have forced austerity upon us. TINA ("There Is No Alternative," as Mrs Thatcher famously put it) has been reanimated for the twenty-first century. But the reality is that expanding inequality is a consequence of deliberate state policies that accelerate polarization.

All of this ran, and continues to run, against the necessity to give priority to full employment and redistribution. The unrelenting expansion of market income inequality witnessed over the past three decades has become so uncomfortably problematic that Thomas Piketty's *Capital in the Twenty-First Century* (2014) became the subject of front-page mainstream media discussion and commentary. Oddly, examining inequality has become fashionable after decades of neglect by opinion leaders. There is no "invisible hand" at work here, but rather business enterprises have rapidly expanded their use of low-waged work and non-standard employment arrangements as a matter of business strategy. And in the aftermath of the financial crisis, the policy response of the state was not to address the social crisis but rather to stabilize the financial sector. In the EU, state-led support for the financial sector was estimated at 37 per cent of EU GDP. As policy is about choice, the policy decision to substantially lessen support for employment during this crisis sharply expresses the balance of forces, class, and otherwise in play (see Peters, Wilks, chapters 3 and 13).

As such, the ahistoric framing of "the public debt made me do it" does not stand up to scrutiny. In the United Kingdom, the current austerity regime is the legacy of the public (and private) debt accumulated through four decades of constructing the "neoliberal developmental market." The previous Coalition Government drew on the narrative of an "unavoidable deficit reduction plan" as the only strategy to restore fiscal balance and market-led growth. This obfuscates the fact that there would never have been a British Empire had such orthodoxy ruled the Treasury in centuries past (see Lee, chapter 6). And the pre-crisis celebrity of Ireland as a model of neoliberal development, despite recurring policy failure, can be attributed to a deeply embedded and institutionalized commitment to "sound money" and austerity through the Irish state, which runs through the history of the republic (see O'Rourke and Hogan, chapter 7). But the political strategy throughout is to employ the state and its array of institutions to deliberately navigate the shifting terrain of class and other social forces to the advantage of capital. In the period of the 2008 crisis, the goal was to transform private liabilities into state debt (see Teeple, chapter 2), a manoeuvre that established the political foundation from which to launch the next phase of neoliberal state building.

A second theme is concerned with the reconfiguration of the state. There is a certain iterative relationship to the foregoing theme, in that structural roots of austerity inform the reconfiguration of the state just as the reconfiguration of the state informs the structuration of austerity. Taken as a whole, the focus is on the internal processes of neoliberalization within the state itself, which are first transforming the redistributional post-war Keynesian welfare state by eroding redistributional policies and allied capacity, but second strengthening its capacities and roles concerned with capital accumulation, competitiveness, and coercion. The state may be crucial in managing the turn to austerity but is itself being transformed by the processes it is initiating and supervising. In essence, this commodification of the state, expressed though privatization, marketization, and corporatization, solidifies the ongoing neoliberal paradigm of governance and state transformation. This type of state presides over a particular type of society – one characterized by inequality and the assertion of the interests of private business, finance, and capital generally at the expense of other social actors. In this situation, the interests of capital lie in acquiring state assets, colonizing the public sector in pursuit of profit-making opportunities, and ensuring the state can service or pay the public debt. A number of chapters deal with the reconfiguration of the state and its relations with capital. Its fiscal capacity is undermined by (1) its tolerance of tax evasion; (2) its ability to manage or monitor outsourced provision of public services compromised by its own cutbacks to the public service; (3) its ideological disempowerment through acceptance of notions that public is always less efficient than private; (4) its future capacity limited and a need for future austerity embedded through long-range contracts associated with P3s; and (5) innovations in the financing of program delivery provide new space for profit.

Meanwhile, the state plays an active role in ideologically legitimizing the contentious politics of austerity. The adage "Never let a crisis go to waste" seems applicable here. The crisis has created opportunities for capital to profit as states restructure and reduce public expenditure through privatization, outsourcing, and infrastructure "partnerships." The crucial point of these strategies, however, is more than simply cost reduction; rather it involves deep structural and institutional transformation in the role of the state and its relationship to capital. Despite an appearance of sometimes being imposed from outside, it is clear that austerity has deep domestic roots in elite attitudes and interests. Within the state, key sites of policy framing, occupied by market fundamentalists, work as the ideational agents constructing the policy parameters of what is acceptable in policy terms and what is filtered out. Indeed, the very structure of the policy advisory system within the state has become exceptionally closed to contestation in any form, leading some to point not just to policy failures but even to the prospect of failing or failed states (see Evans, Wilks, chapters 10 and 13).

The reconfiguration of the state has significant implications for democracy. One of the most effective strategies employed is that of

constitutionalization. This does not refer to the sovereign legal codifi-
cation of fundamental principles of governance in a document, though
the effect may not be that different; it instead refers to a process where
critical powers are situated in agreements and/or institutions far
removed from popular and government influence, and perhaps not
even under observation. And the rules flowing from these processes
are the vehicles for neoliberal policy preferences and serve to block any
future change as a result of a change in a government. This set of policy
outcomes – irrespective of changes in governing party, electoral coalition or public opinion – become "locked in" and become what amounts
to an ideological gene sequence (see McBride, chapter 8). The embedding of neoliberalism within the structures of the state is reinforced by
the critical role of economists in the policy process and the policy process architecture of the neoliberal state, which differs significantly from
the one that prevailed through the Keynesian era. These features serve
to insulate the state from alternative, non-neoliberal policy ideas that
are effectively crowded out by the architecture of the neoliberal state
(see Evans, chapter 10). For example, Canada's commitment to expansionary austerity as state policy can be traced back to the mid-1990s
when cuts to social spending were the deepest in the nation's history.
Since the 1990s, Canada's social expenditure as a percentage of GDP
has stagnated, and even regressed slightly. In the face of modest social
expenditure growth in other OECD countries, Canada has fallen from
close to the average, to well behind it in the last twenty-five years. The
result is that the pace of growing income inequality has quickened. This
fact alone disputes the argument that expansionary austerity leads to
growth or, if it does, the benefits are not particularly well distributed. In
the Canadian case, the general conclusion is that expansionary austerity does not work (see Cohen, chapter 4).

   The ideational contest is further constrained and homogenized
through the role of influential neoliberal think tanks whose purpose is
to manufacture the evidence and arguments advocating for one policy
prescription over another. The case of the European Monetary Union in
the 2008 crisis offers a case study in both the homogenization of options
and big arguments over technical, as opposed to ideological, differences. Those differences are amplified by differing political objectives
of distinct ruling-class fractions (see Plehwe, chapter 9). Moreover, the
applied policy and program delivery outcomes emerging from the neoliberalized state reflect the hegemonic status that "zombie" ideas have
achieved within the state apparatus. The ascent of finance capital and

the resulting financialization of all that exists further demand a reconsideration of approaches to policy design and implementation across a spectrum of policy sectors as well as for public administration itself. As a case in point, a public services industry has emerged, constructed through an alliance of party-political and corporate elites who see the public sector as a new site from which to extract profits by outsourcing what were previously public sector functions carried out "in-house" by public servants (see Wilks, chapter 13). This entrepreneurship is further expressed in a variety of policy innovations that reflect the primacy of markets and business values and practices. The advent of Social Impact Bonds dramatically illustrate the marketization of social policy where private investment is pooled to finance social service projects with the objective of returning a profit to those investors where identified project objectives are met (see Joy and Shields, chapter 14). The private financing of public infrastructure through public-private partnerships (referred to as Public-Private Partnerships or P3s in Canada; Public Finance Initiative [PFI] in the United Kingdom) is one strategy that conforms to austerity and is consistent with the logic of financialization. Through this financing mechanism, necessary infrastructure – whether roads, bridges, public transit, hospital buildings, maritime ports, or airports, etc. – are constructed without recourse to public funds. P3 financing converts public infrastructure into a monetized asset, one where private investors can expect a return on investment over time.

This presents an additional instrument to the austerity toolkit. To the usual methods of public expenditure cuts, marketization, and privatization of state assets and programs can now be added a for-profit revenue-generating instrument linked to global capital markets (see Whiteside, chapter 12). Thus public infrastructure assets are sold, revenue streams are monetized, and profits accumulate to private investors. Given the strategic and long-term importance of such assets, the risk to private investors is minimal, as governments will ensure completion of projects regardless of the challenges and crises that inevitably emerge. While not a component of the state directly, tax havens are both creatures of the state policy that allows them to exist and, perhaps more counterintuitively, a means to advance neoliberal economic policy. Following the 2008 crisis, a tax justice movement emerged to regulate tax havens and ensure that the wealthy could not evade taxation while mere mortal citizens were loaded with additional taxes combined with social program cuts. Campaigns for tax justice represent if not an alternative to austerity then at the very least a perspective that its cost should and can be shared more equitably. However, the efforts of G20 and OECD states to act on tax havens have yielded few tangible results. Ultimately, tax havens manage austerity in several valuable ways. First, tax havens provide pools of investment capital that can be injected into P3/PFI projects. Second, as a source of loan capital, given the shrinking availability of credit. And third, by providing a shield for foreign investors in the host country (see Woodward, chapter 11).

The reconfiguration of the state is derivative from the structural roots of neoliberalism and hence austerity in the current context but, further, the reconfigured state leads in establishing the structural reality that further deepens the ideational, political, and institutional logic of austerity.

The third theme, concerned with the limited availability of alternative policy options to austerity, is addressed in several contributions. It is not that there are no alternatives to austerity but rather a variety of structural, ideational, and institutional arrangements that block these alternatives from reaching the policy agenda or from being taken seriously. Consequently, existing austerity policies are unchallenged in any meaningful way and thus enjoy hegemonic status.

Paradoxically, because of their failure to address deep structural problems, austerity policies, in conjunction with their apparent unassailability, are likely to lead to more crises or increased economic volatility. The instrumental and authoritarian aspects of neoliberalism expressed here inform an increasingly anti-democratic tendency within the state and the broader society (see Peters, McBride, and Wilks, chapters 3, 8, and 13). The automatic stabilizers of the Keynesian era, even though subject to erosion during the neoliberal period, were able, even in 2008, to mitigate the effects of recession. Under austerity they are being further diminished (see Cohen, chapter 4). In Europe, mildly reformist proposals, representing a pragmatic austerity alternative to the harder-line version, are dismissed by the European Commission and central bank (see Plehwe, chapter 9). Instead, efforts are underway to constitutionalize not just fiscal consolidation, but the other components of austerity as well – structural reform of the public sector and flexibilization of labour markets (see Peters, Cohen, and McBride, chapters 3, 4, and 8). The effect is to further restrict the democratic space for contestation. This can be seen in the variety of coercive policy instruments, including balanced budget and expenditure control legislation, the central bank policy of privileging of inflation control, and, in the case of the EU, monetary and fiscal policy instruments that are increasingly triggered automatically rather than at the discretion of a national government (see McBride, chapter 8). Whether these automatic mechanisms are capable of stabilizing the system in the manner of their Keynesian predecessors is open to question.

The immense weight of this regime in ideological, theoretical, and institutional terms feeds a general internalization of the values, insights, and understandings at a popular and cultural level. It is not simply institutions that have been reconstructed but also political culture. Through these processes, austerity becomes "common sense," as even contemplating a different reality becomes inconceivable (see McBride and Mitrea, chapter 5).

The book is organized into two distinct sections. Section 1 addresses how states have responded to the 2008 crisis and contribute to our understanding of austerity policy construction; section 2 deals with how the state has been reconfigured through the interaction between states and mechanisms of global governance. Opening section 1, Gary Teeple (chapter 2) points out the temporary and contingent nature of the Keynesian post-war compromise that brought to the working classes of the industrial nations an unprecedented high standard of living, largely disguising the underlying class conflict. In the 1970s, the contradictions in Keynesianism and liberal democracy between the demands of workers and capital accumulation surfaced in the form of economic stagnation. This was addressed by a shift away from Keynesianism to the adoption of neoliberal policies, reflecting new conditions underlying capital accumulation. Decades of retrenchment and economic crises followed, culminating in near financial collapse in 2007–8. To confront the changing conditions that had brought global capital to this point, the industrial states introduced austerity policies, accelerating neoliberalism and the use of the national debt to shift wealth from the working class to the corporate sector. Teeple argues that the world's working classes now confront global corporate monopolies, cartels, and statelike institutions, and yet are defined by national labour laws and institutions, near-powerless states, global labour markets, declining union density, and stagnant or falling wages.

Chapter 3 by John Peters explores the politics of inequality in five North American and Western European countries after the Financial Crisis of 2008–9. Comparing financial policies to job and income-related programs in Canada, the United States, and a number of leading Western European economies, the argument is made that governments affected the distribution of market income in immediate and substantial ways. The central argument advanced is that global and domestic power imbalances between corporate interests and those of other organized groups explain these outcomes.

Chapter 4, from Marjorie Griffin Cohen, contends that austerity is related to a profound shift in government policy, from a sense that economic crises should be prevented, to one where crisis containment after the fact is the focus. This shift is closely aligned with austerity measures in government institutions of social reproduction, particularly those that have had counter-cyclical effects in the past.

Stephen McBride and Sorin Mitrea's chapter 5 examines how people have coped with state sponsored precarity as part of their daily lives. The post–Global Financial Crisis period witnessed a devolution of social support to the individual, lower labour costs, and entrenchment of austere policies. They argue that this strategy has been partially accepted or, as they put it, "internalized" by the strata targeted by the austerity measures. Starting with state policies to restructure the labour market, the chapter explores the argument that the material realities ("precarity") that result from austerity (flexibilization, outsourcing, privatization, concentration of wealth, inequality) create *necessary conditions* for acceptance of those very policies. The result is a "common sense" enabling the legitimation of austerity. The result is the declining role of institutions of social reproduction as automatic stabilizers.

Simon Lee, in chapter 6, analyses how the Cameron-Clegg Coalition Government used the financial crisis of 2007–8 as justification for its austerity program. Lee's analysis effectively explains how this is a flawed strategy that has been implemented by a failed and failing British state. The chapter demonstrates that the neoliberal developmental market has created Generation Debt by shifting public debt, accumulated over forty years of neoliberalism, onto individuals and households. The narrative that there is a crisis in state finance is found to be historically unsound. A key theme through modern British history is the use of public debt to finance state development projects, whether military adventures or the National Health Service.

Chapter 7 moves to the Republic of Ireland, where Brendan O'Rourke and John Hogan show that Irish "successes" with austerity are marginal and marginalizing. Taking a historical perspective, the chapter situates austerity in Irish elite thinking and traces this from the 1921 conservative revolution's inheritance of the British pre-Keynesian Treasury model, through to the 2008 crisis and beyond. An examination of Ireland's "expansionary fiscal contraction" of the 1980s demonstrates that the claim that austerity succeeds is fragile. The impacts of the current crisis on Ireland and the elite's adoption of austerity measures are appraised.

Section 2 is composed of contributions that illuminate how the state has been reconfigured in the construction and implantation of austerity and neoliberalism more broadly, and how attempts at global governance are implicated in these processes. Chapter 8 by Stephen McBride sets the political context. This chapter posits that the persistence with which austerity policies have been pursued when they clearly fail to achieve their stated objectives presents a public policy puzzle. Rather than prompting a reconsideration of the policy, there is a clear trend to render austerity a permanent, constitutionalized response to economic challenges "for all seasons." The chapter links the drive to austerity within the "new constitutionalism" literature, which depicts procedurally the removal of important decisions from the realm of liberal democratic politics and their relocation behind impenetrable and unaccountable barriers; and, in terms of content, which embed neoliberal practices and policies, and the power relations that underpin them, as "normal."

The role of think tanks in shaping the debate is taken up in chapter 9, where Dieter Plehwe analyses the debate following the proposal that Eurobonds be employed to end speculation against national bonds issued by indebted European countries. By linking the ideas and arguments advanced for and against Eurobonds to relevant constituencies, different discourse coalitions become visible. Interestingly, these are not identical with European party alliances. At the same time, the major coalitions in favour of and against Eurobonds turn out to be not quite as different as presented.

Chapter 10 by Bryan Evans illustrates how neoliberal ideas and those associated with austerity go unchallenged within the policy advisory system of the state. What makes this more perplexing is that the 2008 crisis did nothing to expand the cracks in the edifice of neoliberalism. This neoliberal resiliency is explained here as a function of how ideas are linked to state structures through policy actors, the privileging of certain ideas as common sense, and specifically in this regard the role of economists and the power of scientization of economics as a body of "expert" knowledge. And ultimately, the architecture of the neoliberal state apparatus restricts who and what is "heard."

Richard Woodward in chapter 11 situates tax havens as critical instruments in the age of austerity. The G20's pledge to "end the era of banking secrecy" prompted excited talk of the "end of offshore" tax havens. Unfortunately this is at odds with the empirical evidence that offshore finance centres continue to thrive in the era of austerity. Instead, the flourishing of offshore tax havens was necessitated by demands for states, international financial institutions, and corporate actors to develop instruments to manage the instabilities and contradictions intrinsic to the neoliberal economic project. Although many leading actors have made a rhetorical commitment to a clampdown, the reality, it is argued here, is that offshore financial instruments are central to the delivery of the austerity policies. In this regard, it is worth pointing out that even if states (individually and collectively) became less tolerant of outright tax evasion, they are still willing to tolerate (and indeed encourage) tax avoidance, especially by corporate actors whom they systematically incorporate into their decision-making processes.

With chapter 12, Heather Whiteside links the fiscal austerity in the 1980s and 1990s with significant underfunding of infrastructure development and maintenance, leaving all manner of public works in need of substantial (re)development. The return of austerity post-2008, Whiteside explains, leads to the financialization of public infrastructure: budgetary crises in some jurisdictions are being addressed not only through cuts to expenditures but also through generating revenue by opening up public infrastructure to private investment. The chapter, in this context, examines how, why, and to what effect public sector budgetary pressures are being framed as opportunities to profit from austerity.

Stephen Wilks follows with chapter 13, in which he traces the emergence of a New Corporate State since the 1990s. He discerns a secular trend in anglophone countries where the transfer of public services to the private sector has taken place. This trend has been intensified by austerity, with the result that a qualitative change in the nature of the state is underway. The consequent shrinking of government and the implications of this are the focus here. Specifically, the chapter charts the reciprocal creation and growth of a private, for-profit "public services industry." Implications include (1) a reinvention of the civil service where responsibility for policymaking is transferred to the private sector; and (2) the development of a distinct industrial sector, dependent on government but politically powerful and integrated into a corporate elite as a key component of the New Corporate State.

In chapter 14, Meghan Joy and John Shields examine how neoliberalism seeks to marketize the non-profit sector. The sector performs a key role in austerity rhetoric in the wake of the 2008 crisis, which blends neoliberalism and philanthropic localism. Innovations in social financing have created an opportunity for the private market to profit from those whom the market had previously left behind. One of these new tools, Social Impact Bonds (SIBs), was developed to pool private investment to support social service projects with the attendant promise of a profit. SIBs provide a case study here of the marketization of the non-profit sector in an austerity context and outline the challenges and contradictions that this new policy tool poses.

The volume concludes with a chapter by McBride and Evans summing up the main findings and reviewing interpretations of austerity's apparent intractability.

The central preoccupation of this volume is the role of the state. Taken together, the contributions address the puzzle of continued reliance on policies that, at many levels, have failed miserably. The power structure supporting austerity has been sketched and presents a daunting, though perhaps not impregnable prospect to those who reject austerity's assumptions and practices. But there is obviously more to the picture. The conclusion makes connections to our companion volume, *Austerity: The Lived Experience*, that develops greater consideration of the impact of state policies on populations by concentrating on the lived experience of austerity. There, we examine theories and illustrations of how austerity is articulated and becomes accepted/internalized in subject populations. This involves discussion of the ways austerity is framed to draw upon deeper moral economies and concepts, with the effect that consent (even if disaffected consent) is obtained. That book also addresses in some detail and with reference to particular groups the consequences of austerity, and explores the nature and prospects of resistance to it.

REFERENCES

Albo, G. 2002. "Neoliberalism, the State, and the Left: A Canadian
    Perspective." *Monthly Review (New York)* 54 (1): 46–55. http://dx.doi.org/
    10.14452/MR-054-01-2002-05_4.
– 2008. "Neoliberalism and the Discontented." *The Socialist Register: Global
    Flashpoints*. Pontypool: Merlin.
Bakker, I. 1996. *Rethinking Restructuring: Gender and Changes in Canada*.
    Toronto: University of Toronto Press.

Benford, James, Stuart Berry, Kalin Nikolov, Chris Young, and Mark Robson. 2009. *Quantitative Easing*. Bank of England Quarterly Bulletin.

Boychuk, Gerard W. 2015. "'US Incremental Social Policy: Expansionism' Response to Crisis." In *After 08: Social Policy and the Global Financial Crisis*, ed. Stephen McBride, Rianne Mahon, and Gerard W. Boychuk, 292–312. Vancouver: UBC Press.

Crouch, Colin. 2011. *The Strange Non-Death of Neoliberalism*. Cambridge: Policy.

Davis, Owen. 2016. "State of the Union 2016: A Closer Look at Obama's Economy." IBT, 12 January. http://www.ibtimes.com/state-union-2016-closer-look-obamas-economy-2262164.

Esping-Andersen, G. 1990. *The Three Worlds of Welfare Capitalism*. Princeton: Princeton University Press.

Gamble, Andrew. 1979. "The Free Economy and the Strong State: The Rise of the Social Market Economy." *Socialist Register* 16:1–25.

Giavazzi, Francesco, and Marco Pagano. 1990. "Can Severe Fiscal Contractions Be Expansionary? Tales of Two Small European Countries." Working Paper 3372, National Bureau of Economic Research. http://www.nber.org/papers/w3372.

Hall, P. 1993. "Policy Paradigms, Social Learning and the State: The Case of Economic Policy-making in Britain." *Comparative Politics* 25 (3): 275–96. http://dx.doi.org/10.2307/422246.

Hall, P., and D. Soskice. 2003. *Varieties of Capitalism: The Institutional Foundations of Comparative Advantage*. Oxford: Oxford University Press.

Harvey, D. 2005. *A Brief History of Neoliberalism*. New York: Oxford University Press.

Jessop, B. 2004. "Hollowing Out the 'Nation-State' and Multi-Level Governance." In *A Handbook of Comparative Social Policy*, ed. P. Kennett, 11–25. Northampton, MA: Edward Elgar Publishing. http://dx.doi.org/10.4337/9781845421588.00010.

Konings, Martijn. 2012. "Neoliberalism and the State." In *Neoliberalism: Beyond the Free Market*, ed. Damien Cahill, Lindy Edwards and Frank Stilwell, eds., 54–66. Cheltenham, UK: Edward Elgar.

Kregel, Jan. 2011. "Resolving the US Financial Crisis: Politics Dominates Economics in the New Political Economy." *PSL Quarterly Review* 65:23–37.

Larner, W. 2000. "Neo-liberalism: Policy, Ideology, Governmentality." *Studies in Political Economy* 63 (1): 5–25. http://dx.doi.org/10.1080/19187033.2000.11675231.

Macartney, H. 2011. *Variegated Neoliberalism: EU Varieties of Capitalism and International Political Economy*. London: Routledge.

Palley, Thomas. 2011. "Quantitative Easing: A Keynesian Critique." Working Paper 252. University of Massachusetts Amherst Political Economy Research Institute. https://www.peri.umass.edu/media/k2/attachments/WP252.pdf.

Piketty, Thomas. 2014. *Capital in the Twenty-First Century*. Cambridge, MA: Belknap.

SECTION 1

State Responses to Crisis

2 Austerity Policies: From the Keynesian to the Corporate Welfare State

GARY TEEPLE

The financial crisis of 2007/9 jeopardized the entire global credit system that underlies capitalist production and distribution. At the height of the crisis, the very corporations that had caused it, being central to the system, were able to demand solutions that provided guarantees against their insolvency. Among other actions, they had their debts "nationalized" by means of massive bailouts (Baker 2014), and then "quantitative easing" was provided (Palley 2011) to ensure the viability of credit and prevent systemic collapse.

As the crisis unfolded, more than fifteen national governments assumed some or all of the assets of failed banks or otherwise provided support for their faltering, not to mention corrupt and bankrupted, financial institutions in order to forestall a breakdown, and in the process greatly expanded their public debts (Laeven and Valencia 2012). The actual cause of the debts was obscured by suggestions that the state, and by implication the public, was living beyond its means because debt servicing began to take a larger and growing share of revenues. Greece was used as a frequent example, adding widespread corruption by officials and tax avoidance to the list of causes, feeding the moralism of the German position, and so helping to divide the European working classes. In the Greek case, the "odious" debts (Adams 1991) and fraudulent accounting of a corrupt elite and questionable activities by Goldman Sachs were rarely raised as explanations (Hartmann and Sacks 2012; Bloomberg Business 2012). The real origin of the rising debt – the bailout of the financial institutions that were at once the cause of the crisis and yet central to the system ("too big to fail") – was largely ignored.

The increased state debts required lenders, and here many of the same financial corporations that were being bailed out stepped in to purchase the growing debt; the corporate debtors were becoming the creditors to their state lenders. As the ratio of national debt to GDP rose, reducing the credit-worthiness of the state, questions about the ability to repay also grew. To guarantee their loans, the corporate lenders demanded '"austerity," threatening higher interest rates or restrictions to future purchases of debt if governments did not act (Wolff 2010, 2013).

Austerity policies, then, were introduced and promoted throughout Europe and North America to address rising national budget deficits and debts. They amounted to a mix of state spending cuts in salaries, staff, pensions, and services – including reductions in health care, education, and unemployment insurance – and further restructuring of the labour market to increase "flexibility." They also included tax breaks for the rich and tax hikes for the rest (Johnson 2003), more deregulation, and privatization of state corporations.

Such policies were paraded as an act of necessity to save the system from growing indebtedness, and as means to facilitate needed economic growth by the private sector. And they came with their own academic rationales to justify the cutting of the budgets: one argued that a debt of more than 90 per cent of GDP would stall growth (Reinhardt and Rogoff 2010); another reasoned that spending cuts would likely result in expansion rather than contraction (Alesina et al. 2002; Alesina and Ardanga 2009); and yet another stated that every dollar of government spending "corresponded" to a dollar less of private spending (Cochrane 2009). The perennial idea of tax cuts was also reasserted, as if thirty years of evidence that cutting taxes led to falling revenues and higher deficits were non-existent. All these theories were taken seriously and widely used to validate the budget cuts.

Before long, these academic justifications were exposed as based on faulty research, or mistaken reasoning contradicting even standard textbook economics, i.e., spending cuts during recessions lower an already low aggregate demand. Cursory examination of trends in national debts, moreover, suggested that some had actually been declining before the crisis, and where not, it was largely because of cuts to corporate tax revenue (Krugman 2013, 15; Cassidy 2012; Wolf 2013).

Numerous studies and reports, moreover, began to appear pointing to the negative impacts of austerity policies (Callinicos 2012; Boyer 2012; Whitfield 2014; Stuckler and Basu 2013). In the social domain, they documented declining mental and physical health, growing poverty, and rising rates of alcoholism and suicide; in the political sphere, they lamented eroding state power over policy and falling popular legitimacy; and in the economic arena, they noted stagnant or falling economic growth and wage rates, and increasing numbers of precarious jobs, unemployed, and underemployed. The policies were largely an acceleration of the decades-long dismantling of the post-war compromise between labour and capital, with the added measure of using state debt to subsidize the corporate sector directly and indirectly. Nowhere, however, did the promised return to economic growth materialize; the results have been the opposite of the claims (Fanelli et al. 2010; Blyth 2013). Yet governments continued to carry on with more of the same.

To condemn or lament these policies, or to show how mistaken or ineffectual they have been, or even to offer viable alternatives within the system is, to be sure, part of their critique, but these positions imply that austerity policies are reversible products of liberal democratic politics. And this is to miss the point, as we will argue. If we take our cues from numerous commentators (Radice 2011; Pirsch 2011; Rich 2011), austerity policies are the product of class war, albeit a battle waged largely through legislation via liberal democratic legislatures, and thus disguised as democratic measures. The events leading to the crisis of 2007–8 point to a losing battle for the working classes that will not likely be reversed in the near future. Preceding the crash, there were almost three decades of neoliberal policies systematically retrenching every aspect of the Keynesian welfare state that represented the countervailing rights benefiting the working class and largely won through struggle at a time when they were financially possible and necessary to forestall significant class conflict. Austerity policies have carried this legislative war a step further by accelerating the previous policies and increasing the use of the national debt as a means of shifting wealth from the working class to the corporate sector and the rich (Lahart 2014; Magdoff and Foster 2014; Akerlof et al. 1993).

The war was also advanced through the use and misuse of legal measures. The crisis was partly a product of lax government oversight, overlooked criminality, and unregulated over-extension of financial operations by corporations (Lewis 2010) for which the corporations and their principals, with minor exceptions, were not prosecuted (Garrett 2014). It has been argued that they structured their "products" with the knowledge of the moral hazard entailed, in that they would not bear the consequences of their dealings and, given their size and centrality in the system, would be able to demand state assistance in the event of failure, spreading the results of their illegal actions over the whole of society (Baker 2014). Indeed, their prosecution was very limited, the state support extensive, and abrogation of rule of law self-evident (*Huffington Post* 2013; Will, Handelman, and Brotherton 2013).

No Return

Despite the well-documented negative effects on the well-being of the working class, on economic growth, and on political legitimacy (Whitfield 2014; Stuckler and Basu 2013), there has been little respite from the promulgation and application of austerity policies. The explanation lies largely in the nature of the times; these policies are the only acceptable alternative currently available, given the prevailing structure of capital (Johnson 2009; Lynn 2010) and the working classes. Although the use of state debt and increased taxes has led some to suggest that they represented the return of Keynesian policies, nothing could have been further from the intent of austerity. Keynesianism was possible in the post-war period because of the particular historical juncture that included the memory of the Depression and the sacrifices of war, decolonization or opening global markets, post-war reconstruction, the threats of "actually existing" socialism, a Fordist mode of production, persistent economic growth and expanding markets, continuing high labour demand, and national policies within national boundaries. The use of the redistributive powers of government to produce the welfare state rested on the combination of these elements that marked the period. By the 1970s, however, they were all coming to an end, and with them, Keynesianism. The post-war era was a historical moment of extensive economic growth with complex preconditions that made the welfare state possible; it was not a set of political policies arising merely from political decisions.

In the early 1980s, the introduction of neoliberal policies in the forms of Thatcherism and Reaganism reflected the corporate reaction to the economic stagnation, which was produced by the growing realization of the contradiction in the Keynesian welfare state between social reforms and economic growth brought on by the coming of new economic and political conditions. For the next roughly three decades, these policies incrementally but systematically retrenched the programs and institutions that comprised the welfare state and labour rights, in concert with the changing conditions and the progressive decline of the organized working class and transformation of its political representation. Despite working-class militancy and radicalism, union leaders and social democratic political parties remained committed to Keynesianism and class compromise that were increasingly impossible goals, given the changing conditions, making them unwittingly a factor in the disempowering of the working class.

At the same time, neoliberal policies progressively opened new possibilities for capital accumulation, consistent with changes in the economy that had already begun to take shape in the 1970s. These changes were harbingers of a new stage in the development of capitalism that would transform the forces of production and distribution, political and economic jurisdictions, the labour market, the nature of occupations, and the role of the state. Capital in the late twentieth century and early twenty-first century present us with a new set of conditions that no longer provides the necessity or possibility of an extensive welfare state.

Central to these changes, and what makes the 1970s the decisive decade for these changes, was the *invention of the computer chip* and its rapid application in production and distribution. This was the beginning of the end of Fordism and precipitated a rapid and continuous increase in the organic composition of capital, leading to the invention and application of industrial robots even before the end of that decade. Hereafter, economic growth, if defined as simply increased productivity and output, would no longer create a corresponding demand for labour, as in the past. The ensuing decades began to see a secular rise in chronic un- and under-employment, partly explained by computerization, with a growth in aggregate consumer demand resting increasingly on rising personal debt; but there would be no prospect of a return to levels of employment or wages of the post-war era.

Computer-based technological changes accelerated *the growth of globalization* by making all facets of economic activity cheaper and faster. The progressive expansion of production, distribution, and accumulation at regional and global levels was already evident in the post-war rapprochement decided at Breton Woods, which established a key set of global economic institutions to oversee the development of transnational corporations (TNCs). This enabling framework – the International Monetary Fund (IMF), World Bank, and later the General Agreement on Tariffs and Trade (GATT) – gradually expanded policies and oversight at global and regional levels, correspondingly usurping national economic control. With new technological developments in the 1970s, the TNCs grew rapidly in the 1980s, transforming into monopolies, oligopolies, cartels, etc., at the global level (Foster, McChesney, and Jonna 2011; Vitali, Glattfelder, and Battiston 2011). As they expanded, along with the power and reach of the global frameworks, so too did "investor-state" policies that gave a legal right to corporations to challenge the right of governments to set policy and determine their own priorities (Sinclair 2015; ISDS n.d.). Globalization brought a shift in the role of the state, decreasing national political powers and eroding the integrity of national economies.

An important part of corporate globalization was the rise of *the global labour market*. The promotion of free trade zones in the 1960s expanded into whole regions, and then gradually entire countries such as China began to open their economies to foreign capital in approximately 1979. When the whole of the Soviet Bloc finally fell by 1991, the world had nearly doubled its labour force available to capital (Freeman 2005). With persisting displacement of peasant labour in China, India, and throughout the underdeveloped world, the growth of the global labour force continues, as does its availability, given neoliberal policies. Taking advantage, manufacturing corporations in the industrial nations began in the 1980s to "off-shore" and "out-source" their operations in search of lower costs and non-union labour. This movement of global labour arbitrage led to a measured decline in well-paying (and unionized) jobs, the heart of what was dubbed the "middle class" – referring merely to a standard of material life based on high wages and salaries, in turn based on unequal national trade relations. By the 1990s, the decline of manufacturing jobs and high wages led to enduring high rates of unemployment, underemployment, declining union density, and rising consumer debt in the industrial nations. The "real economy," i.e., the production of value largely in manufactured goods in the industrial nations, was contracting, producing a secular fall in consumer demand, except where supported by the expansion of credit, lower taxes, and increased state welfare expenditures. But demand based on these factors has its limits, and significant implications. Chief among these is the slow decline in consumer demand, particularly evident in the United States, the world's largest economy, for which the main driver of growth is consumer demand. The historic basis of this demand was the "real economy," which has been in decline with little prospect of reversal because of corporate access to the global labour market and computer-aided manufacturing and distribution.

The shift of the capitalist mode of production away from Fordism and a national base was accompanied by another major change – *financialization*. After the war, there was a vast increase in international trade that led to a growing commensurate accumulation of capital at the global level (Cypher 1979, 514). Enormous sums of state-mobilized capital for reconstruction, furthermore, were made available by the United States and later by the European states themselves (Milward 2006; Hogan 1987). These state-leveraged funds – raised through deficit financing – increased taxes, and resulting debased money soon added to the capital that was surplus to productive investment. To these funds were added the overseas spending by the United States for the Korean and Vietnam wars and its European military bases, recycled petro-dollars, the stolen assets of Third World elites, and illicit funds from corporations, state officials, and criminal networks (Naylor 1994). The end of the US dollar gold convertibility and fixed exchange rates in 1971 and 1973 (respectively), moreover, produced a rapid growth in the foreign-exchange markets, facilitating the use of more capital for speculative ventures.

These were the main sources of what came to be called "Eurocurrency" – not referring to the "euro," but instead referring to funds effectively freed from national jurisdiction and regulation, largely beyond the control of central banks or other regulatory bodies. Such was the beginning of financialization, the growth of money capital at the global level with declining prospects for productive investment. This caused banks to turn to credit, speculation, brokerage, arbitraging, hedge funds, etc., not to mention the creation of "new products," like "credit default swaps," and complex forms of securitization. The "casino economy" was taking form (Costello and Michie 1989).

A large new means for accumulation as *centralization* had opened up in the form of speculative capital flows, traded by a large number of banks with global networks (Pardee 1987). The growing size and influence of this independent money capital was now a reality without any obvious barriers to its continued expansion, other than the persistence of national regulations, which it actively strove to abolish.

Financialization, then, points to changes in a pattern of accumulation with roots in the immediate post-war era but growing rapidly in the 1980s. Although the "real" or value-producing sectors of the economy still provide the source of the majority of profits, financialization signals a marked reallocation of the use of capital: to facilitate its expansion as a mechanism to make profits in the sphere of circulation and to enrich its managers. It marks a shift in sources of profits from the sphere of value creation to operations of value centralization. To emphasize the point, there is little production of surplus value in this process, but rather it is a centralization of the surplus value created in the production process or found in pools of existing funds (Johnson 2009).

Accumulation in this manner adds enormously to the growing inequality of wealth by enriching the managers of these vast funds of "freed" capital. The irony in this is that they are no longer predominantly privately owned, but rather accumulations of socialized capital composed of stocks, bonds, pension funds, sovereign wealth funds, state, corporation, and individual debt, embezzled national funds, and other forms of illicit money from many sources. The rich and corporate managers employ forms of socialized capital to enrich themselves further.

By the 1980s, the global economy had considerable money capital surplus to profitable investments in the sphere of production. So began the more or less rapid movement of money capital into every aspect of economic life, fuelling speculative possibilities and coming to prevail over the whole of the system (Dunbar 2011, xi, xii). Striving to find new means to extract surplus or capitalize other forms of wealth or redistribute existing assets, this money capital also pointed to the end of national capital markets and to many aspects of national policy that constrained its operations (Eatwell and Taylor 2000, 2). The Eurocurrency system and international branch banking, for example, undermined national counter-inflation policies by creating a chronic global oversupply of money. National economic and social planning and policies, moreover, were thwarted by these large volumes of "denationalized" capital that could be moved more or less at will, and by unregulated international credit. In order to offset falling profits, furthermore, these available funds were invested in speculative ventures and in large loans to Third World nations, increasing their debt loads and helping to cripple their development by siphoning off their surpluses and existing wealth (Buckley 2002/3). Currency crises increased because exchange rates became determined by shifts in this speculative money capital and by the inadequacy or absence of regulatory mechanisms (Eatwell and Taylor 2000, xi). With global finance able to destabilize national economies, governments were obliged to begin to act in ways to guarantee the confidence of the "investors," and liberal democracy increasingly began to appear an empty exercise, recognized implicitly in declining voter turnouts around the world.

This transformative shift in the capitalist mode of production rested on the expanding interrelations of computer-based technology, globalization of markets and policies, and the rising pre-eminence of vast amounts of unregulated global money capital with ever fewer places to invest productively. Global capital challenged the integrity of national economies, and global labour markets undermined the Keynesian welfare state, which was predicated on the high wages that included a "social wage" for redistribution in national labour markets. By the late 1980s, Fordism and its policy counterpart, Keynesianism, appeared increasingly like vestiges of the past. A "new reality" had opened for the working class, which now found itself encumbered with union leaders and social democratic political parties stuck in the mindset of the post-war era.

Why Austerity after the Crisis of 2007–2009?

The trends outlined above underlay the crisis, while the questionable and criminal activities behind money capital provided the immediate cause. But given that money capital was central to the economy and held sway over state debts, and that global regulation was weak and without enforcement mechanisms, there was little possibility that capital formations at the global level could be restructured or re-regulated. Instead, we find state promulgation of austerity policies that explicitly involved a massive shift of wealth from the public to the private sector in order to save global financial corporations from themselves. The crisis presented an opportune moment to accelerate the process of dismantling the Keynesian welfare state and increasing the opportunities for accumulation.

But this new emphasis was not accumulation or economic growth in the usual sense. Growth as the increase in the value of goods and services continued to be the measure of economic well-being. But now, "growth" as centralization, which has always been a part of the expansion of capital, began to play an increasingly large role. In a world characterized by computer-aided production and distribution and dominated by money capital, "accumulation" was increasingly taking form as the redistribution of existing wealth. This was the key to understanding financialization and the essence of austerity policies.

In the past, despite periodic crises, there was always secular economic growth that produced an increased demand for labour, albeit in new spheres and with different skills. This continued to be the case as long as changes in the mode of production produced a corresponding need for more labour. After the 1970s, increased economic output became possible in all sectors without the previous concomitant increase in demand for labour.

Predicated on a computer-aided mode of production and corresponding new forms of economic-political jurisdictions, economic growth produced relatively less new value and so capital had to find other means of augmentation. "Growth" as redistribution was to become one of the few options, and it took many forms. State regulations over corporations, for example, were scaled back, allowing for massive new "externalities," i.e., the shifting of costs and risks away from the corporate sector onto society in general and nature. Offsetting the costs of transforming nature into capital by means of environmental destruction has brought us to the point of a "metabolic rift" between nature and humans (Foster, Clark, and York 2010). Already in the 1980s, a United Nations report could refer to the irreversible destruction of the environment due to corporate activities (Brundtland 1987). Privatization of the public sector, another form of redistribution, often amounted to giveaways and opened enormous opportunities for private accumulation from what were once public enterprises operating for public interest and benefit (Hagen and Halvorsen 2009). Corporate tax concessions of all sorts added to the systematic and ongoing reduction of state activities, outsourcing them for the benefit of capital (Ascher 1987). Governments also tolerated the rise of tax havens and low-tax jurisdictions, creating significant loss of state revenues but gains for the rich and corporate sector (Deneault 2011; Shaxson 2010; Hampton and Abbott 1999). Mergers and acquisitions, once characteristic of recessions and crises, now became a constant feature of the global economy, increasing the assets and power of the TNCs, shifting wealth upwards within the corporate sector, and concentrating power in ever fewer offices (Gaughan 2015). While capital has always grown by various forms of dispossession of existing wealth, new avenues now opened up with respect to the working classes as pensions were looted (Sirota 2013; Heyes 2014), wages stolen (Meixell and Eisenbrey 2014), and labour standards retrenched (Panitch and Swartz 2003). With fewer opportunities to invest in the "real" economy, the systematic creation of "bubbles" grew (Taibbi 2009; Baker 2009; Brenner 2003; Briys and Varenne 2000), as did much more speculation in stock markets and the invention of questionable new financial "products" (Briys et al. 1998).

Following the bailouts and "quantitative easing" in the aftermath of the 2007–8 crisis, governments were "encouraged" to adopt "austerity" programs, an expansion of the preceding decades of neoliberal policies, in order to guarantee these debts by retrenching working-class rights, reducing pensions and saved assets, and disregarding unpaid wages. When these policies, along with record low interest rates, failed to stimulate economic growth, governments returned to "quantitative easing." This amounted to central banks buying the financial instruments of private financial corporations, mainly bonds and mortgages, thereby increasing their liquid capital in the hope of promoting lending and so economic growth. The theory was that more and cheaper money for corporations would encourage investment, thereby reversing economic stagnation (Magdoff and Foster 2014). But this became economic "growth" in the form of "growth" as central bank bailouts with a form of fiat money that distributed value to the large corporations and the rich, not growth as value added in the "real economy."

The idea that more liquidity in the corporate sector and greater state debt would result in economic stimulus for the productive sector is difficult to grasp when the cause of the crisis was not about credit shortfall but about vast amounts of money capital surplus to the needs of the productive sector searching for profits in the sphere of circulation. More money would simply add to the liquid reserves of the financial institutions and fuel the "casino economy." It was already known that the Bank of Japan had tried this approach to stimulate its stagnant economy for years, long prior to the crisis of 2007/9, and it had not worked (OECD 2007).

The use of "quantitative easing" to stimulate the economy, as widely admitted (Allen 2015), does not work, and it does not because there is little incentive to invest in the "real economy" with relatively sluggish aggregate demand. There is sufficient supply or even surpluses in every sector of the global economy with current levels of demand. The recent rise of the "sharing economy" points to a vast oversupply on the consumption side, implying much "unused capacity" in housing, transportation, food, clothing, etc. In addition, in many industrial countries, individual debt is already high and growing, and real wages are stagnant or falling, making it increasingly difficult to borrow or repay. Much of the corporate sector is already highly leveraged or sitting on large money hoards with little need to invest productively (Isfeld 2014; Kiladze 2011). These central bank purchases ("quantitative easing") are simply forms of increasing money supply that can do little else than increase the degree of wealth inequality without much impact on new value or job creation. This is the conclusion drawn by many, including some in the Bank of England (White 2012; Elliott 2012). And near-zero interest rate policies have simply allowed the corporate sector and rich to borrow cheap money for speculative purposes, while working-class savings and pensions stagnate. In short, if "quantitative easing" and near-zero interest rates do not work as intended, it points to a poverty of economic policies for a system with nowhere to go, except to promote "growth" as redistribution, i.e., to shift wealth by means of state debt and low interest rates, from the working class to the corporate sector and the rich – redistribution as growth for some and contraction for others. If neoliberal policies were designed to "give back" to the corporate sector the socialized state capital and retrench the "costly" rights the working class had gained after the Second World War, they were relatively successful in shifting social wealth upwards (Glyn 2006; Diwan 2006; Guscina 2006; Russell and Dufour 2007), but they were not policies that were sufficient to address the new dilemmas of the twenty-first century. Now, the computer-based mode of production is able to produce a surfeit of everything, but with decreasing numbers of workers and relatively less new value. Global labour arbitraging, furthermore, progressively undermines the organized power of the working classes, by increasing the global reserve army of labour and intensifying the contradiction between national labour legislation and a global labour market. Falling union density and wage stagnation contribute to the secular lowering of consumer demand. And the national state, whose historical role was to serve the interests of national capital, is now increasingly obliged to be the instrument of corporate demands at the national and global levels (Nichols and McChesney 2013; Wolin 2008). It has sought to privatize all the forms of capital not yet in private hands, not to mention "outsourcing" the public service, and to deregulate their operations and retrench the rights of workers as costs to the corporate sector. And it turned, moreover, to an increased use of public debt.

Before the 1980s, public debt was usually incurred to mobilize capital, usually for the private sector, to promote "nation-building" – infrastructure, colonization, military operations, bailouts, etc. – or for public debt-servicing, as was the case in the formation of Canada as a confederation of deeply indebted provinces (Smiley 1963). The use of "odious" debts also has a long history (Adams 1991; Jayachandran and Kremer 2006) as a means of transferring capital from the public to private sectors. By the 1980s, the public debt had become a major instrument of the IMF and World Bank for plundering the so-called Third World (Buckley 2011); these institutions, along with other financial agencies, have continued to employ them as powerful mechanisms for such transfers. As a condition for loans to stem a financial crisis, these institutions oblige the state to borrow funds that are transferred to the corporations that were responsible for the crisis. The working classes, unable to protect their assets from taxation, end up paying for these new debts in the form of higher taxes, reduced pensions, lowered wages, higher unemployment, fewer benefits, decaying infrastructure, and cutbacks to health care and education (Buckley 2002/3). Considerable corporate debt, in this way, is turned into a state debt, or private liabilities are made public ones, or corporations have their debts "nationalized" and the working classes are forced to pay in one way or another. A profound redistribution of wealth takes place; the Keynesian welfare state is gradually replaced with a corporate welfare state. Keynesian policies, increasingly corporate-centric in the name of "austerity," redistribute assets and revenues from the working classes to the corporate sectors and the rich (Baker 2006).

If Keynesian policies had to be introduced to save capitalism from a critically conscious working class during and after the war, neoliberal policies had to be pursued in the 1980s to save capitalism from the success of Keynesianism that contributed to stalled economic growth in the 1970s. By the early twenty-first century, austerity policies had to be adopted to save capitalism from its excesses under neoliberalism by further impoverishing the working classes.

For now, the working classes have little ability to resist; they suffer handicaps on all sides. They confront global corporations and global labour markets, while their actions and organizations are defined by national or local legislation. Their formal political representatives seem transfixed by social democratic ideologies from the twentieth century, policies framed by specific historical conditions and past modes of production that no longer obtain and will not return. Union leadership seems similarly wedded to such policies and to past political victories and is uncertain about how to organize in the "new economy" marked by "precarious" work (Standing 2014). Liberal democracy has become a living example of "institutional lag" (Veblen 1961) – the form remains but the original content is disappearing. Political policies are increasingly defined by and for the benefit of global corporations, in part taking the form of transnational trade agreements that allow for corporations to override political policies generated at any level of government, and to sue national states where state policies infringe on real or imagined returns on investment (Stiglitz 2014; Sinclair 2015).

Without the economic and political conditions that made the postwar welfare state possible and necessary, and faced with declining prospects for global economic growth, governments in the industrial world will have to push forward with austerity and other authoritarian policies. "Permanent austerity" is high on their political agendas as a means of advancing accumulation as redistribution. This predicament, coupled with an increasingly plundered working class, also makes pervasive and permanent war one of the few options left for the future of capital, creating another rationale for austerity.

REFERENCES

Adams, P. 1991. *Odious Debts: Loose Lending, Corruption, and the Third World's Environmental Legacy*. London: Earthscan/Probe International.
Akerlof, G.A., P.M. Romer, R.E. Hall, and N.G. Mankiw. 1993. "Looting: The Economic Underworld of Bankruptcy for Profit." *Brookings Papers on Economic Activity*. Cambridge: National Bureau of Economic Research.
Alesina, A., and S. Ardanga. 2009. "Large Changes in Fiscal Policy: Taxes versus Spending." NBER Working Paper no. 15438. http://dx.doi.org/10.3386/w15438.
Alesina, A., Silvia Ardagna, Roberto Perotti, and Fabio Schiantarelli. 2002. "Fiscal Policy, Profits, and Investment." *American Economic Review* 92 (3): 571–89. http://dx.doi.org/10.1257/00028280260136255.
Allen, K. 2015. "Quantitative Easing around the World: Lessons from Japan, UK and the US." *Guardian*, 22 January.
Ascher, K. 1987. *The Politics of Privatisation: Contracting Out of Public Services*. London: Macmillan. http://dx.doi.org/10.1007/978-1-349-18622-8.
Baker, D. 2006. *The Conservative Nanny State: How the Wealthy Use the Government to Stay Rich and Get Richer*. Center for Economic and Policy Research. http://cepr.net/documents/cns_policies_2006_07.pdf.
– 2009. *Plunder and Blunder: The Rise and Fall of the Bubble Economy*. Sausalito, CA: PoliPoint.
– 2014. "The Myth That Sold the Financial Bailout." OurFuture.org, 17 September. http://ourfuture.org/20140917/the-myth-that-sold-the-financial-bailout.
Bloomberg Business. 2012. "Goldman Secret Greece Loan Shows Two Sinners as Client Unravels." *Bloomberg Business*, 5 March.
Blyth, Mark. 2013. *Austerity: The history of a Dangerous Idea*. Oxford: Oxford University Press.
Boyer, Robert. 2012. "The Four Fallacies of Contemporary Austerity Policies: The Lost Keynesian Legacy." *Cambridge Journal of Economics* 36 (1): 283–312. http://dx.doi.org/10.1093/cje/ber037.
Brenner, Robert. 2003. *The Boom and the Bubble: The US in the World Economy*. London: Verso.

Briys, Eric, Mondher Bellalah, Huu Minh Mai, and François de Varenne. 1998. *Options, Futures, and Exotic Derivatives: Theory, Applications and Practice.* New York: Wiley.

Briys, Eric, and Francois de Varenne. 2000. *The Fisherman and the Rhinoceros: How International Finance Shapes Everyday Life.* New York: Wiley.

Brundtland, Gro. 1987. *Our Common Future: World Commission on Environment and Development.* New York: Oxford University Press.

Buckley, Ross P. 2002/3. "The Rich Borrow and the Poor Repay." *World Policy Journal* 19, no. 4.

– 2011. *From Crisis to Crisis: The Global Financial System and Regulatory Failure.* Frederick: Aspen Publishers: Kluwer Law and Business.

Callinicos, Alex. 2012. "Contradictions of Austerity." *Cambridge Journal of Economics* 36 (1): 65–77. http://dx.doi.org/10.1093/cje/ber026.

Cassidy, John. 2012. "It's Official: Austerity Economics Doesn't Work." *New Yorker*, 6 December.

Cochrane, John. 2009. "'Fiscal Stimulus, Fiscal Inflation, or Fiscal Fallacies?'" 27 February. http://faculty.chicagobooth.edu/john.cochrane/research/Papers/fiscal2.htm.

Costello, Nicholas, and Jonathan Michie. 1989. *Beyond the Casino Economy: Planning for the 1990s.* London: Verso.

Cypher, J.M. 1979. "The Transnational Challenge to the Corporate State." *Journal of Economic Issues* 13 (2): 513–42. http://dx.doi.org/10.1080/00213624.1979.11503657.

Deneault, Alain. 2011. *Offshore: Tax Havens and the Rule of Global Crime.* New York: New.

Diwan, I. 2006. *Debt as Sweat: Labor, Financial Crises, and the Globalization of Capital.* Washington, DC: World Bank.

Dunbar, Nicolas. 2011. *The Devil's Derivatives.* Boston: Harvard Business Review.

Eatwell, J., and L. Taylor. 2000. *Global Finance at Risk: The Case for International Regulation.* New York: New.

Elliott, Larry. 2012. "Britain's Richest 5% Gained Most from 'Quantitative Easing' – Bank of England." *Guardian*, 23 August.

Fanelli, Carlo C. Hurl, P. Lefebvre, and G. Ozcan, eds. 2010. *Saving Global Capitalism: Interrogating Austerity and Working Class Responses to Crises, Alternate Routes.* Ottawa: Red Quill Books.

Foster, John Bellamy, Brett Clark, and Richard York. 2010. *The Ecological Rift: Capitalism's War on the Earth.* New York: Monthly Review.

Foster, John Bellamy, Robert W. McChesney, and R. Jamil Jonna. 2011. "Monopoly and Competition in Twenty-First Century Capitalism." *Monthly Review* 62 (11): 1–39. http://dx.doi.org/10.14452/MR-062-11-2011-04_1.

Freeman, Richard. 2005. "China, India and the Doubling of the Global Labor Force: Who Pays the Price of Globalization?" *Globalist*, 3 June.

Garrett, B.L. 2014. *Too Big to Jail: How Prosecutors Compromise the Corporations.* Cambridge, MA: Harvard University Press. http://dx.doi.org/10.4159/9780674735712.

Gaughan, Patrick A. 2015. *Mergers, Acquisitions, and Corporate Restructurings.* http://www.productmanualguide.com/acquisitions/mergers-acquisitions-and-corporate-restructurings.html.

Glyn, A. 2006. *Capitalism Unleashed.* Oxford: Oxford University Press.

Guscina, A. 2006. "Effects of Globalization on Labor's Share of National Income." IMF Working Paper 06/294. Washington, DC: International Monetary Fund.

Hagen, Ingrid, and Thea Halvorsen, eds. 2009. *Global Privatization and Its Impact.* New York: Nova Science Publishers.

Hampton, Mark, and Jason P. Abbott, eds. 1999. *Offshore Finance Centres and Tax Havens: The Rise of Global Capital.* Basingstoke, UK: Macmillan. http://dx.doi.org/10.1007/978-1-349-14752-6.

Hartmann, T., and S. Sacks. 2012. "Goldman Sachs' Global Coup d'Etat." *Daily Take*, 27 November.

Heyes, J.D. 2014. "The Mass Looting of Pension Plans Begins as Federal Law Altered to Reduce Pension Payouts." *Global Research*, 17 December. http://www.globalresearch.ca/the-mass-looting-of-pension-plans-begins-as-federal-law-altered-to-reduce-pension-payouts/5420343.

Hogan, M.J. 1987. *The Marshall Plan: America, Britain, and the Reconstruction of Western Europe, 1947–1952.* Cambridge: Cambridge University Press. http://dx.doi.org/10.1017/CBO9780511583728.

Huffington Post. 2013. "Michael Lewis: Authorities' Response to the Financial Crisis 'Bizarre.'" 8 March.

International Trade Union Confederation (ITUC). 2014. *ITUC Global Rights Index: The World's Worst Countries for Workers.* http://www.ituc-csi.org/IMG/pdf/survey_ra_2014_eng_v2.pdf.

Investor-State Dispute Settlement (ISDS). n.d. "Case Studies: Investor-State Attacks on Public Interest Policies." http://www.citizen.org/documents/egregious-investor-state-attacks-case-studies.pdf.

Isfeld, Gordon. 2014. "Canadian Corporate Cash Hoard Rises to $610 Billion in First Quarter." *Financial Post*, 19 June.

Jayachandran, Seema, and Michael Kremer. 2006. "Odious Debt." *American Economic Review* 96 (1): 82–92. http://dx.doi.org/10.1257/000282806776157696.

Johnson, David Cay. 2003. *Perfectly Legal: The Covert Campaign to Rig Our Tax System to Benefit the Super Rich – and Cheat Everybody Else.* New York: Portfolio.

Johnson, S. 2009. "The Quiet Coup." *Atlantic*, May. http://www.theatlantic. com/magazine/archive/2009/05/the-quiet-coup/307364/.

Kiladze, Tim. 2011. "Corporate Cash Hoard in the Trillions: Moody's." *Globe and Mail*, 27 July.

Krugman, P. 2013. "How the Case for Austerity Has Crumbled." *New York Review of Books*, June.

Laeven, L., and F. Valencia. 2012. "Systematic Banking Crises Database: An Update." IMF Working Paper WP/12/163. Washington, DC: IMF.

Lahart, J. 2014. "The Next Problem: Too Much Profit." *Wall Street Journal*, 27 March.

Lewis, Michael. 2010. *The Big Short: Inside the Doomsday Machine*. New York: Allen Lane.

Lynn, Barry. 2010. *Cornered: The New Monopoly Capitalism and the Economics of Destruction*. Hoboken, NJ: John Wiley and Sons.

Magdoff, F., and J.B. Foster. 2014. "Stagnation and Financialization." *Monthly Review* 66 (1). http://dx.doi.org/10.14452/MR-066-01-2014-05_1.

Meixell, Brady, and Ross Eisenbrey. 2014. "An Epidemic of Wage Theft Is Costing Workers Hundreds of Millions of Dollars a Year." Economic Policy Institute, Issue Brief #385. http://www.epi.org/publication/epidemic-wage-theft-costing-workers-hundreds/.

Milward, A.S. 2006. *The Reconstruction of Western Europe 1945–51*. Berkeley: University of California Press.

Naylor, R.T. 2004. *Hot Money and the Politics of Debt*. Montreal and Kingston: McGill-Queen's University Press.

Nicholas, Shaxson. 2012. *Treasure Islands: Uncovering the Damage of Offshore Banking and Tax Havens*. London: Vintage Books.

Nichols, John, and Robert W. McChesney. 2013. *Dollarocracy*. New York: Nation Books.

OECD. 2007. "Employment Outlook 2007: How Does Japan Compare?" http://www.oecd.org/employment/emp/38797332.pdf.

Palley, Thomas I. 2011. "Quantitative Easing: A Keynesian Critique." *Investigacion Economica* 70 (277): 69–86.

Panitch, Leo, and D. Swartz. 2003. *From Consent to Coercion: The Assault on Trade Union Freedoms*. Aurora: Garamond.

Pardee, S.E. 1987. "Internationalization of Financial Markets." *Economic Review*, February, 3–7.

Pirsch, Michael. 2011. "Class Warfare, the Final Chapter." Truthout. http://truth-out.org/archive/component/k2/item/94744:class-warfare-the-final-chapter.

Radice, Hugo. 2011. "Cutting Government Deficits: Economic Science or Class War?" *Capital and Class* 35 (1): 125–37. http://dx.doi.org/10.1177/0309816810389593.

Reinhardt, C., and K. Rogoff. 2010. "Growth in a Time of Debt, National Bureau of Economic Research," Working paper 15639. Cambridge, MA.

Rich, Frank. 2011. "The Class War Has Begun." *New York Magazine*, 28 October. https://aidsoversixty.wordpress.com/2011/10/28/frank-rich-new-york-magazine-the-class-war-has-begun/.

Russell, E., and M. Dufour. 2007. "Rising Profit Shares, Falling Wage Shares." Canadian Centre for Policy Alternatives. https://www.policyalternatives. ca/publications/reports/rising-profit-shares-falling-wage-shares.

Seymour, Richard. 2014. *Against Austerity*. London: Pluto.

Shaxson, N. 2012. *Treasure Islands: Tax Havens and the Men Who Stole the World*. London: Vintage Books.

Sinclair, Scott. 2015. *Democracy under Challenge: Canada and Two Decades of NAFTA's Investor-State Dispute Settlement Mechanism*. Canadian Centre for Policy Alternatives.

Sirota, David. 2013. "The Plot against Pensions." Institute for America's Future. http://ourfuture.org/wp-content/uploads/2013/09/Plot-Against-Pensions-final.pdf.

Smiley, Donald, ed. 1963. *Royal Commission Report on Dominion-Provincial Relations*. Toronto: McClelland and Stewart.

Standing, Guy. 2014. *The Precariat: The New Dangerous Class*. London: Bloomsbury.

Stuckler, D., and S. Basu. 2013. *The Body Economic: Why Austerity Kills*. New York: Basic Books.

Stiglitz, Joseph E. 2014. "On the Wrong Side of Globalization." *New York Times*, 15 March.

Taibbi, Matt. 2009. "The Great American Bubble Machine." *Rolling Stone*, 9 July.

Veblen, Thorstein. 1961. *The Place of Science in Modern Civilization*. New York: Russell & Russell.

Vitali, S., J.B. Glattfelder, and S. Battiston. 2011. "The Network of Global Corporate Control." PLOS. http://arxiv.org/PS_cache/arxiv/pdf/1107/1107.5728v2.pdf http://dx.doi.org/10.1371/journal.pone.0025995.

White, William R. 2012. "Ultra Easy Monetary Policy and the Law of Unintended Consequences." Federal Reserve Bank of Dallas, Globalization and Monetary Policy Institute, Working Paper no. 126. http://www.dallasfed.org/assets/documents/institute/wpapers/2012/0126.pdf.

Whitfield, D. 2014. *Unmasking Austerity: Lessons for Australia*. Adelaide: Australian Workplace Innovation and Social Research Centre, in association with ESSU, University of Adelaide.

Will, Susan, Stephen Handelman, and David C. Brotherton, eds. 2013. *How They Got Away with It: White Collar Criminal and the Financial Meltdown*. New York: Columbia University Press.

Wolf, Martin. 2013. "How Austerity Has Failed." *New York Review of Books*, July, 13.

Wolff, Richard. 2010. "Austerity: Why and for Whom?" In These Times, 15 July. http://inthesetimes.com/article/6232/austerity_why_and_for_whom/.

– 2013. "Austerity: Another 'Policy Mistake' Again." Truthout, 8 March. http://www.truth-out.org/opinion/item/14917-austerity-another-policy-mistake-again.

Wolin, Sheldon S. 2008. *Democracy Incorporated: Managed Democracy and the Specter of Inverted Totalitarianism*. Princeton: Princeton University Press.

3 Post-Democracy and the Politics of Inequality: Explaining Policy Responses to the Financial Crisis and the Great Recession

JOHN PETERS

Theoretically, democracy offers citizens opportunities to participate in shaping the agenda of public life, and ensures that public policies provide accountability and fairness in the distribution of adequate jobs and disposable income. But over the past three decades, not only have the economic forces of globalization created widening inequalities, but many governments have appeared to slip under the control of powerful economic interests far more hostile to regulation, taxes, and the mixed economy than in the post-war era, and retreated from efforts to improve income redistribution and jobs. In the wake of the Financial Crisis (2008–9), these trends have often worsened.

Despite unprecedented bailouts of financial institutions and wide public debate on the failures of market economies, governments in Canada and other rich world democracies returned to the neoliberal policy models that prompted many of the key problems that caused the crisis – tax cuts and deregulation, '"flexibility" policies that lowered labour costs and aggregate demand, and limited regulation of the financial sector. Then, contrary to popular demands for redistribution and employment, public officials began to advance policies for an even "leaner" and less interventionist state, implementing a series of austerity policies that included reductions in public employment and cutbacks to services. To many commentators, such as the Nobel Prize–winning economists Joseph Stiglitz and Jeffrey Sachs, such developments have shown that there are very real limits to the extent to which inequality can be eliminated or improved in rich world democracies (Sachs 2012; Stiglitz 2010).

Understanding why such persistent inequalities remain and why government responses to rising inequality have been inadequate is now at the heart of a number of academic, policy, and political debates on income inequality. This chapter draws on the recent work of Colin Crouch about "post-democracy" to explore the politics of inequality in North America and Western Europe after the Financial Crisis of 2008–9. Comparing tax and credit policies to job- and income-related programs, as well as to labour market deregulation policies, the argument is made that governments affected the distribution of market income in immediate and substantial ways. On the one hand, policymakers provided massive bank bailouts and aid to the financial sector in order to uphold global financialization and the upward distribution of income, as well as upheld favourable tax policies for business and liberalized capital and credit markets. On the other, government officials backed corporate plans for wage and job concessions while forwarding efforts at labour market deregulation and the erosion of employment protection. On the basis of literature exploring the dynamics of "post-democracy" in advanced industrial countries, the chapter claims that global and domestic power imbalances between corporate interests and those of other organized groups explain these outcomes.

Governments, it is argued, gave primacy to the goal of improving the business environment because powerful economic interests were able to influence policy and because public officials had a structural dependence on the business and financial community for economic success. By contrast, unions and labour market "outsiders" (immigrants, the unskilled, and the precariously employed) bore the brunt of the economic downturn, and had little effect on policymaking. This response was in line with earlier developments over the past three decades, where governments forwarded neoliberal policies that restructured markets and labour management relations in ways that created new profit opportunities for capital.

Beginning in the 1970s – in reaction to economic slowdowns, external challenges, and the globalization of business and finance – governments consistently introduced a number of pro-business neoliberal reforms. These included states acting forcefully to make their labour markets more competitive. They also included public officials deregulating finance and institutionalizing free trade and international investment agreements in order to stimulate macroeconomic demand and improve the global business environment for multinational corporations and finance. Across advanced industrial countries, such changes to policy were introduced incrementally or were enacted in a more sweeping fashion in response to economic shocks.

Since the Financial Crisis, national policymakers have reacted to the latest economic downturn in a more comprehensive fashion to re-establish the conditions for business growth and profitability by advancing policy models of public sector austerity and structural labour market reform. Such policy measures, the chapter concludes, far from questioning finance and neoliberal policy models, have done much to reinforce them, deepening the extent and intensity of income inequality and low-wage work across advanced industrial economies. The chapter begins first by reviewing recent trends in income inequality, declining wages, and low-wage work before and after the crisis.

Market Income Inequality and Low-Wage Work

During the past two decades, income inequality and low-wage work have increased significantly in advanced industrial countries, most notably in Canada and the United States but also across Western Europe as well (OECD 2008, 2011a). The Financial Crisis of 2008–9 has only exacerbated these trends. Today, throughout the Organization for Economic Cooperation and Development (OECD) countries, 40–53 per cent of workers are employed in occupations that are strongly affected by unemployment and/or atypical employment (Emmenger et al. 2011). Across OECD countries, the share of atypical employment in the overall workforce (part-time and fixed-term employment) has grown from an average of around 10 per cent to 25–35 per cent (Gautie and Schmitt 2010). Since the Financial Crisis, these negative changes have often only worsened in the majority of rich world democracies.

At the very top, over the past generation, the share of top-income recipients in total earned income has soared from approximately 6 per cent in 1974 to more than 10 per cent in 2010 (Atkinson and Piketty 2007; Saez and Veall 2005). If capital gains such as investment and dividend income are included, the share of income that the top 1 per cent of earners have received has gone from just over 9 per cent to 17 per cent (Atkinson and Piketty 2010). The global crisis in 2008 did bring about a fall in top income shares in many countries. But this fall appears to have been temporary (see figure 3.1). This reversal was most marked in the United States, where the share of the richest 1 per cent fell by 12 per cent in 2009, but rose by more than 15 per cent in 2011 and quickly surpassed the top income share rate of 2007 (OECD 2014). But rich households have recovered exceedingly well in a number of other countries including Sweden and Denmark, where the top 1 per cent income share

Figure 3.1. Trends in Top Income* Shares in the English-Speaking Countries

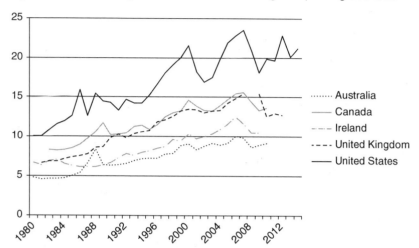

*Income refers to pre-tax incomes as well as capital gains.
Source: World Wealth and Income Database – WID.

fell only briefly in 2009, before rapidly increasing to approximately 7 per cent in both countries in 2010–11.

As Thomas Piketty (2014) and others have recently argued, a key reason for this rapid rise in income inequality – and its recovery after the Financial Crisis – was the growing share of economic growth captured by the rich both before and after the crisis. Over the period 1976–2007, the average incomes of the top 1 per cent earners grew at a rapid rate as they secured the majority of all income and economic growth (OECD 2011a). Across a number of advanced industrial economies over this period, more than half of many countries' economic gains went to the richest 10 per cent (OECD 2014) – the United States, Canada, and Great Britain had the greatest disparities in income distribution, the Nordic countries and the Netherlands the least. But in terms of income captured by the top 1 per cent of earners, the richest individuals in the United States accrued more than 47 per cent of all economic growth over this thirty-year period; in Canada, the richest received more than 37 per cent (ibid.). In other countries, the trend of increased concentration of income at the top was less marked but still significant (OECD 2011a, 2014). In Continental Europe, for example, the slow and steady rise in income going to the top 10 per cent of earners reached 35 per cent in 2010 as CEOs, financial specialists, and managers appropriated ever greater gains (Piketty and Saez 2014).

But in the wake of the Financial Crisis, the key reason for rising market income inequality at the top was firms' use of cash holding to invest in bonds, stocks, and money markets, which boosted corporate returns and executive compensation but did little to spur new investment (Dumenil and Lévy 2011). Cash holdings increased markedly in Europe following the global crisis, accompanied by a considerable fall-off in investment across firms of all sizes (ILO 2012). In the United States, the share of cash holdings in total assets in medium-sized firms increased from around 5.2 per cent in 2006 to around 6.2 per cent after the crisis, while in larger firms it rose from 4.2 per cent in 2006 to 5.3 per cent in 2010. At the same time, despite the decline of nominal interest rates to historic lows, firm investment in capital goods fell to its lowest level in the wake of the financial crisis (Brufman, Martinez, Pérez Artica 2013). By contrast, investment in stock and money markets soared, especially in emerging markets, leading to increasing fees, equity returns, and wealth returns for top income earners (UNCTAD 2012). Buoyed by public injections of trillions of dollars into financial markets, stock and money market indexes reached new heights, stimulating financial gains for top income earners. The result has been rising top income shares since the crisis.

But equally important for increasing market income inequality has been the failure of incomes to grow for the majority of low and middle-class income earners. Across the rich world democracies, the labour share of income declined in relation to the capital share (OECD 2012). The wage share in the business sector demonstrates this best, with recent OECD data showing steady deterioration over the past three decades. In the 1970s and early 1980s, wage share of income reached highs of 89 per cent in Sweden and Austria, and the peak average for the thirteen countries reached 78 per cent (see figure 3.2). Since then, the wage share in the business sector has steadily fallen as income from profits, stocks, shares, and rents have risen. In 1990, wage share had fallen to 71 per cent on average. In 2005, it fell further to 63 per cent. For the thirteen advanced industrial countries surveyed in figure 3.2, the average decline in labour share was 10.6 per cent, with the steepest declines seen in the Nordic countries.

The decline in wage share contributed strongly to the rise in household income inequality across the OECD, as the majority of households

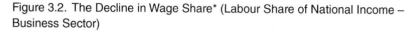

Figure 3.2. The Decline in Wage Share* (Labour Share of National Income –
Business Sector)

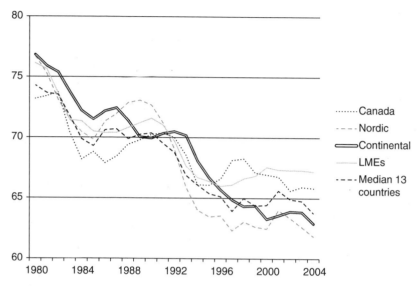

*Wage share is defined as total labour compensation share in the national income
generated by the business sector.
Note: Averages and median based on (Nordic) Denmark, Finland, Norway, Sweden;
(Continental) Austria, Belgium, France, Germany, Italy, the Netherlands; (liberal market
economies) Canada, Great Britain, and the United States.
Source: OECD Economic Outlook, custom request.

had little wealth, and the majority of household income – typically
more than 80 per cent – was derived from labour income (Salverda and
Haas 2014). In general, across the thirteen OECD countries surveyed
here, a 1 per cent decline in wage share correlated with a 0.7 per cent
rise in the Gini coefficient for market income 1995–2005, a number that
could be even higher if all countries removed the gains of the top 1 per
cent income earners that skew wage share data (OECD 2012, chap 3).
Moreover, the OECD estimates that the major decline of the wage share
was accounted for by within-industry developments and declines in
real wages – unrelated to structural shifts away from labour-intensive
and higher-paying industries within countries (OECD 2012, 120–2).
Declines in wage share were also strongly correlated with globalization and the decline in the ability of workers' collective bargaining

institutions to counter employer pressures for wage reductions, a situation that led to the growth in wages lagging productivity in the majority of rich world democracies, regardless of skills or labour relations (ILO 2013).

Across the OECD, this decline in wages relative to income growth was part of another common trend: "job polarization," flat or falling incomes for the majority of middle-income earners and the loss of good jobs. Examining changes to the ratio of median to average income, the income of middle-class earners fell in the bulk of rich world democracies (see figure 3.2). Overall, the decline in the ratio of median to average income was 2 per cent, with the ratio falling to 88 per cent in the mid-2000s as the growth rate of low-paying jobs surpassed that of high-paying jobs, and intermediate-paying jobs either disappeared or changed little (Goos, Manning, and Salomons 2009). Sweden and Denmark did witness some improvement in wages in the mid-2000s, but this had little to do with differences in educational or skill requirements. As Goos, Manning, and Salomons (2009) as well as the OECD (2012) have confirmed, the share of the low-educated fell throughout the rich world economies, while the percentage of workers with upper education remained stable. Instead, the decline in intermediate occupations was due to how educated workers – many overqualified – were increasingly ending up in low-pay jobs and displacing workers with lower skills (Kalleberg 2011).

One of the main reasons for declines in annual median income was that firms were rapidly expanding their use of low-wage work and non-standard employment. Calculating those in full-time employment earning less than two-thirds of the median wage, as well as shares of temporary and part-time employment, analysts have shown how all advanced industrial countries increasingly came to rely on what is now called "cheap labour" (Gautie and Schmitt 2010; King and Rueda 2008). In the aftermath of the Financial Crisis these trends continued. As table 3.1 shows, throughout North America and Western Europe the total number of employees in full-time low-wage work climbed from 14 per cent of the labour force to more than 17 per cent, irrespective of bargaining coverage, skills, or economic competitiveness (1990–2009/10) (see also ibid.). Western European countries such as Germany (the major European exporter) saw the most rapid increases.

But in looking at changes over time, one key overall trend before and after the crisis was increasing low-pay, full-time employment. While the increase in low pay was relatively small in the United Kingdom,

Figure 3.3. Ratio of Mean-to-Median Income, Mid-1970s to Mid-2000s

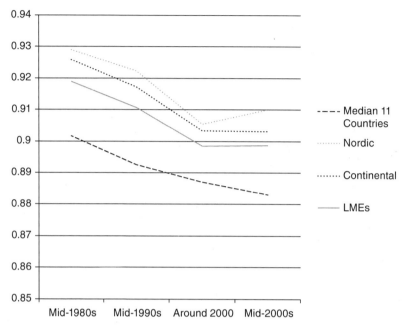

Source: OECD 2008. Averages and median eleven countries based on (Nordic) Denmark, Finland, Norway, Sweden; (Continental) France, Germany, Italy, the Netherlands; (liberal market economies) Canada, Great Britain, and the United States.

increases were substantially greater in many others like Denmark, Finland, Germany, and the United States, indicating that full-time low-wage earners lost ground to median wage-earners. The global recession worsened the situation for many low-paid workers, especially young workers, women, and immigrants, as they were among the first to experience layoffs or be displaced by workers with more seniority and education (ILO 2011a). These trends contributed then to the widening gap between high-wage/high-skill workers and those in low-wage and low-skill occupations, as the D9/D1 ratios across rich world democracies also increased on average from a ratio of 3 to 3.3 in 2011 (see table 3.1)

Another reason for the decline in wages was the growth of non-standard employment. It is well established that the majority of part-time and temporary jobs are remunerated at a rate below average wages (OECD 2012, 2011a). After 2008, net job growth has been primarily in

Table 3.1. Inequality and Low-Wage Work

	Low-pay ratios*		D9/D1 ratios**	
	2001–9	2011	2001–9	2011
Austria	14.5	16.4	3.1	3.3
Belgium	12.1	12.7	2.8	2.8
Canada	22.1	20.3	3.7	3.8
Denmark	11.1	16.7	2.6	2.7
Finland	4.6	9.3	2.3	2.3
Germany	19.2	21.2	3.2	3.3
Netherlands	14.3	17.0	2.9	2.9
Sweden	6.2	6.2	2.3	2.3
United Kingdom	20.6	20.6	3.5	3.6
United States	23.8	25.2	4.8	5.2
Median	14.4	17.0	3.0	3.3

*Low-pay ratios are defined as the percentage of full-time workers earning two-thirds or less of the gross hourly median wage.
**D9/D1 ratios are comparisons of the wage or salary earned by individuals at the nine-tieth percentile (those earning more than 90 per cent of other workers) compared to the earnings of workers at the lowest tenth percentile.
Sources: ILO Global Wage Report 2010/11 OECD Employment and Labour Market Statistics online.

part-time jobs, affecting earnings and annual incomes (Huwart and Verdier 2013). Employers who have sought to offset investment uncertainty have responded by increasing the flexibility of their workforces, driving the rise of non-standard employments (Milberg and Winkler 2013). Across Western Europe, full-time jobs fell annually by more than 2.5 million between 2008 and 2010 (see figure 3.4). But part-time jobs grew annually by 465,000 as employers replaced full-time workers with part-time. By contrast, in North America, the layoffs were far steeper between 2008 and 2010, as North America lost more than 8 million jobs. However, full-time employment began to pick up in 2012 while part-time employment continued to grow in both Canada and the United States to more than 23 per cent of all jobs.

A number of current comparative political economy theories suggest that variations in wage dispersion and employment are shaped by growth in industry sectors, skills, the strength of collective bargaining, and partisan politics (Pontusson 2005; Rueda 2008; Thelen 2014). But rising non-standard employment and increasing wage and income inequality among full-time workers throughout the different models of capitalism make such claims questionable. Certainly women, young

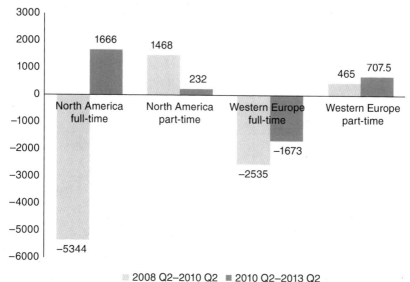

Figure 3.4. Job Destruction and Creation in North America and Western Europe, Annual Averages, by Working Time, 2008–13 (000s)

2008 Q2–2010 Q2   ■ 2010 Q2–2013 Q2

Sources: ETUI 2014; OECD Employment and Labour Market Statistics online.

workers, immigrants, and ethnic minorities found themselves relegated to low-wage work and non-standard employment, often characterized by low pay, little job security, and few opportunities for advancement (OECD 2011a). But non-standard contracts accounted for a large share of newly created jobs for all workers, and workers in low-skill service jobs experienced the largest variation in pay, job security, and benefits across North America and Western Europe (OECD 2012).

In developed economies, the OECD estimates that temporary contracts grew annually by 15–20 per cent, almost ten times the overall rate of employment growth over the period 1990–2005, even in manufacturing and public sectors – areas traditionally seen as having higher-quality jobs. After the crisis, part-time work increased considerably in both North America and Western Europe, indicating that employers were far more likely to lay off full-time workers, and were also more likely to begin rehiring by converting former full-time positions into part-time ones (OECD 2011b). These employer strategies affected

Figure 3.5. Change in the Gini Coefficient* of Market and Disposable Incomes, 2007 and 2011 (%)

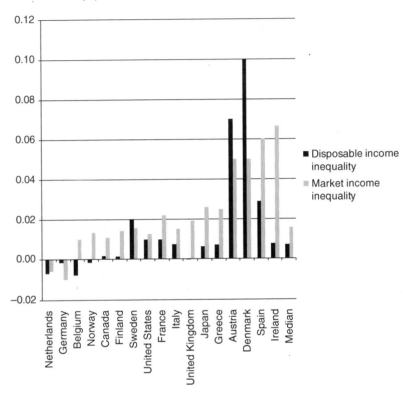

*Gini coefficient measures the extent to which the distribution of income among individuals deviates from a perfectly equal distribution. A Gini index of 0 represents perfect equality, an index of 100 implies perfect inequality. Disposable income inequality measures inequality after tax and transfers.
Source: OECD Income Distribution Database Online.

hourly and annual earnings, as well as increasing earnings inequality across national economies.

Between 2007 and 2011, market income inequality widened considerably, rising by nearly 2 percentage points in seventeen OECD countries (see figure 3.5). The increase was especially notable in countries most affected by the collapse of banks, construction, and housing industries such as Ireland and Spain, where unemployment soared with the global slowdown. But in these and many other countries, the rising number of unemployed, the decrease in earnings, and the slowdown in growth contributed to rising incoming inequality. Interestingly, income inequality rose most rapidly in Denmark and Austria. Only Germany and its two neighbouring economies closely tied to its manufacturing and export markets – Belgium and the Netherlands – saw declines in market and disposable income inequality as high incomes fell more than median incomes across their economies. It appears these jobs and income trends will continue, for after employment gains in 2012, unemployment and non-participation in labour markets have risen again, while the numbers of those in involuntary part-time and temporary employment have grown. This suggests that employment levels, job quality, and income inequality will remain problems for a number of countries in the short and medium term.

Global Firms and Inequality in the Wake of the Financial Crisis

What accounts for the continuing rise in inequality after the Financial Crisis? Why did firms continue to expand the flexibility of their workforces? And why did governments continue to support policies that lowered labour and social costs rather than enhance employment? One key to explaining the rise in inequality was the unbalanced policy responses across advanced industrial economies. In size and scope, government support of the financial sector through a loan guarantees, purchase of bad debt, recapitalization of banks, and guarantees on bank liabilities far exceeded social program spending in many countries. In the United Kingdom, Belgium, and the Netherlands, direct state aid to the financial sector totalled more than 25 per cent of GDP, and in Ireland totalled more than twice its GDP (Grossman and Woll 2013). The majority of government measures were short-term and there were few structural reforms imposed on the financial sector. Between 2008 and 2011, it is estimated that the United States committed $12.6 trillion in government assistance to the financial sector, and more than $4 trillion with the Federal Reserve purchasing mortgage-backed and agency security as well as other long-term securities – or approximately 32 per cent of GDP (Atkinson, Luttrell, and Rosenblum 2013). In Europe, public support for the financial sector is estimated to have been equivalent to 37 per cent of EU GDP (European Commission 2012).

In contrast, despite making commitments to "fiscal" stimulus and support for growth and employment, for the majority of governments, tax cuts were the key focus of the packages intended to keep individuals spending even if unemployed or working part-time. Together, it was estimated that fiscal stimulus packages across the largest rich world economies would total 3.5 per cent of GDP (OECD 2009). Tax cuts on average contributed two-thirds of aggregate fiscal stimulus; labour market measures such as unemployment insurance and short-time work schemes less than 15 per cent (ILO 2011b). However, despite the fact that tax cuts are known to be less redistributive than spending and program increases, governments more readily adopted these measures than spending increases that had been more widely used during previous economic recessions (see Cohen, chapter 4; Pontusson and Raess 2012). Assessments of the tax-cut led packages showed they had little stimulus effect, while significantly worsening the budgetary position of governments. The economic and political weight of the banking sector on macroeconomic conditions and on public officials provides one suggestive explanation for these responses, and why – despite causing the Financial Crisis – rescue packages were designed to save finance at the cost of other interests and priorities.

But of equal importance in explaining the ongoing changes to employment and income distribution were global corporate strategies and multi-national corporations operational capacities. In the wake of the Financial Crisis, firms immediately withheld foreign direct investment from the developed countries, but by 2009 began to increase it towards non-OECD countries, and by 2013 cross-border acquisitions and large retained earnings in foreign affiliates in non-OECD countries were central drivers of global foreign direct investment growth (Economist Intelligence Unit 2014). Another key corporate strategy in response to the slowdown in growth and increased economic uncertainty was to lay off workers and then shift to more flexible and non-standard employment contracts. A third MNC tack was to significantly reduce export and inter-firm trade volumes along their global value chains, resulting in declines in trade and employment in developed and emerging economies alike.

Such corporate strategies were unique in the response to economic shocks. They also had significantly negative impacts on the labour markets of advanced industrial countries. In contrast to previous crises and recessions with comparable declines in GDP growth, what makes such corporate strategies notable in response to the Financial Crisis of 2008–9 was the ability of firms to use layoffs, and short-time work schemes in Western Europe, as a means of adjustment (Pontusson and Raess 2012). In the mid-1970s and early 1980s, changes in the unemployment rate were relatively modest, given the size of the decline in GDP. But from

2008 to 2010, in countries such as the United States, Greece, Spain, and Italy – as well as across the EU-28 – unemployment rose by more than 4 per cent at a minimum and more than 15 per cent at a maximum. These figures would be even higher if "discouraged" workers who have ceased looking for work were included in unemployment rates (ETUI 2014). Jonas Pontusson and Damien Raess (2012) have argued this "disproportionate" increase was due to weaker unions and more flexible labour markets that provided firms with greater opportunities to lay off workers and adjust working hours.

However, an equally likely explanation was the capacity of MNCs to adjust employment and working hours with little regard for domestic consequences. Moreover, unlike in the past, when governments could more easily regulate or press firms for employment-generating investments, governments now face global competition and the integrated production markets of global MNCs in the wake of the Financial Crisis. As such, governments quickly accommodated firm demands by lowering the costs for firms to restructure as well as reducing long-term labour costs (and labour-related social costs) to ensure global competitiveness. This suggests that rather than simply a case of policy deregulation as the reason for higher unemployment, it was the new global powers of business and the reliance of governments on MNCs for employment that explain policymakers' adoption of business-oriented structural reforms in the wake of the crisis. Where in the past firms were restricted by a range of trade, labour regulations, and "national champion" industrial goals, after the economic downturn of 2008–9, individual giant firms set their own priorities with little reference to international or national authorities, and did so deliberately to lower costs.

Such an explanation suggests significant transformation to political economic power across advanced industrial economies. As recent critical literatures have highlighted, the rise of finance and global MNCs has challenged the balance between government and business, and now there are concerns that neither pluralism nor neo-corporatism can prevent the increasingly skewed influence of business on policy (Crouch 2006, 2011; Streeck 2014). Increasingly it is argued that it is necessary to reconceptualize large firms and finance as political entities. This is because policy rather than electoral victory is the grand prize of political conflict, and the main competitors are not, for the most part, individual voters; rather, the main combatants today are organized groups of business and labour. Business organizations wield real clout in daily political life through advocacy campaigns and lobbying, fundraising, and the development of policy and legal expertise (Horn 2012; Streeck and Visser 2006). High concentrations of wealth are also easily converted into political influence through political financing and global regulatory agencies (Moran 2009; Wilks 2013).

Furthermore, the size and influence of MNCs in national political economies grew dramatically in importance. Throughout the post-war Keynesian era of capitalism, nationally embedded firms were more likely to compromise with organized labour and workers because of their interests in avoiding externalities such as layoffs affecting local consumer demand and long-term investment, or government intervention in industries facing economic difficulty (Crouch 2014). This is decreasingly common as global firms have the capability to operate in many jurisdictions, and do not need to consider the negative implications for consumer demand of low wages or flexible employment among their national, regional, or international workforces (ibid.). Consequently, in the context of global competition or economic downturn, government officials have had to accommodate firm demands for lower labour costs and greater employer discretion in workplaces by deregulating labour markets and fostering higher levels of non-standard employment

In addition, recent structural developments to business and their new operating priorities have also led, governments to be more accommodating to business (Dicken 2011; Dixon 2014). Leading global firms – in the advanced capitalist countries as well as the rapidly growing economies of China, Brazil, and India – have readily adopted new global financial models to run their operations and have developed global operations through mergers and acquisitions as well as greenfield investments in China and South East Asia (UNCTAD 2012). Pushed by institutional investors and the involvement of private equity firms, global multinationals have quickly adopted outsourcing, offshoring, subcontracting, and franchising arrangements as central modes of operation (Milberg and Winkler 2013). And to take advantage of global operations for lower costs, MNCs have integrated human resource departments, developed financial procedures to pressure affiliates to lower labour costs, or used outsourcing across their operations to shift production to the most efficient locales (Edwards, Marginson, and Ferner 2013). Such new economic realities have been critical in making governments compete for new investment and jobs by decentralizing collective bargaining, facilitating non-standard labour contracts, and introducing "activation" measures into social policy programs by

Table 3.2. Share of Foreign-Controlled Affiliates in Manufacturing, 2007 and 2011
(% total turnover in corporate operating revenues)

	Turnover 2007	Turnover 2011
Ireland	79.0	76.0
Canada (2006)	51.5	52.0
United Kingdom	45.1	45.0
Netherlands (2005)	41.3	40.0
Sweden	39.6	39.9
Austria	39.3	41.0
Spain	30.4	26.9
France	29.7	28.5
Norway	27.8	25.0
Germany (2006)	27.2	28.5
Denmark	26.0	26.1
United States	21.2	23.0
Italy	18.7	17.8
Finland	18.4	16.5
Median	30.1	28.5

Sources: OECD (2010) and OECD AMNE Database.

tying income support to job requirements, irrespective of the terms and conditions of employment.

As table 3.2 suggests, firms' global capacities and operations are now substantial and remained so after the Financial Crisis. Prior to the crisis in 2007, global multinationals and their affiliates accounted for 30 per cent of gross operating revenues ("turnover") in host economies; more than 79 per cent in Ireland and approximately 20 per cent in the United States as well as Finland and Italy. After the crisis, global firms still accounted for more than 28 per cent of turnover. While full employment data are still unavailable, it appears that many MNCs were able to adjust operations by retrenching in core markets and expanding in non-OECD countries without affecting corporate revenues (Milberg and Winkler 2013).

In a number of leading manufacturing countries, such as the United States, Germany, and small exporting countries of high-tech and pharmaceuticals such as Switzerland, Sweden, and Finland, multinational operations and sales far outstrip domestic operations, giving firms options on how to best generate returns, despite declines in home country operations (OECD 2010). That firms were able to retain considerable cash and liquid asset holdings – as well as increase dividend payouts as strategies for profitability (Milberg and Winkler 2013) rather than invest in new capital and hiring – further supports the argument that global firms had far more options than previously nationally located firms, and that such flexibility gave them far more leverage in dealing with governments and reacting to the economic downturn.

Such developments suggest that the emergence of global firms has allowed them to shed labour and restructure in the wake of the crisis, while boosting profitability and shareholder returns. With the ability to shift production and investment to lower-cost producing regions on more flexible terms, firms were able to reform their workplaces either by laying off workers or by taking advantage of state-enforced changes to collective bargaining arrangements – often both. Where firms were limited in the capacities to adjust global operations, they took the opportunity the crisis afforded them to shed workers and use government support to bargain major wage and benefit concessions with their unionized workforces (Crouch 2014; Hermann 2014). These developments across rich world democracies strongly suggest that rather than diversity of firms and employment systems, the Financial Crisis has contributed to the increasing convergence of global firm operations around more hierarchical systems that privileged short-term financial objectives, labour shedding, and – where possible – non-union operations or workforces where union representatives and institutions could be more easily circumvented.

Moreover, unlike governments in the past, because of the global size and flexibility of firms, policy officials systematically privileged MNCs while allowing inequality, low-wage work, and poverty to expand. Instead of seeking to advance protection or – in the case of Western Europe – social citizenship, governments used their policy tools to foster more competitive labour markets and lower the labour and social costs for firms. As part of the ongoing shift towards "post-democracy," these political outcomes strongly imply a more uncompromising neoliberal stance towards labour markets and collective bargaining – a stance that no longer accepts the need to balance the extension of business and markets by broader labour institutions and employment protection.

Trade Unions in Decline

New analysis has also begun to explore why unions have been decreasingly able to respond to or resist neoliberal politics and policy – before or after the crisis. Since the crisis, governments have placed new restrictions on union organizing and bargaining in North America, and firms have sought to advance the decentralization of collective bargaining institutions while seeking concessions throughout North America and

Table 3.3. Deregulation of Employment Protection, 2008–2012

	Countries with change (%)	Countries with negative change (%)
Permanent contracts	49	76
Temporary contracts	26	44
Collective dismissals	29	50

Source: ILO (2012).

Western Europe (Marginson, Keune, and Bohle 2014; Milkman 2013; Peters 2012). At the same time, governments have imposed liberalizing and deregulatory measures on their public sectors in order to reduce labour costs and public expenditures. In the United States, a number of state-level governments removed collective bargaining rights from public sector employees, restricted bargaining to wages, and banned strikes and binding arbitration (Milkman 2013; Rosenfeld 2014). In the EU, policymakers used "country-specific recommendations" and bilateral agreements to push for changes to national bargaining outcomes and procedures (Hermann 2014). In exchange for financial support, countries like Greece, Spain, Portugal, Latvia, Romania, and Ireland have had to reduce their minimum wages, downwardly adjust wages in the public sector, and decentralize collective bargaining (ETUI 2014). Added to this have been new reform efforts by the EU to restrict minimum wages and formally end wage indexation.

More widely, government officials continued their efforts to relax employment protection rules (Milberg and Winkler 2013). During the 1990s and 2000s, governments made extensive efforts to liberalize terms for fixed-term contracts, increase temporary foreign work permits, and reduce the level of protection afforded to temporary workers (Avdagic 2012). Since 2008, these endeavours have only increased (see table 3.3). As reported by the ILO, more than 50 per cent of advanced countries deregulated legislation for employees on permanent contracts; 26 per cent introduced further liberalizing reforms for fixed-term contracts (also known as temporary contracts) (ILO 2012). Most national policymakers increased the maximum length of fixed-term contracts, while widening the number of reasons for their conclusion and reducing the level of protection ascribed to them. Other governments reduced administrative procedures on collective dismissals, increasing the numerical benchmarks for a dismissal to trigger legislative intervention. Overall, these policy reforms have expanded the opportunities open to employers to increase their part-time and temporary workforces.

The declining influence of organized labour on public officials provides one suggestive reason for these developments, and why government responses did little more than expose more workers to higher levels of unemployment and non-standard employment. Over the past few years, scholars have explored the impacts of globalization and labour market deregulation on democratic mobilization and how internationalization has led to a notable deterioration in the power resources of organized labour (Gumbrell-McCormick and Hyman 2013; Hacker and Pierson 2010; ILO 2011a; Streeck 2014). Trade unions and the growing number of workers in low-wage work and non-standard employment, it is claimed, face increasing challenges to their political effectiveness while making it even more difficult to jointly act as "coalitions of influence" within mainstream politics (Moody 2007; Tattersall 2010). Above all, organized labour has borne the brunt of flexibilization and non-standard employment, and unions have lost members and seen their contracts fragmented or weakened (Baccaro and Howell 2011; Sisson 2013). This has led to an erosion in the capacities of organized labour to mobilize more widely within communities and among low-wage workers, and has limited the ability of organized labour to influence public officials or limit the concessions demanded by firms (Baccaro and Avdagic 2014; Peters 2012; Pontusson 2013; Rosenfeld 2014). These problems have been only magnified since the Financial Crisis of 2007–8.

Traditionally, unions played major political roles in their democracies, educating members about politics and policy, reaching out to citizens through advocacy campaigns and community support, and acting as valuable allies for political parties of the left. But the current erosion in trade union power has come just at the time that rising inequality has disadvantaged a growing majority of citizens, who now feel that government is passing beyond popular involvement and control (Mair 2013; McBride and Whiteside 2011). More and more, it is claimed, the decline in the reach and clout of organizations representing workers and lower-income citizens is compounding the crisis in voter confidence in government and worsening the widespread political disengagement and withdrawal of citizens from the political process (Gumbrell-McCormick and Hyman 2013; Crouch 2006). The results have been increasing government indifference to the concerns of organized labour as well as significant attempts by public officials to deregulate labour

relations and minimize the scope of collective bargaining and employment protection – even in Western Europe, where in the wake of the
Financial Crisis a number of governments have imposed severe austerity measures (Albo and Evans 2011; Heyes, Lewis, and Clark 2012;
Keune and Vandaele 2013; Nolan 2011).

Since the onset of the global recession in 2008, labour movements in
both North America and Western Europe have faced a number of challenges. In the United States, state governments have cut public sector
jobs and wages, and led by Wisconsin, public officials have liberalized
public sector industrial relations by limiting union rights for public
employees, banning strikes and arbitration, and restricting bargaining
for wages (Moody and Post 2014). State governments in the Midwest
have also introduced "right to work" legislation (clauses that require
union-represented workers to pay dues or equivalent fees for union
representation) in labour-management contracts, seriously restricting
the long-term viability of workplace unionization.

In Western Europe, initially short-time work agreements were bar-
gained with government support and maintained jobs through a combination of measures including reduced hours, freezes in basic pay,
suspension of pay premiums, and alternatives to redundancy such as
redeployment (Glassner and Keune 2010). But since 2010, business has
demanded new concessions and the generalization of flexible employment and decentralized bargaining (Marginson, Keune, and Bohle
2014). Governments have accommodated by freezing wages and
laying off public sector employees, as well as by undertaking measures to erode centralized or coordinated bargaining across Europe. In
the countries most affected by the crisis – Spain, Portugal, Ireland,
Greece – the EU/ECB/IMF have offered financial assistance only on
the condition that governments dismantle their current labour market regulations and bargaining systems, and privatize their transport
and energy sectors (Hermann 2014). But more widely, many countries
including Germany and Sweden have introduced structural reforms
in order to extend the downward flexibility of wages and improve cost
competitiveness. The result has been a continuing decline of union
density and members (table 3.4).

Prior to the crisis from 1990 to 2008, union density declined on average by 16 per cent across Western Europe and by 4 per cent in the United
States. After the crisis, density continued to decline, as did bargaining
coverage. But most notable were the membership drops. In the United
States, from 2008 through 2013, public sector union membership fell

Table 3.4. Declining Union Densities and Collective Bargaining Coverage

	Union density (change 1990–2008)	Bargaining coverage (change 1990–2008)	Union density (decline 2008–11)	Bargaining coverage (decline 2008–11)
Austria	-17.8	1.0	-1.3	–
Belgium	-2.0	–	-2.5	–
Canada	-5.5	-7.5	–	-3.0
Denmark	-11	-3.7	-0.3	–
Finland	-1.9	10.3	1.5	1.3
France	-11.4	-1.75	–	–
Germany	-15.9	-11.1	-1.1	-3.0
Italy	-16.2	-2.9	2.2	–
Netherlands	-15.1	0.4	-0.6	1.0
Norway	-5.2	3.3	1.3	–
Sweden	-11.2	2.2	-1.8	–
Spain	2.1	-3.6	1.0	-7.0
UK	-12.5	-20.4	-1.5	-2.4
US	-4.0	-4.7	-0.3	-0.7
Average	-9.1	-2.8	-0.2	-1.0

Sources: OECD Labour Market Statistics and ICTWSS Database.

by 622,000, a result of public worker job cuts and labour law reforms (Moody and Post 2014). Union membership in the private sector fell even further between 2008 and 2012 with a decline of 1,228,000. In Western Europe, union membership also declined significantly. In the EU 15, the number of unionized workers fell by 1.1 million, with the steepest declines occurring in the United Kingdom, Ireland, and Spain after the collapse of their housing and construction sectors, but equally significant declines in Germany, Greece, Denmark, and the Netherlands occurred as employers laid off workers, and governments sold off public utilities and infrastructures (ETUI 2014).

Part of the reason that organized labour was unable to halt the loss of unionized jobs and the fragmentation of bargaining systems was its inability to mobilize as widely and as militantly as in the past. In the 1970s and 1980s, the most effective weapon of organized labour against government and employer attempts to undermine wages and erode conditions of employment was to use economic and political strikes (Rosenfeld 2014). Strike waves reached their peaks during the recessions of the mid-1970s and early 1980s. However, these incidences of industrial conflict have continued to decline over the past generation, often by more than eighty in terms of workdays lost from strike activity for many countries. And with a few notable exceptions in the wake of the Financial Crisis – such as Greece, Spain, Ireland, and Portugal – strikes have declined even further in size and frequency (Streeck 2013). Without the wider mobilization of workers, unions have often been unable to build wider public support or pressure government officials to enact alternative policies.

Another problem faced by unions has been the internal difficulties created by trying to maintain employment while bargaining wage concessions and job flexibility. In facing more aggressive MNCs and firms demanding concessions, and governments seeking efficiencies, unions have been under enormous pressures to make concessions in order to retain jobs. But in dealing with these circumstances, unions have often adopted defensive strategies that have led to bargaining agreements that have "two-tiered" their memberships, disenchanted activists, and put national and international union locals in competition with one another over wages and benefits. In return for job security for those members not laid off or offered retirement packages, unions have given wage, pension, and employment concessions often while also accepting speed-up, job-loading, and more irregular hours. Such bargaining and workplace arrangements have not only limited internal solidarity within unions, they have also made it far harder for unions to expand external solidarity within their localities. Splits between "insiders" and "outsiders" are thus limiting the development of new forms of union representation, organization, and activity. And in the wake of the crisis, where bargaining has been increasingly concessionary, unions have found it difficult to actively support the upsurge of resistance and campaigning in the global Occupy Wall Street movement, or to be seen by the activists themselves as critical for a wider progressive coalition.

There is also evidence that international strategies of global unionism and coordinated bargaining and advocacy failed to limit the reach of MNCs and often led to further internal and international conflicts of interest, both before and after the crisis (Fairbrother, Levesque, and Hennebert 2013). In North America, unions have combined public advocacy and awareness campaigns at shareholder meetings with protests and job actions (Murnighan and Stanford 2013). In Western Europe, global union federations such as IndustriALL have sought to coordinate bargaining across Europe to prevent auto and steel makers from using concessionary agreements in one country to attain wage and jobs reductions in another. But one such problem unions have faced is that greater effort at international campaigning and bargaining have not made up for lack of local mobilizing, education, and external solidarity (Peters 2010). In Western Europe, there has been a shift in the internal power balance between trade unions and works councils, with the latter increasing their influence over bargaining outcomes at the expense of the former – the works councils' first priority is employment security, and they have been more willing to make concessions than industrial unions would. This has led to internal battles and the fragmentation of workforces as employers exploit union fears with job loss, demanding opt-out clauses from higher-level collective agreements, striking deals with unions to pay new entrants less than stipulated by collective agreements, and increasing outsourcing in plants. The consequences of such defensive postures, internal conflict, and limited returns for global unionism has been to make unions increasingly hollow organizations with declining capacities to engage in collective practices (Baccaro and Avdagic 2014).

Overall, the aggregate evidence points to a growing number of problems for the organizational fortunes of labour across North America and Western Europe. Inequality is increasing, union bargaining strength and coverage are slowly eroding, and workers are increasingly finding themselves in non-standard, part-time, and temporary jobs. There is still variety with differences in the political and institutional strength of firms and organized labour. Labour movements in the Nordic countries, for example, have coped best with the challenges of globalization and neoliberalism, even going some way to maintaining an employment model that continues to uphold wages and limits inequality while maintaining strong employment insurance and training programs (Thelen 2014). But even in these countries, there are growing numbers of temporary workers, and unions have been forced to take major bargaining concessions, while governments have introduced a wide range of privatization and outsourcing reforms in the public sector that have undermined jobs and union solidarity.

In other countries though, like the United States, unions have been so weakened that they are unable to accomplish much (Rosenfeld 2014), while in Canada, Italy, Spain, and the United Kingdom, unions protect only a minority of workers but are unable to counter wider trends of low-wage work, de-unionization, and declining wages and benefits (Baccaro and Howell 2011; Peters 2012). In the wake of the crisis, union density has continued to fall, most notably in the largest economies as well as in the countries deepest in economic difficulty. This has been matched with a falloff of industrial conflict, and a tendency for bargaining to be either further restricted or become more differentiated and accommodating to company demands for wage and employment concessions. Meanwhile, public officials' restrictive microeconomic policies have focused on wage restraint, alongside renewed emphasis on market forces, both of which have further eroded labour's position in national political economies. The results have been that inequality continues to grow, job quality declines, and citizens' ability to make meaningful demands on firms or policymakers erodes.

Conclusion

Taking a wider comparative view, this chapter seeks to make transparent two structural roots of major policy shifts in the wake of the Financial Crisis and to show how they furthered neoliberal, supply-side reforms in the majority of rich world democracies. The argument here suggests that the economic shock provided by the crisis gave powerful organized interests yet another lever to make further incremental shifts to policy that advantages business and finance at the cost of organized labour and citizens more generally. The size and scope of powerful MNCs within national economies appears critical in public officials' decision-making, leading to policy responses that backed firm efforts to shed unionized workers and restructure with lower-cost non-standard labour. So too the decline in organizing and mobilizing capacities of organized labour shaped government responses. With limited abilities to conduct strikes and coordinate bargaining and international actions, unions were unable to influence policymakers or sway the public more generally of the need for greater distributive measures and more employment-oriented policies.

Consequently, a crisis caused by the deregulation of financial markets has contributed to wider firm demands for more neoliberal deregulation of labour markets and ongoing downward pressure on union density and protective labour market institutions. The results have been a continuing decline in measures that provided people with some security in income and employment, and a substantive rise in non-standard employment and income inequality – trends that continued the transformations of state and society into a more neoliberal and inegalitarian direction. Understanding the economic forces and the structural changes to the relationships between government, business, and finance is critical to explaining these outcomes and the ongoing reforms to states and public policies in North America and Western Europe.

REFERENCES

Albo, Greg, and Bryan Evans. 2011. "From Rescue Strategies to Exit Strategies: The Struggle over Public Sector Austerity." In *Socialist Register 2011: The Crisis This Time*, ed. L. Panitch, G. Albo, and V. Chibber, 283–308. Pontypools, Wales: Merlin.
Atkinson, Anthony B., and Thomas Piketty, eds. 2007. *Top Incomes over the Twentieth Century: A Contrast between Continental European and English-Speaking Countries*. New York: Oxford University Press.
– eds. 2010. *Top Incomes: A Global Perspective*. New York: Oxford University Press.
Atkinson, Tyler, David Luttrell, and Harvey Rosenblum. 2013. *How Bad Was It? The Costs and Consequences of the 2007–2009 Financial Crisis*. Dallas: Federal Reserve Bank of Dallas.
Avdagic, Sabina. 2012. "Partisanship, Political Constraints, and Employment Protection Reforms in an Era of Austerity." *European Political Science Review* 5 (3): 431–55. http://dx.doi.org/10.1017/S1755773912000197.
Baccaro, Lucio, and Sabina Avdagic. 2014. "The Future of Employment Relations in Advanced Capitalism: Inexorable Decline?" In *The Oxford Handbook of Employment Relations: Comparative Employment Systems*, ed. A. Wilkinson, G. Wood, and R. Deeg. New York: Oxford University Press. Online.
Baccaro, Lucio, and Chris Howell. 2011. "A Common Neoliberal Trajectory: The Transformation of Industrial Relations in Advanced Capitalism." *Politics & Society* 39 (4): 521–63. http://dx.doi.org/10.1177/0032329211420082.
Brufman, Leandro, Lisana Martinez, and Rodrigo Pérez Artica. 2013. *What Are the Causes of the Growing Trend of Excess Savings of the Corporate Sector in Developed Countries?* New York: World Bank.
Crouch, Colin. 2006. *Post-Democracy*. Malden, MA: Polity.
– 2011. *The Strange Non-Death of Neo-Liberalism*. Malden, MA: Polity.
– 2014. "The Neo-Liberal Turn and the Implications for Labour." In *The Oxford Handbook of Employment Relations: Comparative Employment Systems*, ed. Adrian Wilkinson, Geoffrey Wood, and Richard Deeg. New York: Oxford University Press. Online.

Dicken, Peter. 2011. *Global Shift: Mapping the Changes Contours of the World Economy*. New York: Sage Publications.

Dixon, Adam D. 2014. *The New Geography of Capitalism: Firms, Finance, and Society*. New York: Oxford University Press. http://dx.doi.org/10.1093/acprof:oso/9780199668236.001.0001.

Duménil, Gérard, and Dominique Lévy. 2011. *The Crisis of Neoliberalism*. Cambridge: Harvard University Press.

Economist Intelligence Unit. 2014. *What's Next: Future Global Trends Affecting Your Organization: Evolution of Work and the Worker*. New York: Economist.

Edwards, Tony J., Paul Marginson, and Anthony Ferner. 2013. "Multinational Companies in Cross-National Context: Integration, Differentiation, and the Interactions between MNCs and Nation States." *Industrial & Labor Relations Review* 66 (3): 547–87. http://dx.doi.org/10.1177/001979391306600301.

Emmenger, Patrick, Silja Hausermann, Bruno Palier, and Martin Seeleib-Kaiser. 2011. "How We Grow Unequal." In *The Age of Dualization: The Changing Face of Inequality in De-industrializing Societes*, ed. P. Emmenger, S. Hausermann, B. Palier, and M. Seeleib-Kaiser, 3–26. New York: Oxford University Press.

European Trade Union Institute (ETUI). 2014. *Benchmarking Working Europe 2014*. Brussels: ETUI.

European Commission. 2012. *Tackling the Financial Crisis: Banks*. Brussels: European Commission.

Fairbrother, Peter, Christian Levesque, and Marc-Antonin Hennebert, eds. 2013. *Transnational Trade Unionism*. Routledge Studies in Employment and Work Relations. New York: Routledge.

Gautie, Jerome, and John Schmitt, eds. 2010. *Low-Wage Work in the Wealthy World*. New York: Russell Sage Foundation.

Glassner, Vera, and Maarten Keune. 2010. *Negotitating the Crisis? Collective Bargaining in Europe after the Economic Downturn*. Geneva: ILO.

Goos, Maarten, Alan Manning, and Anna Salomons. 2009. "Job Polarization in Europe." *American Economic Review* 99 (2): 58–63. http://dx.doi.org/10.1257/aer.99.2.58.

Grossman, Emiliano, and Cornelia Woll. 2013. "Saving the Banks: The Political Economy of Bailouts." *Comparative Political Studies* 47 (4): 574–600.

Gumbrell-McCormick, Rebecca, and Richard Hyman. 2013. *Trade Unions in Western Europe: Hard Times, Hard Choices*. New York: Oxford University Press. http://dx.doi.org/10.1093/acprof:oso/9780199644414.001.0001.

Hacker, Jacob, and Paul Pierson. 2010. *Winner-Take-All Politics: How Washington Made the Rich Richer – And Turned Its Back on the Middle Class*. New York: Simon & Schuster.

Hermann, Christoph. 2014. "Structural Adjustment and Neoliberal Convergence in Labour Markets and Welfare: The Impact of the Crisis and Austerity Measures on European Economic and Social Models." *Competition & Change* 18 (2): 111–30.

Heyes, Jason, Paul Lewis, and Ian Clark. 2012. "Varieties of Capitalism, Neoliberalism and the Economic Crisis of 2008–?" *Industrial Relations Journal* 43 (3): 222–41. http://dx.doi.org/10.1111/j.1468-2338.2012.00669.x.

Horn, Laura. 2012. *Regulating Corporate Governance in the EU.* Basingstoke, UK: Palgrave Macmillan. http://dx.doi.org/10.1057/9780230356405.

Huwart, Jean-Yves, and Loïc Verdier. 2013. *Economic Globalisation: Origins and Consequences.* Paris: OECD Publishing. http://dx.doi.org/10.1787/9789264111905-en.

International Labour Organization (ILO). 2011a. *Global Employment Trends 2011: The Challenge of a Jobs Recovery.* Geneva: ILO.

– 2011b. *Global Wage Report 2010/2011.* Geneva: ILO.

– 2011c. *A Review of Global Fiscal Stimulus.* EC-IILS Joint Discussion Paper Series no. 5. Geneva: ILO/International Institute for Labour Studies.

– 2012. *World of Work Report 2012.* Geneva: ILO.

– 2013. *Global Wage Report 2012/13.* Geneva: ILO.

Kalleberg, Arne L. 2011. *Good Jobs, Bad Jobs: The Rise of Polarized and Precarious Employment Systems in the United States, 1970s to 2000s.* New York: Russell Sage Foundation.

Keune, Maarten, and Kurt Vandaele. 2013. "Wage Regulation in the Private Sector: Moving Further Away from a Solidaristic Wage Policy." In *The Transformation of Employment Relations in Europe,* ed. J. Arrowsmith and V. Pulignano, 88–110. New York: Routledge.

King, Desmond, and David Rueda. 2008. "Cheap Labor: The New Politics of 'Bread and Roses' in Industrial Democracies." *Perspectives on Politics* 6 (2): 279–97. http://dx.doi.org/10.1017/S1537592708080614.

Mair, Peter. 2013. *Ruling the Void: The Hollowing of Western Democracy.* New York: Verso.

Marginson, Paul, Maarten Keune, and Dorothee Bohle. 2014. "Negotiating the Effects of Uncertainty? The Governance Capacity of Collective Bargaining under Pressure." *Transfer: European Review of Labour and Research* 20 (1): 37–51. http://dx.doi.org/10.1177/1024258913514356.

McBride, Stephen, and Heather Whiteside. 2011. *Private Affluence, Public Austerity: Economic Crisis and Democratic Malaise in Canada.* Halifax: Fernwood Publishing.

Milberg, William, and Deborah Winkler. 2013. *Outsourcing Economics: Global Value Chains in Capitalist Development.* New York: Cambridge University Press. http://dx.doi.org/10.1017/CBO9781139208772.

Milkman, Ruth. 2013. "Back to the Future? US Labour in the New Gilded Age." *British Journal of Industrial Relations* 51 (4): 645–65. http://dx.doi.org/10.1111/bjir.12047.

Moody, Kim. 2007. *US Labor in Trouble and Transition: The Failure of Reform from Above, the Promise of Revival from Below*. New York: Verso.

Moody, Kim, and Charles Post. 2014. "The Politics of US Labour: Paralysis and Possibilities." *Socialist Register 2015: Transforming Classes* 51:295–317.

Moran, Michael. 2009. *Business, Politics, and Society*. New York: Oxford University Press.

Murnighan, Bill, and Jim Stanford. 2013. "'We Will Fight This Crisis': Auto Workers Resist an Industrial Meltdown." In *From Crisis to Austerity: Neoliberalism, Labour and the Canadian State*, ed. T. Fowler. Ottawa: Red Quill Books. Online.

Nolan, Peter. 2011. "Money, Markets, Meltdown: The 21st Century Crisis of Labour." *Industrial Relations Journal* 42 (1): 2–17. http://dx.doi.org/10.1111/J.1468-2338.2010.00594.x.

OECD. n.d. Activity of Multi-National Database (AMNE). Paris: OECD. http://www.oecd.org/sti/ind/amne.htm.

– n.d. OECD Income Distribution Database (IDD). Paris: OECD. http://www.oecd.org/social/income-distribution-database.htm.

– 2008. *Growing Unequal: Income Distribution and Poverty in OECD Countries*. Paris: OECD.

– 2009. *OECD Economic Outlook Interim Report March 2009*. Paris: OECD.

– 2010. *Measuring Globalisation: OECD Economic Globalisation Indicators*. Paris: OECD.

– 2011a. *Divided We Stand: Why Inequality Keeps Rising*. Paris: OECD.

– 2011b. *OECD Employment Outlook 2011*. Paris: OECD.

– 2012. *Employment Outlook 2012*. Paris: OECD.

– 2014. *Tackling High Inequalities, Creating Opportunities for All*. Paris: OECD.

Peters, John. 2010. "Down in the Vale: Corporate Globalization, Unions on the Defensive, and the USW Local 6500 Strike in Sudbury, 2009–2010." *Labour (Halifax)* 66:73–106.

– 2012. "Free Markets and the Decline of Unions and Good Jobs." In *Boom, Bust and Crisis: Labour, Corporate Power and Politics in Canada*, ed. J. Peters, 16–54. Halifax: Fernwood Publishing.

Piketty, Thomas. 2014. *Capital in the Twenty-First Century*. Cambridge: Harvard University Press.

Piketty, Thomas, and Emmanuel Saez. 2014. "Inequality in the Long Run." *Science* 344 (6186): 838–43. http://dx.doi.org/10.1126/science.1251936.

Pontusson, Jonas. 2005. *Inequality and Prosperity: Social Europe vs Liberal America*. Ithaca, NY: Cornell University Press.

– 2013. "Unionization, Inequality, and Redistribution." *British Journal of Industrial Relations* 51:797–825.

Pontusson, Jonas, and Damian Raess. 2012. "How (and Why) Is This Time Different? The Politics of Economic Crisis in Western Europe and the United States." *Annual Review of Political Science* 15:13–33. http://dx.doi.org/10.1146/annurev-polisci-031710-100955.

Rosenfeld, Jake. 2014. *What Unions No Longer Do*. Cambridge, MA: Harvard University Press. http://dx.doi.org/10.4159/harvard.9780674726215.

Rueda, David. 2008. "Political Agency and Institutions: Explaining the Influence of Left Governments and Corporatism on Inequality." In *Democracy, Inequality, and Representation: A Comparative Perspective*, ed. P. Beramendi and C.J. Anderson, 169–200. New York: Russell Sage Foundation.

Sachs, Jeffrey D. 2012. *The Price of Civilization: Economics and Ethics after the Fall*. Toronto: Vintage Canada.

Saez, Emmanuel, and Michael R. Veall. 2005. "The Evolution of High Incomes in North America: Lessons from the Canadian Evidence." *American Economic Review* 95 (3): 831–49. http://dx.doi.org/10.1257/0002828054201404.

Salverda, Weimar, and Christina Haas. 2014. "Earnings, Employment, and Income Inequality." In *Changing Inequalities in Rich Countries*, ed. W. Salverda, B. Nolan, D. Checchi, I. Marx, A. McKnight, I. Toth, and H. van de Werhorst. New York: Oxford University Press. http://dx.doi.org/10.1093/acprof:oso/9780199687435.003.0003.

Sisson, Keith. 2013. "Private Sector Employment Relations in Western Europe: Collective Bargaining under Pressure." In *The Transformation of Employment Relations in Europe*, ed. J. Arrowsmith and V. Pulignano, 13–32. New York: Routledge.

Stiglitz, Joseph E. 2010. *Freefall: America, Free Markets, and the Sinking of the World Economy*. New York: W.W. Norton.

Streeck, Wolfgang. 2013. "The Crisis in Context: Democratic Capitalism and Its Contradictions." In *Politics in the Age of Austerity*, ed. A. Schafer and W. Streeck, 262–86. Malden, MA: Polity.

– 2014. *Buying Time: The Delayed Crisis of Democratic Capitalism*. New York: Verso.

Streeck, Wolfgang, and Jelle Visser, eds. 2006. *Governing Interests: Business Associations Facing Internationalization*. New York: Routledge.

Tattersall, Amanda. 2010. *Power in Coalition: Strategies for Strong Unions and Social Change*. Ithaca, NY: Cornell University Press.

Thelen, Kathleen. 2014. *Varieties of Liberalisation and the New Politics of Social Solidarity.* New York: Cambridge University Press. http://dx.doi.org/ 10.1017/CBO9781107282001.

United Nations Conference on Trade and Development (UNCTAD). 2012. *World Investment Report 2012.* New York: United Nations.

Wilks, Stephen. 2013. *The Political Power of the Business Corporation.* Northampton, MA: Edward Elgar Publishing. http://dx.doi.org/10.4337/9781849807326.

4 Austerity's Role in Economic Performance: The Relationships between Social Reproduction Spending, the Economy, and People[1]

MARJORIE GRIFFIN COHEN

Introduction

The idea of "expansionary austerity" has had a considerable revival, especially in Canada, since the initial "expansionary" attempts to deal with the Great Recession of 2008–10. The desperation of governments in both Europe and North America, when it almost looked as if the capitalist financial world would collapse, initiated a short-lived inversion of the austerity approach to fiscal policy. In Canada, "austerity" had been widely accepted for the past twenty years as the most sensible approach for government policy in normal times – something that was set aside briefly during the Great Recession of 2008–10.[2]

Austerity as a permanent feature that would progressively deepen became embedded in public policy in tandem with abandoning the idea that economic crises could or should be prevented. More proactive government policy was based on the idea that when the economy went through periodic crises, the presence of automatic stabilizers could either prevent or mitigate serious economic damage.

This smoothing of economic volatility, as is well known, was associated with Keynesian policy and was originally designed as a counter-cyclical approach to stimulate demand when it was deficient. Over time, the conditions under which Keynesian policy worked

1 I would like specifically to thank Mike Kim for his extremely helpful research assistance.
2 It is usually set aside during election years as well.

relatively well changed, and stagflation soured governments on Keynesian solutions. The most significant change in conditions related to global influences and free trade: as economies became more open, the effectiveness of stimulus spending decreased. The result was that inflationary pressures tended to rise, and these economic factors, combined with the political influence of the corporate sector, shaped a rejection of Keynesian approaches and the popularity of "austerity" – at least for government spending on policies related to social reproduction. Social reproduction includes the activities of both males and females, and the ways that the market, the state, the community, the household, and the individual are involved in meeting the direct needs of people. The state's role includes activities that directly and universally support the household (medical care, education, pensions, labour regulation, and support), as well as specific programs that are more targeted to meet the needs of specific populations (social assistance, disability aid, employment insurance, pensions, childcare, housing). At various capitalistic stages, each share undertaken by the actors in this process is different, with the state assuming a larger or smaller influence on the social security systems designed to support social reproduction, depending on the time, state of development, and political ideology in ascendance (Cohen 2013, 235).

This chapter examines the impact of austerity policies on economic performance and the effect that reductions in the significance of spending on social reproduction programs have on people and economic outcomes. The question of the impact of austerity on performance arises because of the debate among economists about the economic impacts of "expansionary austerity," and whether it helps or hinders an economy (Blyth 2013). Generally these studies do not look at the composition of reductions in government spending and instead deal with total spending, even though it would be important to know if the type of government spending and programs that were reduced influenced outcomes. Another influence on understanding the impact of austerity is the recent publication of *Capital* by Thomas Piketty, and his work on the rise of unequal wealth and income in capitalist countries (Piketty 2014). There is much to say about the significance of this book (a powerful exposé of inequality in capitalism), but in it he does not attempt to correlate any negative economic effects to increasing disparities over time. Rising inequality is bad for people, but he does not show it is bad for the capitalist economy; or rather, he shows that it is bad only because if it becomes *bad enough* people will rebel.[3] That, as we know, is not guaranteed and a very, very long time can lapse before social unrest has economic repercussions.[4]

This chapter will discuss the shift away from ideas about countercyclical social spending as instruments to either prevent or mitigate economic crisis to the sense that "expansionary austerity" can have positive economic consequences. Also explored is whether the inversion of "expansionary austerity" policies will necessarily have positive economic or social results. It seems that there are several possibilities for policy, depending on the findings. One most frequently raised by more progressive economists is that the economic policies of expansionary austerity ultimately are bad for both the economy and people, and that reversing these policies will markedly improve economic performance and help prevent crises in the future. The other is that the neoclassical economists are more or less right and that austerity, especially as it relates to social reproduction, does not have a negative impact on the economy as expressed through long-term performance and ultimately could be beneficial to people as well. Another possibility is that capitalism can tolerate fairly dramatic swings in economic activity so that even if austerity policies are disruptive, there is no need to try to prevent crises – instead, we should manage them as they arise.

The question to test is whether the relative deterioration of public institutions supporting social reproduction has a negative effect on the domestic economies. Clearly there are important immediate implications for people when institutions of social reproduction are cut or minimized, and these cannot be ignored, although the supporters of "austerity" argue that people will be better off in the long run. In contrast, the argument generally from the progressive political spectrum is that austerity is bad policy for people and the economy and is precisely the wrong policy to pursue when there is an economic crisis. Usually when the effect of austerity policy is examined, the focus is on total government spending. This chapter will focus on whether the composition of that spending (such as spending through tax reductions or from

---

3 For a discussion of this aspect of Piketty's analysis, see Cohen (2016).

4 This does not mean that others have not tried to deal with the relationship between economic inequality and the rise of financial instability in recent periods. See, for example, Papadimitriou et al. (2014); Causa, de Serres, and Ruiz (2014).

social programs) has an impact on economic performance and will use the experiences in Canada to analyse the issue.

Policy/Crisis Nexus

Economic failure prevention was prominent in ideas about the role of the state in the United States and other countries, especially during and after the Second World War. This has changed since the shift towards austerity. Now, the major understanding of the policy/crisis nexus is to devise tools to manage the crisis once it has occurred (Panitch and Gindin 2012). That is, failure containment rather than failure prevention is now consciously the key and the policies – even when expansionary policies are distinctly different and, except for tax cuts, temporary.

In the post–Second World War period, Canada and the United States worked specifically at avoiding the kind of economic disaster that had occurred during the 1930s, which was all-too-painfully familiar and recent. Even more significant was government interest in preventing the long-term problems similar to those that accompanied demilitarization after the First World War. The recession that followed the First World War was widely understood in later years to have been preventable by having an active labour policy that would ensure that returning soldiers were integrated into an expanding economy and by managing fiscal policy prudently, mainly through not demanding budget surpluses too rapidly (Vernon 1919). The almost inevitable rise in unemployment could be lessened, and demand could be stimulated if governments acted to steer the economy.

Attempts to prevent or mitigate the severity of potential crises would require planning, and Canada and the United States gained considerable experience at planning the economy during the Second World War, an exercise that was not abandoned as soon as the war was over. The planning was substantial and extended beyond war work to include activities ranging from industrial to social reproduction aspects of the economy. The planning for social reproduction was new to capitalist economies, at least to the extent that was undertaken during the war itself, but it did become a permanent feature of the system in the immediate post-war period.

Going into the war, capital was about as weak as it had ever been, and this relatively weak capitalist class, which had almost destroyed the system during the Great Depression, strengthened the ability of the institutionalists and Keynesians within governments to shape a new system. These governments recognized that ongoing institutions dealing with a variety of aspects of social reproduction were crucial to economic and political stability and could be engines of growth itself.[5] These were powerful tools that made it seem as though the dramatic depressions of the past would be confined to the past and that, with the proper instruments, governments could prevent economic disaster in the future.

In Canada, the significance of government activity on issues related to social reproduction began early in the war itself. As early as December 1939, the government established a Committee on Demobilization and Re-Establishment. The minister of pensions and national health, Ian Mackenzie, led this, indicating the significance of social reproduction to the concept of avoiding economic instability. He was also instrumental in establishing a national unemployment insurance program in 1940 (Canada War Museum n.d.). While a variety of factors led to development of a national social security protection in the post-war period, economic stability was understood to be a major outcome of these developments.

The significance of policy instruments in the neoliberal period is distinct from that associated with the period of Keynesian influence. They are usually confined to two main types of approaches: one relates to the idea of "expansionary austerity" and the other to temporary stimulus to be undertaken primarily when markets fail. This is certainly how "expansion" has been interpreted by both Canada's Action Plan, and the Obama administration's 2009 American Recovery and Investment Act. These programs were designed to be typically short-term activities, focusing mainly on so-called shovel-ready projects that do not get embedded into the economic functioning of the system (as would, for example, a national disability, drug, housing, or childcare scheme). In this sense, they have little ability to temper the onset of economic crises in the ways that were characteristic of social institutions that are integral to the system.

Institutions of social reproduction in the past appear to have had important functions for the economy in tempering economic crisis in

---

5 The distinction between Keynesian and institutionalist economic approaches was important in this period. The Keynesians tended to focus on aggregate employment and macroeconomic issues, and while these were significant also for the institutionalists, they tended to be more cognizant of the issues related to social spending, specific sectors of the economy, and relationships between these sectors.

counter-cyclical ways. Recent analysis of OECD countries indicates that the current focus on unemployment compensation and tax reductions as the primary automatic stabilizers should be expanded. Although usually dismissed as significant aspects of automatic stabilization, other kinds of government spending often respond to business cycles and move together with employment insurance when there is an economic downturn (Darby and Melitz 2007). The most often-discussed expenditures that operate in this way appear to be pension benefits (people tend to retire early during economic downturns), health benefits (sick benefits may be used rather than unemployment benefits), and payments for disability (which tends to increase during economic downturns) (Darby and Melitz 2011). Similarly, government funding for education and housing could also be used to track economic downturns if, as is true in Canada, more people tend to pursue post-secondary education and more people need social housing during an economic crisis. Increasingly, social expenditures have become important for the economy itself, particularly with regard to levels of employment, although public expenditures related to social reproduction are often characterized by neoliberal governments as just items of consumption that are only "paid for" by resource and manufacturing economic activity. However, it is precisely these kinds of activities that tend not to be supported during economic downturns and are increasingly whittled away when the economy is in relative health.

Expansionary Austerity

There is something decidedly contradictory about the term *expansionary austerity*, and intuitively seems wrong. Yet the argument for "austerity" in government policy, despite its frequent historical failures, has experienced a revival among neoliberal governments since the 1980s.[6] This is partially because it is a natural complement to the arguments in favour of free trade and has similar intellectual origins. The underlying idea is that the private corporate sector is best situated to determine the direction of production and distribution of goods and services worldwide – and the less that governments are involved in restricting

---

6 Others in this volume discuss the production, resilience, and power of the idea of "expansionary austerity." See Evans, chapter 10; Plehwe, chapter 9; and McBride, chapter 8.

or competing with these activities, the healthier will be all of the economies of the world.

Deliberately depressing wages and restricting the size and output
of the public sector in order to reduce government debt and taxes
were theorized to ultimately stimulate growth for two main reasons.
One was that the export-oriented economies where this occurred, characterized by low taxes and low government debt, would be seen as
more competitive in world markets, and an inflow of investment funding would ensue. This would increase exports and in turn stimulate
long-term growth. The other reason for seeing austerity as a stimulus
for growth is based on the assumption that people and corporations
will think differently about the future when government spending and
taxes fall. People will expect to retain a larger proportion of their income
in anticipation of lower taxes in the future, so will revise their current
and future spending habits, whereas corporations will no longer experience the "crowding-out" that government activity engenders and will
increasingly step into the void left by government cuts and expand their
production spending. Associated with these actions is the argument
that these types of expansions will actually lead to larger government
revenues through more taxes as a result of increased economic activity.
Generally the theory is that there would be a small contraction period
initially, but this is expected to be short-lived, and thus both austerity
and economic expansion can be a permanent feature of an economy.

The evidence-based justification that spurred governments towards
more aggressive austerity politics in the 1990s came largely from a
paper written by Francesco Giavazzi and Marco Pagano, wherein they
compared the experiences of Ireland and Denmark and found that "fiscal consolidations" in the 1980s did improve economic performance
(Giavazzi and Pagano 1990). This was the first study to critically look
at the empirical evidence of whether the Keynesian or German view
of fiscal contraction was more appropriate.[7] The Keynesian view posited that fiscal contraction would reduce domestic demand, and unemployment would rise and have a dampening effect on the economy.
The German view was that fiscal contraction, rather than raising taxes
in order to control debt, would have a benign effect on demand and
would inspire confidence. Giavazzi and Pagano used the cases of

---

7 The "German" view was termed by Giavazzi and Pagano to describe the most
prominent non-Keynesian effect of fiscal contraction. For a discussion, see Lucke (1997).

Ireland and the Denmark, primarily because of their very contradictory contexts, to understand the conditions under which fiscal contractions can be expansionary. Their findings were convincing, at least for the short term. Ireland had tried fiscal contraction with disastrous results earlier in the 1980s (supporting the Keynesian conclusion), but on the second attempt it appears to have been successful and turned around the downward spiral. In Ireland, the critical difference in the two time periods was the use of monetary policy and the exchange rate to stimulate domestic demand. In Denmark, cuts to government spending and an increase in taxes did not lead to a decrease in demand, primarily because a dramatic deflation meant households holding the public debt increased their wealth dramatically. Apparently this kept domestic demand from falling, and highlights "the importance of monetary and exchange rate policies that accompanies the fiscal stabilization" (82). What is very clear in this article is that the authors are not arguing that fiscal contractions inevitably can be expansionary, as their example of Ireland in the early 1980s makes clear, but can be expansionary when other policy makes the conditions amenable to this approach. They certainly did not argue that fiscal contraction could be a long-term project for capitalist governments.

A great deal has been written about the success or failure of expansionary austerity and the intent here is not to show the permutations of the arguments of the debate. But one recent example of the case against the positive effects of expansionary austerity is an IMF paper that compares the short-term effects of fiscal consolidation on economic activity in OECD economies (Guajardo, Leigh, Pescatori 2011). The findings from the collective experience of these countries are that the methods used by others to prove that fiscal contraction stimulates demand in the short run (because it relies on cyclically adjusted data) overstated the expansionary effects. Their evidence did not support the expansionary hypothesis and found that fiscal consolidation reduces both real private consumption and GDP within two years. They also found that the decline in both GDP and private consumption is mitigated by a fall in the value of the domestic currency, which gives a rise in net exports. This analysis is in line with that of Giavazzi and Pagano, who see that the economic context, particularly with regard to monetary and exchange rate policies, can offset the austerity measures.

It should be recognized that the justification Giavazzi and Pagano gave for government program cuts was not the tipping point for countries like Canada: the economic directions associated with free trade agreements and the ideological perspectives of the political parties in power certainly supported the downsizing of government, particularly as it relates to reduced taxes on corporations and relative lower spending on social reproduction. These were things, once the trade agreements (CUFTA and NAFTA) were signed, that became the consensus of the corporate sector, government, and media.[8]

Canada was reported to have performed well under a regime of budget cuts and balanced budgets, restrictive monetary policy focusing solely on inflation, and various wage suppression tactics[9] (Blyth 2013b). And most recently, during the 2008–10 economic crisis, its austerity regime was credited for the relative ease with which the country weathered the economic crisis (Barro 2014). But government and business acknowledged the good news about the success of austerity even earlier, in response to Canada's austerity measures related to the recession of the early 1980s. This was the period when the major tax changes were put into motion, including reductions in the income tax brackets from ten to three; reductions in corporate taxes; tying program financing to 2 per cent below GDP increases; the beginnings of massive privatization initiatives; and the complete withdrawal of the federal government in the shared funding of the Unemployment Insurance program (Cohen 1997). Nevertheless, as figure 4.1 shows, total spending on social programs continued to rise until the early 1990s, something that may have accounted for the success of the "fiscal consolidations" so applauded at the time.

Canada's Experience with Austerity

As most of the studies examining austerity acknowledge, getting a clear picture of the effect of austerity policies on economic growth

---

8 Before the free trade deals were signed, the promise was that under the conditions of free trade, more revenue would come to governments and, as a result, social programs could be strengthened and expanded. Arguments prominent in Canada during the free trade debates to show how social reproduction needs could be reconciled with the macroeconomic objectives in Canada – i.e., that free trade would bring greater wealth that would allow for expanded social programs – disappeared once the agreements were signed.

9 Note that part of the period considered a success during the 1990s was a time of very serious currency devaluation, in an attempt to recover from the disastrous first years of the Canada-US Free Trade Agreement. The value of the Canadian dollar went from US$0.872 in 1991 to US$0.645 in 2001. See Canadian Foreign Exchange Services.

Figure 4.1. Public Social Expenditures as Percentage of GDP (Select Countries)

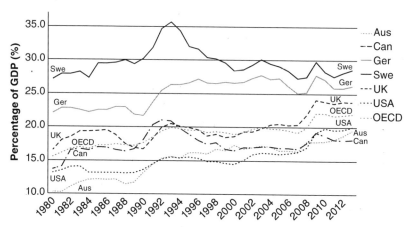

Source: OECD.Stat (2017).

is not straightforward. It is rare when austerity policies are taken in isolation from other policies (such as currency devaluation), and the general economic conditions of both the country and the world economy have an impact as well. This means that for very open economies, like Canada and Germany, the impact of currency changes will be large, and for a resource and commodity export–dependent country like Canada the state of international demand will be very significant.

What follows will examine what has happened in Canada since austerity was instituted in a major way in the 1990s. The primary concern is to see if there is a relationship between a relative reduction in government spending, and spending specifically on social reproduction on economic performance. I will also look at the impact of tax reduction on long-term government revenues and on the significance of reductions in compensation to labour and rising inequality.

Public Spending Record

Figure 4.1 shows the standing of six OECD countries and the OECD average from 1980 to 2013 in public social expenditures relative to national income.[10] The pattern for most countries is similar, although Canada stands out for the most dramatic changes. In 1980, Canada's standing was third from the bottom with 13.7 per cent of GDP accounted for by social spending, but this increased dramatically until 1992 when social spending accounted for 21 per cent of the GDP. At this point Canada was third, after Sweden and Germany, in the proportion of national income spent on social programs, and for the first time, Canada's spending was above the OECD average, a distinction that did not last long. It should be noted that Germany has one of the highest social expenditures to GDP of any country, something that contradicts the idea that Germany is a good example of austerity's success, since its "austerity" is light compared with other countries. On the other hand, Germany's total government expenditures are lower than in other countries. Together, these might give an indication of the significance of social expenditures to successfully mitigating economic crises and altogether producing more healthy economic growth.

The decline in social spending for Canada during the 1990s was steep – the steepest of any country. Some of the dramatic decline was a result of structural changes in the way social programs were funded. Most significant was the change from direct spending by the federal government on specific areas within provinces (health, education, social assistance) to transferring programs to provinces that did not specify the nature of program expenditure and that actually amounted to total cuts to dollar amounts (Rice and Prince 2000, 126). But also significant were total federal government program cuts, such as the abolishing of the federal monthly family allowance, the confiscation of Unemployment Insurance surpluses to pay down the debt and the subsequent reduction in insurance coverage for the unemployed, and the provincial roll-back of wages for workers in the public sector, especially in Ontario, the most populous province in the country.

By the end of the Canadian Action Plan, designed to help the country recover from the 2008–10 recession, Canada fell from being third-highest to the bottom of the ranking in social spending as a proportion

---

10 This includes expenditures for all levels of government. The comparison between countries is always difficult, and even among OECD nations the data have problems. In this case expenditures on education, other than through the federal transfers to the provinces, do not seem to be included, nor are they included for other nations. (For notes on the OECD database by country on social expenditure, see OECD 2016.)

Figure 4.2. Canadian Public Social Expenditure as Percentage of GDP

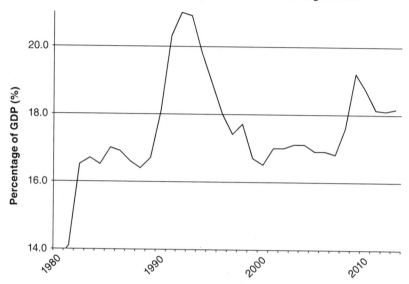

Source: OECD.Stat (2017a).

of GDP for these six OECD countries and was considerably below the OECD average.[11] Figure 4.2 shows Canada's record of social expenditures as a percentage of GDP without the comparisons. As a result of the one-off stimulus spending, Canada's record on social spending did improve after sinking to 16.8 per cent of GDP in 2007, but the spike in the 2008–9 period has levelled off at considerably less (18.1 per cent) than the high point in 1992 at 21 per cent.

Canada's record on total government spending is slightly different from its record on social spending, at least relative to that of other countries, in that it has more or less retained its ranking as third-highest among the six OECD countries and considerably higher than the OECD average (see figure 4.3). Like all other countries, total spending as a proportion of GDP in Canada has dropped considerably since the high points in the early 1980 and 1990s. The difference after the effect of the

---

11 Jim Stanford convincingly shows that while Canada is often applauded for having weathered the 2009 economic crisis relatively well, this basically is not true (Stanford 2013).

Figure 4.3. Government Spending as Percentage of GDP (Select Countries)

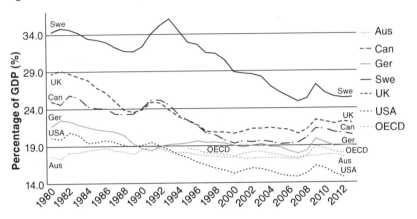

Source: OECD.Stat (2017b).

2009–10 stimulus efforts, in comparison with other countries, shows Canada to be on a downward trajectory again as the federal and provincial governments resume their efforts towards balanced budgets.

The Multiplier Effect

There is a strong likelihood that the decline in social expenditures could affect economic performance. This was indicated as a possibility by the government itself through the published multiplier effect of government stimulus policies during the 2008–10 recession. The multiplier is the reference to the total increase in income from a particular type of increase in spending. A dollar of spending can have fairly little impact if it is spent outside the country (such as buying fighter jets), but a dollar spent within the country related to populations who tend to spend all they earn will have a magnified impact.

The report on the activities of Canada's Action Plan lists the multiplier effect of various types of stimulus activities, as shown in table 4.1. These figures are instructive, because it is clear that there are significant differences between money that is foregone because of tax cuts, and money spent on low-income households and the unemployed. The actions having no stimulus effect (and in fact, are actions that withdraw money from the economy) are tax reductions for business, reductions in EI premiums, and personal income tax cuts.

Table 4.1. Canadian Expenditure and Tax Multipliers

	2009	2010
Infrastructure investment	1.0	1.5
Housing investment	1.0	1.4
Other spending	0.8	1.3
Measures for low-income households and the unemployed	0.8	1.5
EI premiums	0.4	0.5
Personal income tax measures	0.4	0.9
Business tax measure	0.1	0.2

Source: Department of Finance (2011, table A.1).

The government explains the very low impact of business tax cuts by saying that while they had little impact on demand over the period under review, over the long run they would have the highest multiplier effects, because they would increase the incentive to invest and accumulate capital, which would lead to greater capacity in the ability to produce goods and services (Canada 2011). This is particularly interesting in the case of Canada's stimulus program because the largest single item of the program was devoted to tax cuts. The government, in its report on the Action Plan, includes $200 billion in tax reductions on individuals, families, and business from various budgets that give tax relief from 2008 to 2013, in addition to the $46 billion in federal government stimulus that in itself included tax cuts (33).

Tax cuts were the only items in the stimulus plans that were retained as permanent features: all other programs ended in 2011, when the economy was assumed to be on the road to recovery. It should also be noted that at this time the recovery was deemed sufficient so that some of the money on infrastructure was not spent. The expenditures actually having a stimulus effect (increased money for the unemployed and those with limited income, infrastructure spending, and increased housing subsidies) were all short-term measures designed only to deal with the crisis itself. In the case of Employment Insurance benefits, the stimulus package expanded coverage for those unemployed only during the recession, and many of those who would have been eligible for benefits during the recession were not eligible when it was declared over.

Impact of Economic Change through Austerity

Austerity measures in Canada, represented as a percentage of both total social spending and total government spending to GDP, have decreased steadily since the early 1990s and are interrupted only occasionally by stimulus programs (figures 4.1 and 4.3). The stimulus programs are short-term initiatives designed to counter the most devastating effects of economic crisis. The relationship between the effects of declining relative government expenditures is not entirely clear, in that a wide variety of factors contribute to Canada's declining growth rates. But one major claim of "austerity" theory is that, over time, economic growth will be affected in a positive way. This does not appear to be the trend in Canada.

As figure 4.4 indicates, Canada's growth rates fluctuate considerably in relatively short periods of time. Figure 4.5 shows the changes a little differently, and while the changes look less dramatic than in figure 4.4, it demonstrates a way to understand trends in volatility. This measures the difference in growth by year. Aside from the dramatic recession in the early 1980s, one can see in figure 4.5 that the changes from year to year appear to be increasing, with the negative changes becoming larger since the 1990s. Certainly nothing definitive about the effects of specific government spending over a long period can be taken from these correlations. But one thing is certain: Canada's growth rate has been decreasing, especially since 2000, and recovered only in the post-2008–10 recession because of extraordinary government spending on special short-term programs.

Government Social Spending and Inequality

The effect of relative decreases in government spending on social programs appears to be closely related to an increase in gross levels of inequality in Canada. As can be seen in figure 4.6, Canada had relatively low levels of inequality when government social spending relative to GDP was high. This figure measures inequality by using Canada's Gini coefficient, where 0 indicates a state where everyone would have the same income and 1 is a state when total inequality exists and one person has all income. This figure shows that government social spending is fairly closely correlated to levels of inequality and that inequality decreases only when government social expenditures rise. This did occur during the increased temporary spending in the course of the 2008–10 economic crisis, a period where the level of inequality dropped somewhat. But since this was a temporary occurrence, it is unlikely to be a sustained trend.

Income inequality increased in Canada considerably between 1995 and 2011. It coincided with the change in provision of social

Figure 4.4. GDP Growth Rate – Canada

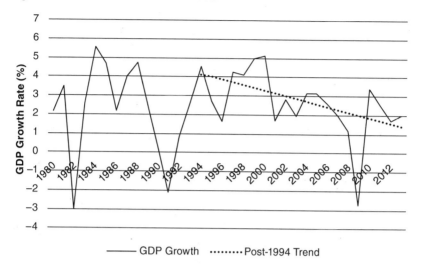

——— GDP Growth ········· Post-1994 Trend

Source: OECD.Stat. National Accounts > Main Aggregates > Gross Domestic Product.
Filters: Transaction: GDP (Expenditure Approach); Measure: Growth Rate; Time: 1980–
Latest Available.

Figure 4.5. Canadian Growth Volatility

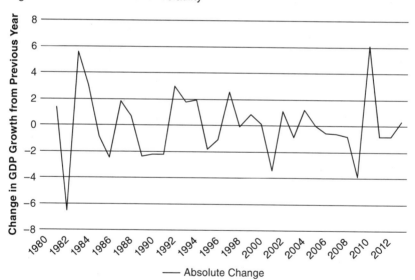

——— Absolute Change

Source: OECD.Stat. Volatility = Change in growth in absolute difference by year. Filters:
Transaction: GDP (Expenditure Approach); Measure: Growth Rate; Time: 1980–Latest
Available.

Figure 4.6. Canadian Social Expenditure as a Percentage of GDP Compared to Gini Coefficient

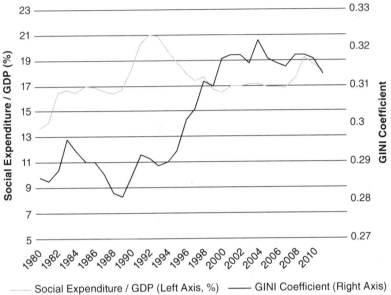

—— Social Expenditure / GDP (Left Axis, %)   —— GINI Coefficient (Right Axis)

Source: OECD.Stat (2017a); Statistics Canada (2013).

programming with the federal government's shift of major funding to the provinces. The resulting inequality was primarily because the after-tax income of the top income group rose much more than that of other groups. A rise in inequality is clearly not beneficial for most people, but it may also be harmful for economic performance. In the past, the common economic wisdom was that inequality was necessary in a capitalist economy, because there is a trade-off between economic efficiency and inequality. However, more recently, as a result of an expanded understanding of the nature and effects of inequality, there is a growing sense even among institutions such as the International Monetary Fund that greater levels of equality is important for sustaining growth over a long period. Two reasons in particular relate to Canada's growth record. One is that inequality itself can accentuate financial crisis, because people at the bottom end of the income scale are forced to borrow more, and that increases over-all financial risk; and the second is that growth can be diminished if people's skills are not being adequately employed

(Berg and Ostry 2011). In Canada, the rate of household borrowing has increased at rapid rates since austerity measures accelerated in the mid-1990s. Also, the rise of low-wage and non-standard employment, despite high education levels, indicates the rise in underemployment.

The rise of inequality that has accompanied austerity in social spending is a clear indication that austerity cannot lead to prosperity for a substantial proportion of the population.

Revenue Effects of Tax Cuts

One significant claim of those advocating government cutbacks and tax reductions is that austerity can eventually lead to not only expansion of the economy, but also increased revenues to government. The argument is that when individuals have more money in their pockets they will spend more, which will have a stimulating effect on the economy. Also, it is assumed that when corporate taxes are cut, corporations will use the money to increase investment. Both actions would increase the national income, and that in turn will result in greater total tax returns.

Tax cuts in Canada have been considerable, and the result can be seen in figure 4.7, which shows tax revenues as a percentage of GDP for select OECD countries. In the 1990s, Canada's tax revenues were slightly above the OECD average, but the decline was clearly correlated with the tax cuts that occurred since 1996. In 1997 and 1998, revenues from taxes were 36 per cent of GDP and dropped steadily so that in 2012 total taxes were 30.7 per cent of GDP. Canada is now considerably below the OECD average in tax revenues as a percentage of GDP.[12]

The tax cuts to businesses in Canada have been particularly dramatic and, according to the accounting firm PricewaterhouseCoopers, Canada now has one of the lowest business tax rates in the world (Canadian Press 2012). Altogether, the assumption that tax decreases could, over a long term, increase revenues because of higher economic activity is not born out in the case of Canada. As figure 4.7 shows, the revenue to GDP has decreased steadily since 1997. Although governments have assiduously pursued balanced budgets and total debt reduction, the reduction in the tax share seems oddly immune to policy considerations. In fact, when balanced budgets are achieved, as seems to be the case for Canada for 2014, the government then proceeds with a new round of tax cuts.

---

12 The tax cuts have occurred at the federal and provincial levels. For an indication of the impact of shift in tax fairness in one province, see Lee, Ivanova, Klein (2011).

Figure 4.7. Tax Revenue as Percentage of GDP

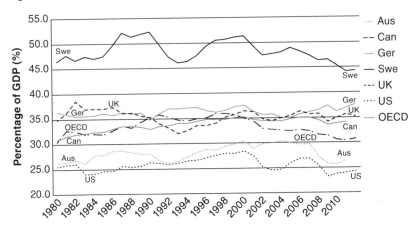

Source: OEC2017-05-01.Stat. Public Sector, Taxation and Market Regulation > Taxation > Revenue Stats - OECD Members > Comparative Tables.

Labour

The decline in labour's share of the national income since the early 1990s is well-known in Canada. Government policy to reduce wages for all except senior management has been successful through government cutbacks in the public sector, but also through changes in legislation related to employment standards and the labour code within provinces (Fairey 2012; Mackenzie 2012; Peters 2012; Ross and Savage 2012). As can be seen in figure 4.8, there has been a fairly steady decline in labour compensation to GDP since the high point of 1991–2, with an increase during the government's stimulus policies associated with the 2008–10 recession.

The comparison with other countries shows that Canada has always lagged behind most other countries (all except Australia) in the proportion of the national income that goes to labour. The largest proportion to labour was in 1991 and 1992, when it accounted for 54.4 per cent of the national income. The low point over the past three decades was in the twenty-first century, where it dipped as low as 49.2 per cent. This improved when government specifically targeted the auto, housing, and resource sectors in the stimulus package associated with the 2008–10 recession. But also significant was the increased use of Employment

Figure 4.8. Employee Compensation in Canada (% of GDP)

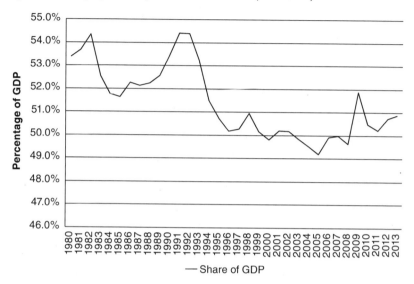

— Share of GDP

Source: National Accounts, Main Aggregates, GDP; Compensation of Employees, Current prices, Millions. OECD.Stat.

Insurance so that a greater proportion of people who became unemployed received insurance benefits.

Conclusion

Since 1990, Canadian governments have consistently avoided expanding or creating new social programs, and have cut the importance of most of them. This includes relative cuts to those that are most often considered counter-cyclical stabilizers, such as pension benefits, housing programs, social assistance, and employment insurance. They have also downsized employment in the public sectors, instituted a range of policies that have suppressed wages, and have embarked on radical reductions to taxes. Altogether government social spending as a percentage of GDP has declined steadily since the early 1990s, then increased briefly during the attempts to stimulate the economy over the recent recession, and subsequently seems to be resuming the downward trend.

The obvious observation from this chapter is that these approaches to "expansionary austerity" have not improved the performance of the economy, particularly in its growth and the volatility of growth. The increases in spending to countermand the recession were confined to permanent tax cuts, very short-term expansions of social programs, and support for specific industries. The economy did improve during the short period that Canada's stimulus program was in effect. This was not related to tax cuts (which have a poor multiplier effect), but to other initiatives that had a greater impact. Government spending can have a positive effect on growth rates, as the government obviously anticipated and that occurred in response to the recession. But the experience of the recession was very short-lived, and confirms the tendency for Canadian governments to focus on short-term crisis management, rather than on long-term stability.

The assumption associated with a Keynesian analysis would be that reductions to government social spending and tax cuts should, under normal circumstances, have increased economic volatility, and there is evidence that economic volatility has increased in Canada. But it also needs to be noted that other kinds of economic policy affected the impact of social and total public spending on volatility. For a considerable length of time, the expansionary austerity of both program and tax cuts was accompanied by either massive currency devaluation (as during the 1990s) or expansionary monetary policy (as in recent years). That is, the use of monetary policy and the value of the dollar may offset the effect of fiscal policy – specifically the reductions in government social spending – on growth rates.

These findings do contradict the assertions that expansionary austerity through the approach Canada has used (tax reductions and smaller government social spending/GDP) will both create more government revenues and improve growth rates. Higher taxes have not stimulated investment as claimed would happen, and growth rates not only are decreasing but also are more volatile.

My final observation would be that it seems entirely possible that expansionary austerity could continue for a very long time, as long as governments and people are willing to tolerate substantial uncertainty in the economy and the deterioration of services that people need. The automatic stabilizers that could temper the volatility and its consequences for people are decreasingly significant as a proportion of the total economy. This means that governments will continue to focus on containing crises as they arise for short periods of time and resume austerity measures once the economy is more stable.

REFERENCES

Barro, Josh. 2014. "Conservatives Fall in Love with Canada." *New York Times*, 21 September.

Berg, Andrew G., and Jonathan D. Ostry. 2011. "Equality and Efficiency." (International Monetary Fund) *Finance & Development* 48 (3): 1–15.

Blyth, Mark. 2013. *Austerity: The History of a Dangerous Idea*. Oxford: Oxford University Press.

– 2013b. "The Austerity Delusion." *Foreign Affairs* 92 (3): 41–56.

Canada. 2011. *Canada's Economic Action Plan Year 2: A Seventh Report to Canadians*. http://www.actionplan.gc.ca.

Canada War Museum. n.d. "Canada at War: Post-war Planning." http://www.warmuseum.ca/cwm/exhibitions/newspapers/canadawar/postwar_e.shtml.

Canadian Foreign Exchange Services. "Yearly Average Exchange Rates for Currencies." http://www.canadianforex.ca/forex-tools/historical-rate-tools/yearly-average-rates.

Canadian Press. 2012. "Canadian Business Tax Rate among the World's Lowest," 3 December. http://www.cbc.ca/news/business/canadian-business-tax-rate-among-world-s-lowest-1.1173662.

Causa, Orsetta, Alain de Serres, and Nicolas Ruiz. 2014. "Can Growth-Enhancing Policies Lift All Boats? An Analysis Based on Household Disposable Incomes." OECD Economics Department Working Papers, OECD Publishing, Paris.

Cohen, Marjorie. 2016. "How Useful Is Picketty's Analysis for Political Action?" *Social Studies* 11 (1): 212–15.

Cohen, Marjorie Griffin. 1997. "From the Welfare State to Vampire Capitalism." In *Women and the Canadian Welfare State*, ed. Patrica M. Evans and Gerda R. Wekerle, 28–67. Toronto: University of Toronto Press. http://dx.doi.org/10.3138/9781442683549-005.

– 2013. "Neo-Liberal Crisis/Social Reproduction/Gender Implications." *University of New Brunswick Law Journal* 64:234–52.

Darby, J., and J. Melitz. 2007. "Labour Market Adjustment, Social Spending and the Automatic Stabilizers in the OECD." 47th Panel Meeting of Economic Policy, 18–19 April, Ljubljana. www.econpapers.repec.org/RePEc:cpr:ceprdp:6230.

– 2011. "Joint Estimates of Automatic and Discretionary Fiscal Policy: The OECD, 1981–2003." Paris: Centre d'Études Prospectives et d'informations Internationales.

Department of Finance. 2011. "Canada's Economic Action Plan: A Seventh Report to Canadians." http://www.fin.gc.ca/pub/report-rapport/2011-7/ceap-paec-a-eng.asp.

Fairey, David. 2012. *Why BC's Lower-Wage Workers Are Struggling: The Case for Stronger Employment Standards.* Vancouver: Canadian Centre for Policy Alternatives.

Giavazzi, Fransesco, and Marco Pagano. 1990. "Can Severe Fiscal Contractions Be Expansionary? Tales of Two Small European Countries." *NBER Macroeconomics Annual* 5:75–111. http://dx.doi.org/10.1086/654131.

Guajardo, Jamie, Daniel Leigh, and Andrea Pescatori. 2011. *Expansionary Austerity: New International Evidence.* IMF working Paper, July.

Joël, Cariolle. 2012. *Measuring Macroeconomic Volatility: Applications to Export Revenue Data, 1970–2005.* Auvergne: Fondation pour les Études et Reserches sur le Development International. http://www.ferdi.fr/sites/www.ferdi.fr/files/idi/I14_eng.pdf.

Lee, Marc, Iglika Ivanova, and Seth Klein. 2011. "BC's Regressive Tax Shift." In *Behind the Numbers.* Vancouver: Canadian Centre for Policy Alternatives, June.

Lucke, Bernd. 1997. "Non-Keynesian Effects of Fiscal Contractions: Theory and Applications for Germany." ResearchGate. https://www.researchgate.net/publication/228637644_Non-Keynesian_effects_of_fiscal_contractions_theory_and_applications_for_Germany.

Mackenzie, Hugh. 2012. *Canada's CEO Elite 100.* Ottawa: Canadian Centre for Policy Alternatives.

OECD. 2016. "Social Expenditure Database (SOCX)." http://www.oecd.org/social/expenditure.htm.

OECD.Stat. 2017a. "Social Expenditure: Aggregated Data." OECD. http://stats.oecd.org/Index.aspx?datasetcode=SOCX_AGG#.

– 2017b. "Welcome to OECD.Stat." http://stats.oecd.org.

Panitch, Leo, and Sam Gindin. 2012. *The Making of Global Capitalism: The Political Economy of American Empire.* London: Verso.

Papadimitriou, Dimitri B., Michais Nikiforos, Gennaro Zezza, and Greg Hannsgen. 2014. *Is Rising Inequality a Hindrance to the US Economic Recovery?* Annandale-on-Hudson, NY: Levy Economics Institute.

Peters, John. 2012. *Boom, Bust and Crisis: Labour, Corporate Power and Politics in Canada.* Halifax: Fernwood.

Piketty, Thomas. 2014. *Capital in the Twenty-First Century.* Cambridge, MA: Belknap. http://dx.doi.org/10.4159/9780674369542.

Rice, James J., and Michael J. Prince. 2000. *Changing Politics of Canadian Social Policy.* Toronto: University of Toronto Press.

Ross, Stephanie, and Larry Savage, eds. 2012. *Rethinking the Politics of Labour in Canada*. Halifax: Fernwood.

Statistics Canada. 2013. "Table 202-0709: Gini Coefficients of Market, Total and After-Tax Income of Individuals, Where Each Individual Is Represented by Their Adjusted Household Income, by Economic Type." http://www5. statcan.gc.ca/cansim/a26?id=2020709&retrLang=eng&lang=eng.

Vernon, J.R. 1919. "The 1920–21 Deflation: The Role of Aggregate Supply." *Economic Inquiry* 29 (3): 572–80.

5 Internalizing Neoliberalism and Austerity

STEPHEN MCBRIDE AND SORIN MITREA

You are in charge of your career all the time, every day, in every situation. Workers can rely on "skills security" rather than long-term job security. Career self-management means not relying on any business, organization, government or union to look after your interests.

British Columbia Ministry of Advanced Training and Technology, June 1999

This message exemplifies the neoliberal approach to the labour market. Assuming the market is functioning properly, and that any rigidities posed by over-regulation have been removed, then success or failure within it is individually determined. Not long ago, the prevailing wisdom was that labour market problems experienced by individuals, such as unemployment, were largely systemic – the product of structural factors. One question this chapter asks is, How did we get to here from there? More specifically it focuses on whether and in what ways the individualist account of labour market success or failure has been internalized. To what extent have the state policies that have reconfigured the labour market, which will be briefly described in the first parts of the chapter, been accepted by those who have experienced them, often to their disadvantage when compared to labour market experiences in the previous period. We engage in a comparative analysis of the United Kingdom and Canada as both countries have long narratives of austerity – dating back to the 1980s and 1990s – defined as fiscal consolidation and structural reforms that include labour market restructuring and flexibilization (Berry 2014; Blyth 2013). Labour market policies (LMP) operate at the intersection of social construction and coercion, making social support for the precarious contingent on undertaking training and attitudinal adjustment. Rather than simply responding to exogenous economic conditions (e.g., post-Fordist production and globalization), these policies are best understood as responsibilizing projects, materially and rhetorically devolving any social or collective responsibility for well-being to the subject. We use the literature to parse the ways in which people have reacted to the exigencies brought on by austere labour market policy.

Canada and the United Kingdom are excellent cases for a comparative analysis. Although the latter is a unitary and not federal system, both states are parliamentary, representative liberal democracies; both are residual liberal welfare states and industrially advanced liberal market economies; both are mid-sized powers internationally; and both have long histories of austerity and voluntarily undertook it after the global financial crisis (GFC) (Berry 2014; Blyth 2013; Macdonald 2014; Dunk 2002).

From Keynesianism to Neoliberalism: Full to Flexible Employment and the Individualization of Labour Market Performance

John Maynard Keynes considered most of the mass unemployment of the 1930s to be caused by a lack of effective aggregate demand – spending on consumption, investment, government, and net exports. If effective aggregate demand fell below the capacity of the economy to supply goods and services, then unemployment would occur. Contrary to the neoclassical orthodoxy of his day, Keynes argued that without effective demand the economy might remain in depression or recession. Government should therefore act to raise the level of aggregate demand, either through spending, intervening in the private economy to raise exports, or adjusting consumption or investment. The corollary of this approach was that, outside of exceptions, individual unemployed persons suffered from the shortfall in aggregate demand (a structural factor) rather than their own "failings."

Keynes's ideas were widely adopted after 1945. The "Golden Age" imaginary of post-war welfare capitalism, often depicted as an era of full employment managed by a benevolent state, came to define the Keynesian era. It came to an end, depending on place, somewhere between 1975 and 1995. Although this imaginary was somewhat inflated, it does provide a contrast with the increasingly austere neoliberal period that succeeded it.

100 The Austerity State

Leaving aside the issue of how to explain this shift in policy paradigms, we can briefly summarize the neoliberal approach as involving
the idea that state intervention in the economy obstructs the efficiency
of the market and should therefore be reduced to a minimum. The primary means of constraining the state include privatization, deregulation, devolution, debt, and balanced budgets (austerity). The preferred
method of achieving the last is through spending restraint rather than
increased revenues via taxes, indicating that the overarching goal is not
a balanced budget per se, but a reduced role for the state. Conversely,
neoliberals tend to favour a strong but limited state, and so spending is
maintained in areas like law and order, defence, and protection of property rights, while spending restraint typically befalls social programs,
which redistribute through in-kind, free, or subsidized benefits such as
education, health, pensions, and income security (Gamble 1998). With
respect to the labour market, neoliberals argue that various problems,
including unemployment, result from "rigidities" (typically measures
that confer security to workers through negotiated settlements or regulation). Removal of these rigidities will overcome labour market problems by allowing the market to function efficiently (flexibly) with the
onus on individuals to be flexible and adjust to changing circumstances.

This diffusion of market logics *through* the state has increased the
diffusion of neoliberal "common sense" – a Gramscian concept that
can be defined as a spontaneous, naturalized way of experiencing and
living in the world (Knight 1998, 106; Hall and O'Shea 2013, 8). This
common sense has several components: (1) the individual is the normative centre of society and should be as unencumbered by rules and
collective responsibilities as possible; (2) the market is the most effective means through which individuals can maximize their own utility; (3) state actions that interfere with individual autonomy or market
relations lead to an autocratic society; (4) these logics frame entrepreneurial practices and subjectivities as the rightful and necessary (for
survival and success) culmination of individual responsibility, rational
calculation (oriented towards self-interest), disciplined consumption,
and "self-work" (Pierre 1995; Herd, Lightman, and Mitchell 2009).
Consequently, dependence ("laziness") is an immoral individual failing (Clarke and Newman 2012, 311).

Between the end of the Second World War and the mid-1970s, the Canadian labour market exhibited relatively full employment (compared to
the preceding and subsequent periods) and security. Security refers to
low unemployment levels, increased protection due to unionization,

and low incidence of part-time or temporary work as compared to full-time, ongoing work. In the neoliberal period unemployment was generally higher and, equally important, the labour market was restructured towards less security for workers and more flexibility for employers (an umbilical linkage). In broad terms, therefore, we have moved from full employment to flexible employment. While flexibility can be advantageous for employees who have other time commitments, they rarely have control over scheduling (Lewchuk et al. 2013). Indeed, flexibility is typically in the interest of employers who determine the allocation and conditions of working time (Standing 1999).

Concurrently, consumption and survival continued to shift from wages – which stagnated – to debt, which prompted individual responses in overtime work and reduced consumption to meet rising debt obligations (Pathak 2014, 91). Indeed, the pre-GFC Anglo-American economies experienced a rapid rise in and proliferation of financialization via consumer credit, increasingly in unsecured (e.g., non-mortgage) liabilities (Montgomerie and Williams 2009, 100). As a result, individuals became further integrated into financial markets via more dangerous instruments (3). The state's retreat from mitigating precarity (or regulating financial markets) permitted rising debt to take on a disciplinary character, necessitating consistent individual efforts to manage obligations so as to maintain consumption and survival (Pathak 2014, 93).

The degree to which workers enjoy security depends ultimately on their relative power vis-à-vis capital and the state, influenced by the mode of labour market regulation. Standing (1999) identifies three modes: regulation by the state, regulation by "voice" (through direct negotiations or bargaining between employers and workers), and regulation by the market. Although there are pros and cons to each regulatory mode, Standing argues that the post-war period (of full employment) was characterized by state regulation of the labour market that tended to extend labour's rights and security. Regulation by the state or by voice are essentially collectivist forms of regulation. Regulation by a market stripped of its rigidities leads to labour market flexibility and the individualization of responsibility, described on the BC government website with which we opened the chapter.

Austerity: Policy and Morality

Austerity proponents claim that exorbitant public indebtedness is ruining the major economies and that neoliberal measures such as cutting spending (wages, prices, and general spending while cutting taxes) to eliminate deficits and debts would result in economic growth (Levinson 2013, 93; Blyth 2013, 2). Austerity policies also have "lock-in effects," wherein cuts to public expenditures, revenue, and less economic stimulus leave governments with fewer options to address economic downturns (Levinson 2013, 91).

However, austerity is more than a policy orientation – it is a moral economy built around practices of consumption that frame individual responsibility for reduced consumption and resilience as practices of "good citizenship" (Knight 1998; Clarke 2005). Failing to make the virtuously necessary shared sacrifices compelled by crisis threatens the future of the subject and the community (Clarke and Newman 2012, 316). Moral austerity is tutelary insofar as it works to shape the behaviour of subjects through broad social relations or through the state (MacGregor 1999, 108).

Material precarity (financial/employment insecurity, debt, etc.) and the retrenchment of the social state contribute to psychological and physical trauma and cause the subject to "retreat inward," increasingly abandoning social (let alone political) relations (Lewchuk et al. 2013; Slay and Penny 2013). Austerity intensifies precarity (through its effects of lower growth and subsequently lower-quality jobs, shrinking the state, and raising unemployment) and, through its own narrative of reduced consumption and individual responsibility, puts more pressure for individuals to be resilient, "lower their expectations," and survive rather than strive to change austere trajectories. Assistance from the state is contingent on taking part in LMP training programs, and other support is dependent on social relations and existing assets, both of which are rapidly stretched in precarity (Berry 2014; Vrankulj 2012; Harrison 2013; Herd, Lightman, and Mitchell 2009). As labour protections retrench, wages stagnate, and precarity and unemployment rise, people must find a way to survive, and neoliberal austerity delineates the psychological and material mechanisms by which people may cope. Neoliberal LMP provides a "common sense" narrative of responsibilization: making the self employable, remaining flexible, and reducing consumption and expectations so as to be a resilient entrepreneurial subject (Read 2009; Pathak 2014).

Austerity unravels safety nets, with benefits and tax credits becoming less generous and more conditional and punitive, bifurcating the vulnerable between those who responsibilize (the "deserving poor") and those who do not (Slay and Penny 2013, 11; Macdonald 2014). In the United Kingdom with budget 2014/15, this has taken the form of £19 billion per year in cuts to incapacity benefits (the hardest hit), tax credits, child benefits, housing benefits, disability living allowances, deductions, and introduction of benefit caps (Slay and Penny 2013, 11). In Canada, the 2014 federal budget enacted $14 billion in spending cuts or freezes to federal departments and operating budgets, continuing years of social service retrenchment, privatization, and devolution (putting more pressure on the provinces, such that Ontario's 2014 budget forecast $2.1 billion in cuts and spending reductions) (Macdonald 2014; Tiessen 2014).

Relatedly, precarity has physiological, psychological, and social consequences, particularly for those with multiple disadvantages (e.g., unemployment, poverty, poor education, networks, and supports), which have been found to isolate individuals by compromising social networks, again driving them inward for survival (Benach et al. 2014). In a sample of 36,984 individuals aged fifteen and over in Canada, 28 per cent of those in the low-income population experienced high psychological distress, compared to 19 per cent in the non-low-income population (Caron and Liu 2011, 318). Similarly, in the United Kingdom, the least-skilled workers – disproportionately represented in precarious employment – are 21.6 per cent more likely to experience anxiety, are 288 per cent more likely to be depressed, are 121 per cent more likely to develop alcohol dependence, and have a 188 per cent higher mortality rate (all of these figures are exacerbated by unemployment and poverty) (Murali and Oyebode 2004, 218).

Social Construction and Responsibilization

Social construction describes the ways that policy design and implementation have material and psychological effects on subjectivity as a result of particular framings and discourses. Policies normatively construct subjects and their conditions by allocating resources and mobilizing narratives towards particular goals (Schneider and Ingram 1993, 93). Social construction in policy has "feedback" effects, wherein positive construction correlates strongly with political power resource (material and discursive) outcomes and more active political participation (98). In the case of austerity and neoliberal LMP, these policies operate as a moral project to conduct citizens' behaviour and attitudes towards individual responsibility and employability as conditions for social support. As former UK prime minister Tony Blair said,

"We accept our duty as a society to give each person a stake in its future. And in return each person accepts responsibility ... to work to improve themselves" (Dam Sam Yu 2008, 386; Wainwright et al. 2010, 490). This is paralleled in Canada, as Stephen Harper recently noted: "We have to govern ourselves responsibly [and] the wealth we have today [has] to be earned in a very competitive ... future" (Harper 2013). Subjects are increasingly expected to be independent, but hard working; autonomous, but responsible (e.g., avoiding binge drinking or over-eating); and to manage their lifestyles so as to promote their own health and well-being (Clarke 2005, 451).

The state utilizes supply-side[1] LMP to construct responsibilized individuals: subjects who internalize a culture of self-discipline and are individually active in cultivating their success, health, and well-being, while making them responsible for it and to society (Knight 1998; MacGregor 1999). Responsibilization is based on the assumption that rises in inequality and poverty are a result of individual failings rather than structural design and morally equates self-care, discipline, responsibility, and self-containment ("you are responsible for yourself, but also for your effect on others") with good citizenship and the realization of future security (MacGregor 1999, 108; Whitworth and Carter 2014, 110). In the case of supply-side LMP, individuals are called upon to answer to their moral responsibility for self-care (survival) and independence through discipline, sacrifice, and reduced consumption so as to secure their future (Herd, Lightman, and Mitchell 2009; Harrison 2013). Thus, while responsibility can operate in non-individualizing discursive regimes and has done so, it is framed through autonomy (individualization) and personal choice by neoliberalism and austerity as "common sense" (Knight 1998, 125; Whitworth and Carter 2014, 110).

In the context of labour, neoliberalism expands the logic of neoclassical economic theory to all social relations and behaviours, or, as Foucault said, "Homo economicus is an entrepreneur, an entrepreneur of himself" (Read 2009, 26). Supply-side LMP socially constructs "human capital," not workers, through responsibilization: attempting to inculcate the idea of self-actualized ("activation") "investment" in one's skills or abilities so as to make oneself employable through market-based pedagogies (e.g., training, education, mobility, flexibility) (Pathak 2014, 105). Crucially,

---

1 Supply-side measures focus on individual employability rather than job creation ("demand side") (Lightman, Herd, and Mitchell 2006).

via supply-side LMP's focus on individual will and dependency, entre-preneurial subjectivity is a moral enterprise whose outcomes in upward mobility, well-being, and independence are framed as utterly contingent on integration into the market, and failure as a result of a lack of indi-vidual will, responsibility, and moral conscience (105).

The Austere Worlds of Labour Market and Welfare Policy in the Neoliberal Era

In the 1970s, limitations emerged to Keynesian aggregate demand man-agement in ensuring full-employment alongside global pressures to flexibilize labour markets and roll back the social state that protected and supported workers. As a result, labour market policy shifted from demand side to "active (e.g., training programs) supply side (focus-ing on individuals)," focusing on individuals' employability, responsi-bility, and attitudes as responses to narratives of welfare dependence, rising fiscal deficits, and structural unemployment in the late 1980s and 1990s (Lightman, Herd, and Mitchell 2006; Nicholls and Morgan 2009). The OECD is an epistemic community that can be viewed as a principal architect promulgating flexible LMP by cultivating a con-sensus on these policies as "best practices" and providing a forum for the exchange and reinforcement of ideas. It became a strong sponsor of free market ideologies and, although it has no authority to enforce its recommendations or sanction non-compliance, it had considerable persuasive power (Kuruvilla and Verma 2006). The OECD Jobs Study reports, notwithstanding some internal differences, advocated a "one size fits all" set of policy recommendations for members' labour, eco-nomic, and finance ministers to address rising unemployment through deregulation, market liberalization, activation of the unemployed, and removal of labour market rigidities (Noaksson and Jacobsson 2003, 31; Hodson and Maher 2002).

While compliance varied (e.g., among social market economies attempting to combine flexibility and security) and the OECD's own benchmark indicators suggested their strategies do not produce pre-dicted benefits, the liberal group of countries, which included our case studies in Britain and Canada, were the most compliant with OECD recommendations (McBride and Williams 2001).[2] Liberal states provide

---

2 See Mahon (2011) for an alternative view.

minimal standards and focus on "activating" people to adapt to labour market conditions through means-tested assistance, modest social transfer to the working class and poor, stigmatized benefits, and heavy emphasis on employability rather than employment.

Consequently, equity objectives contended with efficiency motives in Canada[3] (Little 2001) and the United Kingdom (Berry 2014), eventually leading to dilution of training, privatization of service delivery, and the individualization of labour market success. Responsibilization informs contemporary supply-side LMP in Canada and the United Kingdom, both of which tie welfare to LMP ("workfare") and privilege rapid job placement ("work-first"), consequently forgoing substantial skill investment (Herd, Lightman, and Mitchell 2009; Harrison 2013). In the context of austerity, "activation" in LMP refers to "self-work," wherein welfare recipients and the unemployed are required to take part in workfare programs that encourage individual solutions such as self-responsibility and attitudinal adjustment to lower expectations, reduced consumption, and be flexible (Clarke 2005; Read 2009).

Moral and fiscal austerity inform the devolution of labour market policy in Canada and the United Kingdom with the shift to work-first workfare models. In Canada in the mid-1990s, the federal government devolved more financial responsibility to the provinces for social support provision with the end of the Canada Assistance Plan (CAP) and the shift to the Canada Health and Social Transfer (CHST) in 1995 (Lazar 2006). The 1996 federal Employment Insurance Act similarly retrenched support and eligibility for employment insurance (EI) while devolving increasing responsibility for training to the provinces (who subsequently privatized many services) (Haddow and Klassen 2006). The provinces, then, typically devolved the implementation – and increasingly, financial burden – onto municipalities (who then often employed private contractors) (Herd, Lightman, and Mitchell 2009, 133).

Similarly, in January 1998 the UK government launched the first of twelve "New Deals," which devolved increasing implementation and management of workfare to local authorities and applied to anyone who was claiming an out-of-work benefit (Berry 2014; Nicholls and Morgan 2009). As with the Canadian shifts, the New Deals shifted financial benefits based on automatic entitlement of citizenship to users' efforts to re-enter the labour market (Dam Sam Yu 2008; Smith 2013). In both

---

3 See McBride (1992, chap. 5).

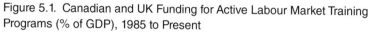

Figure 5.1. Canadian and UK Funding for Active Labour Market Training Programs (% of GDP), 1985 to Present

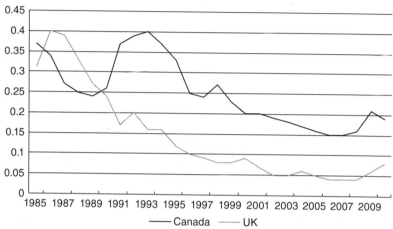

Note: Most recent data for Canada were 2011 and 2010 for the United Kingdom. The OECD considers training programs, placements, and incentives (including unemployment support).
Source: OECD Statistics 2014.

Canada and the United Kingdom, the shift towards supply-side LMP devolves program responsibility to lower levels of government and responsibility for labour market outcomes to the individual, shifting eligibility based on an unconditional determination of need to market-based selectivity (Herd, Lightman, and Mitchell 2009; Slay and Penny 2013). Individualization and privatization in neoliberal LMP has been consistent with the fiscal consolidation of austerity, shifting emphasis to compulsion over voluntarism, sanctions over incentives, and individualized obligations over collective rights (Little 2001; Nicholls and Morgan 2009). The long-term effect on active labour market spending can be seen in figure 5.1.

Liberal market economies such as Canada and the United Kingdom pursued "work-first" (the New Deals in the United Kingdom and programs such as Ontario Works in Canada) workfare models,[4]

---

4 Welfare support for post-secondary education was abolished in 1996 in Ontario, and support for full-time education or vocational training drifted with the United Kingdom's "New Deals" in 1998 (Little 2001, 21; Berry 2014, 598).

which place priority on rapid labour force entry through compulsory participation,[5] attitudinal adjustment, minimal retraining, and job search skills in short-term, low-cost programs (Herd, Lightman, and Mitchell 2009; Berry 2014). These measures – along with politicians, the media, and the public – push the idea that unemployment and poverty were individual failings in lacking skills, education, attitudes, morality, responsibility and flexibility[6] (Dam Sam Yu 2008, 384; Herd, Lightman, and Mitchell 2009, 129). This approach individualizes blame and elides structural forces and policies that create unemployment and poverty, which results in individuals remaining in poverty and "cycling" between poor-paying jobs of low quality, with low retention and unemployment (Herd, Lightman, and Mitchell 2009, 134; Wainwright, Buckingham, and Marandet 2010, 495). Work-first programs privilege job search skills, "soft" skills (e.g., communication, problem-solving, assertiveness, and time management) and attitudinal adjustment (Herd, Lightman, and Mitchell 2009; Berry 2014). Compliance is obtained through a mixture of ideology (via attitudinal adjustment as social construction) and coercion, with the latter reinforcing the former.

For example, with the United Kingdom's New Deal for Young People (NDYP), individuals were required to take part in either full-time education or vocational training for a year or subsidized employment in the private, voluntary, or public sector for six months (Berry 2014, 598). However, over 90 per cent of services were dedicated to job-search and related services such as job counselling, CV-writing, and search assistance (598; Nicholls and Morgan 2009, 83). The NDYP used soft social control (e.g., one-to-one advice) and hard sanctions such as the withdrawal of benefits for persistent "refusal to conform" by not completing programs, being late, or leaving early (Dam Sam Yu 2008, 385). Similarly, with Ontario Works (whose funding was cut by 17 per cent in 1996–7), the emphasis was disproportionately on job-seeking skills and attitudinal adjustment: in a 2009 study of four municipal programs in Ontario, all focused primarily on "life skills" such as résumé preparation, job coaching, interview preparation, and employers' expectations;

---

5 Failure to attend, not completing sufficient hours, leaving early, or refusing employment results in the withdrawal of benefits in both the United Kingdom and Canada (Herd, Lightman, and Mitchell 2009, 136; Smith 2013, 162).
6 While welfare receipt would "engender laziness," resulting in long-term reliance on public assistance and a drag on social services, the state, and society (moral austerity) (Little 2001; Diprose 2014).

some focused specifically on work ethics, increased motivation, positively adjusting attitudes, and developing coping strategies; and failure to attend resulted in financial sanctions (Herd, Lightman, and Mitchell 2009, 139; Mendelsohn and Medow 2010). For those who cannot find work, "community participation" or unpaid work placements (which may not be covered by employment standards or EI) are required in exchange for welfare in the United Kingdom and Canada (Little 2001, 22; Nicholls and Morgan 2009, 83). Reduced consumption is enforced, as the state requires access to financial statements for up to a year, potentially forcing participants to sell assets (at the time, allowed liquidity was $520). Also, all income must be declared, including any help from others (Herd, Lightman, and Mitchell 2009).

These low-cost programs disseminate neoliberal ideology, encouraging workers to lower ("realistic") expectations by adjusting individuals' attitudes from "passivity and poor working habits" towards "activation" (Herd, Lightman, and Mitchell 2009, 136). Programs focus primarily on shaping participants' attitudes, focusing daily on the financial and psychological value of work, independence, work ethic, and individual responsibility to develop "realistic expectations" about the labour market: as an Ontario facilitator said, "Take a lower-paying job at this time. Be realistic. It's common sense" (146).[7] Similarly, in the United Kingdom, programs were built around lowered expectations. As a policymaker said, "Our view [was] that retention depended on getting people job ready [more than] it did in the kind of support they had after they got a job" (Nicholls and Morgan 2009, 88). Negative situations, such as job loss, poverty, and even family death, could be "resolved" through attitudinal adjustment, according to Ontario facilitators: "You can be sad, depressed, angry ... you have to find another road" (Herd, Lightman, and Mitchell 2009, 145).

Neoliberal Labour Market Policy Post-GFC

Around the time of the Global Financial Crisis and onward, workfare policies in the United Kingdom under the Coalition government pivoted towards correcting "individual failings" by addressing "the incentives

---

7 Throughout the experience in Ontario, researchers did not observe participants ask any questions or resist: "The practice made sense to all involved," exhibiting internalization (Herd, Lightman, and Mitchell 2009, 142).

and disincentives of benefits" (Slay and Penny 2013). However, the shift to "universal credit" as part of the 2012 Welfare Reform Act further retrenched social supports by cutting certain subsidies, introducing benefit caps and new sanctions (for not complying with workfare measures or not getting off welfare), and locking tax credits to only a 1 per cent increase a year instead of tying to inflation (Slay and Penny 2013, 1). As recently as May 2015, a Labour Party leadership contender in the United Kingdom expressed support for the Tories' £12 billion cuts to social supports, including dropping benefit caps from £26,000 to £23,000 (Beattie 2015). In Canada after the GFC, the federal government extended EI benefits temporarily by five weeks, and five to twenty weeks of additional EI benefit were provided to the long-term unemployed, while active LMP spending rose only temporarily (see figure 5.1) (Bernard 2014, 34). Further, 2013 EI reforms forced claimants to take jobs with up to as much as a 30 per cent pay cut, and EI receipt has been falling 200 per cent faster than unemployment (Canadian Press 2013; Weir 2013). The results included a decline in coverage, such that while in 1987 some 87 per cent of the unemployed received benefits, only 36 per cent did in 2014 (PressProgress 2014). Similar results can be found in the United Kingdom,[8] with approximately 86 per cent of the unemployed receiving benefits in 1987 compared to 50 per cent in 2014 (Office for National Statistics 2015). Again, the message of individual responsibility for labour market outcomes is reinforced by continued ideology and the depletion of benefits as a form of coercion.

Internalizing Neoliberalism and Austerity

In the remainder of this chapter, we provide an early-stage comparative content and statistical analysis to determine how people have reacted to precarity and LMP under neoliberalism and austerity in Canada and the United Kingdom. In looking at secondary sources, results will be organized under headings of attitudes towards the vulnerable, individual responsibility, market solutions, reduced expectations, moral judgments, and reduced consumption.

We are interested in how effective these policies have been in shaping individuals' perspectives through the logics of neoliberalism and austerity. Faced with precarity and the individualizing and responsibilizing

---

8 This is a general comparison of trends and does not account for the differences between Canadian Employment Insurance and the UK Job Seeker's Allowance.

narrative offered by neoliberalism, austerity, and supply-side LMP, we propose that people will react on a spectrum of internalization (*embracing* responsibilization), disaffected consent (embodying responsibilization as primary survival recourse),[9] and resistance (contesting responsibilization). On the basis of a review of secondary literature, we hypothesize that disaffected consent will be the most common response, speaking to the degree to which neoliberal austerity and LMP have undermined other forms and options of surviving and being, providing one main "path" (and narrative) for survival.

Attitudes towards the Vulnerable

Attitudes towards the unemployed and impoverished typically follow narratives of individual irresponsibility, laziness, dependency, and immorality that correlate with increased support for social service retrenchment (Krahn et al. 1987; Diprose 2015). These findings are validated in perceptions of poor and unemployed people in Canada (Fournier, Zimmermann, and Gauthier 2011) and in the United Kingdom (Taylor-Gooby and Taylor 2014):

- Benefits for the unemployed "discourage work" and self-sufficiency (2011): Canada 55.9 per cent agree; UK 62 per cent;
- "If people really want to work, they can find a job" (2011): Canada 70.9 per cent agree; UK 57 per cent;
- "People who don't get ahead should blame themselves, not the system" (2011): Canada 56.8 per cent agree; UK 23 per cent[10] (a 53.3 per cent increase since 1994).

The 2011 Canada Election Study found that 66.3 per cent of people believe that people should move if they can't find work, a sentiment mirrored by participants in a UK study on perception of poverty: "Don't go by what the Government says, but by what you see out there

---

9 A conditional and grudging, rather than enthusiastic, consent (Clarke and Newman 2012, 316).
10 It is beyond the scope of this chapter to address the difference between Canada and the United Kingdom in this measure, but the 1993 Canada Election Study showed 50.5 per cent support for the statement, so it appears both countries are becoming more comfortable with individualist attributions for precarity.

on the street, if people try to get a job they can get one" (Fournier, Zimmermann, and Gauthier 2011, 114; Castell and Thompson 2007, 18).

In several Canadian studies (Herd, Lightman, and Mitchell 2009; Little 2001; Collins 2005), the least privileged members of society (unskilled manual labour, poorly paid individuals, and even welfare recipients) appeared to internalize neoliberal perspectives, exhibiting the most negative and individualistic attitudes towards the unemployed. They cognitively and emotionally distance themselves from the "undeserving poor" who "have too many children, have never worked before, and who don't try to better themselves" – results that are mirrored in the United Kingdom (Diprose 2015; Castell and Thompson 2007). These studies demonstrated a growing concern with "the future" of the polis, informing moral criticism of the "dependent" who would undermine the structure and sustainability of the community.

Individual Responsibility for Circumstances

Supply-side LMP as workfare frames culminate in narratives of "no legitimate dependency," wherein almost "everything about people's lives are deemed to be the responsibility of the individual" (Peacock, Bissell, and Owen 2014, 176). As a result, workfare socially constructs coping with precarity as an activity of individual resilience in practices and attitudes.

In a study in the United Kingdom, participants understood their own precarity as a result of individual failure (eliciting self-blame), and any attempt to use a non-individualistic lens was "seen as a way to shirk responsibilities and duties" (Peacock, Bissell, and Owen 2014, 176):

> "It's like making excuses, yeah? Because only I can do [change my circumstances], it's all down to me ... But it is about making the choices ... so I am responsible aren't I?" (UK participant; 176)

This is similar in the Canadian context:

> "I'm not very happy with myself. I feel like I'm not doing anything worthwhile, I feel useless." (Canadian participant; Fournier, Zimmermann, and Gauthier 2011, 322)

Without social support, unemployment and poverty put tremendous pressure on time, energy, and resources, which foreclose social, let alone political, relations in an effort to simply survive, while "no

legitimate dependency" and the need for "responsibilization" disseminated by supply-side LMP may see people turn inward (Fournier, Zimmermann, and Gauthier 2011; Chase and Walker 2012; Little 2001, 17).
Indeed, research has shown that experiences of poverty and unemployment rarely lead to heightened class consciousness (Dunk 2002, 233).
In a Canadian study, unemployment (worse when poverty intersects)
had negative effects on social relations and health, as 47 per cent felt
depressed about their circumstances, 29 per cent reported that most of
the days in the past month were stressful, and 47 per cent reported that
family relations had become stressful (Vrankulj 2012, 22).

Accepting Market Solutions

Supply-side LMP engenders a sense of individual responsibility for
precarity so as to socially construct subjects to be employable, mobile,
flexible, and constantly "working on themselves" ("entrepreneurial
subjectivity") (Dunk 2002; Wainwright et al. 2010). At its core, supply-
side LMP disseminates a narrative that what is fair, right, and reasonable is determined by the market:

> "Life is what you make it if you can. Like nobody's going to give you
> anything ... Like they should give me a job ... It doesn't work that way."
> (Canadian participant; Dunk 2002, 888)

> "My career is rather unusual inasmuch as I've had probably three or four
> careers ... I think it's just the circumstances that you have presented to you
> in your life [and what you make of them]." (UK participant; Gabriel, Gray,
> and Goregaokar 2010, 1698)

Subjects in a Canadian study illustrated the intersection of austerity
(via reduced consumption) and entrepreneurial subjectivity by "investing" in their "human capital" so as to render themselves employable:
one respondent now saw "tuition fees as a form of investment and
understood that he must forgo other spending to afford this," and
another saw negative events as "an opportunity to learn" (Buckland,
Fikkert, and Gonske 2013, 345). Here subjects internalize the futurity of
austerity in projecting the realization of sacrifice to the future ("investment") and resilience in reframing vulnerability as opportunity.
   There is an inherent futurity in retraining, letting go of expectations rooted in the past to prepare yourself for the new future, as was

articulated in an Ontario retraining program: "Success is said to require 'letting go of old patterns and behaviors' and 'looking forward to change as a challenge, taking risks and innovating'" (Dunk 2002, 887). Supply-side measures and "getting over" layoffs were accepted by some workers:

> "[The retraining program] was good ... they helped with the resumes and they [helped] people realize that the place was shut down ... I think that was the whole point." (Canadian participant; Dunk 2002, 888)

Reduced Expectations

One effect of the flexibilization of labour, precarity, and supply-side LMP is that expectations and aspirations for control over work (let alone for gratifying work) and the future are lowered so as to inure people to repeated deprivation and frustration (Dunk 2002). Indeed, reservation wages – the lowest that a worker will accept – decline over time as expectations degrade and needs increase (Nichols, Mitchell, and Lindner 2013, 4).

In a Canadian three-year longitudinal study, precarious employment and unemployment led workers to accept jobs for which they were overqualified and that offered little or no social protection (e.g., retirement plans, health insurance), paid a low and/or irregular wage, and were unfulfilling and precarious (Fournier, Zimmermann, and Gauthier 2011). There were similar findings in the United Kingdom (Slay and Penny 2013; Gabriel, Gray, and Goregaokar 2010) and other Canadian studies (Lewchuk et al. 2013; Vrankulj 2012). People's feelings of precarity led to disaffected consent to labour market conditions:

> "I'm feeling down, disappointed, lost. This is what work has become for me: I'm going to get a job I won't hate too much for the next 15 years and that's going to put money in my pocket, PERIOD ... Before, I was passionate about work, it fulfilled my need to give and create." (Canadian participant; Fournier, Zimmermann, and Gauthier, 2011, 322)

> "Your dreams and your aspirations go out the window ... I suppose for me it took a while for me to psychologically come to grips with the fact that I'm not longer going to be able to go out and [find] work." (UK participant; Brown and Vickerstaff 2011, 539)

The restructuring of labour relations in Canada and the United Kingdom by capital and the state, which intensified during the 1980s, was also a form of social construction that inured subjects (particularly labour) to neoliberal capitalism (Dunk 2002, 884). Workers have been said to define their interests in relatively narrow and individualistic terms – what Lenin referred to as "trade union consciousness" – which by definition accepts the capitalist paradigm, even if conflicts over wages, benefits, and working conditions occur (885). Younger and more educated workers expressed more neoliberal interpretations and anti-union sentiments:

> "[The union] were totally ridiculous in their expectations, totally unreasonable ... There's no reason in the world why guys with grade eight training should have been uh getting uh you know 20 bucks an hour, 22, 25 dollars an hour." (Canadian participant; Dunk 2002, 893)

Moral Judgments

As mentioned previously, the least privileged members of several studies exhibited the most individualistic attitudes towards the unemployed, cognitively and emotionally distancing themselves from the "undeserving poor" so as to "attribute their relative success to personal factors that explain the failure of the unemployed" (Krahn et al. 1987, 229). Indeed, the surveillance and micromanagement (via sanctions, attendance, activity reports, and completion of program hours) of workfare LMP socially construct the poor as morally suspect – a view that they may internalize (Little 2001; Berry 2014). In this way, subjects internalize the dichotomies promulgated by workfare policies and their underlying ideologies.

However, the precarious are also likely to blame themselves, as several studies in the United Kingdom (Chase and Walker 2012; Smith 2013; Gabriel, Gray, and Goregaokar 2010) and Canada (Fournier, Zimmermann, and Gauthier 2011; Collins 2005; Little 2001) indicate that the poor and unemployed score statistically higher on anxiety, blame, shame, and guilt (also articulated through feeling "awkward, embarrassed, useless, worthless, a failure"). Self-blame of and in combination with precarious conditions often leads to a downward spiral of negative mental and health outcomes, reduced expectations, social isolation, and retreating inward:

> "Many of the single mothers I interviewed were ... desperate to prove that they are *deserving and faithfully* feeding their children." (Canadian study; Little 2001, 19)

Impoverished participants in a 2005 Canada study categorized the precarious as "withdrawn and afraid" while expressing a sense of guilt "for every little thing you do," while others spoke of "daily humiliations from government agencies" (Collins 2005, 21). These subjects felt as if they lived "under a giant microscope" (a kind of panopticism) which added to the "stress, guilt, shame, and self-blame about living on inadequate income" (18).

Reduced Consumption

Studies in the United Kingdom (Chase and Walker 2012; Harrison 2013) and Canada (Vrankulj 2012; Buckland, Fikkert, and Gonske 2013; Collins 2005) illustrate that, once unemployed, people typically react first by reducing consumption. Further, the long-term unemployed displayed 16–24 per cent lower consumption than the unemployed (Nichols, Mitchell, and Lindner 2013, 3). Common survival strategies include reducing consumption of non-essentials and then essentials, spending savings/retirement funds, selling assets, borrowing from friends, going into debt, and putting off needed health care. In a Canadian longitudinal analysis of laid-off workers, 48 per cent reported reducing consumption ("done without something you needed") to make ends meet, with 40 per cent having difficulty with debts (Vrankulj 2012, 22). Similarly, in a UK study, participants did more than reduce consumption in having to choose between bills, food, or shelter for their children (Chase and Walker 2012, 742; Harrison 2013, 105). There are limits to the resourcefulness of reduced consumption, such that with very limited social assistance or funds, stress and sacrifice intensifies towards the end of each month (Collins 2005, 18).

> "When my bills come in I have to sit down and rummage through my cupboards just to see what I can stretch for a week ... when [utilities] bills come in that's the worst, I cannot afford it. Simple. I have to turn off the heating and get out of the house because it is too cold." (UK participants; Slay and Penny 2013, 4)

Although reduced consumption is frequently framed as a mechanism to secure the future, for many it elicits another kind of disaffection, limiting their abilities to imagine survival, let alone something more (Clarke and Newman 2012):

"There is no money coming in. I keep worrying: 'What's going to happen to me? Where will I end up?'" (Canadian participant; Fournier, Zimmermann, and Gauthier 2011, 321)

Conclusion

The structural shifts in Canadian and UK (and beyond) labour conditions and LMP require a modicum of acceptance by citizens to be sustained. The ever-increasing precarity wrought by austerity and the neoliberal labour market put subjects in a position where they *have* to find a way to survive. The ephemeral stimulus post-GFC was merely a blip in a continued trajectory of austerity. The state utilizes supply-side LMP to devolve responsibility for precarity to the individual, legitimated by a powerfully resonant narrative of coping via a moral responsibility to be flexible, to work on the self, and to discipline consumption (Hall and O'Shea 2013). Our analysis has illustrated how workers, the unemployed, and the impoverished live by neoliberal and austere ideas even if they do not *embrace* them: in a paradigm that strips social support and opportunity, all that is left is individual resilience. Perhaps the ultimate success of the neoliberal and austere state is in defining the conditions of life, regardless of the conditions of thought.

REFERENCES

Beattie, Jason. 2015. "Andy Burnham Vows to Get Tough on Benefits If He Wins Labour Leadership Race." *Mirror (Stafford, TX)*, 29 May. http://www. mirror.co.uk/news/uk-news/andy-burnham-vows-tough-benefits-5786479.

Benach, J., A. Vives, M. Amable, C. Vanroelen, G. Tarafa, and C. Muntaner. 2014. "Precarious Employment: Understanding an Emerging Social Determinant of Health." *Annual Review of Public Health* 35 (1): 229–53. http://dx.doi.org/10.1146/annurev-publhealth-032013-182500.

Bernard, Prosper M., Jr. 2014. "Canadian Political Economy and the Great Recession of 2008–09: The Politics of Coping with Economic Crisis." *American Review of Canadian Studies* 44 (1): 28–48. http://dx.doi.org/10.1080/02722011. 2014.885542.

Berry, Craig. 2014. "Quantity over Quality: A Political Economy of 'Active Labour Market Policy' in the UK." *Policy Studies* 35 (6): 592–610. http:// dx.doi.org/10.1080/01442872.2014.971730.

Blyth, Mark. 2013. *Austerity: The History of a Dangerous Idea*. Oxford: Oxford University Press.

Brown, Patrick, and Sarah Vickerstaff. 2011. "Health Subjectivities and Labour Market Participation: Pessimism and Older Workers' Attitudes and Narratives around Retirement in the United Kingdom." *Research on Aging* 33 (5): 529–50. http://dx.doi.org/10.1177/0164027511410249.

Buckland, Jerry, Antonia Fikkert, and Joel Gonske. 2013. "Struggling to Make Ends Meet: Using Financial Diaries to Examine Financial Literacy among Low-Income Canadians." *Journal of Poverty* 17 (3): 331–55. http://dx.doi.org/10.1080/10875549.2013.804480.

Canadian Press. 2013. "Employment Insurance Canada Changes in Effect as of January 6, 2013." *HuffPost Politics*, 6 January. http://www.huffingtonpost.ca/2013/01/06/employment-insurance-canada-changes-2013_n_2421333.html.

Caron, Jean, and Aihua Liu. 2011. "Factors Associated with Psychological Distress in the Canadian Population: A Comparison of Low-Income and Non Low-Income Sub-Groups." *Community Mental Health Journal* 47 (3): 318–30. http://dx.doi.org/10.1007/s10597-010-9306-4.

Castell, Sarah, and Julian Thompson. 2007. *Understanding Attitudes to Poverty in the UK: Getting the Public's Attention*. York: Joseph Rowntree Foundation.

Chase, Elaine, and Robert Walker. 2012. "The Co-construction of Shame in the Context of Poverty: Beyond a Threat to the Social Bond." *Sociology* 47 (4): 739–54. http://dx.doi.org/10.1177/0038038512453796.

Clarke, John. 2005. "New Labour's Citizens: Activated, Empowered, Responsibilized, Abandoned?" *Critical Social Policy* 25 (4): 447–63. http://dx.doi.org/10.1177/0261018305057024.

Clarke, John, and Janet Newman. 2012. "The Alchemy of Austerity." *Critical Social Policy* 32 (3): 299–319. http://dx.doi.org/10.1177/0261018312444405.

Collins, Stephanie Baker. 2005. "An Understanding of Poverty from Those Who Are Poor." *Action Research* 3 (1): 9–31. http://dx.doi.org/10.1177/1476750305047983.

Dam Sam Yu, Wai. 2008. "The Normative Ideas That Underpin Welfare-to-Work Measures for Young People in Hong Kong and the UK." *International Journal of Sociology and Social Policy* 28 (9/10): 380–93. http://dx.doi.org/10.1108/01443330810900211.

Diprose, Kristina. 2015. "Resilience Is Futile: The Cultivation of Resilience Is Not an Answer to Austerity and Poverty." *Soundings: A Journal of Politics and Culture* 58:44–56. http://dx.doi.org/10.3898/136266215814379736.

Dunk, Thomas. 2002. "Remaking the Working Class: Experience, Class Consciousness, and the Industrial Adjustment Process." *American Ethnologist* 29 (4): 878–900. http://dx.doi.org/10.1525/ae.2002.29.4.878.

Fournier, Genevieve, Helene Zimmermann, and Christine Gauthier. 2011. "Instable Career Paths among Workers 45 and Older: Insight Gained from Long-term Career Trajectories." *Journal of Aging Studies* 25 (3): 316–27. http://dx.doi.org/10.1016/j.jaging.2010.11.003.

Gabriel, Yiannis, David E. Gray, and Harshita Goregaokar. 2010. "Temporary Derailment or the End of the Line? Managers Coping with Unemployment at 50." *Organization Studies* 31 (12): 1687–712. http://dx.doi.org/10.1177/0170840610387237.

Gamble, Andrew. 1998. *The Free Economy and the Strong State.* London: Palgrave Macmillan.

Hall, Stuart, and Alan O'Shea. 2013. "Common-Sense Neoliberalism." *Soundings: A Journal of Politics and Culture* 55:8–24.

Haddow, Rodney, and Thomas Klassen. 2006. *Partisanship, Globalization, and Canadian Labour Market Policy: Four Provinces in Comparative Perspective.* Toronto: University of Toronto Press.

Harper, Stephen, interview by Robert E. Ruben. 2013. "A Conversation with Stephen Harper," 16 May. Council on Foreign Relations. http://cfr.org/canada/conversation-stephen-harper-prime-minister-canada/p35473.

Harrison, Elizabeth. 2013. "Bouncing Back? Recession, Resilience and Everyday Lives." *Critical Social Policy* 33 (1): 97–113. http://dx.doi.org/10.1177/0261018312439365.

Herd, Dean, Ernie Lightman, and Andrew Mitchell. 2009. "Searching for Local Solutions: Making Welfare Policy on the Ground in Ontario." *Journal of Progressive Human Services* 20 (2): 129–51. http://dx.doi.org/10.1080/10428230902871199.

Hodson, Dermot, and Imelda Maher. 2002. "Economic and Monetary Union: Balancing Credibility and Legitimacy in an Asymmetric Policy-Mix." *Journal of European Public Policy* 9 (3): 391–407.

Knight, Graham. 1998. "Hegemony, the Media, and New Right Politics: Ontario in the Late 1990s." *Critical Sociology* 24 (1–2): 105–29. http://dx.doi.org/10.1177/089692059802400106.

Krahn, H., G.S. Lowe, T.F. Hartnagel, and J. Tanner. 1987. "Explanations of Unemployment in Canada." *International Journal of Comparative Sociology* 28 (3–4): 228–36.

Kuruvilla, Sarosh C., and Anil Verma. 2006. "International Labour Standards, Soft Regulation, and National Government Roles." *Journal of Industrial Relations* 48 (1): 41–58.

Lazar, Harvey. 2006. "The Intergovernmental Dimensions of the Social Union: A Sectoral Analysis." *Canadian Public Administration* 49 (1): 23–45. http://dx.doi.org/10.1111/j.1754-7121.2006.tb02016.x.

Levinson, Mark. 2013. "Austerity Agonistes." *Dissent* 60 (3): 91–5. http://dx.doi.org/10.1353/dss.2013.0071.

Lewchuk, Wayne, Michelynn Lafleche, Diane Dyson, Luin Goldring, Alan Mesisner, Stephanie Procyk, Dan Rosen, John Shields, Peter Viducis, and Sam Vrankulj. 2013. "It's More Than Poverty: Employment Precarity and Household Well-being." Poverty and Employment Precarity in Southern Ontario (PEPSO). https://pepso.ca/case-studies/case-study-1/.

Lightman, Ernie, Dean Herd, and Andrew Mitchell. 2006. "Exploring the Local Implementation of Ontario Works." *Studies in Political Economy* 78 (1): 119–43. http://dx.doi.org/10.1080/19187033.2006.11675104.

Little, Margaret. 2001. "A Litmus Test for Democracy: The Impact of Ontario Welfare Changes on Single Mothers." *Studies in Political Economy* 66 (1): 9–36. http://dx.doi.org/10.1080/19187033.2001.11675209.

Macdonald, David. 2014. "Budget 2014: Let Stagnation Reign." Behind the Numbers: A Blog from the CCPA, 11 February. http://behindthenumbers.ca/2014/02/11/budget-2014-let-stagnation-reign/.

MacGregor, Susanne. 1999. "Welfare, Neo-Liberalism and New Paternalism: Three Ways for Social Policy in Late Capitalist Societies." *Capital and Class* 23 (1): 91–118. http://dx.doi.org/10.1177/030981689906700104.

Mahon, Rianne. 2011. "The Jobs Strategy: From Neo- to Inclusive Liberalism?" *Review of International Political Economy* 18 (5): 570–91. http://dx.doi.org/10.1080/09692290.2011.603668.

Mendelsohn, Matthew, and Jon Medow. 2010. *Help Wanted: How Well Did the EI Program Respond during Recent Recessions?* Toronto: Mowat Centre for Policy Innovation.

Montgomerie, Johnna, and Karel Williams. 2009. "Financialised Capitalism: After the Crisis and beyond Neoliberalism." *Competition & Change* 13 (2): 99–107.

Murali, Vijaya, and Femi Oyebode. 2004. "Poverty, Social Inequality and Mental Health." *Advances in Psychiatric Treatment* 10 (3): 216–24. http://dx.doi.org/10.1192/apt.10.3.216.

Nicholls, Rachel, and W. John Morgan. 2009. "Integrating Employment and Skills Policy: Lessons from the United Kingdom's New Deal for Young People." *Education, Knowledge & Economy* 3 (2): 81–96. http://dx.doi.org/10.1080/17496890903132453.

Nichols, Austin, Josh Mitchell, and Stephan Lindner. 2013. *Consequences of Long-Term Unemployment.* Washington, DC: Urban Institute.

Noaksson, Niklas, and Kerstin Jacobsson. 2003. *The Production of Ideas and Expert Knowledge in OECD: The OECD Jobs Strategy in Contrast with the EU Employment Strategy.* Stockholm: Stockholm Centre for Organizational Research.

OECD Statistics. Organisation for Economic Cooperation and Development. 2014. http://stats.oecd.org/.

Office for National Statistics. 2015. "Key Economic Time Series Data," 17 April. http://www.ons.gov.uk/ons/site-information/using-the-website/time-series/index.html#3.

Pathak, Pathik. 2014. "Ethopolitics and the Financial Citizen." *Sociological Review* 62 (1): 90–116. http://dx.doi.org/10.1111/1467-954X.12119.

Peacock, Marian, Paul Bissell, and Jenny Owen. 2014. "Dependency Denied: Health Inequalities in the Neo-Liberal Era." *Social Science & Medicine* 118:173–80. http://dx.doi.org/10.1016/j.socscimed.2014.08.006.

Pierre, Jon. 1995. "The Marketization of the State: Citizens, Consumers, and the Emergence of the Public Market." In *Governance in a Changing Environment*, ed. Guy Peters and Donald Savoie, 55–81. Montreal and Kingston: McGill-Queen's University Press.

PressProgress. 2014. "Unemployed? Good Luck Getting EI as Eligibility Hits All-Time Low," 2 August. http://www.pressprogress.ca/en/post/unemployed-good-luck-getting-ei-eligibility-hits-all-time-low-0.

Read, Jason. 2009. "A Genealogy of Homo-Economicus: Neoliberalism and the Production of Subjectivity." *Foucault Studies* 6:25–36. http://dx.doi.org/10.22439/fs.v0i0.2465.

Schneider, Anne, and Helen Ingram. 1993. "Social Construction of Target Populations: Implications for Politics and Policy." *American Political Science Review* 87 (2): 334–47. http://dx.doi.org/10.2307/2939044.

Slay, Julia, and Joe Penny. 2013. *Surviving Austerity: Local Voices and Local Action in England's Poorest Neighbourhoods*. London: New Economics Foundation.

Smith, Fiona. 2013. "Parents and Policy under New Labour: A Case Study of the United Kingdom's New Deal for Lone Parents." *Children's Geographies* 11 (2): 160–72. http://dx.doi.org/10.1080/14733285.2013.779443.

Standing, Guy. 1999. *Global Labour Flexibility*. London: Macmillan. http://www.palgrave.com/us/book/9780333773147.

Taylor-Gooby, Peter, and Eleanor Taylor. 2014. *British Social Attitudes 32: Benefits and Welfare*. London: NatCen Social Research.

Tiessen, Kaylie. 2014. "Austerity 2.0: Kinder and Gentler, but a Cut Is Still a Cut." Canadian Centre for Policy Alternatives, 1 October. http://behindthenumbers.ca/2014/10/01/austerity-2-0-kinder-and-gentler-but-a-cut-is-still-a-cut/.

Vrankulj, Sam. 2012. *Finding Their Way: Second Round Report of the CAW Worker Adjustment Tracking Project*. Toronto: Canadian Auto Workers.

Wainwright, Emma, Susan Buckingham, Elodie Marandet, and Fiona Smith. 2010. "'Body Training': Investigating the Embodied Training Choices

of/for Mothers in West London." *Geoforum* 41 (3): 489–97. http://dx.doi.org/
10.1016/j.geoforum.2009.12.006.

Weir, Erin. 2013. "EI Benefits Falling Faster Than Unemployment." Canadian
Centre for Policy Alternatives, 18 July. http://behindthenumbers.
ca/2013/07/18/ei-benefits-falling-faster-than-unemployment/.

Whitworth, Adam, and Elle Carter. 2014. "Welfare-to-Work Reform, Power
and Inequality: From Governance to Governmentalities." *Journal of
Contemporary European Studies* 22 (2): 104–17. http://dx.doi.org/10.1080/
14782804.2014.907132.

6 Expansionary Fiscal Consolidation and the "Smarter State": An Evaluation of the Politics of Austerity in the United Kingdom, May 2010 to February 2016

SIMON LEE

Introduction: A Political Choice, Not an Economic Necessity

Austerity, when it has meant a process of fiscal consolidation and an ideological belief in rolling back the frontiers of the state to prevent the "crowding-out" of market, has been acknowledged to be a dangerous idea, with a long history (Blyth 2013). It is also an idea that, when used as the basis for economic policy in the aftermath of a major financial crisis, can be extremely divisive and the harbinger of hard times rather than economic recovery (Clark and Heath 2014). However, for the political proponents of austerity in public expenditure, notably the Conservative Party under the leadership of Prime Minister David Cameron and Chancellor of the Exchequer George Osborne, the combination of a financial crisis followed by economic recession has presented a dual opportunity. First, it has provided a context for a political narrative that has deflected attention away from the major fiscal consequences of an unprecedentedly massive £1162 billion taxpayer bailout of failing United Kingdom banks, which had loaned recklessly. This narrative attributes the rise in government borrowing and public sector debt not to these banks but to the purportedly reckless borrowing undertaken by the previous Labour governments led by Tony Blair and Gordon Brown prior to the onset of the financial crisis in September 2007 (Lee 2009, 2011, 2015b). Second, it has provided the economic and political rationale for the implementation of a decade-long program of fiscal consolidation via austerity in government spending, and an accompanying major reform of the role of the state in the United Kingdom, whose legacy will be a significantly different political economy.

At the time of writing, the United Kingdom finds itself only half-way through a decade-long period of fiscal consolidation that is redefining the role of the state and market. This chapter therefore seeks to evaluate the strategy of fiscal consolidation under both the Cameron-Clegg coalition government and (from 8 May 2015) the Cameron government. The chapter also demonstrates how the implementation of George Osborne's plans for fiscal consolidation, while firmly ideologically rooted and presented as a series of long-term strategic choices, frequently have been a matter of political expediency. While George Osborne promised the British people a new economic model founded upon a "rebalancing" of the national economy – away from its over-dependence upon unsustainable levels of government spending and debt, and the financial services of London and the Southeast of England, towards one rooted in higher private business investment, savings, and exports, especially from the manufacturing industries of the whole of the United Kingdom – it has not been forthcoming. Instead, austerity has yielded the slowest economic recovery in modern British economic history from a major recession, and has strengthened and deepened an economic model founded upon ever-higher debt-financed consumer spending, an unsustainable asset bubble rooted in the domestic property market, and a return to the very pattern of highly speculative trading in the City of London's financial markets that brought about the 2007–8 financial crisis.

The Three Phases of Coalition Austerity: From Contractionary Fiscal Expansion to the "Long-Term Economic Plan"

From the very outset, the decision to implement austerity in the United Kingdom, like the decision to use taxpayers' cash, loans, and guarantees to rescue UK banks from the consequences of their own reckless lending, was a deliberate political and ideological choice. Austerity was not necessitated by the state of the United Kingdom's public finances. As the official government statistics for public sector finance have attested, public borrowing and debt under the Blair and Brown governments prior to the onset of the financial crisis had not risen as recklessly as portrayed by the subsequent austerity-based political narrative of governments since May 2010. The UK net public sector debt had actually risen by £212.9 billion or an annual average of just over £40 billion, from a low of £324.6 billion or 28.8 per cent of GDP in July 2002 to £537.5 billion or 36.0 per cent of GDP at the end of August 2007, immediately prior to the onset of the financial crisis at Northern Rock, and the first run on a British bank for more than a century (Office for National Statistics 2016, table PSA4). By contrast, following a series of taxpayer bailouts of British banks during 2008 and the ensuing recession – which had witnessed a parallel collapse in tax revenue and a compensatory increase in government spending and borrowing to stimulate effective demand – public sector net debt (which now included the liabilities of the banks taken into state ownership) had rocketed from the onset of the financial crisis in September 2007 by £1748.5 billion or 112 per cent of GDP, to a total of £2286.0 billion or 148 per cent of GDP by the end of April 2010 (ibid.). Indeed, the cost of rescuing the banks had added more to the UK national debt in peacetime than had been added during either of the two world wars.

Initially, austerity was presented politically as a matter of overriding national economic necessity and an ineluctable course of action. The British power elite, in the form of the Brown government and the Cameron-Clegg coalition government formed in May 2010, agreed upon the need to rescue the banks and to impose austerity. All they disagreed about was the pace at which fiscal consolidation was to be undertaken, and the appropriate balance between expenditure cuts and increases in taxation (Lee 2011). To begin with, austerity was termed "the unavoidable deficit reduction plan" in the Cameron-Clegg Coalition's May 2010 Program for Government (Cabinet Office 2010). The coalition also adopted the mantra deployed in the Conservatives' 2010 General Election manifesto, namely "We're all in this together" (Conservative Party 2010, vi), and presented austerity as a shared national burden. Subsequently, when it became increasingly apparent to the electorate that the impact of fiscal consolidation would be far from uniform across all taxpayers and income groups, this mantra was quietly abandoned.

The process of fiscal consolidation implemented in the United Kingdom since May 2010 has progressed through four phases. During the first three phases, the Cameron-Clegg Coalition Government failed in its twin objectives of eliminating the current budget deficit and creating a new "rebalanced" growth model, and instead bequeathed a legacy of greater indebtedness and unbalanced economic growth (Lee 2015b, 2017). The first phase of austerity from the publication of the coalition's May 2010 *Program for Government*, June 2010 "Emergency" Budget, and October 2010 Spending Review, was characterized by the implementation of a strategy of expansionary fiscal contraction. This strategy assumed that, as the frontiers of the state retreated and no longer crowded out entrepreneurship and investment by the private sector, the frontiers of the market would roll forward to deliver sustained economic recovery based upon private business investment, and a recovery in exports and manufacturing.

It should be noted that the thesis of "crowding out" was not new to British politics. From May 1979 until June 1983, the first Thatcher government had tested the thesis in its macroeconomic policies in general and its 1981 Budget in particular (Needham and Hotson 2014). Furthermore, by the time the coalition took office, there was already a long-standing debate among economists and politicians about the efficacy of "expansionary austerity" or "expansionary fiscal contraction," i.e., cutting government spending (with the promise of future lower taxes) as a means of entrenching economic recovery, while simultaneously redressing the high levels of public debt incurred during, and in the immediate aftermath of, major financial crises. Moreover, there was far from consensus about the efficacy of fiscal austerity. Indeed, at the very juncture the coalition was embracing expansionary fiscal contraction, others, including the International Monetary Fund (IMF), were pointing out its flaws and risks.

In its October 2010 World Economic Outlook, the IMF reported, "Fiscal consolidation typically has a contractionary effect on output. A fiscal consolidation equal to 1 percent of GDP typically reduced GDP by about 0.5 percent within two years and raises the unemployment rate by about 0.3 percentage points" (IMF 2010, 94). Subsequent IMF research would assert that the contractionary impact of austerity might be greater, and that a 1.0 per cent of GDP fiscal consolidation would not only reduce real private consumption by 0.75 per cent within two years, but also cut real GDP by 0.62 per cent (Guajardo, Leigh, and Pescatori 2011, 29). Indeed, an IMF paper co-authored by its chief economist, Olivier Blanchard, asserted that "actual multipliers were substantially above 1 percent early in the crisis" (Blanchard and Leigh 2013, 19).

Despite these concerns about the contractionary impact of fiscal consolidation, the October 2010 Spending Review duly detailed the United Kingdom's "unavoidable deficit reduction plan," forecast to be the tightest squeeze on total spending since the end of the Second World War (Crawford 2010). It would entail a total of £80.5 billion of expenditure savings by 2014–15, with total managed expenditure planned to fall from 47.3 per cent of GDP in 2010–11 to 41.0 per cent of GDP in 2014–15. With tax increases of £29.8 billion by 2014–15, the plan would deliver a total fiscal tightening of £110.3 billion by 2014–15, composed of 73 per cent in spending cuts and 27 per cent in tax rises. Because the UK economy was forecast to grow by 2.7 per cent in 2014–15, but the state was planned to contract by around 6.3 per cent of GDP, the coalition's plans assumed a "crowding in" by the private sector equivalent to 9 per cent of GDP, or around £180 billion in output by 2015.

In practice, rather than expansionary fiscal contraction, what the politics of austerity actually delivered was contractionary fiscal expansion. During the coalition's first two years in office, a collapse in business investment and tax revenue accompanied the coalition's own cuts in public capital investment, which led to lower than forecast economic growth and an increase in the UK public sector net debt. The latter had risen from £1009.7 billion or 65.3 per cent of GDP at the end of April 2010 to £1242.2 billion or 75.0 per cent of GDP at the end of April 2012, as the coalition borrowed more than £265.1 billion during its first two years in office (Office for National Statistics 2016, tables PSA3, PSA4).

When the coalition's first two years in office failed to yield the forecast economic expansion from its strategy of fiscal consolidation, and indeed threatened to push the UK economy back into recession, austerity in the United Kingdom entered a second phase. Chancellor of the Exchequer George Osborne used his 5 December 2012 Autumn Statement to loosen the pace of planned fiscal contraction, through additional borrowing. During the first phase of its economic policy, in 2010–11 the coalition's additional fiscal tightening had amounted to 1.5 per cent of national income, followed by a further 2.3 per cent during 2011–12. However, the recognition that a further acceleration in fiscal consolidation might drive the economy into recession rather than expansion led Osborne to loosen fiscal policy, with the result that fiscal consolidation was planned to be only 0.7 per cent of GDP in 2014–15 and 0.6 per cent in 2015–16 (Emmerson and Tetlow 2015, 25). Moreover, the December 2012 Autumn Statement planned borrowing of 5.2 per cent of GDP in 2014–15, whereas the coalition's November 2010 Autumn Statement had originally planned for public borrowing of only 1.9 per cent of national income (22).

Osborne also implemented measures, notably the Funding for Lending scheme (FLS) launched in July 2012 in partnership with the Bank of England, to boost the economy. It was designed to incentivise banks and building societies to increase their lending to the real economy. However, while by the end of January 2014, almost £42 billion of loans were outstanding under the FLS, most of this finance had been channelled into the overheating domestic property sector, while very little had been loaned to small and medium-sized enterprises (SMEs). Indeed, Bank of England statistics disclosed that whereas in 2007 and 2008, net lending to UK businesses had increased by annual rates of 16.8 per cent and 17.9 per cent respectively, during the subsequent years, and under the coalition's austerity, there had been net repayment by businesses to banks rather than net lending. Indeed, net repayments during 2011 and 2012 had grown by 3.3 per cent and 3.1 per cent respectively (Bank of England 2014, 5).

In September 2013, austerity in the United Kingdom entered its third phase of "the long-term economic plan," as both Cameron and Osborne acknowledged in keynote speeches that fiscal consolidation would now take fully ten years to rebalance the nation's finances. On 9 September 2013, Osborne chose 1 Commercial Street, a private sector development in the City of London, to denote that austerity was entering a new phase. Having begun in 2007, construction on the development had stopped in 2008, but resumed during 2012, symbolizing the sporadic and partial nature of economic recovery in the United Kingdom: one confined to London and the Southeast of England. Osborne's explanation of austerity was composed of four elements. First, "The economic collapse was even worse than we thought," an open admission of miscalculation and the coalition's complacency in thinking austerity could rebalance the public finances and national economy within the confines of a single parliamentary term. Second, "Repairing it will take even longer than we hoped," not least because of the coalition's erroneous faith in expansionary fiscal contraction, and its fundamentally flawed "crowding out" thesis. Third, "We held our nerve when many told us to abandon the plan," an attempt to make a virtue out of his own intransigence and coalition obstinacy in the face of overwhelming evidence of the failure of expansionary fiscal contraction. Fourth, "Thanks to the efforts and sacrifices of the British people, Britain is turning a corner," a highly dubious assertion overlooking the fact that the majority of the people would have to continue to suffer falling real living standards for many further years, given his plans for deeper and prolonged austerity (Osborne 2013b).

The third phase of austerity was marked by two important new developments in the political narrative surrounding austerity. First, the long-term economic plan was now underpinned by an increasingly overt commitment by Cameron and Osborne to roll back the frontiers of the state further than had previously been detailed in the coalition's plans.

Their intention was to establish clear blue water, ideologically, between themselves and their principal political opponents in the Labour Party and Liberal Democrats, and thereby open up the possibility of a majority Conservative government after 7 May 2015. For Cameron, this ambition meant "building a leaner, more efficient state. We need to do more with less. Not just now, but permanently" (Cameron 2013). For Osborne, it meant "we will have a surplus in good times as insurance against difficult times ahead. Provided the recovery is sustained, our goal is to achieve that surplus in the next Parliament" (Osborne 2013a).

The true scale of Cameron and Osborne's ambition was not fully apparent until the onset of the campaign for the 7 May 2015 General Election, and the publication of the December 2014 Autumn Statement. It affirmed the new objective in fiscal policy "to reach a small surplus of 0.2% of GDP in 2018–19 and 1.0% of GDP in 2019–20" (Her Majesty's Treasury 2014, 7). Indeed, total public spending was now projected "to fall to 35.2 percent of GDP in 2019–20, taking it below the previous post-war lows reached in 1957–58 and 1999–00 to what would probably be its lowest level in 80 years" (Office for Budget Responsibility 2014, 6–7). Moreover, "Between 2009–10 and 2019–20, spending on public services, administration and grants by central government is projected to fall from 21.2 percent to 12.6 percent of GDP and from £5650 to £3880 per head in 2014–15 prices" (7). Since only 40 per cent of this planned austerity had been delivered under the coalition, around 60 per cent would have to be implemented during the tenure of the next government.

The second key development during the third phase of austerity was Osborne's 23 June 2014 personal political epiphany and his discovery of the "Northern Powerhouse," and a commitment to "deliver a real improvement in the long term economic performance of the north of England" (Osborne 2014). The Northern Powerhouse was a bolt from the blue. It had not featured in either the 2010 Conservative Party or the Liberal Democrat General Election manifestos. Nor had it been mentioned in the Coalition Agreement, the Program for Government, the 2010 and 2013 Spending Reviews, or any of Osborne's previous Budget statements. Osborne claimed, "A true powerhouse requires true power. So today I am putting on the table and starting the conversation about serious devolution of powers and budgets for any city that wants to move to a new model of city government – and have an elected Mayor" (ibid.).

In effect, having failed to rebalance the UK economy in a sectoral sense – away from financial services, private consumption, public and private debt towards private business investment, manufacturing and exports – Osborne was now redefining his commitment to "re-balancing" towards a geographical and English constitutional "rebalancing." With the 18 September 2014 Scottish independence referendum imminent, Osborne was offering the people of the North of England the opportunity to participate in a heavily diluted form of devolution. More importantly, through brokering a series of "city deals" between the Treasury and major urban local governments from outside London and the Southeast, Osborne was entrapping a new generation of civic leaders in the politically toxic task of implementing local fiscal consolidation through further cuts to spending and public services during a fourth post–2015 General Election phase of austerity (Lee 2015a).

The Fourth Phase of Austerity: Towards the "Smarter State"

Between May 2015 and May 2016, both David Cameron and George Osborne, when confronted with the opportunity of governing alone as a single party of government, chose a very different political narrative to justify austerity. They couched their fiscal choices in terms of the opportunity to craft a smaller, "smarter state" (Cameron 2015) and a "new settlement across the political spectrum" (Osborne 2015a). Indeed, during the 2015 UK General Election campaign, the 2015 Conservative Party Manifesto actually championed the economic dividend from austerity, proclaiming,

> The Great Recession has given way to a Great Revival, which is creating on average 1,000 new jobs every day: more than the rest of the European Union combined. This is no accident. It is the product of hard work by people in every part of the country and it is thanks to the success of our long-term economic plan. By halving the deficit, we have helped to restore confidence to the economy. (Conservative Party 2015, 7)

Far from abandoning a strategy of austerity in relation to public spending and a diminished role for the state, the Conservative Party promised that, if elected for a further five-year term of office, it would "control spending, eliminate the deficit, and start to run a surplus" (Conservative Party 2015, 8). Government spending would be reduced "by one per cent each year in real terms for the first two full financial years of the next Parliament, the same rate as over the last five years" (8). This would necessitate "a further £30 billion in fiscal consolidation over the next two years," composed of £13 billion in departmental savings, a further £12 billion from welfare savings, and at least another £5 billion from tackling tax evasion (8).

Moreover, far from being content with achieving a budget surplus in 2019–20, the Conservatives promised to implement "a new fundamental principle of fiscal policy," namely "that in normal economic times, when the economy is growing, the government will always run a surplus in order to reduce our national debt and keep our economy secure, with a state neither smaller than we need nor bigger than we can afford" (Conservative Party 2015, 9).

The fact that following in the 7 May 2015 UK General Election, the Conservative Party emerged victorious as a single party government under the leadership of David Cameron with a parliamentary majority of twelve seats could be been seen as a vindication of this continuing commitment to fiscal consolidation and a politics of austerity. This is especially true when compared with the fate of the Conservatives' coalition partners from May 2010 to April 2015, the Liberal Democrats, who saw their representation at Westminster collapse disastrously from fifty-seven seats to a mere eight seats (including the loss of twenty-seven of those seats to the Conservatives), and their share of the vote collapse from 23.1 per cent in 2010 to only 7.9 per cent in 2015.

However, the result of the general election should not be viewed as an unmitigated triumph for the politics of austerity. First, the Conservatives' share of the vote was only 36.8 per cent (up just 0.8 per cent from 2010). Only the vagaries of the United Kingdom's first-past-the-post voting system allowed such a low share of the vote to be converted into 330 seats or 50.8 per cent of the seats at Westminster. Second, political parties whose manifestos included an anti-austerity agenda, notably the Scottish National Party (SNP), were markedly more popular. In Scotland, the SNP won 50 per cent of the votes (an increase of 30 per cent compared to 2010), and no fewer than 56 out of 59 seats, reducing the Labour Party's representation in Scotland from forty-one MPs to just one solitary MP. Labour's share of the vote in Scotland collapsed from 42 per cent in 2010 to just 24.3 per cent in 2015, itself an indictment of its failure to develop a credible critique and alternative to austerity.

On 11 September 2015, David Cameron outlined his vision for "a smarter state," itself the answer to "thinking properly about the state – what it does and how it does it" (Cameron 2015). Cameron claimed that while achieving a budget surplus and reducing high debt would "build our resilience," to not do so would mean "repeating the mistakes of the period that led up to the financial crash" (ibid.). This analysis overlooked the fact that numerous official inquiries into the causes of the 2007–8 financial crash, including those conducted by the Financial Crisis Inquiry Commission and at the behest of the United Nations (Financial Crisis Inquiry Commission 2010; United Nations 2009) that had attributed its cause not to reckless government debt and borrowing, but to reckless private speculation and lending, and a failure of the state to be smart enough to regulate the excesses of private market actors, not least major banks.

Cameron identified twin principles of "a smarter state." First, the need to demonstrate "absolute clarity on what government should prioritise in an era of obviously finite resources," for "to govern is to choose – and we have made clear choices" (Cameron 2015). This statement overlooked the many instances where official government policy had displayed inconsistency at best. For example, the government had initially provided generous incentives to encourage a switch to low-carbon, renewable technologies such as solar power, carbon capture, and onshore windfarms – and then abruptly announced the withdrawal of public subsidy, threatening investor confidence. Second, the principle that where government does act, it should "ensure that it does so as effectively as possible" (ibid.). Here, it could be noted that the Cameron-Clegg Coalition government had acted repeatedly to implement fiscal consolidation, and yet its record in office in failing to rebalance either public finances or economic growth had suggested that expansionary fiscal contraction had not amounted to a smart choice for either the state or the British people.

The New Settlement: From Long-Term Plan to Short-Term Fixes

The fourth phase of austerity under the Cameron government was implemented through the 8 July 2015 Budget and the 25 November 2015 Spending Review. Although the accompanying political narrative during the third phase of austerity had been that of the "long-term economic plan," what was evident during the fourth phase of austerity was a series of short-term changes in government plans for public spending, borrowing, and the date by which the nation's finances would be returned to a surplus. In his pre-election 18 March 2015 Budget, Osborne had announced an important change in fiscal policy. Previously, in his 3 December 2014 Autumn Statement, Osborne had forecast "a surplus of 0.2% of GDP in 2018–19, increasing to 1.0% of GDP in 2019–20," and that public debt would fall as a percentage of GDP in every year (Her Majesty's Treasury 2014, 23–4). With the 7 May

2015 General Election imminent, Osborne now announced that from 2019 to 2020, a future majority Conservative government would allow public spending to grow in line with national income. However, he failed to specify how either the planned £12 billion annual cuts in welfare spending by 2017–18 would be delivered or how the more than 5 per cent cuts in "unprotected" public spending (i.e., budgets other than those for the NHS, schools, and overseas aid) would be achieved in 2016–17 and 2017–18 (Johnson 2015a, 1).

When Osborne delivered the post-election 8 July 2015 Budget, he announced further changes in the Cameron government's fiscal strategy. First, while the budget deficit would continue to be cut by the same annual rate of 1.1 per cent as it had been cut during the previous Parliament, the budget would now not return to surplus until 2019–20, a year later than previously promised, and an additional £18 billion would be borrowed over the lifetime of the Cameron government, compared to the 18 March 2015 Budget forecast (Her Majesty's Treasury 2015a, 2). This would mean that between 2015–16 and 2019–20, for departmental spending beyond the "protected" budgets of the NHS, schools, overseas aid, and defence, the Cameron government would seek further real-terms cuts of around £19 billion a year or 12.6 per cent (Tetlow 2015). Second, to achieve its vision of "a higher wage, low tax, lower welfare society" (Her Majesty's Treasury 2015a, 32) he would introduce a new National Living Wage of £7.20 per hour for adults aged twenty-five and over from 1 April 2016 ("to make work pay"), but would introduce a range of measures to cut working-age tax credits by £4.4 billion in 2016–17 (this saving was later corrected to £3.4 billion), and working-age welfare spending by 2.3 per cent in real terms in every year of the Parliament, compared to real-terms cuts averaging 0.6 per cent under the previous government (26). In short, the burden of rebalancing the nation's budget would fall disproportionately upon the working poor, and public sector workers, whose pay increases would be limited to a maximum of 1 per cent annual increases until at least April 2020 (32).

The political implications of Osborne's "new settlement" were potentially politically toxic for Osborne's ambitions to succeed Cameron as Conservative Party leader and prime minister. Cameron had previously announced his decision not to serve a full term or to lead his party into the May 2020 General Election. The 8 July Budget appeared to penalize the working poor unduly, the very constituency of "strivers" to whom the Conservative Party's 2015 General Election manifesto and campaign political narrative had been seeking to appeal. Unsurprisingly, when Osborne delivered the 25 November 2015 Spending Review and Autumn Statement, his fiscal plans had once again changed significantly over the course of only four months, and for the fourth time since the 3 December 2014 Autumn Statement.

Announcing that forecasts of higher tax receipts and lower debt interest charges would mean that the public finances would be £27 billion better off than at the time of his 8 July 2015 Budget, Osborne declared that his proposed changes to working tax credits would be avoided altogether and that day-to-day government spending would fall by an annual average of 0.8 per cent in real terms under the Cameron government, compared to a 2 per cent annual average fall under its predecessor (Osborne 2015b). The Office for Budget Responsibility now estimated that the cumulative impact of the measures in Osborne's 8 July Budget and 25 November 2015 Spending Review would mean that, over the five-year lifetime of the Parliament, real departmental expenditure limits (RDEL) would increase by £129 billion and taxes would be cut by £36 billion. This additional expenditure would be paid for "by £91 billion of tax increases, £43 billion of welfare cuts, £19 billion of indirect revenue and spending effects and £21 billion more borrowing" (Office for Budget Responsibility 2015, 20–1).

Although Osborne's fiscal plans constituted a somewhat diluted phase of austerity compared to what had been suggested in both the 2015 Conservative Party General Election manifesto and his 8 July 2015 Budget statement, it should not be thought that they signified the conclusion to the United Kingdom's encounter with austerity via planned fiscal consolidation. As one sage commentator observed,

> July's fiscal arithmetic implied average cuts of 27% to the resource spending of "unprotected" departmental spending – that is to day-to-day spending other than that on health, schools, ODA and defence which was explicitly protected. The comparable figure after yesterday's announcements is "just" 18%, one third less than implied in July. Yet the planned surplus for 2019–20 is largely unchanged. The first thing to say is that this is not the end of "austerity." This spending review is still one of the tightest in post war history. Total managed expenditure is due to fall from 40.9% of national income in 2014–15 to 36.5% in 2019–20. A swathe of departments will see real terms cuts." (Johnson 2015b, 1)

To deliver this new fiscal and political settlement, the fourth phase of austerity was marked by the introduction of a new fiscal framework in the form of an updated version of the Charter for Budget Responsibility (Her Majesty's Treasury 2015b). The Treasury's mandate for fiscal policy under the Cameron government was to be defined in terms of two targets. The primary target was for "a surplus on public sector net borrowing by the end of 2019–20," supplemented by "a target for public sector net debt as a percentage of GDP to be falling in each year" (7). However, these targets were not to apply if the Office for Budget Responsibility determined that there was "a significant negative shock to the UK," which in turn was defined as "real GDP growth of less than 1% on a rolling 4 quarter on 4 quarter basis" (7).

At this juncture, it should be remembered that Osborne had experienced a messianic conversion to the cause of fiscal charters in government, having been a vocal opponent when in opposition. Indeed, when the Brown government had sought to introduce a similar measure through its Fiscal Responsibility Bill in January 2010, Osborne had told Parliament, "Let us remember what one of the economists whom the Prime Minister himself appointed to the Monetary Policy Committee has said about the Bill. Willem Buiter has said: 'Fiscal responsibility acts are instruments of the fiscally irresponsible to con the public'" (Osborne 2010, c.72). Osborne's embracing of a fixed, rigid target of a budget surplus by the end of March 2020 was a major political risk to his own ambitions to become prime minister and to the Cameron government's prospects of re-election in May 2020. Historically, the United Kingdom has not managed to achieve three years of consecutive budget surpluses since 1952 (Emmerson, Johnson, and Joyce 2016, 2). If Osborne duly proceeded to be fiscally irresponsible, and repeated the same failure to hit his forecast targets for public spending, tax revenue, government borrowing, and public debt as during the tenure of the Cameron-Clegg Coalition Government, the financial outcomes of any failure to deliver the forecast budget surplus would be patently evident to the electorate immediately before the May 2020 General Election. In the event, following the outcome of the 23 June 2016 European Union referendum, the resignation of David Cameron as prime minister, and his succession by Theresa May, led to Osborne's departure from government, but not before he had abandoned his target to achieve a current budget surplus by the end of 2019–20.

The Legacy of Austerity: The Failure to Rebalance

Austerity via the process of fiscal consolidation undertaken by United Kingdom governments since May 2010 has failed in its own terms.

First, it has failed to rebalance the nation's public finances by eliminating the annual public budget deficit in the time span that George Osborne had so confidently predicted in his June 2010 "Emergency" Budget. Then, Osborne forecast that by the end of March 2015, UK public sector net debt (excluding the "temporary" liabilities on the national accounts arising from nationalization of failed United Kingdom banks) would be £1284 billion or 69.4 per cent of GDP, and that the government would borrow £453 billion between 2010–11 and 2014–15 (Her Majesty's Treasury 2010, 72). In the event, by the end of March 2015, UK public debt stood at £1546.8 billion or 83.7 per cent of GDP, with the government having borrowed around £90 billion more than forecast (Office for National Statistics 2016, table PS4). Moreover, even if the Treasury's optimistic forecasts for economic growth, tax receipts, and public spending were met by the end of March 2020, after two terms of austerity, the UK public debt was forecast to be £1708 billion or 74.3 per cent of GDP, well above the £1009.7 billion or 65.3 per cent inherited from the Brown government in May 2010 (table PSA4).

Second, austerity has failed to rebalance the UK economy away from economic growth driven by consumer spending, debt, and an over-dependence upon the financial services of London and the Southeast towards an economic recovery built upon private business investment, manufacturing, exports and the economies of all parts of the United Kingdom. Indeed, the economic growth has continued to be driven by the very same "accumulation of unsustainable levels of private sector debt and rising public sector debt" identified in the coalition's June 2010 "Emergency" Budget statement (Her Majesty's Treasury 2010, 2). In every month and year since May 2010, under austerity the United Kingdom has run parallel deficits on its overall current account, i.e., its financial transactions with the rest of the world, and its balance of payments in trade. Thus, in the three months to the end of September 2015, the United Kingdom's current account recorded a deficit of £17.5 billion or 3.7 per cent of GDP. The United Kingdom's net liabilities with the rest of the world totalled £348.8 billion (its assets totalling £9677.5 billion and its liabilities £10,026.3 billion). During 2015, the United Kingdom ran a deficit in its trade in goods of £125.3 billion and a surplus on its trade in services of £88.7 billion, leading to an overall trade deficit of £36.6 billion, and a cumulative trade deficit of more than £165 billion from 2011 to 2015 (Office for National Statistics 2016). Austerity has failed to reverse the long-term trend of the United Kingdom having run current and capital account deficits in every year since 1983, and every three-month quarterly period since the third quarter of 1998. To that extent, its failure is shared with the economic policies of every UK government since the first Thatcher government (1979–83), and every prime minister from Margaret Thatcher onwards.

In June 2010, the coalition had forecast that business investment and trade, rather than private consumption or government spending, would drive its new "rebalanced" economic model. That forecast has proven illusory. For example, from the start of the fourth quarter of 2012 until the end of the second quarter of 2015, real business investment grew by only 1.2 per cent of GDP and real trade by only 0.9 per cent of GDP (compared to the 2.7 per cent of GDP and 1.4 per cent of GDP respective forecasts in June 2010). By contrast, private consumption and total government activity contributed to 4.3 per cent and 1.1 per cent to real GDP growth during the same period (compared to the June 2010 forecasts of 3.5 per cent and -1.4 per cent of GDP respectively) (Office for Budget Responsibility 2015, table 2.5).

The UK economy has also remained heavily imbalanced in favour of the financial and commercial interests of London and the Southeast. For example, official statistics for average annual per capita income in 2014 (measured by gross value added – GVA) have shown that only two administrative regions of England – London and the Southeast – possessed regional GVA per capita above the United Kingdom's average GVA per capita of £24,616. The Southeast's regional GVA per capita was £27,012 (109.7 per cent of the UK GVA), but London's was no less than £42,666 (173.3 per cent of the UK GVA). All seven other English administrative regions had regional GVA per capita well below the average UK GVA, ranging from the East of England at £23,063 or 93.7 per cent of the average UK GVA, to the Northeast at a lowly £18,216 per capita or 74.0 per cent of the average UK GVA (Office for National Statistics 2015, 7). Among the constituent nations of the United Kingdom, only England with an average GVA per capita of £25,367 (103.1 per cent of the UK figure) was above the average UK GVA. By comparison, the GVA per capita for Scotland was £23,102 (93.9 per cent of the UK GVA); for Northern Ireland, £18,682 per capita (75.9 per cent of the UK GVA); and for Wales £17,573 (71.4 per cent of the UK GVA) (7). More importantly, from 1997 to 2014 (including the years of austerity from May 2010 onwards), only London (up 13.5 per cent) had experienced a significant increase in its income. All other nations and administrative regions of the United Kingdom (with the exception of the Northeast, which had witnessed a 0.9 per cent increase in its income) had actually experienced a decline in their average income per capita (9–10). Far from "rebalancing," the UK economy had actually become more imbalanced in favour of London.

A further definitive but paradoxical feature of the pursuit of austerity by UK governments since May 2010 has been that it has been "one-eyed." On the one hand, there has been a fixation with the need to reduce public sector debt, and not to pass a burden of debt on to future generations. In practice, under austerity UK public sector net debt (excluding public sector banks) has increased from £1009.7 billion or 65.3 per cent of GDP (at market prices) at the end of April 2010 to £1581.6 billion or 82.8 per cent of GDP at the end of January 2016 (Office for National Statistics 2016, table PSA4). On the other hand, during the tenure of both the Cameron-Clegg Coalition and (from 7 May 2010) the Cameron government, there has been a steadfast refusal to acknowledge the growth of private household debt, and the way in which the impact of austerity (e.g., through the trebling of student university tuition fees in England) has brought about a huge intergenerational transfer of wealth from those under the age of thirty to those over the age of sixty-five. Indeed, every Budget and Spending Review delivered since June 2010 has been accompanied by forecasts from the Office for Budget Responsibility assuming that economic recovery will be founded upon a major increase in private household debt. Thus, for example, the November 2010 Spending Review forecast that household debt would increase from £1566 billion or 160 per cent of income in 2010 to £2113 billion or 173 per cent of income in 2015 (Office for Budget Responsibility 2010, table 1.8), while the November 2015 Spending Review has encompassed an official Office for Budget Responsibility forecast that private household debt will rise from £1702 billion at the end of March 2015 to £2262 billion or 159 per cent of income at the end of March 2020 (Office for Budget Responsibility 2015, table 1.11). In short, not only will two parliamentary terms of austerity policies have added a forecast £700 billion to public sector net debt by the time of the May 2020 UK General Election (since the Treasury has predicted public sector net debt will be £1708 billion or 74.3 per cent of GDP by the end of March 2020), but also more than £700 billion in private household debt will have been accumulated. Far from rebalancing the economy away from overdependence upon public borrowing and debt, ten years of austerity is forecast to add around £1.4 trillion to public and private debt.

Conclusion

When the Cameron-Clegg Coalition took office in May 2010, it embraced austerity just at the very point when influential actors and policymakers, led by the International Monetary Fund, were admitting that expansionary fiscal consolidation was a flawed policy. Following the May 2015 General Election, the Cameron government's commitment to delivering a smaller, "smarter" state threatened to leave it isolated against the growing tide of opinion among key policymakers, both past and present, that austerity in the form of fiscal consolidation is not the route to lasting prosperity.

In advance of the 26–7 February 2016 meeting of G-20 finance ministers and Central Bank governors in Shanghai, the IMF published a report on global economic prospects and policy challenges. It argued, "The fragile conjuncture requires a comprehensive policy response both at the national and the G-20 level" (IMF 2016a, 5). Indeed, "To avoid over-reliance on monetary policy, near-term fiscal policy should support the recovery where appropriate and provided there is fiscal space, focusing on investment" (6). In its February 2016 analysis of UK economic policy and performance, while acknowledging that fiscal consolidation had halved the UK's annual fiscal deficit, the IMF also observed that "the fiscal path may need to be eased if growth slows markedly," and that "the government may need to show some flexibility in finding alternative fiscal measures if anticipated spending efficiency gains fail to materialize" (IMF 2016b, 11).

In a similar vein, the Organization for Economic Cooperation and Development (OECD) had asserted that, when confronted by the prospect of the slowest global economic growth for five years and substantial risks of financial instability, there was an urgent need for a stronger collective policy response at both the national and international levels. The OECD had also highlighted the contractionary impact upon economic growth of fiscal policy in many major economies, not least the United Kingdom (OECD 2016). Consequently, the OECD's chief economist, Catherine Mann, had suggested, "With governments in many countries able to borrow for long periods at very low interest rates, there is room for fiscal expansion to strengthen demand in a manner consistent with fiscal sustainability" (Mann 2016). Furthermore, "A commitment to raising public investment would boost demand and help support future growth" (ibid.).

Some of George Osborne's fellow economic policymakers had also advocated an economic policy agenda far removed from further austerity, which had focused attention upon the failures of borrowing and lending by private financial institutions, rather than by the British state. Mervyn King, governor of the Bank of England from 2003 until 2013 (including during Osborne's tenure as Chancellor of the Exchequer from May 2010), had attributed the causes of the 2007–8 financial crisis to a mistaken faith in the financial alchemy of the banking system, and the disequilibrium, radical uncertainty, "prisoner's dilemma" barriers to best outcomes and cooperation, and insufficiency of trust characteristic of modern markets (King 2016). Since, in his judgment, that financial alchemy had remained largely untouched by policy developments since 2008, King's analysis pointed towards an economic policy reform agenda far removed from austerity.

In a similar vein, Adair Turner, former chairman of the Financial Services Authority, the United Kingdom's key regulator of financial services until its abolition in 2013, had highlighted how austerity does not offer the way forward for economic policy. Turner attributed the 2007–8 financial crisis to excessive free market private credit creation resulting in "too much of the wrong sort of debt, crisis, debt overhang, and post-crisis recession" (Turner 2016, 250). In short, it had been "a fatal conceit that produced the disaster of 2007–2008" (251), but that fatal conceit was not excessive government spending, borrowing, or debt, but rather "the idea that free financial markets plus simple macroeconomic rules will ensure social optimality" (251).

David Cameron had claimed that "with a smarter state, we can spend less and deliver more," and by so doing not just balance the books, but "lay the foundations for the most radical and most progressive government of our recent history" (Cameron 2015). However, it is hard to see what is progressive or smart about running a budget surplus and capping capital investment at a time of historically low interest rates, when government could instead borrow to finance essential infrastructure projects, with a major benefit for private sector growth and investment, and avoid having to source infrastructure from private sector sources at a much higher capital cost to taxpayers and service users alike. The very reason why governments historically had intervened to fund public infrastructure and services in the first place was because they had recognized that it was the smarter thing to do, and that if they didn't, the market itself would not be smart enough to supply such infrastructure and services in sufficient volume or at an affordable price. In their ideological determination to roll back the frontiers of the state, UK governments since May 2010 have also overlooked the fact that there is no historical evidence whatsoever that past austerity programs have yielded a lasting reduction in either public borrowing or debt.

REFERENCES

Bank of England. 2014. *Trends in Lending: January 2014*. London: Bank of England.

Blanchard, Olivier, and Daniel Leigh. 2013. "Growth Forecast Errors and Fiscal Multipliers." IMF Working Paper WP/13/1. Washington, DC: International Monetary Fund. http://dx.doi.org/10.3386/w18779.

Blyth, Mark. 2013. *Austerity: The History of a Dangerous Idea*. Oxford: Oxford University.

Cabinet Office. 2010. *The Coalition: Our Programme for Government*. London: Cabinet Office.

Cameron, David. 2013. "Lord Mayor's Banquet Speech." Mansion House, London, 11 November.

– 2015. "My Vision for a Smarter State Speech." Leeds ONE, Leeds, 11 September.

Clark, Tom, and Anthony Heath. 2014. *Hard Times: The Divisive Toll of the Economic Slump*. New Haven, CT: Yale University Press.

Conservative Party. 2010. *Invitation to Join the Government of Britain: The Conservative Manifesto 2010*. London: Conservative Party.

– 2015. *The Conservative Party Manifesto 2015*. London: Conservative Party.

Crawford, Rowenna. 2010. *Where Did the Axe Fall?* London: Institute for Fiscal Studies.

Emmerson, Carl, Paul Johnson, and Robert Joyce, eds. 2016. *The IFS Green Budget: February 2016*. London: Institute for Fiscal Studies.

Emmerson, Carl, and Gemma Tetlow. 2015. "Public Finances under the Coalition." In *The IFS Green Budget: February 2015*, ed. Carl Emmerson, Johnson Paul, and Robert Joyce, 10–32. London: Institute for Fiscal Studies.

Financial Crisis Inquiry Commission. 2010. *Financial Crisis Inquiry Report*. Washington, DC: US Government.

Guajardo, Jaime, Daniel Leigh, and Andrea Pescatori. 2011. "Expansionary Austerity: New International Evidence." IMF Working Paper 11/158. Washington, DC: International Monetary Fund.

Her Majesty's Treasury. 2010. *Securing the Recovery: Economic and Fiscal Strategy Report and Financial Statement and Budget Report, HC.451*. London: Stationery Office.

– 2014. *Autumn Statement 2014, HC.8961*. London: Stationery Office.

– 2015a. *Budget 2015, HC.1093*. London: Stationery Office.
– 2015b. *Charter for Budget Responsibility: Autumn 2015 Update*. London: Her Majesty's Treasury.
International Monetary Fund. 2010. *World Economic Outlook: Recovery, Risk, and Rebalancing*. Washington, DC: International Monetary Fund.
– 2016a. *Global Prospects and Policy Challenges*. Washington, DC: International Monetary Fund.
– 2016b. *United Kingdom: 2015 Article IV Consultation*. IMF Country Report No.16/57. Washington, DC: International Monetary Fund.
Johnson, Paul. 2015a. "IFS Post-Budget Briefing: Opening Remarks." London, Institute for Fiscal Studies, 19 March.
– 2015b. "IFS Post-Spending Review/Autumn Statement Briefing: Opening Remarks." London, Institute for Fiscal Studies, 26 November.
King, Mervyn. 2016. *The End of Alchemy: Money, Banking and the Future of the Global Economy*. London: Little, Brown.
Lee, Simon. 2009. "Convergence, Critique and Divergence: The Development of Economic Policy under David Cameron." In *The Conservatives under David Cameron*, ed. Simon Lee and Matt Beech, chap. 5. London: Palgrave Macmillan. http://dx.doi.org/10.1057/9780230237025_5.
– 2011. "No Plan B: The Coalition Agenda for Cutting the Deficit and Rebalancing the Economy." In *The Cameron-Clegg Government: Coalition Politics in an Age of Austerity*, ed. Simon Lee and Matt Beech, 59–74. London: Palgrave Macmillan. http://dx.doi.org/10.1057/9780230305014_4.
Lee, Simon. 2015a. "The Condition of England under the Coalition." In *Coalition Politics Evaluated: Examining the Cameron-Clegg Government*, ed. Matt Beech and Simon Lee, 145–61. London: Palgrave Macmillan. http://dx.doi.org/10.1057/9781137461377_10.
– 2015b. "Indebted and Unbalanced: The Political Economy of the Coalition." In *Coalition Politics Evaluated: Examining the Cameron-Clegg Government*, ed. Matt Beech and Simon Lee, 16–35. London: Palgrave Macmillan. http://dx.doi.org/10.1057/9781137461377_2.
– 2017. *The State of England: The Nation We're In*. London: Palgrave Macmillan.
Mann, Catherine. 2016. "Stronger Growth Remains Elusive: Urgent Policy Response Is Needed." Presentation at the launch of the OECD Interim Economic Outlook, Paris, 18 February.
Needham, Duncan, and Anthony Hotson, eds. 2014. *Expansionary Fiscal Contraction: The Thatcher Government's 1981 Budget in Perspective*. Cambridge: Cambridge University Press. http://dx.doi.org/10.1017/CBO9781107337626.

Office for Budget Responsibility. 2010. *Economic and Fiscal Outlook October 2010: Economic Supplementary Data: Table 1.8: Household Borrowing and Debt*. London: Office for Budget Responsibility.

– 2014. *Economic and Fiscal Outlook December 2014, Cm.8966*. London: Her Majesty's Stationery Office.

– 2015. *Economic and Fiscal Outlook November 2015: Supplementary Economy Tables: Table 1.11 Household Balance Sheet, PNFC, Balance Sheet and Bank Lending*. London: Office for Budget Responsibility.

Office for National Statistics. 2015. *Regional Gross Value Added (Income Approach), 1997 to 2014*. Newport, UK: Office for National Statistics.

– 2016. *Public Finances: January 2016*. Newport, UK: Office for National Statistics.

Organization for Economic Cooperation and Development. 2016. "Elusive Global Growth Outlook Requires Urgent Policy Response." News release, Organization for Economic Cooperation and Development, 18 February.

Osborne, George. 2010. Fiscal Responsibility Bill Debate. *Hansard*. 5 January.

Osborne, George. 2013a. "Autumn Statement." 5 December.

– 2013b. "Speech to the Conservative Party Conference." Manchester, 30 September.

– 2014. "We Need a Northern Powerhouse." Speech, Museum of Science and Industry, Manchester, 23 June.

– 2015a. "Budget Statement." 8 July.

– 2015b. *Spending Review and Autumn Statement 2015*.

Tetlow, Gemma. 2015. "The End of Austerity Is Nigh?" IFS Post-Budget Briefing 2015, Institute for Fiscal Studies, London, 19 March.

Turner, Adair. 2016. *Between Debt and the Devil: Money, Credit, and Fixing Global Finance*. Princeton, NJ: Princeton University Press. http://dx.doi.org/10.1515/9781400873326.

United Nations. 2009. *The Stiglitz Report: Reforming the International Monetary and Financial System in the Wake of the Global Crisis*. New York: New.

7 Frugal Comfort from Ireland: Marginal Tales from an Austere Isle

BRENDAN K. O'ROURKE AND JOHN HOGAN

Introduction

In the early twentieth century, Ireland seemed poised at the forefront of progress, committing itself to national independence, universal adult suffrage, and confronting poverty and inequality. Yet, at crucial times, both before and in the austerity period after the 2007 international economic crisis, Ireland has been celebrated as a model for liberal and post-liberal policies that impose harsh consequences for many of its people. These policies have been advocated by a section of the Irish policymaking elite, a marginal group, on a peripheral island, connected to the globally hegemonic liberal discourses – and, more specifically in recent times, neoliberal discourses. Ireland's elite can apply these hegemonic discourses to advocate neoliberal cures and also acquire international status and acclaim among post-liberals in celebrating their alleged successes. These "successes" are very marginal and provide frugal comfort for those seeking to use Ireland as an example of either the benefits of postliberal austerity, or excess.

To explain neoliberal discursive success in Ireland, despite neoliberal policy failures, it is essential to understand its historical context. For that reason we begin with explaining how a rather austere British economic liberalism, and its treasury model, were preserved through the establishment of the new state, its protectionist period, and even through its more internationalizing and expansionist phase until 1972. This focus on context is needed to see how economic institutions and ideas prominent prior to independence, along with early post-independence economic policy decisions and circumstances, had long-lasting implications on policy. Keynesian current account deficit-financed demand management arrived in Ireland only in 1973, and it is the tales of booms, busts, and growth from then until 1996 that we examine as a second source of Irish post-liberal hegemony. The third phase we look at is the Celtic Tiger's period of Neoliberal Excess (1997–2007) – an orgy of tax reductions and spending. We then examine how Ireland (2008–14) once again donned sackcloth and ashes and became an exemplar of how post-liberal austerity "works." Finally, we draw some conclusions about these post-liberal fables from Ireland and raise some possible implications of our analysis.

Tales of a Revolutionary Marginal Isle: 1922–1972

Conservative Revolution, Context, and Consolidation: Independent Ireland until 1932

Ireland's War of Independence (1919–21) was revolutionary. It confronted the world power of the time, promising more democracy, greater economic equality, and national independence. The democratic program of the First Dáil (parliament formed in Dublin in January 1919 by the majority of Irish MPs who boycotted Westminster) declared, "All right to private property must be subordinated to the public right and welfare ... no child shall suffer hunger or cold from lack of food, clothing, or shelter ... all shall be provided with the means and facilities requisite for their proper education and training as Citizens of a Free and Gaelic Ireland" (Dáil Debates 1919).

Despite such revolutionary zeal, implementing universal adult suffrage and the winning of, if not a republic, an independent state (Irish Free State 1922–37), unimaginable a few years before, was still difficult. The new polity was "notable for a stultifying lack of social, cultural and economic ambition ... a prudent acquiescence before the inherited realities of the Irish social order and a conservative determination to shore up aspects of that order" (Brown 2004, 4). The first fifteen years of the new state have even been described as the "Irish Counter-Revolution" (Regan 1999). At least some of its leaders seemed to want to fashion the new state in the image of British society (Valiulis 1992). One factor explaining the conservatism of the Irish Free State is the context in which its revolutionary elites emerged. Victorian Ireland was an austere society whose population had been shrinking from the middle of the nineteenth century when the "Great Famine set off a population decline unmatched in any other European country" (Ó'Gráda 1994,

213). A million perished of starvation and disease and another million emigrated (Guinnane 1997; McHale 2010). The result was sustained outflows over the second half of the nineteenth and into the twentieth century. By 1901, the population (twenty-six counties) had fallen to 3.22 million – a 51 per cent fall since 1841 (McHale 2010). No longer were small holdings divided among multiplying descendants. These consolidated holdings were eventually inherited by an eldest son, who often remained unmarried until his parents died (Smyth 2000). Emigration functioned as a release valve, allowing for greater political stability (McHale 2010) as the remaining population became more prudent and puritanical (Foster 1988, 338). While the rising Catholic middle class revived their Gaelic roots, they were aware that their rising prosperity could be attributed to this liberal austerity. The power of this ideology is seen in an Irish land agent's account to economist Nassau Senior shortly after the famine: "Nothing but the successive failures of the potato, its failure season after season, could have produced the emigration which will, I trust, give us room to become civilized" (Ó'Gráda 1983, 76).

Ireland's revolutionary leaders emerged from a deeply damaged and conservative society with a widespread acceptance of liberal economics' explanations (Kissane 2002). Nevertheless, among the leadership for independence there were some alternatives to the liberal economists. The original Sinn Féin vision included a robust conception of nationalistic enterprise (O'Rourke 2010), while James Connolly, a founder of Ireland's Labour Party, promoted a socialist alternative (Nevin 2006). Yet the period took a heavy toll on Ireland's leadership, with a first set of leaders (Irish Parliamentary Party) discarded in the aftermath of the 1916 Rising, a second leadership cadre killed in that rebellion, and a third set of chiefs consumed by the First World, Irish independence and Irish civil wars (Lee 1989). Thus alternative economic visions were weakened just as the country gained independence, and the new government's energy was limited to restoring order, and its depleted leadership did not have the appetite for radical social change (Regan 1999, 97).

One element of this conservatism was a continuity in public administration in the form of a strong Department of Finance with a pre-Keynesian British Treasury orthodoxy (Bielenberg and Ryan 2013) – an orthodoxy that had more to do with liberal imaginaries of British development than the prominent role of debt-financed state investment in that development (Lee 2015). Initially, W.T. Cosgrave acted as both prime minister[1] and minister for finance, underlining finance's centrality. This centrality continued under Ernest Blythe, who served as minister for finance between 1923 and 1932, and was noted for sacrificing welfare services "on the altar of fiscal responsibility" (Lee 1989, 140). The Department of Finance's top civil servant was Joseph Brennan. Educated by Jesuits in the elite Clongowes school, Brennan attended Cambridge before securing a top position in finance at Dublin Castle, then the centre of British rule in Ireland (Fanning 2007, 10). While still employed by the British, Brennan started working for the Irish side in its treaty negotiations and so was welcomed into the Free State administration, where he "indulged an austere ideal of the civil servant perched above the public morass, immune from vulgar self-interest, holding the scales of public justice between conflicting selfish private interests" (Lee 1989, 107). Brennan asserted the primacy of finance with much success and contributed to ensuring that the 1922 constitution and, later, the 1937 constitution would "enshrine what have been called the 'fundamental principles' of the British financial system" (Fanning 2007, 10). By 1930, the Treasury model, with its policy of liberal austerity, was a well-worn path, since the famine, along which the new state continued travelling.

In addition to the institutionalization of the Treasury model, the basic shape of the Irish political party landscape, persisting until at least 2011, emerged at this time. Following a treaty granting most of Ireland independence from the United Kingdom (UK), Cuman na nGaedheal (CG), governed until 1932. CG, with its "stoicism and forbiddingly austere public aspect" (Brown 2004, 129), increasingly relied on the "urban middle class and more substantial farmers" (Ó'Gráda 1994, 386). Subsequently, CG merged with a smaller centre-right party and a quasi-fascist organization to form Fine Gael (FG), the Christian Democratic group that leads the current government (2011–16). A large minority opposed the treaty, leading to a civil war because it did not go far enough, primarily in terms of severing the British link but also, for many, because of failure to deliver social progress. As military defeat in the civil war became clear, many opposing the treaty formed themselves into Fianna Fáil (FF), which was to be the largest party in the state until 2011. There

---

1 *President of the executive council* was the official title between 1922 and 1937. This office and title was subsequently changed to *taoiseach*, a significantly more powerful position.

were also vibrant but small parties that continued to hold out against the treaty, including the progenitor of the Sinn Féin (SF), now led by Gerry Adams, one of many parties that had laid claim to that name and to which all the large Irish parties can trace their origins. This national question tended to marginalize and divide the Left. Labour, a persistent but small European socialist party, shares the space with a changing array of more radical socialist parties and nationalist parties in progressive phases.

Frugal Isolationism to Investment and Internationalism: 1932–1972

When elected to government in the early 1930s, FF's choices were constrained by the national formation that preceded it, the Great Depression, and the global trend towards economic isolationism. This is an example of how, according to historical institutionalism, earlier events and decisions delimit the range of choices policymakers find themselves subsequently able to make (Hogan 2006). Without accepting the determinism that such an approach can imply, we see throughout this chapter that choices and discourses that dominated early on, together with those elements that were not altered when the state was established, have had a persistent influence on the construction of austerity in Ireland. Yet, even with such limited constructions, no lesser an authority than Keynes (1933, 185) declared that during this time Ireland was one of the countries engaged in economic experimentation and exploring "new modes of political economy."

Ireland's experimentation included protectionism. While much of Western Europe went into a period of economic protectionism in the 1930s, Ireland's lasted longer, and, given its small size, autarky cost it more. Whatever the potential benefits of such protectionism, memories of its utter failure in Ireland meant widespread support for international trade, whatever its neoliberal forms. Ireland's mid-twentieth-century economic experimentation also involved state enterprise. Added to the Electricity Supply Board, established in 1927, were state enterprises such as peat harvesting (1933), sugar production (1933), and air travel (1936). Some were successful, bequeathing companies that prosper into the twenty-first century. While Ireland's state-owned commercial ventures did not surpass its private ones, the experience was successful enough to weaken any rhetoric that denies such economic possibilities. There was also some weakening of the centrality of the Department of

Finance during this period (Bielenberg and Ryan 2013, chap. 2), though it is hard to agree that Finance lost its premier position. However, it would be a mistake to think of this period as one of purely progressive policy. FF's dominant leader expressed his conservative vision that Ireland "would be the home of a people who valued material wealth only as a basis for right living, of a people who were satisfied with frugal comfort and devoted their leisure to the things of the spirit" (de Valera's 1943 St Patrick's Day broadcast, quoted in Aldous 2007, 93). By the 1950s, the extreme isolationist policies were recognized as failing, and politicians, including FF, were turning outwards. This process, though late in Western European terms, was embraced enthusiastically from 1957 onwards. While this outward turn was important for future neoliberalism in Ireland, particularly in how, in increasing its attraction of foreign direct investment, this outward shift also involved expansive moves in state capital investments, public education, and engagements with Europe that adulterated the purity of Ireland's Anglo-American free market influences.

Tales of Boom, Bust, and Growth: 1973–1996

By 1973, Ireland had opened up and effectively joined Western Europe with accession to what is now the European Union (EU).

Success and Failures in Demand Management: 1973–1986

Ireland first used a current deficit-financed demand boost to counter, with some success, the immediate effects of the early 1970s crises. As the government, in a correct use of Keynesian technique, cut back in response to recovery, they became unpopular. Ironically, the greater Keynesian project was falling apart just as Ireland caught up with it. From 1977 to 1981, FF led Ireland in a poorly planned and ill-executed state investment and taxation-cutting demand-boosting bid for growth, this at a time when the economy was already growing. By 1981 the economy was in serious trouble (Bielenberg and Ryan 2013, chap. 2).

Between June 1981 and November 1982, three general elections each brought a change of government. Apart from crisis-induced cutbacks and tax increases, no coherent idea/policies emerged. The November 1982 general election was won by a FG-Labour Coalition that remained in power until 1987. This coalition was marked by compromise with a mixture of tax increases and cutbacks. Whether due to circumstance or inappropriateness, these policies had little success.

During the 1980s, Irish economists were unusually prominent in public debate. The Dublin Economic Workshop became an annual austerity sermon. The Doheny and Nesbit school of economics – named after a bar in Dublin where many economists and journalists drank – advocated fiscal rectitude by way of cutbacks in expenditure, not tax increases.

Elite Unity and the Triumphs of Economists: 1987–1996

FF's Charles Haughey was re-elected as taoiseach in 1987. Despite Haughey's increasing corruption, and although they were bitter enemies on Northern Ireland policy, FG under Alan Dukes supported FF's austerity. As early as 1980, Haughey had preached, "Taking us all together, we have been living at a rate which is simply not justified by the amount of goods and services we are producing" (Aldous 2007, 143). In opposition, Haughey had campaigned against austerity, yet once back in government his austerity was reborn and he was "listening to economists with greater care" (Ferriter 2005, 698).

Economic recovery came in 1987 and with it, extraordinary claims: "Fiscal retrenchment led not to recession but to recovery. The poor did not suffer. Rather their numbers were reduced" (McAleese 1990, 29). Beneath this hyperbole is a claim that the direct effects of fiscal contraction are outweighed by an expansion in private spending induced by the confidence-boosting effects of government austerity. That "expansionary fiscal contraction" has been largely explored using small open economies, where government spending is not as significant for overall demand as in larger countries, gives a favourable bias to the thesis (Giavazzi and Pagano 1990). While reduced government spending can, in times of high government debt, give rise to increases in private spending, this is unlikely to outweigh the direct effects of decreased government spending (Guajardo, Leigh and Pescatori 2014). The more extreme contention, that the poor do not suffer from government cutbacks, is delusional.

Ireland's 1987 recovery is often portrayed as the Irish elite's heroic achievement in taking control of a feckless populace. By embracing austerity, Ireland's elite apparently renewed their entitlement to their leadership. The return of Haughey is seen as the economic turning point, with implementation by his finance minister (Ray MacSharry) of neoliberal austerity policy constructed as providing the essential element needed for recovery. The "noble sacrifice" of electoral opportunism by FG's leader Alan Dukes gave austerity its needed "political cover" (Barry 2010, 37).

Whereas Patrick Honohan, a respected academic economist and governor of the Central Bank (2009–15), credits this "decisive action" with contributing to the Celtic Tiger, he notes, "It was not only the domestic action: the external environment improved dramatically ... interest rates fell at home and abroad ... the UK boom sucked in migrants from Ireland ... appreciation of sterling helped Irish wage competitiveness ... the doubling of EU structural funds offered a new source of revenue" (Honohan 1999, 81–2).

Amidst the decisive action, Honohan notes a not-so-austere measure: "An effective tax amnesty (combined with credible threats for those who did not comply) brought in a huge revenue windfall, especially in 1988, and also helped secure improved collection in subsequent years" (Honohan 1999, 82). Regardless of the subtleties of what actually occurred, for Ireland's elites "the lessons of the failed fiscal experiments are important and have been largely internalised: fiscal rectitude is important for long term growth, and taxes cannot be pushed too high" (Haughton 2011, 23–4).

The Celtic Tiger: A Tale of Neoliberal Excess (1997–2007)

Profligate Neoliberal Policy

Where Ireland would turn next was signalled by the 1997 abolition of the modest Residential Property Tax (RPT). RPT had been levied only on principal private residences, not on investment properties, and only on those above a certain income with higher-priced properties. As house prices rose, particularly in the Dublin area, and collection methods improved, RPT came under attack. FF attacked RPT as "born out of the confused social thinking so beloved in Irish politics, the typical old Labour Party doctrine of begrudgery" (Dáil Debates 1996). The FG-led rainbow coalition government (1994–7) abolished the tax a few months later as house prices rose, reminding some of FF's abolition of local property taxes in the late 1970s. Profligate neoliberalist tax reductions were back.

In June 1997, FF returned to office, together with the right-of-centre Progressive Democrats (PD). FF's Charlie McCreevy became minister for finance, and his neoliberal tax reductions became central to the governments of Bertie Ahern (1997–2002, 2002–7, 2007–8). That these governments were profligate is widely agreed. Even former finance minister Ray MacSharry, neoliberal hero of Ireland's late 1980s austerity, summarizes thus: "The focus of that FF-PD government was all wrong … That Government felt that they could afford both massive increases in public pay and huge reductions in income tax because of the enormous revenues that property-related taxes were bringing in … When I suggested this was a mistake, McCreevy was far from happy" (MacSharry 2014).

Increased public spending is often seen as a left-wing activity, inevitably redistributing from the lucky to the unfortunate. This has even been implied to be a key factor in Ireland's recent crisis, where "Ireland's fiscal meltdown was triggered by a conscious policy decision of the government to 'spread the bounty' of the property and construction boom throughout the wider population" (Donovan and Murphy 2013, 114). Yet this excess between 1998 and 2008 was not left-wing, but fundamentally neoliberal. Yes, there were increases in social welfare and public service numbers and pay. Without these it would have been hard to sell the core policies to the public. However, the more discretionary spending was strongly neoliberal. This included the National Pension Reserve Fund (NPRF), introduced in 2001, a sovereign wealth fund that invested state money in the stock market to provide for future pensions. For a state to invest its future in private stocks, rather than public infrastructure, is innovative. Regardless of its merit, the NPRF was a "reform" that valued the market and the individualized more than the collective and relational. That makes the NPRF an undoubtedly neoliberal policy. Another scheme on which the government spent was the Special Saving Incentive Accounts (SSIA), introduced in 2001. SSIA gave those who saved up to €250 per month a 25 per cent state top-up. Thus, SSIA combined neoliberalism in subsidizing those who could save with political guile, as the bounty's release was timed for the 2007 election. Large reductions in tax were introduced in 1996–2008. From 1996, the FG-led coalition declared they would seek to introduce a low tax rate for all corporations. The FF-led government continued this policy, with the rate reduced to 12.5 per cent by 2006. Arguably this was less a neoliberal choice and more a pragmatic move by a small open economy in a neoliberal world, though admittedly Ireland plays this game rather well. The neoliberal world order did not, however, force the reductions in Irish income tax rates, where the top rate was lowered from 48 per cent in 1997 to 41 per cent in 2008, and the standard rate went from 26 per cent in 1997 to 20 per cent by 2008. In 1998, Capital Gains Tax was cut from 40 to 20 per cent, where it remained until 2008. True to the tenets of the neoliberal creed, the 1997–2007 governments preferred principle-based light touch corporate regulation. This was true in law (e.g., the Central Bank and Financial Services Act 1987) and in regulatory practice (Maguire 2010; Nyberg 2011). The manner in which the highly restrictive regulation of Dublin taxis ended in 2000 was celebrated as an example of how Ireland showed that, even for non-international trading sectors, "there should be full and immediate deregulation" (Barrett 2003, 39). Where the law might accidentally allow regulation, as in the revenue commissioners' proposal in 2006 to tax contracts for difference, there was quick political action to ensure enterprise was facilitated (Kingston 2010).

Ignoring Economists

Many contend that economists did not warn sufficiently of dangers during the Celtic Tiger (Donovan and Murphy 2013). We disagree. In addition to academic economists, the Economic and Social Research Institute (ESRI), the EU, the Organisation for Economic Cooperation and Development (OECD), and the International Monetary Fund (IMF) all "frequently pointed to the risks of overheating prices and wages in Ireland ... Signals of overheating were especially loud in the early 2000s" (Wright 2010, 20). Despite his conclusions that the Department of Finance warnings should have been more insistent, Wright (21) states, "Generally speaking, we found that advice prepared by the Department for Cabinet did provide clear warnings on the risks of pro-cyclical fiscal action. These views were signed-off by the Finance Ministers of the day ... This advice was more direct and comprehensive than concerns expressed by others in Ireland, or by international agencies."

In February 1999, the ESRI warned of "dangers, of which the principal threat is that the degree of overheating in the economy could become more widespread" (Baker, Duffy, and Smyth 1999, 5). These remarks were received with derision. Undeterred, in March 2000 the ESRI called for measures to slow the economy. This was reported by RTÉ (Ireland's public service broadcaster) as being "flatly rejected" by the taoiseach, Bertie Aherne, while the minister for finance, Charlie McCreevy, was quoted as saying he was not worried about the ESRI, but that the times showed a "sign of our economic manhood" (Lee 2000). If the advice of the ESRI could be dismissed, academic economists' arguments could be easily marginalized (see Kelly 2007). Most famously, in March 2007 Taoiseach Ahern poured scorn on those who warned of an overheated economy: "Sitting on the sidelines, cribbing and moaning is a lost opportunity. I don't know how people who engage in that don't commit suicide" (RTÉ 2007). Ahern quickly apologized to those hurt by suicide, but not to those warning of excess. Other neoliberal entrepreneurial types from politicians, to stockbrokers, to bankers were dismissive of those who did not share their optimistic viewpoint (see, for example, the compilation of clips aired on RTÉ 2009).

Championing "Freedom"

Charlie McCreevy, Ireland's minister for finance (1997–2004), has declared, "My belief fundamentally is that people do better when they get the chances to do better, that you don't have the tyranny of say higher taxation, you don't have the tyranny of overregulation" (quoted in O'Rourke and Hogan 2013, 230). McCreevy's language positions him as a neoliberal entrepreneur, a man of the people, of action, who need not pay attention to intellectuals, public servants, or calls for social justice. Despite irregular grammar, skipped-over words, and half-finished clauses, McCreevy is a master of neoliberal discourse (ibid.).

McCreevy departed as minister for finance to take up the office of European commissioner for internal market and services. He was replaced by the more conventional Brian Cowen, who, without the same neoliberal rhetorical flare, continued McCreevy's policies, including a further reduction of the top rate of income tax to 41 per cent.

The neoliberal discourse of McCreevy may not have been as pervasive throughout the government, but calling the period 1997–2008 one of neoliberal excess is justified. Indeed, it was a period of "starving the beast" – the neoliberal tactic (Barlett 2007) of reducing the tax base so that future governments will be forced to shrink progressive programs and have to rely upon privatized neoliberal policies. Whereas the government accounts showed only modest deficits, or even surpluses, during 1997–2008 the lowering of tax rates, proliferation of tax reliefs, reliance on boom revenues, and increased spending all left the public finances vulnerable to even a gradual slowdown in the economy. Alas, there was a massive crash.

The Celtic PIIG: 2008–2014

Before turning to the post-liberal austerity discourse applied by the Irish elite, it is worth considering how extreme Ireland's crash was: "Ireland has experienced a cumulative nominal gross domestic product (GDP) decline of 21% from quarter 4 2007 to quarter 3 2010, while its primary fiscal balance shifted to baseline deficits of 11%–12% of GDP in 2009 and 2010. The Irish economy experienced the largest compound decline in gross national product (GNP) of any industrialised economy over the 2007–10 period" (Kinsella 2012, 224). Considerable reconstruction of what had happened was needed to apply neoliberal austerity to this result of neoliberal excess.

Reconstructing the Context for Neoliberal Austerity

The economic crisis was constructed as a problem of excessive public spending, with only minor roles for property bubbles and banking imprudence. Neoliberalism, an apparently powerful omnipresence in the good times, seemed strangely absent from discussions of what caused the crisis. Thus, neoliberalism was able, with the broader post-liberal family, including ordo-liberalism, to impose its austerity solution on the crisis (Dardot, Laval, and Elliott 2014). After all, there is no point letting a crisis go to waste (Mirowski 2013). Austerity has a powerful appeal globally, and Ireland was part of that general trend, both as a developed neoliberal and peripheral state (Blyth 2013; Harvey 2005).

The work of casting Ireland's 2008 crisis in terms of the need for austerity, and austerity's past "successes," was pursued on many fronts. Analysis of two 2008 radio interviews, one with former finance minister McCreevy and the other with economist Brendan Walsh, shows an almost pincer movement of discourses (one populist, the other expert) in drawing out the virtue and alleged success of neoliberal austerity (O'Rourke and Hogan 2013). An analysis of the print media also shows how the newspapers supported neoliberal solutions: "Since 2008, the media have strongly endorsed austerity and accompanying structural reforms. For example, a *Sunday Independent* piece asserts that 'Deep reform of the civil and public sector has to be the starting point,' including redundancies, but we must go 'well beyond' public sector wages by privatizing state-owned companies and micro-managing 'every line of spending.'" (Mercille 2014, 127).

The stress on public sector cutbacks is unsurprising for a conservative "quality" newspaper like the *Sunday Independent*, but the piece by Alan Ruddock, to which Mercille refers, was published on 28 September 2008 – just days before the minister for finance announced the state would guarantee all loans to Irish banks, risking a comparison that might make even a hardened neoliberal advocate blush. Even before the banks were dealt with, the public sector is declared to be the starting point for action because, as Ruddock's piece was headlined, "Wall Street is not to blame for our recession." This portrayal of Irish economic woes was not confined to Ireland's media. On 23 January 2009, a *Daily Mail* (a mid-range UK newspaper) columnist, Mary Ellen Synon, approvingly quoted an anonymous Irishman describing Ireland as "a sick, diseased, wretched and immoral corner of Europe. Self-government for the Irish is merely an excuse to thieve, to lie, to indulge in corruption, to destroy everything that is precious and beautiful. The most enchanting landscapes in Ireland have been covered in bungalows. This is a land without any values."

Constructing Ireland's problem as one of feckless inability to self-govern was a moral tale that remained attractive in the twenty-first century. The business press was not as crude, although the acronym *PIIGS* was popular in describing Portugal, Ireland, Italy, Greece, and Spain, who were now suffering from excessive appetites and an absence of prudence (Allen 2010). The economics profession seemed to prefer the more human *GIPSY* (Greece, Ireland, Portugal, Spain, and Italy) to discuss the "adjustment difficulties" of such societies (Gros 2010). Under pressure in his neoliberal defence of public money being used to bail out banks, the minister for finance preferred in RTÉ radio interviews to move on to the need for austerity: "The banks are out of the way, now let's have a clear debate on the public finances and how they can be adjusted" (quoted in O'Rourke and Hogan 2014, 53).

Betting on Neoliberal Cures

From 2008 to 2014 there were massive cuts in public expenditure in the usual neoliberal targets of welfare expenditure, public servants, and labour costs (Allen and O'Boyle 2013). However, even post-crisis, there is neoliberal excess. Below, the banking guarantee, the National Asset Management Agency (NAMA), and the destruction of social partnership are examined.

The banking guarantee was announced by the minister for finance on 30 September 2008 and gave a state guarantee to all creditors of Irish banks for two years. The decision to provide a blanket guarantee was defended vigorously in neoliberal terms (O'Rourke and Hogan 2014), yet it transformed "an enormous private debt into a sovereign debt, thereby doubling and potentially tripling the liabilities incurred by the state" (Mair 2013, 148). Those who provide the most persuasive defence of the bank guarantee are reduced to arguments that depend on the insufficient information then available, the understanding that the EU and European Central Bank (ECB) would not tolerate any Eurozone bank failure, and the fact that cost may not turn out to be as high as some argued (Donovan and Murphy 2013).

Another generous move was the establishment of NAMA, a state agency designed to transfer poorly performing assets from the main banks to state ownership, so the banks would, even if largely owned by state, not be tarnished by nationalization. Mainstream economists beseeched the government to nationalize the banks instead of engaging in this generosity: "Every additional euro that the State pays for bad assets is an additional euro for the current capital holders and one euro less of valuable equity for the state" (Whelan et al. 2009). Yet NAMA went ahead, and bank shares retained some value for investors who might have expected nothing from such mismanaged businesses. The state's ownership of properties through NAMA tied its finances to property and incentivizes the state to favour higher prices.

More resources were spent on the neoliberal destruction of social partnership. Ireland's social partnership deals had meant tax reductions and wage constraint that might justify such centralized compacts as a short-term tactic of the right. The mechanism of conflict resolution and industrial dispute dissipation could be valuable in times of austerity. Yet, in clearing the decks for the coming austerity, neoliberalism destroyed social partnership. The report on strengthening the capacity of the Department of Finance (Wright 2010) emphasized how it was "overwhelmed" by social partnership. The decisive battle on social partnership started with an attack on a proposal for a reduction in public services that might have been expected to be met with neoliberal approval. In negotiations, the unions seemed open to reducing public service through unpaid leave. One might have thought that such a US-style furlough of public servants would have been welcomed by neoliberals. Initial reports of the idea seemed calm and neutral about this flexibility, especially since it was suggested, according to an earlier report on 2 December 2009 in the *Irish Times* (the second-largest-selling Irish "quality" newspaper), by Stephen Collings and Martin Wall, "that where it is not practical for staff to take 12 days' unpaid leave next year they would in effect be asked to work for nothing in 2010 with the leave being added to holidays at a later date, possibly over a three to four year period."

Two days later, the same newspaper reported that FF politicians viewed such unpaid absences (or possible attendances) as an unacceptable indulgence of the public sector. In the same issue, 4 December 2009, the *Irish Times* editorialized about such "out of touch" proposals. That the subsequent near-death of social partnership was premeditated is evidenced by a quote from FF's minister for finance: "The Department of Finance has concluded that the dominance of the social partnership process did enormous damage to our financial system. This is something I intend to fix" (Culpepper and Regan 2014, 1). The bank guarantee, NAMA, and social partnership's destruction show that even as austerity was being applied to some, neoliberalism meant that others had to be indulged. The question of to whom austerity is applied always needs to be asked (McBride and Whiteside 2011). Investors' confidence in banks was prioritized, while expectations of social partners could be easily cast aside.

Administering Austerity

As the crisis deepened, Irish neoliberalism let slip its pretence of the politician as entrepreneurial hero (O'Rourke and Hogan 2013) and the news of the imminent surrender of economic sovereignty was left to a public servant (Donovan and Murphy 2013, 241–5). Patrick Honan, by then governor of the Central Bank of Ireland, declared in a radio interview from Frankfurt, on 18 November 2010, that he expected the IMF, the ECB, and the European Commission (subsequently known as the Troika) to negotiate a substantial loan package with the government. Governor Honan was believed, despite contrary statements by politicians.

The details of the bailout deal, announced on 28 November 2010, harked back to old school pre-Keynesian liberalism's austerity. Fintan O'Toole, an influential columnist writing the following day in the *Irish Times*, summarized the deal: "Yesterday's bailout of broken and delinquent Ireland is much more Versailles than Marshall. There is no sharing of the burden. There is no evidence of a single thought for the consequences of mass unemployment, mass emigration and war on the most vulnerable, there is no European solidarity. And there is not even a genuine sense of self-interest."

A general election was held in February 2011. The incumbent FF lost fifty-one of its seventy-one parliamentary seats. FG won seventy-six seats, just short of the eighty-four required for an overall majority. FG, though critical of the period of neoliberal excess, since the late 1980s shared FF's policies of austerity in public spending, lower income taxes, and promotion of free markets. FG had been even less friendly to social partnership and supported the bank guarantee. Labour, opposed to the bank guarantee and austerity, won thirty-seven seats. The left had been strengthened, but the post-liberal parties remained dominant, and though Labour entered government with FG it was clearly the junior partner.

Prospects for radical change in government policy in 2011, like in the 1930s, seemed limited. Again there seemed to be an element of path dependency, where by 2011 the state had given a commitment to guarantee most bank debts, NAMA had been established, trust in social partnership has been destroyed, and a treaty, this time with the Troika rather the British, had been agreed to by government. The new FG-Labour government sought to restore economic independence at least formally within the treaty with the Troika. In 2014, that government produced the country's first budget, after six years of increasing austerity, that included a 1 per cent drop in the top rate of income tax: clearly, any generosity was going to be as post-liberal as the austerity.

Conclusion and Discussion

Neoliberal's hegemony in Ireland's political discourse is historically embedded. This is not to imply a fatalistic determinism, or a denial of the importance of discourse and ideas vital in Irish policy development (Hogan and O'Rourke 2015). In particular, the conservative nature of the Irish revolution established a narrowly economistic pre-Keynesian model as the foundation from which public discourses would emerge and on which, following 1987, a neoliberal tale of expansionary fiscal contraction became a dominant fable. Ireland's period of neoliberal excess (1997–2007) was censured by many, including economists. Given these criticisms, economists' role in Ireland cannot simply be read off as a straightforward replication of the US profession's entanglement with neoliberalist politics, even if Irish economists, in differentiated ways, largely give ideological succour to similar policies. With economic downturn, austerity was advocated by a range of voices that seemed all the more broad, due to previous difference. Post-liberals were now united: neoliberals forgave ordo-liberals for not shouting loudly enough about an overheating economy, and ordo-liberals forgave the overenthusiastic tax reductions and deregulation, which, after all, are good liberal things in themselves. Economists play pivotal roles in supporting post-liberalism, and more work is needed in understanding the precise nature of how this is done, as Evans (2014), FitzGerald and O'Rourke (2016) and Plehwe (2014) show. Ireland's positioning geographically and culturally between Boston and Berlin means that two forms of post-liberal austerity – neoliberal and ordo-liberal – are present. The Irish experience shows that these forms of austerity are overlapping but not the same, and formed a pincer movement once the bubble burst, to strengthen their shared strain of austerity.

The hegemonic power of Irish right-wing austerity is uncontaminated by, for example, Britain's experience of war and post-war austerity, where collective sacrifices contributed to beating the Nazis and built institutions like its National Health Service. Austerity can be an attractive personal choice (see Mitrea 2014, for an exploration). De Valera's frugality might have been embraced as a virtue by some, but it was a virtue born of necessity – backward-looking and rejected by his successors. Nevertheless, such alternative austerities show that current post-liberal austerity is assembled from particular ideological storehouses for particular political purposes, in particular times and spaces (Clarke 2014). Ireland's austerities are less associated with choice and more with a "constitutionalizing of austerity" (McBride 2016) that marginalizes small states in particular. The early integration of austerity into the Irish state was due to its close relationship, as a smaller state, to the world power of its time. Ireland's large US direct investment and membership of the Eurozone contributed to Ireland's adoption of post-liberal austerity after 2007. The agreement with the Troika, monetary union, and continual monitoring of its finances by the EU push certain economic questions "beyond politics," or at least beyond Irish domestic politics, much as the inheritance of the British Treasury model did previously.

A less constitutionalized but powerful influence on small state policy selection is the need to compete in a neoliberal globalized market. Ireland's bid for foreign direct investment through low corporate tax produced a generalized strategy of low tax. Though small states vary along many dimensions, discourse may be particularly important in understanding their policy development (Schmidt 2003), so analysis of Ireland's tales may provide insights in understanding how states can be captured by, or escape from, particular post-liberal prescriptions. Applying those insights to cases such as, for contrast, the small states of Scandinavia, may require much adjustment, but might also demonstrate how much post-liberal discourses can serve twists and turns in the strategic advance of neoliberal practice, even with a background of alternative discourses

Post-liberal forms of austerity are enormously successful as discourse. They draw our attention to what is being cut, but not what is being built (see Whiteside 2014; and Joy and Shields 2014). They throw opponents into defence, while advocates can advance. In good times, neoliberalism can be enthusiastic and excessive in lowering taxes, deregulating, and privatizing. This ensures that the neoliberal bête noire of progressive public spending is incapacitated. In bad times, excess for some can still be justified – after all, post-liberal structural reforms require cutting, merging, and managing. These all cost money, sometimes lots of money. Explicating post-liberal austerity and promoting alternatives to it requires not only a critique of its claims that the world is free of Keynesian macroeconomic effects, but also a careful critique of post-liberal excess and the pay-offs it claims for its investments in its very particular notions of "structural reform."

REFERENCES

Aldous, Richard. 2007. *Great Irish Speeches*. London: Quercus.

Allen, Katie. 2010. "Acronym Acrimony: The Problem with Pigs." *Guardian*, 12 February. https://www.theguardian.com/business/2010/feb/12/pigs-piigs-debted-eu-countries.

Allen, Kieran, and Brian O'Boyle. 2013. *Austerity Ireland: The Failure of Irish Capitalism*. London: Pluto.

Baker, Terence J., David Duffy, and Diarmaid Smyth. 1999. "Quarterly Economic Commentary, February 1999." *ESRI Forecasting Series* (February).

Barlett, Bruce. 2007. "'Starve the Beast': Origins and Development of a Budgetary Metaphor." *Independent Review* 12:5–26.

Barrett, Sean D. 2003. "Regulatory Capture, Property Rights and Taxi Deregulation: A Case Study." *Economic Affairs* 23 (4): 34–40. http://dx.doi.org/10.1111/j.1468-0270.2003.00441.x.

Barry, Frank. 2010. "Politics and Economic Policy Making in Ireland." In *Irish Business & Society: Governing, Participating & Transforming in the 21st Century*, ed. John Hogan, Paul F. Donnelly, and Brendan K. O'Rourke, 28–43. Dublin: Gill & McMillan.

Bielenberg, Andy, and Raymond Ryan. 2013. *An Economic History of Ireland since Independence*. London: Routledge.

Blyth, Mark. 2013. *Austerity: The History of a Dangerous Idea*. Oxford: Oxford University Press.

Brown, Terence. 2004. *Ireland: A Social and Cultural History, 1922–2002*. London: HarperCollins Publishers.

Clarke, John. 2014. "Imagined Economies: Austerity and the Moral Economy of 'Fairness.'" *TOPIA: Canadian Journal of Cultural Studies* 17 (30–1): 1–14. https://topia.journals.yorku.ca/index.php/topia/article/view/38417.

Culpepper, Pepper D., and Aidan Regan. 2014. "Why Don't Governments Need Trade Unions Anymore? The Death of Social Pacts in Ireland and Italy." *Socioeconomic Review* 12 (4): 723–45. http://dx.doi.org/10.1093/ser/mwt028.

Dáil Debates. 1919. "Democratic Programme." Dáil Éireann, 21 January. http://oireachtasdebates.oireachtas.ie/debates%20authoring/debateswebpack.nsf/takes/dail1919012100016.

Dardot, Pierre, Christian Laval, and Gregory Elliott. 2014. *The New Way of the World: On Neoliberal Society*. New York: Verso.

– 1996. Private Members' Business – Residential Property Tax: Motion 2 October. http://oireachtasdebates.oireachtas.ie/Debates%20Authoring/DebatesWebPack.nsf/takes/dail1996100200012.

Donovan, Donal, and Antoine E. Murphy. 2013. *The Fall of the Celtic Tiger: Ireland and the Euro Debt Crisis*. Oxford: Oxford University Press. http://dx.doi.org/10.1093/acprof:oso/9780199663958.001.0001.

Evans, Bryan. 2014. "The Ideational Foundations of Economic Policy in an Age of Austerity: Ideas, Agents, Institutions and the Neoliberal State." Paper presented at the Manufacturing and Framing Austerity Workshop, McMaster University, Canada, 30 October–1 November.

Fanning, Ronan. 2007. "Picturing the Public Services in 1922." In *Ireland 2022: Towards One Hundred Years of Self-Government*, ed. Mark Callanan, 6–15. Dublin: Institute of Public Administration.

Ferriter, Diarmaid. 2005. *The Transformation of Ireland, 1900–2000*. London: Profile.

FitzGerald, Joseph K., and Brendan K. O'Rourke. 2016. "Legitimising Expertise: Analysing the Legitimation Strategies Used by Economics Experts in Broadcast Interviews." *Journal of Multicultural Discourses* 11 (3): 269–82.

Foster, Roy F. 1988. *Modern Ireland: 1600–1972*. London: Penguin.

Giavazzi, Francesco, and Marco Pagano. 1990. "Can Severe Fiscal Contractions Be Expansionary? Tales of Two Small European Countries." *NBER Macroeconomics Annual* 5:75–111. http://dx.doi.org/10.1086/654131.

Gros, Daniel. 2010. "Adjustment Difficulties in the GIPSY Club." CEPS Working document no. 326. http://dx.doi.org/10.2139/ssrn.1604568.

Guajardo, Jaime, Daniel Leigh, and Andrea Pescatori. 2014. "Expansionary Austerity? International Evidence." *Journal of the European Economic Association* 12 (4): 949–68. doi:10.1111/jeea.12083.

Guinnane, Timothy. 1997. *The Vanishing Irish: Households, Migration, and the Rural Economy in Ireland, 1850–1914*. Princeton, NJ: Princeton University Press.

Harvey, David. 2005. *A Brief History of Neoliberalism*. Oxford: Oxford University Press.

Haughton, Jonathan. 2011. "The Historical Background." In *The Economy of Ireland: National and Sectoral Policy Issues*, ed. John W. O'Hagan and Carol Newman, 2–28. Dublin: Gill & McMillan.

Hogan, John. 2006. "Remoulding the Critical Junctures Approach." *Canadian Journal of Political Science* 39 (3): 657–79. http://dx.doi.org/10.1017/S0008423906060203.

Honohan, Patrick. 1999. "Fiscal Adjustment and Disinflation in Ireland: Setting the Macro Basis of Economic Recovery and Expansion." In *Understanding Ireland's Economic Growth*, ed. Frank Barry, 75–98. London: Macmillian. http://dx.doi.org/10.1057/9780333985052_5.

Hogan, John, and Brendan K. O'Rourke. 2015. "The Critical Role of Ideas: Understanding Industrial Policy Changes in Ireland in the 1980s." In *Policy Paradigms in Theory and Practice: Discourses, Ideas and Anomalies in Public Policy Dynamics*, ed. John Hogan and Michael Howlett, 167–88. Basingstoke, UK: Palgrave.

Joy, Meaghan, and John Shields. 2014. "Austerity and the Non-Profit Sector: The Case of Social Impact Bonds." Paper presented at the Manufacturing and Framing Austerity Workshop, McMaster University, Canada, 30 October–1 November.

Kelly, Morgan. 2007. "On the Likely Extent of Falls in Irish House Price." Working Paper Series WP07/01. Dublin: University College Dublin Centre for Economic Research.

Keynes, John M. 1933. "Nation Self-Sufficiency: The First Finlay Lecture Delivered at University College, Dublin, 19 April 1933." *Studies Irish Review* (June): 177–92.

Kingston, William. 2010. "Need the Irish Economic Experiment Fail?" In *Irish Business & Society: Governing, Participating & Transforming in the 21st Century*, ed. John Hogan, Paul F. Donnelly, and Brendan K. O'Rourke, 69–89. Dublin: Gill & McMillan.

Kinsella, Stephen. 2012. "Is Ireland Really the Role Model for Austerity?" *Cambridge Journal of Economics* 36 (1): 223–35. http://dx.doi.org/10.1093/cje/ber032.

Kissane, Bill. 2002. *Explaining Irish Democracy*. Dublin: University College Dublin Press.

Lee, George. 2000. News report. RTÉ Nine O'Clock News. https://www.youtube.com/watch?v=THWbrFy5NWM.

Lee, Joseph J. 1989. *Ireland, 1912–1985: Politics and Society*. Cambridge: Cambridge University Press.

Lee, Simon. 2015. "Indebted and Unbalanced." In *The Conservative-Liberal Coalition: Examining the Cameron-Clegg Government*, ed. Matt Beech and Simon D. Lee, 16–35. London: Palgrave Macmillan.

MacSharry, Ray. 2014. "The Poisoned Chalice." In *Brian Lenihan: In Calm and Crisis*, ed. Brian Murphy, Mary O'Rourke, and Noel Whelan. Sallins: Merrion / Irish Academic. Kindle edition.

Maguire, Roderick. 2010. "White-Collar Crime: The Business of Crime." In *Irish Business & Society: Governing, Participating & Transforming in the 21st Century*, ed. John Hogan, Paul F. Donnelly, and Brendan K. O'Rourke, 172–93. Dublin: Gill & McMillan.

Mair, Peter. 2013. "Smaghi versus the Parties: Representative Government and Institutional Constraints." In *Politics in the Age of Austerity*, ed. Armin Schäfer and Wolfgang Streeck, 143–68. Cambridge: Polity.

McAleese, Dermot. 1990. "Ireland's Economic Recovery." *Irish Banking Review* (Summer): 18–32.

McBride, Stephen. 2016. "Constitutionalizing Austerity: Taking the Public out of Public Policy." *Global Policy* 7 (1): 5–14.

McBride, Stephen, and Heather Whiteside. 2011. "Austerity for Whom?" *Socialist Studies/Études socialistes* 7:42–64.

McHale, John. 2010. "Achieving Growth in a Regional Economy: Lessons from Irish Economic History." In *Irish Business & Society: Governing, Participating & Transforming in the 21st Century*, ed. John Hogan, Paul F. Donnelly, and Brendan K. O'Rourke, 454–70. Dublin: Gill & McMillan.

Mercille, Julien. 2014. *The Political Economy and Media Coverage of the European Economic Crisis: The Case of Ireland*. Routledge. Kindle edition.

Mirowski, Philip. 2013. *Never Let a Serious Crisis Go to Waste: How Neoliberalism Survived the Financial Meltdown*. New York: Verso Books.

Mitrea, Sorin. 2014. "Austere Bodies: The Morality, Futurity and Responsibility of Consumption." Paper presented at the Manufacturing and Framing Austerity Workshop, McMaster University, Canada, 30 October–1 November.

Nevin, Donal. 2006. *James Connolly, a Full Life: A Biography of Ireland's Renowned Trade Unionist and Leader of the 1916 Easter Rising*. Dublin: Gill & McMillan.

Nyberg, Peter. 2011. *Misjudging Risk: Causes of the Systemic Banking Crisis in Ireland: Report of the Commission of Investigation into the Banking Sector in Ireland*. Dublin: Department of Finance.

Ó'Gráda, Cormac. 1983. "Malthus and the Pre-Famine Economy." In *Economists and the Irish Economy from the Eighteenth Century to the Present Day*, ed. Antoin E. Murphy, 75–95. Dublin: Irish Academic.

– 1994. *Ireland: A New Economic History, 1780–1939*. Oxford: Oxford University Press.

O'Rourke, Brendan K. 2010. "Enterprise Discourse: Its Origins and Its Influence in Ireland." In *Irish Business & Society: Governing, Participating & Transforming in the 21st Century*, ed. John Hogan, Paul F. Donnelly, and Brendan K. O'Rourke, 69–89. Dublin: Gill & McMillan.

O'Rourke, Brendan K., and John Hogan. 2013. "Reflections in the Eyes of a Dying Tiger: Looking Back on Ireland's 1987 Economic Crisis." In *Discourse and Crisis: Critical Perspectives*, ed. Antoon De Rycker and Zuraidah Mohd Don, 215–38. Amsterdam: John Benjamins. http://dx.doi.org/10.1075/dapsac.52.07oro.

– 2014. "Guaranteeing Failure: Neoliberal Discourse in the Irish Economic Crisis." *Journal of Political Ideologies* 19 (1): 41–59. http://dx.doi.org/10.1080/13569317.2013.869456.

Plehwe, Dieter. 2014. "Fighting the Financial Crisis or Consolidating Austerity? The Eurobond Battle Reconsidered." Paper presented at the Manufacturing and Framing Austerity Workshop, McMaster University, Canada, 30 October–1 November.

Regan, John M. 1999. *The Irish Counter-revolution, 1921–1936: Treatyite Politics and Settlement in Independent Ireland*. Dublin: Gill & McMillan.

RTÉ. 2007. "Ahern Apologises for Suicide Remark." RTÉ News, 4 July. http://www.rte.ie/news/2007/0704/90808-economy/.

– 2009. Frontline. https://www.youtube.com/watch?v=0znF8vWUWmA

Schmidt, Vivien A. 2003. "How, Where and When Does Discourse Matter in Small States' Welfare State Adjustment?" *New Political Economy* 8 (1): 127–46. http://dx.doi.org/10.1080/1356346032000078750.

Smyth, William J. 2000. "Nephews, Dowries, Sons and Mothers: The Geography of Farm and Marital Transactions in Eastern Ireland c.1820–c.1970." In *Migration, Mobility and Modernization*, ed. David J. Siddle, 9–46. Liverpool: Liverpool University Press.

Valiulis, Maryann Gialanella. 1992. *Portrait of a Revolutionary: General Richard Mulcahy and the Founding of the Irish Free State*. Dublin: Irish Academic Press.

Whelan, Karl, John Cotter, Don Bredin, Elaine Hutson, Cal Muckley, Shane Whelan, Kevin O'Rourke, Frank Barry, Pearse Colbert, Brian Lucey, Patrick

McCabe, Alex Sevic, Constantin Gurdgiev, Valerio Poti, Jennifer Berrill, Ciarán Mac an Bhaird, Gregory Connor, Rowena Pecchenino, James Deegan, and Cormac Ó Gráda. 2009. "Nationalising Banks Is the Best Option." *Irish Times*, 17 April.

Whiteside, Heather. 2014. "Profiting Off Austerity: Private Finance for Public Infrastructure." Paper presented at the Manufacturing and Framing Austerity Workshop, McMaster University, Canada, 30 October–1 November.

Wright, Robert. 2010. *Strengthening the Capacity of the Department of Finance: Report of the Independent Review Panel*. Dublin: Department of Finance.

SECTION 2

State Reconfiguration

8 The New Constitutionalism and Austerity[1]

STEPHEN MCBRIDE

Given the severity of the shock that the 2007–8 financial crisis posed to the stability of the capitalist system, emergency measures to slow the crisis and to stimulate the economy were adopted in many countries. Apart from automatic stabilizers represented by automatically triggered expenditures on unemployment benefits and other social supports, a variety of discretionary fiscal and monetary measures were put in place. In some countries stimulative monetary measures such as quantitative easing ran counter to austerity fiscal policies, while in other examples they complemented each other, at least for a time.[2] However, almost before the immediate crisis had abated, many states and international organizations turned to policies of austerity and restraint. Much debate on the wisdom, or otherwise, of these policies ensued. Considerable evidence suggests that austerity policies do not work in the way that proponents claim (Blyth 2013; Herndon, Ash, and Pollin 2013; Krugman 2013; Stiglitz 2011). In particular the idea of expansionary fiscal contraction – that cutting spending could generate greater economic activity – is no longer credible. And the idea that a given level of public debt would, once the threshold was exceeded, trigger a massive drop in growth has been similarly debunked (Herndon, Ash, and Pollin 2013).

---

1 Parts of this chapter are drawn from a previously published article, "Constitutionalizing Austerity: Taking the Public Out of Public Policy," *Global Policy* 7, no. 1 (2016): 5–14.
2 For a discussion of quantitative easing and where is sits in the policy arsenal associated with the crisis and austerity, see the Introduction to this volume; also the chapters by Teeple (2), Peters (3), and Cohen (4).

Notwithstanding early reliance on stimulus policies and despite the serious criticisms levelled at austerity as a one-size-fits-all policy for all seasons, long-standing moves to remove fiscal discretion from governments and lock in the austerity option have intensified. To the extent these moves succeed, fiscal policy will join other key economic policy instruments such as monetary policy and trade and investment policy, in being removed from the realm of political choice and consigned to that of prearranged and, by design at least, permanent rules. In some interpretations (Oberndorfer 2014, 28), structural reform policies affecting the public sector and labour markets are undergoing the same process.

Early analyses of globalization posited that the nation-state had lost sovereignty and, explicitly or implicitly, this also implied a loss of democracy and accountability. It could not plausibly be argued that supranational democratic forums had emerged to replace those at the national level. The process was depicted as one in which the nation-state had been hollowed out, losing power upwards to supranational entities, downwards to subnational levels of governments, and sideways to markets, private actors, and sometimes civil society. A second generation of more sceptical globalization scholars conceptually rescued the state from oblivion. They emphasized its role in fostering globalization and states' continued relevance as political actors.

Sceptics were undoubtedly correct in pointing to the exaggerations of early globalization theorists, and in contributing to more nuanced analyses. Yet in applying the lessons of the financial crisis, and reinvigorated efforts to "constitutionalize" austerity policies, it may be useful to revisit the degree to which a continued state role in global processes is removed from the concept of democracy that formerly rationalized liberal democratic theory and practice. This does not imply that the state is the instrument of global forces: it helps shape its own role in response to internal as well as external pressures.

Constitutionalization features in two bodies of literature, one originating in international political economy (Gill 1992), and the other in analyses of the impact of neoliberalism generally and, more specifically, of international economic agreements on domestic institutions (Clarkson 1993; McBride 2003). Much of this North American literature was inspired by US President Reagan's observation that the 1988 Canada-US Free Trade Agreement represented a new "economic constitution" for North America. Under that agreement and its NAFTA successor, and complemented by the World Trade Organization (WTO),

broad swathes of economic policy have become "constitutionalized."
Clearly this does not refer only to codified constitutional documents.
However, if we define a constitution as measures, institutions, and
practices that fit an older and broader concept of constitution, as applying to the entire governmental order involved in governing a polity,
then a variety of instruments can help separate particular policy areas
from the realm of normal politics and establish a higher threshold for
contravening the rules or outcomes established.

In this process, the following tendencies can be noted. First, key
powers are located in ways that are remote from popular or even
governmental influence (Gill 1992, 296; Harmes 2006; Hirschl 2004).
Once remote[3] institutional homes are established, there is little further
accountability. Second, the rules themselves reflect neoliberal policy
preferences and seem designed to protect them against future change.
These rules are intended, therefore, to "lock in" one set of policy outcomes. By rendering the implementation of measures automatic rather
than discretionary, the intention is to depoliticize these policies and, by
removing them from the political realm, act as political stabilizers.

In their discussion of new constitutionalism, Stephen Gill and Claire
Cutler (2014, 7) advance a broad definition comprising four interactive
processes. These are the emergence of a "de facto constitutional governance structure" for the world economy that incorporates public and
private actors and operates at all levels, from regional to global; neoliberal restructuring of state forms, with the effect of extending the power
of capitalist markets and of market forces; specific mechanisms to lock
in institutional and policy measures that support capital accumulation;
and a new set of informal, self-regulatory, and flexible regulations and
legal standards.

This chapter addresses the third of these – measures to lock neoliberal
policy options in place. Notwithstanding its narrower focus, however,
at least four different modes of constitutionalization are readily identi-
fiable. First, nation-states can assume obligations, including observance
of specified rules, as part of binding and enforceable international treaties. Second, they may embed such obligations and rules as part of their
own national or subnational constitutions with special amendment procedures that are more difficult than those associated with the passage of

3 Either spatially, as in an international venue, or functionally, as in a transfer of public
authority to a private body.

normal legislation. Third, they can accept binding but temporally limited obligations as conditions for receiving some form of international assistance. Conceptually at least, once the assistance expires, so does the obligation. Finally, ordinary legislation or regulations can be used to create obstacles to deviating from the obligations, either by strengthening the position of those favouring them within state structures, or by imposing a symbolic cost on those who would deviate from them. If successful, such measures can create a kind of quasi-constitutional convention, not legally enforceable but a habitual and accepted practice with which there is general compliance.

Before focusing on the constitutionalization of fiscal policy generally and austerity specifically, it will be worth reviewing briefly the extent to which other economic policy areas – trade, investment, and monetary policy – have been removed from the arena of politics. This can illustrate some of the constitutional mechanisms by which this has been accomplished and by which the constitutionalization of fiscal policy and austerity is proceeding.

The constitutionalization of trade and investment policies has in some ways proceeded earlier and further than those in place for some other economic policy areas. The whole process of constitutionalizing economic policy has been and remains untidy, and the sequencing probably has as much to do with opportunities arising, and the degree of resistance encountered, as it does with the implementation of any master plan. Nevertheless, institutionalizing mobility of capital through investment agreements, and thus opening the spectre of capital flight or exit should governments fail to provide a conducive context for investors, clearly exerts a disciplinary effect on states and on labour. Similarly, the option of substituting cheap imports, permitted under free trade agreements, for domestic production disciplines both labour and the state. To the extent that widespread use of inexpensive imported consumer goods and food is institutionalized by the agreements, it can also achieve a depressing effect on wages.

Trade agreements' coverage and enforcement now reach beyond national borders much more that those negotiated in the post-war period. Earlier agreements covered mainly at-the-border tariff barriers on goods. Later agreements, exemplified by those under the World Trade Organization (WTO) umbrella, extended to many other subjects, including performance requirements on investment, trade in services, and intellectual property rights. The Dispute Settlement Mechanism of the WTO is designed to increase enforcement of breaches of WTO rules, though the ultimate sanction, if the loser of a case refuses to adhere to a WTO decision, still rests with the winning member state. Starting with the North American Free Trade Agreement (NAFTA), but anticipated in many Bilateral Investment Agreements (BITs) before that, state interference with foreign investment is circumscribed in multilateral trade agreements[4] in a variety of ways. Most significantly, enforcement, at least at the level of obtaining financial damages for adverse regulation, is assigned to investor state dispute-settlement mechanisms, giving foreign investors the right to launch cases against states and have them adjudicated essentially under the rules of international commercial arbitration. Such procedures have been widely criticized as inducing "regulatory chill" on states, and even some commercial arbitrators express disquiet about the process: "When I wake up at night and think about arbitration, it never ceases to amaze me that sovereign states have agreed to investment arbitration at all ... Three private individuals are entrusted with the power to review, without any restriction or appeal procedure, all actions of the government, all decisions of the courts, and all laws and regulations emanating from parliament" (see Perry 2012). An attempt to globalize these rights and procedures failed when a proposed Multilateral Agreement on Investment (MAI) foundered in the 1990s, but they have been included in hundreds if not thousands of BITs and in other multilateral agreements (Van Harten 2005).

Investor-state dispute-settlement mechanisms have been included in two major trade agreements in the 2010s. These are the Canada–European Union Comprehensive Economic and Trade Agreement (CETA), which is widely considered a precursor of an agreement between the United States and the European Union, and the Trans-Pacific Partnership (TPP).

In the case of CETA, the investor-state dispute provisions became a controversial issue, especially in Europe, where public opinion, perhaps belatedly, has discovered that lawsuits launched by foreign investors could challenge or demand compensation for the impact of health, social, and environmental policies (McKenna 2016). The agreement is signed, as of the time of writing, but not ratified. In response to criticisms, some changes were agreed to the investor-state

---

4 Such provisions are found in ongoing multilateral trade agreements under negotiation including TPP, CETA, and presumably the EU-US agreement.

dispute-settlement process. Under the guise of a "legal scrubbing" of the agreement, the changes are substantial, though they still fail to satisfy critics who consider that foreign investors should avail themselves of the domestic court system rather than an essentially private or separate justice system (Walkom 2016). The new procedures include a stronger affirmation of governments' right to regulate, substitutes a roster of fifteen arbitrators, chosen by the EU and Canada, who would not be permitted to represent either companies or states in other investor-state disputes, and established an appeals body (Mazereeuw 2016).

Nevertheless, the CETA includes binding constraints on states' policy options, which will be enforceable by a disputes mechanism. Government procurement policies, often used in economic development strategies, now face a quasi-constitutional obstacle in the form of the CETA. Similarly, should any state opt to reverse previous policies of privatization, it will face action under CETA. As well as constraints, there are injunctions to act. Examples include a requirement to consult foreign governments and investors prior to introducing regulation that could be regarded as trade-related; and to extend the length of patent protection, thus delaying the arrival of cheaper, generic pharmaceuticals (see Sinclair, Trew and Mertins-Kirkwood 2014 for a full analysis of CETA provisions).

The same trends are apparent in the Trans-Pacific Partnership, a thirty-chapter, 3,000-page document. In January 2017 US President Donald Trump signed an executive order withdrawing American participation, a move that was widely seen as ending the initiative, at least for the present. The TPP involved a dozen countries from North America, Asia, and South America, including the United States, Canada, Mexico, and Japan, with several other countries expressing interest in joining. No detailed analysis of this complex document can be offered here. Among its chapters were ones dealing with trade in goods, services, financial services, investment, government procurement, e-commerce, telecommunications, regulatory coherence, and investor-state dispute settlement. The direction of the TPP was clear and consistent with the constitutionalization argument being advanced, one of progressive liberalization that carries the corollary of progressive limitation of states' ability to moderate the effect of markets or to regulate the behaviour of market actors. Canadian commentators highlighted this in comparing the TPP to NAFTA. TPP would have superseded NAFTA and any bilateral agreements, except where "any NAFTA agreements are superior to the TPP provisions ... I think that most of the provisions in the TPP will be superior" (trade lawyer Lawrence Herman, cited in Isfeld 2015). Similarly, Danielle Goldfarb, director of global commerce at the Conference Board of Canada, depicted the TPP as "a bit more ambitious in terms of its liberalization," but NAFTA "essentially remains in place unless these other aspects of the deal are more ambitious" (quoted in Isfeld 2015).

Structural adjustment and conditional loan agreements between international organizations and developing countries typically included measures to lower budget deficits, liberalize prices and trade, and reduce real wages, especially in the public sector (Williams 1994). Here the policy prescriptions of the Washington consensus were imposed on states, at least for as long as they were financial clients of the organizations. Under different nomenclature, since the 2008 crisis the system can now be observed in Europe (Greer 2014). Indebted countries seeking aid have had to contend with the Troika (composed of the IMF, the European Commission, and the European Central Bank). Under memorandums of understanding between the nation-state debtors and these international lenders (Ayhan and McBride 2015), fiscal rules, public spending cuts, and structural labour market reforms to make employment relations more flexible have been imposed as part of the debt relief agreements.

With respect to monetary policy, two broad approaches have been followed. First, in most countries central banks have been made more independent of governments, and hence, even if indirectly, of the public. Central banks play important roles, including setting monetary policy and interest rates, influencing exchange rates, regulating the banking system, and controlling money supply (Picker 2007). Increasingly they exercise their function independently of governments. There is long-standing literature suggesting that autonomous central banks will favour austerity and financial orthodoxy over policies of stimulus (Kurzer 1988). Over the 1989–2010 period there was a steady movement towards central bank independence (CBI) covering advanced countries, emerging economies, and developing countries (Polillo and Guillén 2005; Dincer and Eichengreen 2014). Much of this was accomplished, depending on jurisdiction, by normal legislative or regulatory change. A second route, however, was by international agreements or treaties. Thus within the Eurozone, the European Central Bank (ECB) has been assigned the primary goal of maintaining price stability, and its independence in pursuing it has been given constitutional status in the European System of Central Banks statute and in the European Community Treaty itself.[5]

In the fiscal policy area, a 2009 IMF study reported that the number of countries using fiscal rules had increased dramatically from seven countries in 1990 to eighty in 2009 (cited in Tapp 2010, 3).

Europe

The European Union has been in the forefront of experimenting with limiting governments' ability to pursue expansionary fiscal policies. Thresholds have been imposed that, if exceeded, result automatically in austerity measures. The intention has been to establish rules beyond the reach of politics and thereby to constrain the state and insulate it from democratic pressures that tend in an expansionary direction.

The Maastricht Treaty (MT) and its supranational fiscal and monetary rules were unprecedented at the time of its ratification in November 1993 (Baun 1995–6; Buti and Giudice 2002, 4). From a fiscal perspective, the treaty was particularly focused on debt and balanced budget rules, outlining desired targets of 60 per cent of GDP as maximum allowable public debt and a maximum yearly budget deficit of no more than 3 per cent of GDP, except under exceptional economic circumstances (Schuknecht et al. 2011, 11). These provisions echoed academic dismissal of expansionary policies designed to stimulate growth and sustain employment as outdated (Rogoff 1990; Sandholtz 1993, 34). The new academic and political consensus was that low inflation and price stability obtained through fiscal rules that reduced government budgets, and led to low debt levels, would drive economic growth (Rogoff 1990; Sandholtz 1993, 34).

In addition to political peer pressure for reaching these goals, the member states also provided for enforcement for dissenting members. This enforcement process was run through the European Commission and the Economic and Financial Affairs Council (ECOFIN), and included public shaming, but could escalate all the way to sanctions in extreme circumstances (Buiter et al. 1993).

---

5 The ECB's own account shows its independence to be extremely robust and its accountability to consist of little more than transparency and explaining its actions (see European Central Bank (n.d.)).

ECOFIN proving inadequate, attempts were made in the EU to tighten these limits on fiscal policy discretion through the Stability and Growth Pact (SGP). Technical arguments were advanced positing the value and necessity of sound fiscal policies that can be effectively enforced at the supranational level with a well-functioning monetary union (Balassone and Franco 2000; Buti, Franco, and Ongena 1998; De Haan, Berger, and Jansen 2004; Heipertz and Verdun 2004; Schuknecht 2005). This literature is very narrowly focused on economic targets and is almost completely uncritical of the relevance of strict numerical targets such as a limit on the deficit of 3 per cent of GDP, or the target debt rate of 60 per cent of GDP, or the impact these targets have on member states.

To the extent that sovereignty or democracy issues are considered in the literature on the SGP, it depicts member states as having too much power to ignore the fiscal rules outlined in the MT and the SGP (Artis and Buti 2000; Buti, Franco, and Ongena 1998; von Hagen 2003; Heipertz and Verdun 2004; Hodson and Maher 2001, 8–9). The pact itself was the result of popular concern in Germany among economists, banks, and the public at large that without stronger fiscal rules at the supranational level, the stability of the entire European Monetary Union would be in jeopardy (Heipertz and Verdun 2004, 768–9). The SGP enhanced the fiscal rules laid out in the Maastricht Treaty in a variety of ways. However, it fell short of imposing enforceable sanctions for excess deficits: "The essence of the pact is not a mechanism of 'quasi-automatic sanctions' but the institutionalization of a political pledge to aim for low deficits. The procedures cannot be enforced by legal means" (770).

In 2012, a new Fiscal Compact in the EU was designed to strengthen the earlier pact by providing that "the budgetary position of the general government of a Contracting Party shall be balanced or in surplus," subject to temporary deviations with a correction mechanism, "triggered automatically," for "significant observed deviations." The compact goes on to state, "[These] rules … shall take effect in the national law of the Contracting Parties … through provisions of binding force and permanent character, preferably constitutional, or otherwise guaranteed to be fully respected and adhered to through national budgetary processes. The Contracting Parties shall put in place at national level the correction mechanism."

Under the Fiscal Compact states must keep structural deficits to 0.5 per cent of GDP if their public debt is beyond 60 per cent of GDP, and deficits must be kept to 1 per cent of GDP for states which have public debt below 60 per cent of GDP (Costello 2014, 459). In addition, the Fiscal Compact outlines debt-reduction obligations for any country above a 60 per cent debt limit at a reduction rate of one-twentieth (5 per cent) per annum. In both the MT and the SGP, the budget deficit could be as large as 3 per cent of GDP before Excessive Deficit Procedures (EDP) were enacted, and rules on debt reduction were far more vague.

In addition, the Fiscal Compact contains a correction mechanism that automatically allows the commission to place states into EDP if they deviate from the deficit or debt rules in their yearly budgets, or if it appears they may deviate from their medium-term objectives. Sanctions for repeated deviations from sound budget management can begin at an interest-bearing deposit of 0.2 per cent of GDP (to be returned upon the correction of deviation), and move all the way up to a fine of 0.5 per cent of GDP for repeated deviations from recommended deficit- and debt-reduction strategies. Unlike the MT and the SGP where the ECOFIN Council had to first approve an EDP through a qualified majority, member states within the Fiscal Compact must now operate on a reverse qualified majority basis. Essentially, what this means is that the council must now reach a qualified majority *not* to commence an EDP rather than to begin one, and in addition, the council must reach a reverse qualified majority every time it wishes to block any commission recommendation of any sort (Costello 2014, 459). Thus, although ultimate authority still rests with the state, the process to block commission-recommended reforms is much more difficult.

The intended effect of the combination of treaties and rules on monetary and fiscal policy is to rule out currency devaluation and the use of budget deficits, both of which could play a role in pro-employment policies. Ruling out external devaluation through currency adjustments means that internal devaluation, compressed wages, and unemployment must be the chief adjustment mechanism to deal with imbalances.

States agreed to internalize general commission principles within their constitutions or a comparable piece of legislation (Burret and Schnellenbach 2014, 6). Although the exact way in which these general commission principles are internalized is left up to each member state, the Fiscal Compact intends that similar fiscal rules will nevertheless be highly binding within the legal systems of individual states. This common set of fiscal rules is to be monitored by an independent national supervisory institution that reports directly to the commission and requires nation states to comply or explain if this supervisory institution determines that member states have deviated from the general principles of the compact (ibid.).

In addition, the Fiscal Compact has been complemented by a number of other treaty reforms that have been undertaken in response to the European Debt Crisis. In particular, the compact operates alongside the European Semester, which is essentially an agreement between member states to share and discuss their economic and budgetary plans with one another and the commission at specific times throughout the year (European Commission 2014). The commission uses this information to outline a broad policy guidance report (known as an Annual Growth Survey), which member states are expected to follow. Moreover, the commission is responsible, through the European Semester, for screening all national budgets for potential imbalances. If balances are identified, the commission is obligated to undertake an in-depth review of a member state's budget and finances and can use this information to publicly shame guilty countries, as well as commence a new procedure, known as an Excessive Imbalance Procedure (EIP). The main difference between an EDP and an EIP is that an EIP allows the commission to force member states into corrective action before a country even arrives at a point of "excessive deficit," defined as a structural deficit above 0.5 per cent of GDP (ibid.). Moreover, depending on member-state responses to these early warnings, this information can be used by the commission later in the year as justification to place member states in EDP earlier than otherwise previously possible (Bauer and Becker 2014, 221).

Many of the states subject to these rules have yet to constitutionalize them formally. However, the treaties that contain these measures partially constitutionalize them through binding their signatories, even if they are parliamentary-type systems under which no Parliament can bind its successors. Thus, the Fiscal Compact, signed by twenty-five out of the twenty-seven EU members,[6] "establishes a pervasive legal regime to tighten the budgetary policies of the Contracting Parties, with the goal of ensuring fiscal discipline in the member states as a pre-condition for financial stability in the entire Euro-zone" (Fabbrini 2013, 8).

The Fiscal Compact was negotiated as part of an intergovernmental treaty between member states (The Treaty on Stability, Coordination, and Governance in the Economic and Monetary Union), outside of the European community. Nevertheless states cede an unprecedented

---

6 The exceptions are the United Kingdom and the Czech Republic.

amount of political power upwards to the European Commission and the European Court of Justice. It is part of an effort to strengthen the European Monetary Union through tighter and more consistent fiscal policy across the European Union (Bauer and Becker 2014; Burret and Schnellenbach 2014; Tsebelis and Hahm 2014).

These reforms provide supranational institutions with a great deal of political authority to alter the behaviour of national governments through (1) the obligation of member states to internalize a set of general principles, (2) large sanctions for dissenting members, and (3) a variety of procedures to better monitor and publicly shame deviant countries. This does not mean that the new mechanism is watertight (Burret and Schnellenbach 2014, 12); however, the intention is clear, and it represents a tightening of previous efforts in this area.

United States

Lacking the degree of economic integration that is found in Europe, the situation in North America is different. Nevertheless, long-standing efforts to constitutionalize fiscal policy can be found, especially at the state level in the United States, and provincial level in Canada.

In the United States there is no constitutional balanced budget provision at the federal level, though there have been several attempts to begin constitutional change that would bring this about. In both 1995 and 1997, proposals to initiate the constitutional amendment process fell one Senate vote short of the number that would have initiated the amendment process (Philipps 1996, 683). There was, however, a 1997 Balanced Budget Act (revised as the Balanced Budget Refinement Act in 1999) at the US federal level (Younis and Forgione 2009, 57).

At the state level, balanced budget legislation is legally binding, and restrictive mechanisms apply to the "executive preparation, legislative approval, and implementation stages of the budget cycle" (Hou and Smith 2009, 659). These clearly predate the current focus on austerity and signify the extent to which excluding fiscal discretion has been a part of liberal and neoliberal approaches over the long term. Every state but Vermont has either statutory or constitutional balanced budget legislation (NCSL 2010). At the US state level, such legislation takes three forms: (1) the governor must submit a balanced budget; (2) the legislature must pass a balanced budget; (3) a government cannot carry over a deficit (thirty-eight states) (NCSL 2010, 3). Enforcement mechanisms for balanced budget legislation (BBL) vary, with twenty-two of forty-nine states claiming such a mechanism (3). Most states have a constitutional or statutory limitation on the issuance of general obligation debt ("guaranteed by all government funds and the government's ability to raise taxes") (Kennedy and Robbins 2003, 12). Sixteen states allow this to be amended by a referendum or supermajority vote, while a few prohibit incurring general obligation debt (12; NCSL 2010, 9). Some states hold certain officials liable for imbalances, while others (Alabama and Oklahoma) require mandatory reductions in expenditures to keep budgets in balance (4).

There are three general enforcement provisions among the states: (1) the state constitution allows for appropriations if the treasury lacks money to pay for them; (2) deficits are avoided by reducing unexpended agency allotments, even if it is necessary to defer or suspend statutory obligations; (3) the state constitution requires that the governor continually survey expenditures and implement necessary changes if revenues and reserves will not meet budget requirements (NCSL 2010, 9). At least sixteen states require voter approval of "general obligation debt" through constitutional amendments (9). The most important force, however, is discursive and political: the expectation that budgets will be balanced has proved to be a stronger force than actual BBL (9). The combination of popular support and political salience make amendments unlikely in states that have only statutory BBL (ibid.; Mullins and Wallin 2004). Constitutionalized fiscal rules can be amended only by referendum (NCSL 2014). BBL at the US state level is entrenched insofar as state statutes rarely change, lawmakers must abide by them, and constitutional amendments are difficult to achieve in a short timespan (Hou and Smith 2009, 659).

Twenty-seven states also have tax and expenditure limitations (TEL), which outline and enforce limits on annual revenue or expenditure increases (Kennedy and Robbins 2003, 12). Of those states with expenditure limits, most limit appropriations to some index of inflation (12). Before 1970, only two states had TELs in place, and by 2001 there were fifty-three limitations implemented in thirty-one states (Mullins and Wallin 2004, 10). Twenty-five states allow for legislative override of limits, but usually with a minimum of three-fifths vote (10). Eighteen states have adopted revenue limits, while twenty-four states budget under expenditure limitations; eleven states have adopted both kinds of provisions (10). Most (twenty-four states) state limitations are constitutionalized, and citizen initiative is increasingly the source of state-level tax and expenditure limitations (accounting for half of all limitations adopted since 1990) (10).

Canada

Canada has a track record of trying to insert neoliberal principles into its formal constitutional structure. During constitutional negotiations in the late 1980s and early 1990s, a variety of unsuccessful attempts were made to incorporate economic rules into negotiations that had been triggered by other issues – of nation, region, and language. Specifically, the federal government attempted to alter the Bank of Canada's mandate to make its sole goal one of preventing inflation, rather than the broader one it had that included creating growth and employment. Similarly, attempts were made to incorporate property rights into the constitution.

In the fiscal policy area, the federal government enacted a Spending Control Act, which was in place from 1991 to 1995, and established program spending limits. Similar legislation was in place in Alberta for a short time, and revenue limits were also used in several provinces (Tapp 2010, 5). In its 2013 Throne Speech the federal government signalled its intention to a return to balanced budget legislation at the federal level (Chase 2013).

Balanced budget legislation has been frequent at the provincial level, beginning with British Columbia's 1991 Taxpayer Protection Act, which "prohibited the provincial government from raising tax rates, and required that total revenues meet or exceed total expenditures computed over a five year period." The act was repealed the next year (Philipps 1996, 686). The political discourse engendered by these rules has become part of normal political culture in Canada (e.g., discussions focus on degrees of austerity and budget restriction, not on broader alternatives). Public salience for tax limitations/cuts (which are constitutionalized in some provinces) as well as for "fiscal responsibility" (balanced budgets, debt stigma, "hampering growth," etc.) constitute a disciplinary mechanism over any governments tempted to engage in fiscal stimulus (Mullins and Wallin 2004; Philipps 1996).

Most provinces and territories used balanced budget legislation during the mid-1990s but subsequently amended those laws in various ways (Kennedy and Robbins 2003). The fact that this was ordinary legislation in parliamentary systems and could be easily rescinded or ignored, as the assessment of their effectiveness just cited shows, meant that these measures were partially of symbolic value (McBride and Whiteside 2011). Even so, in the right circumstances they should also have strengthened the negotiating position of fiscally conservative finance ministers in internal governmental deliberations. Compliance with the legislation thus consists mostly of willingness to comply,[7] pushed by political pressures (Philipps 1996, 703). Sometimes legislation stipulates penalties for non-compliance and, in these cases, the courts might play a role. Examples include penalties for cabinet ministers, as in Manitoba, or the potential dismissal of the Executive Council, in the Northwest Territories (704). However, the legislation itself remains instantly amendable or replaceable, given a legislative majority in favour of doing that. Thus balanced budget legislation is not an entirely satisfactory substitute for constitutional entrenchment. That said, BBL legislations are rarely repealed or even lapse. More often, they are amended or superseded with varying shifts to enforcement mechanisms and requirements.[8]

In contrast to BBL, Canadian implementations of tax and expenditure limitations (TEL) have generally closely followed the pattern found in US states in that changes are to be achieved by referenda (Philipps 1996, 705; Tapp 2010, 24; 2013, 63). Six provinces have implemented tax limitations, five of which can be amended only by referendum (Tapp 2010, 24; 2013, 63). Tax limitations are also constitutional in nature because of how fundamentally they alter "the rules of the politico-fiscal game" in constraining the options available to governments to address debts and deficits (Philipps 1996, 705).

Institutional changes like these effectively remove fiscal policy from normal political debate and render it more remote, less accountable, and, by intention at least, impervious to future change. To the extent that this is so, constitutionalizing fiscal policy under the guise of austerity represents the addition of the last significant economic policy area that could be used to challenge the neoliberal policy status quo.

Results

The neoliberal period has seen the constitutionalization of key economic policies, including trade and investment, monetary, and lately fiscal policy. Constitutionalizing them, establishing rules that must

---

7 In the literature, among politicians and with the public, support for fiscal rules relies on the view that they can help correct policymakers' "distorted incentives" and "strengthen their commitment to implement better policies" (Tapp 2013, 46).
8 For details, see Tapp (2010, 2013); Geist (1998); Philipps (1996); Kennedy and Robbins (2003).

be followed, limits the scope for democracy because of the "depoliti-cization" of crucial spheres of policymaking that used, ultimately if imperfectly, to be in the hands of the public (Offe 2013; Hay 2007). Fis-cal policy, and in particular its expression as austerity, is the latest in a series of measures that hollow out democratic decision-making, pre-vent or hinder the use of the state to modify the results of markets, and, as a result, lock in place inequality between social classes. Elections continue to take place, providing an appearance of democracy, legis-latures deliberate over measures proposed, though outside the United States they do so increasingly in the shadow of executive dominance. However, the real substance of democracy, making choices about vital issues – including all the major levers of monetary, fiscal, trade, and investment policy – are increasingly transferred beyond the democratic process and become unaccountable to the people.

REFERENCES

Artis, M.J., and M. Buti. 2000. "'Close-to-Balance or in Surplus': A Policy-Maker's Guide to the Implementation of the Stability and Growth Pact." *JCMS: Journal of Common Market Studies* 38 (4): 563–91.

Ayhan, Berkay, and Stephen McBride. 2015. "Global Crisis and Social Policy in Peripheral Europe: Comparing, Ireland, Portugal and Greece." In *After 08: Social Policy and the Global Financial Crisis*, ed. Stephen McBride, Rianne Mahon, and Gerard W. Boychuk, 237–53. Vancouver: UBC Press.

Balassone, F., and D. Franco. 2000. "Public Investment, the Stability Pact and the 'Golden Rule.'" *Fiscal Studies* 21 (2): 207–29. http://dx.doi.org/10.1111/j.1475-5890.2000.tb00023.x.

Bauer, M.W., and S. Becker. 2014. "The Unexpected Winner of the Crisis: The European Commission's Strengthened Role in Economic Governance." *Journal of European Integration* 36 (3): 213–29. http://dx.doi.org/10.1080/07036337.2014.885750.

Baun, M. 1995–6. "The Maastricht Treaty as High Politics: Germany, France and European Integration." *Political Science Quarterly* 110 (4): 605–24. http://dx.doi.org/10.2307/2151886.

Blyth, M. 2013. *Austerity: The History of a Dangerous Idea*. Oxford: Oxford University Press.

Buiter, W., G. Corsetti, N. Roubini, Rafael Repullo, and Jeffrey Frankel. 1993. "Excessive Deficits: Sense and Nonsense in the Treaty of Maastricht." *Economic Policy* 8 (16): 57–100. http://dx.doi.org/10.2307/1344568.

Burret, H.T., and J. Schnellenbach. 2014. "Implementation of the Fiscal Compact in the Euro Area Member States: Expertise on the Behalf of the German Council of Economic Experts." Working Paper no. 8, German Council of Economic Experts, 2013e.

Buti, M., D. Franco, and H. Ongena. 1998. "Fiscal Discipline and Flexibility in EMU: The Implementation of the Stability and Growth Pact." *Oxford Review of Economic Policy* 14 (3): 81–97. http://dx.doi.org/10.1093/oxrep/14.3.81.

Buti, M., and G. Giudice. 2002. "Maastricht's Fiscal Rules at Ten: An Assessment." *JCMS: Journal of Common Market Studies* 40 (5): 823–48.

Chase, Steven. 2013. "Prime Minister Harper Pledges Balanced-Budget Law in Throne Speech." *Globe and Mail*, 16 October.

Clarkson, Stephen. 1993. "Constitutionalizing the Canadian-American Relationship." In *Canada under Free Trade*, ed. Duncan Cameron and Mel Watkins, 3–20. Toronto: Lorimer.

Costello, T. 2014. "The Fiscal Stability Treaty Referendum 2012." *Irish Political Studies* 29 (3): 457–70. http://dx.doi.org/10.1080/07907184.2014.923842.

De Haan, J., H. Berger, and D.J. Jansen. 2004. "Why Has the Stability and Growth Pact Failed?" *International Finance* 7 (2): 235–60. http://dx.doi.org/10.1111/j.1367-0271.2004.00137.x.

Dincer, N. Nergiz, and Barry Eichengreen. 2014. "Central Bank Transparency and Independence: Updates and New Measures." *International Journal of Central Banking* (March): 189–253.

European Central Bank. n.d. *Facts*. Accessed 11 March 2017. http://www.centralbank.ie/about-us/documents/ecb_facts_presentation.pdf.

European Commission. 2014. "The EU's Economic Governance Explained." European Commission. http://europa.eu/rapid/press-release_MEMO-14-2180_en.htm.

Fabbrini, Federico. 2013. "The Fiscal Compact, the 'Golden Rule,' and the Paradox of European Federalism." Tilburg Law School Legal Studies Research Paper Series 13.

Geist, M.A. 1998. "Balanced Budget Legislation: An Assessment of the Recent Canadian Experience." *Ottawa Law Review* 29 (1): 1–38.

Gill, Stephen. 1992. "Economic Globalization and the Internationalization of Authority: Limits and Contradictions." *Geoforum* 23 (3): 269–83. http://dx.doi.org/10.1016/0016-7185(92)90042-3.

Gill, Stephen, and A. Claire Cutler. 2014. "New Constitutionalism and World Order: General Introduction." In *New Constitutionalism and World Order*, ed. Stephen Gill and A. Claire Cutler, 1–21. Cambridge: Cambridge University Press.

Greer, Scott. 2014. "Structural Adjustment Comes to Europe: Lessons for the Eurozone from the Conditionality Debates." *Global Social Policy* 14 (1): 51–71. http://dx.doi.org/10.1177/1468018113511473.

Harmes, Adam. 2006. "Neoliberalism and Multilevel Governance." *Review of International Political Economy* 13 (5): 725–49. http://dx.doi.org/10.1080/09692290600950621.

Hay, Colin. 2007. *Why We Hate Politics*. Cambridge: Polity.

Heipertz, M., and A. Verdun. 2004. "The Dog That Would Never Bite? What We Can Learn from the Origins of the Stability and Growth Pact." *Journal of European Public Policy* 11 (5): 765–80. http://dx.doi.org/10.1080/1350176042000273522.

Herndon, Thomas, Michael Ash, and Robert Pollin. 2013. "Does High Public Debt Consistently Stifle Economic Growth: A Critique of Reinhart and Rogoff." Working Paper 322, Political Economy Research Unit, University of Massachusetts, Amherst.

Hirschl, Ran. 2004. "The Political Origins of the New Constitutionalism." *Indiana Journal of Global Legal Studies* 11 (1): 71–108. http://www.repository.law.indiana.edu/ijgls/vol11/iss1/4.

Hodson, D., and I. Maher. 2001. "The Open Method as a New Mode of Governance: The Case of Soft Economic Policy Co-ordination." *JCMS: Journal of Common Market Studies* 39 (4): 719–46.

Hou, Yilin, and Douglas Smith. 2009. "Informal Norms as a Bridge between Formal Rules and Outcomes of Government Financial Operations: Evidence from State Balanced Budget Requirements." *Journal of Public Administration: Research and Theory* 20 (3): 656–78.

Isfeld, Gordon. 2015. "Forget NAFTA, the TPP Is the New 'Gold Standard' of Global Trade." *National Post*, 12 October. http://business.financialpost.com/news/economy/forget-nafta-the-tpp-is-the-new-gold-standard-of-global-trade.

Kennedy, S., and J. Robbins. 2001. "The Role of Fiscal Rules in Determining Fiscal Performance: The Canadian Case." Department of Finance Canada. http://www.fin.gc.ca/pub/pdfs/wp2001-16e.pdf.

– 2003. "The Role of Fiscal Rules in Determining Fiscal Performance: The Canadian Case." Department of Finance Canada. http://www.fin.gc.ca/pub/pdfs/wp2001-16e.pdf.

Krugman, Paul. 2013. *End This Depression Now!* New York: W.W. Norton.

Kurzer, Paulette. 1988. "The Politics of Central Banks: Austerity and Unemployment in Europe." *Journal of Public Policy* 8 (1): 21–47. http://dx.doi.org/10.1017/S0143814X00006838.

Mazereeuw, Peter. 2016. "Lukewarm Reception for New EU Trade Deal Investor Rules." *Embassy*, 3 March.

McBride, Stephen. 2003. "Quiet Constitutionalism in Canada: The International Political Economy of Domestic Institutional Change." *Canadian Journal of Political Science* 36 (2): 251–73. http://dx.doi.org/10.1017/S0008423903778603.

McBride, Stephen, and Heather Whiteside. 2011. *Private Affluence, Public Austerity: Economic Crisis and Democratic Malaise in Canada*. Halifax: Fernwood.

McKenna, Barrie. 2016. "Canada's Forgotten Economic Pact with the EU in Limbo." *Globe and Mail*, 15 February. https://secure.globeadvisor.com/servlet/ArticleNews/story/gam/20160215/RBRIMCKENNACOLUMN.

Mullins, D.R., and B.A. Wallin. 2004. "Tax and Expenditure Limitations: Introduction and Overview." *Public Budgeting & Finance* 24 (4): 2–15. http://dx.doi.org/10.1111/j.0275-1100.2004.00344.x.

National Conference of State Legislatures (NCSL). 2010. *NCSL Fiscal Brief: State Balanced Budget Provisions*. NCSL.

– 2014. "Initiative, Referendum and Recall." http://www.ncsl.org/research/elections-and-campaigns/initiative-referendum-and-recall-overview.aspx.

Oberndorfer, Lukas. 2014. "A New Economic Governance through Secondary Legislation? Analysis and Constitutional Assessment: From New Constitutionalism, via Authoritarian Constitutionalism to Progressive Constitutionalism." In *The Economic and Financial Crisis and Collective Labour Law in Europe*, ed. Niklas Bruun, Klaus Lorcher, and Isabelle Schomann, 25–54. Oxford: Hart Publishing.

Offe, Claus. 2013. "Participatory Inequality in the Austerity State: A Supply-Side Approach." In Schafer and Streek, *Politics in an Age of Austerity*, 196–218.

Perry, Sebastian. 2012. "STOCKHOLM: Arbitrator and Counsel: The Double-Hat Syndrome." *Global Arbitration Review* 7 (2).

Philipps, L.C. 1996. "The Rise of Balanced Budget Laws in Canada: Legislating Fiscal (Ir)Responsibility." *Osgoode Hall Law Journal* 34 (4): 681–740.

Picker, Anne D. 2007. *International Economic Indicators and Central Banks*. Hoboken, NJ: John Wiley & Sons.

Polillo, Simone, and Mauro F. Guillén. 2005. "Globalization Pressures and the State: The Worldwide Spread of Central Bank Independence." *American Journal of Sociology* 110 (6): 1764–802. http://dx.doi.org/10.1086/428685.

Rogoff, K.S. 1990. "Equilibrium Political Budget Cycles." Working Paper 2428, National Bureau of Economic Research.

Sandholtz, W. 1993. "Choosing Union: Monetary Politics and Maastricht." *International Organization* 47 (1): 1–39. http://dx.doi.org/10.1017/S0020818300004690.

Schafer, Armin, and Wolfgang Streek, eds. 2013. *Politics in an Age of Austerity.* Cambridge: Polity.

Schuknecht, L. 2005. "Stability and Growth Pact: Issues and Lessons from Political Economy." *International Economics and Economic Policy* 2 (1): 65–89. http://dx.doi.org/10.1007/s10368-005-0028-3-y.

Schuknecht, Ludger, Philippe Moutot, Philipp Rother, and Jürgen Stark. 2011. "The Stability and Growth Pact: Crisis and Reform." ECB Occasional Paper 129.

Sinclair, Scott, Stuart Trew, and Hadrian Mertins-Kirkwood. 2014. *Making Sense of the CETA: An Analysis of the Final Text of the Canada–European Union Comprehensive Economic and Trade Agreement.* Ottawa: Canadian Centre for Policy Alternatives.

Stiglitz, Joseph E. 2011. "Rethinking Macroeconomics: What Went Wrong and How to Fix It." *Global Policy* 2 (2): 165–75. http://dx.doi.org/10.1111/j.1758-5899.2011.00095.x.

Tapp, S. 2010. *Canadian Experiences with Fiscal Consolidations and Fiscal Rules.* Ottawa: Office of the Parliamentary Budget Officer.

– 2013. "The Use and Effectiveness of Fiscal Rules in Canadian Provinces." *Canadian Public Policy* 39 (1): 45–70. http://dx.doi.org/10.3138/CPP.39.1.45.

Tsebelis, G., and H. Hahm. 2014. "Suspending Vetoes: How the Euro Countries Achieved Unanimity in the Fiscal Compact." *Journal of European Public Policy* 21 (10): 1388–411. http://dx.doi.org/10.1080/13501763.2014.929167.

Van Harten, Gus. 2005. "Private Authority and Transnational Governance: The Contours of the International System of Investor Protection." *Review of International Political Economy* 12 (4): 600–23.

von Hagen, J. 2003. *Fiscal Discipline and Growth in Euroland: Experiences with the Stability and Growth Pact.* Mannheim: Zentrum für Europäische Wirtschaftsforschung.

Walkom, Thomas. 2016. "CETA Critics Force Europe, Canada to Revise Trade Pact." *Toronto Star*, 2 March.

Williams, Marc. 1994. *International Economic Organizations and the Third World.* London: Harvester Wheatsheaf.

Younis, M.Z., and D.A. Forgione. 2009. "The Relationship between the Balanced Budget Act and Length of Stay for Medicare Patients in US Hospitals." *European Journal of Health Economics* 10 (1): 57–63. http://dx.doi.org/10.1007/s10198-008-0103-8.

9 Fighting the Financial Crisis or Consolidating Austerity? The Eurobond Battle Reconsidered

DIETER PLEHWE

Introduction: The Eurobonds Controversy

In 2015, newly elected Syriza government leaders in Greece started an international campaign to change the European terms of the Greek deep austerity regime. A key demand of Finance Minister Varoufakis's "modest proposal" (Varoufakis 2013) was the conversion of public debts into European loans in ways conforming to the European treaties. Prime Minister Tsipras and Varoufakis thereby revived the Eurobonds controversy at the centre of earlier (2010–12) struggles over the euro-saving operation. Greece's Secretary of State Nikos Kotzias recently emphasized the significance of the Eurobonds demand due to the related question of recognizing the causes of European financial crisis: If the private, speculative financial-sector origins of the crisis are recognized, the pooling of resulting public debts is an adequate solution, which also shields the primary and most vulnerable victims of the crisis – people dependent on public spending – from recurring speculation on financial markets and a repetition of the vicious circle of international finance. Avoiding Eurobonds instead blames the crisis on "free-spending" (Greek) public authorities and allows (European) political authorities in favour of the austerity regime to maintain external control over public budgets through financial markets on top of whatever conditionality is imposed by the European Union and international monetary fund institutions (private conversation, 23 January 2016; compare Kotzias 2013).

Syriza and its international allies lost this battle. Regardless of the rejection of the deal in a popular referendum, the country's leadership eventually had to succumb essentially to the European institutions. Rather than focusing on the interlinked banking, public debt, low-investment, and social crisis as suggested in the "modest proposal," national public finance remains the primary focus of euro politics in the periphery. European socio-economic asymmetries – between core and periphery, between social market and liberal market rules (Scharpf 2010) – are maintained, even if the Greek exit from the Eurozone has been avoided. While the enormous tensions within Europe's uneven and combined development are presently overlaid with the refugee crisis, the fundamental mismatch between transnational economy and finance, supranational economic and monetary union, and further reduced national public financial authority is hard to miss. But how has the likely temporary solution to the euro crisis been manufactured, and why could such a regime last?

This chapter contributes to answering this question by revisiting the original Eurobond controversy. A clarification of the competing social forces and relevant structural dimensions of the EU since the crisis in light of the Eurobonds controversy is helpful to avoid prevailing (or revitalized) methodological nationalism / inter-governmentalism in European studies. Much of the media presentation in Germany pitted European Union and national officials in the Eurobonds controversy against Merkel and her finance minister Schäuble, who had actually signalled willingness to compromise on debt mutualization in an interview with the *Wall Street Journal* around the same time the Eurobonds proposal was rejected (28 June 2012). Media in Germany and other Northern EU member states played free-spending Italy and Brussels off against fiscally prudent Germany, creating an image of "Southern Sinners" and "Northern Saints" (Matthijs and McNamara 2015). This simplification is utterly unconvincing, because European Commission President Juncker's Eurobond proposal was also backed by the British Prime Minister Cameron and Business Europe, unlikely supporters of "free spending." While it is tempting to blame Germany ("Mr Schäuble," "ordo-liberalism") for the unprecedented European austerity regime, we have to open the black box of European "interstate federalism" (Hayek's term 1980; compare Streeck 2013) in order to better understand the political sociology of Europe's national and transnational power relations. Although German elements form a significant part of Europe's austerity lobby and anti-Eurobond coalition, neither can all of Germany or German austerity forces alone be held responsible for the defeat.

Few scholars have examined the Eurobond controversy so far. The notable exception is Matthijs and McNamara (2015, 229), who argue that "the response to the euro crisis was heavily informed by broader social logics that constructed the problem and the solution heavily toward ordoliberal and neoliberal ideas." The authors emphasize the interplay of economic policymaking, and academic theorizing in general, apply a social perspective of co-production of (austerity) knowledge, and claim to heed the call for analytic symmetry in their effort to analyse why alternative Eurobond proposals were not employed. While I share the general thrust of the argument of Matthijs and McNamara – the defeat of the Eurobonds approach was grounded in a more general knowledge and power regime of austerity – the explanation for the reproduction of economic thought and ideologies behind Europe's austerity regimes, and the varieties of neoliberalism within and across borders deserve closer scrutiny.

Matthijs and McNamara emphasize a rather uniform and continuous knowledge dimension – a policy-related knowledge and advisory regime "frozen in time" (Straßheim 2013, 77). The weight of historical institutionalization, and the resulting social logics of the neoliberal economic knowledge regime in Germany in particular, appear to require little maintenance and adaptation. To the contrary, I am arguing that in addition to the efforts to secure the overall entrenchment of austerity-related expertise and ideas, greater attention needs to be paid to a variety of knowledge and power struggles, the political logics of the reproduction and transformation of Europe's austerity regimes, in order to not let some of the paradoxical agents of austerity off the hook. The Eurobonds controversy cannot be as neatly isolated as Matthijs and McNamara suggest in their analysis, since struggles across Europe, and within Germany in particular, tied different economic policy instruments and objectives together, notably the Eurobond controversy, the financial umbrellas to rescue the euro, and the financial transaction tax controversy. If the battle between Eurobond supporters and detractors is separated too neatly from the broader public finance debate, we get a black-and-white picture of good anti-austerity fighters and consolidation monsters, which amounts to a simple reversal of the Southern sinner and Northern saint metaphor that Matthijs and McNamara (2015) describe.

Since the German government eventually embraced the financial transaction tax and an investment program to integrate the opposition in 2012[1], and defended the transfer components of the financial

---

1 Social Democrats and Greens could have blocked legislation required in Germany in 2012 to establish the European Stability Mechanism due to their majority in the Bundesrat (representing the German states).

umbrellas against right-wing critiques, the conflict lines between more and less pragmatic as well as truly rigid austerity forces cannot be fully explained by a general notion of the social co-production of austerity bias. The call for analytic symmetry, in other words, requires attention to economic policymaking proposals beyond the Eurobonds, and more attention on the ways in which neoliberal hegemonic constellations are (re)produced in social struggles between centre-left and centre-right on the one hand, and within the (centre-)right on the other hand. The social and political logics of the integration of the majority wings of Germany's Greens and Social Democracy into the austerity coalition in particular needs much closer attention.

In the remainder of this chapter I will revisit and reconstruct relevant parts of the Eurobond battle between 2010 and 2012 in order to gain a more detailed understanding of the social forces and alliances involved. While Eurobonds were supported by a formidable alliance of business and political forces, the Eurobond coalition was also full of contradictions in the pending debate on the future of European integration (pro Eurobonds, but against closer union in parts, and in favour of austerity regimes). Within the political party spectrum, nominally pro-Eurobonds (Social Democratic) parties also suffered from asymmetrical distribution of power of real supporters within the parties in the different countries. The opposition to Eurobonds instead appears to be more homogeneous across the whole of the EU – except for the United Kingdom, which needs additional explaining, since the Tory government supports both rigid austerity at home and Eurobonds abroad. Contrary to the pragmatic austerity policy line, which failed to keep the public debate focused on the financial-sector causes of the crisis, the restrictive austerity perspective managed to mobilize moral hazard concerns about public spending in Southern member states. Beyond austerity, the campaigns served to strengthen nationalist worries about deeper integration.

The chapter is structured in the following order. Section 1 serves to refresh the memory of the Eurozone crisis and the original Eurobonds proposal. Section 2 deepens the analysis by providing background on the restricted Economic and Monetary Union established by the Maastricht Treaty, and the dynamics of Europe's pragmatic austerity union leading up to the financial crisis of 2007. Against this backdrop we will take a closer look at the Eurobond proposals in section 3, and will investigate in which ways mainstream economic policy–think tanks in general, and Bruegel in particular, played such an extraordinary role in the debate. Less prominent, though arguably no less important than Bruegel was the right-wing liberal Center for European Politics (CEP) in Freiburg, Germany, which is part of much wider neoliberal think tank networks that supply important normative orientation, and theoretical and empirical ammunition in European policy controversies. Section 4 will look at the intellectual munition supplied to the rigid austerity camp by CEP and others. The broader participation in the pro and contra Eurobond discourse coalitions will be tackled in section 5 by looking at the European consultation following the publication of the Commission Green Book. In section 6 a brief discussion of the difficulties of Bruegel to sustain the Eurobond policy line serves to discuss strength and limits of think tank independence and power. The concluding section sums up the results of this investigation and points to research that still needs to be done to more thoroughly scrutinize the transnational dimensions of the larger discourse coalition of "increasing austerity" in particular.

The Eurobonds Controversy, 2010–2012

The "North Atlantic financial crisis" (Kotz 2011, 44) began in 2007, and rapidly turned into a European sovereign debt crisis due to the bailout of banks deemed "too big to fail." Within a few years, in turn public debt rather than financial speculation and short-term risk-taking occupied centre stage in the European discussion of the Great Recession following the Great Crisis. Although it has been widely acknowledged that the crisis of public finance in most EU member states (and the United States itself) was due primarily to the financial crisis, and decade-long lax regulation (Sorge 2011), the apparent manipulation of public finances in a few EU member countries, most notably Greece, served to shift the blame in public debates to public authorities.[2]

The emphasis on fiscal consolidation quickly replaced Europe's short flirt with coordinated Keynesian stimulus programs (2008–9). Led by the "Troika" (European Central Bank, European Commission, IMF), the recommended policy to deal with public sector deficits henceforth was fiscal restraint, or restrictive austerity, focusing mainly on the reduction

---

2 The chronological monitoring of events and "the German position" by Swiss consultant George Dorgan (penname) (2012) is certainly not objective, but a good indicator of the hegemonic public interpretation.

of public spending, even if some effort was going into improving tax collection, broadening the tax base, and thus somewhat increasing the share of the wealthy in carrying the consolidation burden.[3] Europe, clearly, is on its way to a new type of austerity union far beyond the Maastricht criteria, unless the main thrust of European economic policy developments and the economic governance mechanisms established are revised. Blyth (2013, 51) calls it "permanent austerity," but "increasing austerity" might be more adequate for the cumulative impact of welfare state shrinking and fiscal contraction in general.

Even if the mainstream moved swiftly from stimulus to austerity and fiscal consolidation in 2009 – "Half drew she him, half sank he in," as in Goethe's famous "Fisher" – the discussion still remained divided between those who did not want to forget the financial-sector causes of the public debt crisis on the one hand, and those who were increasingly eager to use the present fiscal crisis of the state to recover private sector ground lost after the crisis on the other hand. The former maintained criticism of financial capital and policy-driven financialization, but refuse to blame the public sector unilaterally (Wolf 2014). In politics, moderate public officials who thought along these lines pursued a *pragmatic* austerity line, which was searching for ways to lift some of the burden from the countries and social classes suffering most. The latter focused on national responsibility and aimed to avoid or at least limit the extent of fiscal solidarity and shared liability instead. This position can be described as the *restrictive* or *radical* austerity line, which aimed to restrain the (welfare) state, shrink public spending, and defend the status quo of globalized capitalism prior to the crisis in general (Plehwe 2010; Mirowski 2013). Between 2009 and 2012, the battle line between pragmatic and restrictive austerity forces was drawn in a particularly lucid way in the debate over a new financial policy instrument: the European sovereign bonds, or Eurobonds, for short.

The present EU Commission president (2016), Jean-Claude Juncker, publicly proposed Eurobonds as a new policy instrument to overcome the European public debt and euro crisis in December 2010.

---

3 OECD data show the decline in public spending and the increase in property and personal income taxes, for example (OECD 2017). The data do not reveal by themselves if the tax income distribution has become more progressive since taxes on goods and services (VAT) have also increased. Since VAT taxes are hitting people with low disposable income most, increasing VAT tax income has to be considered regressive.

Eurobonds are European debt investments. Instead of loaning strictly to a national authority, an investor would lend a certain amount of money, for a certain amount of time, with a certain interest rate, to the members of the Eurozone. Once the instrument would be in place, all or part of public debt (old or new) would be mutualized. With the integration of the European public debt (market), financial speculators could no longer single out public debt of a particular country to create speculator pressures. As a result, the spread of interest paid on public debt across Europe would be greatly reduced, though low rates of less-indebted countries could rise, reflecting a somewhat higher risk of insolvency of particular members of the Eurozone covered by all.

Juncker was Luxemburg's prime minister and treasury minister as well as head of the euro group – members of Europe's monetary union – at the time. He, along with Italy's minister of economy and finance, Giolio Tremonti, advanced a highly contentious proposal in the face of the ongoing crisis: "In spite of recent decisions by European fiscal and monetary authorities, sovereign debt markets continue to experience considerable stress. Europe must formulate a strong and systemic response to the crisis, to send a clear message to global markets and European citizens of our political commitment to economic and monetary union, and the irreversibility of the euro. This can be achieved by launching E-bonds, or European sovereign bonds, issued by a European Debt Agency (EDA) as successor to the current European Financial Stability Facility" (Juncker and Tremonti 2010).

Juncker and Tremonti's proposal went far beyond the established European public policy line on exclusively national public debt, and concomitantly, continued sovereign public finance of the European nation state. Juncker and Tremonti opened a joint European liability perspective, possibly in contradiction to the existing European treaties, since shared liability would no longer be restricted to extraordinary emergency circumstances (no bailout, Article 125 of the Lisbon Treaty).

After a heated debate following, first, the high-profile publication of the sophisticated "blue bond" by the Bruegel think tank in March 2011, and second, a European Green Book on the facility of introducing stability bonds (European Commission 2011) in November 2011, Germany's head of government Angela Merkel eventually ended the ensuing debate over the advantages and disadvantages of Eurobonds by categorically excluding the Eurobond option ("only over my dead body"; *Spiegel* 2012). While the euro-saving operation had compromised European treaty obligations that exclude the bailout of foreign sovereign debt – at least in the eyes of right-wing critics of Merkel in Germany, the German government was still navigating a pragmatic austerity course in continuity with the Maastricht regulatory framework. Harsh in theory, Maastricht still provided considerable room for public finance manoeuvring. Before digging deeper into the Eurobonds controversy, we have to ascertain key aspects of Europe's economic and monetary union.

Europe's Unreliable Economic and Monetary Union

The course of European Integration has been shaped increasingly by supply side economics and neoliberal thought in general, since the passing of the Single European Act in 1987 (single market program). From the creation of a European common market to the euro convergence criteria of the Maastricht Treaty, with its strict overall debt levels (60 per cent of GDP), maximum deficit criterion (3 per cent of GDP), and obligations for member states to keep inflation low (1.5 per cent), a whiff of neoliberal thought, supply side economics, and austerity ideas is evident (McNamara 1999), far beyond the influence of neoliberals in the early history of the European Community in some areas (competition policy in particular; compare Wegmann 2002).

With the introduction of a common currency in 2002, the elimination of trade barriers and monetary integration was taken a step further, and the European Central Bank (ECB) centralized the monetary policy framework across, and arguably beyond, the euro-group. While the move towards the euro and the creation of German-style central banking was regarded as a consolidation of neoliberal monetary politics by many critics on the left, many right-wing liberals, from Germany in particular, expressed strong reservations about the common currency, because they did not trust that Maastricht Treaty stipulations would be sufficiently – let alone rigidly – enforced. The right-wing liberal opposition against the common currency objected to the perceived pragmatism on fiscal discipline – Maastricht was not quite neoliberal or rigid enough for them. Since not only Southern European countries, but indeed Germany and France were missing Maastricht targets regularly, such fears were not just fantasies or neoliberal imagination. Rather, the flexibility on Maastricht criteria expressed the dominance of pragmatic austerity politics, and a moderate version of neoliberalism with an eye for the needs of social integration and compromise with important stakeholders (Europe's trade unions in particular). The early benefits of European monetary integration, low rates for government bonds in the South, and the subsidy effect of an undervalued currency for the export-oriented industries in the North additionally helped to keep down the critics who pointed to abstract principles.

Yet the development of fiscal and monetary integration was challenged heavily by the banking crisis, starting in 2007, which quickly turned into a governmental debt crisis for several European countries. States like Ireland or Spain, and to a lesser extent Portugal and Greece, which had performed quite well overall since the passing of the Maastricht Treaty, faced the collapse of major banks like in the United Kingdom or Germany, but lacked domestic funds to socialize the losses. In order to avoid such bankruptcies, national and foreign governments had to step in, and the result was extremely fast-rising fiscal deficits and growing public debt rates. As triple-A ratings of some national bonds turned into junk overnight, and financial market actors started testing the commitment to the common currency, the Eurozone was drifting apart. While Germany and other Northern European states became low-yield havens of financial stability, the burden for Greece, Spain, Ireland, and Portugal became too heavy to carry. Speculations also started to address the financial situation of France and Italy, which would certainly have exacerbated the already huge problems of the Eurozone.

While the euro had bestowed low interest rates for weaker-currency countries equal to the level of Germany for five years, the euro regime suddenly foreclosed common fiscal instruments for handling the public debt crisis: since the weaker countries cannot simply print money, or increase debt levels beyond certain points to meet obligations (due to speculation against their national bonds, even if they are denominated in euros), the only choice is to cut spending and lower production costs, in the hope that austerity will increase competitiveness as promised by the "expansionary fiscal contraction hypothesis" economics (Giavazzi and Pagano 1990; Alesina and Perotti 1995; and just before the Troika rule, Alesina and Ardagna 2010, critical: Guajardo, Leigh, and Pescatori 2011; Blyth 2013; Krugman 2014).

The extent of the economic downturn in the different countries and the contagious effects of a collapse of a Eurozone member country required transnational financial solidarity, sharing liability and an extended bailout interventionism among the member states. This was encountered by setting up financial umbrellas such as the European Financial Stability Facility being replaced by a more permanent solution in 2011: the European Stability Mechanism.[4] The financial umbrellas ended speculation against the weaker Eurozone members, and thereby secured their refinancing of government debt like the Eurobonds. But such financial transfer pragmatism was accompanied by rigid conditions, introducing radical austerity agendas, which insinuated a temporary character of emergency transfers and aimed to maintain the EMU notions of national self-responsibility and sound finance, disregarding centralization and cross-border socialization under conditions of European monetary union. The parallel effort of the European Central Bank (monetary easing) likewise can be regarded as an effort to "hide the state," namely the extent to which the European monetary union relied on fiscal federalism to function over the long run.

This is the core tension of Europe's austerity union: a de facto need for shared liability and fiscal federalism to accompany monetary union on the one hand, and the normative credo of fiscal sovereignty and national self-responsibility on the other hand; public finance intergovernmentalism versus supranational and multi-level governance regimes in monetary and economic policymaking. These tensions can also be identified in the already mentioned pragmatic and restrictive austerity perspectives. While the Eurobond solution is frequently presented as a departure from austerity capitalism, the proposals were really still part of the effort to align public finance needs and pragmatic austerity perspectives. Even if some of the economists proposing Eurobonds had liked to go beyond austerity, the proposed instruments were designed to meet the fundamental concerns of the critics. Austerity ideas and policies, therefore, are not well represented as a singular or uniform agenda: fiscal consolidation can be achieved in a variety of ways if only we consider both sides of the public finance equation: the spending and the income side of government.

In contrast to the mainstay of Europe's new economic governance regime, however, Eurobonds aim explicitly to directly improve the income side of public finance beyond higher tax income, which

---

4 Under such pressure, the financial umbrella was quickly increased. The nearly unlimited power of the European Central Bank was fully expressed by Draghi (2012).

can help to reduce the need for spending cuts to meet budget and deficit goals. A common bond market would remove the spread of bond rates and lower the cost of financing by creating a very large common bond market. A common Eurobond market, in turn, could even permanently end speculation against individual country bonds, although each of the proposed Eurobond mechanisms resolved to keep pressure on national governments to reduce debts by using a spread in the conversion rate of national to Eurobonds. This makes it difficult to present Eurobonds as a complete departure from austerity politics. The primary aim clearly was to solve the euro crisis, however, and that requires an end to disruptive speculation against the bonds of financially weak member states. Eurobonds thereby also address the perceived private-sector causes of the financial crisis in addition to meeting public finance objectives. Eurobonds would arguably even have lowered the cost of the stabilization of the euro (Verhofstadt 2012). But compared to the required negotiations of conditions of aid with individual debtor states in companion with the transfers of the financial umbrellas, Eurobonds would have reduced the direct pressure from lenders to debtor countries, and lowered the structural position of power of Germany in particular.

While recognizing the differences between pragmatic and rigid austerity voices, the common neoliberal austerity heritage should certainly not be overlooked. Rejecting deficit spending and consolidated budget ideas clearly are a part of the discourse coalition in support of Eurobonds as much as they are a more central part of the anti-Eurobond coalition, expressing the shift from deficit spending to fiscal deficit discourse. Timothy Sinclair's (2000) examination of the social construction of the deficit discourse shows how (public choice) anti-deficit writers – most prominently James Buchanan – rely on methodological individualist frameworks to principally explain excessive deficit spending with a collapse of traditional moral values (of the "responsible classes"). The extension and abstract generalization of historical moral hazard arguments (in the insurance business, compare Baker 1996) in economic theory in turn have been highly relevant in the fight against Eurobonds, even if the proposals themselves addressed moral hazard concerns, once again displaying the battle line between moderate and radical neoliberalism, between pragmatic and rigid austerity perspectives. We will take a closer look at the Eurobond proposals and their political ramifications next.

The Making of the Eurobond Coalition: The Intellectual and Political Discourse

The recent history of Eurobond proposals has been documented first by Erik Jones (2012).[5] Jones credits Paul De Grauwe and Wim Moesen (2009) for launching the Eurobond debate (Jones 2010, 2). De Grauwe and Moesen addressed the sharp widening of yield spreads in the sovereign bond markets and proposed common bonds, possibly issued by the European Investment Bank. National liability would be relative EIB share of the country, and political mechanisms were considered to simulate market discipline. Their paper was published by the Brussels-based think tank CEPS, together with other papers opposing Eurobonds and discussing the idea of a new European Monetary Fund. CEPS is a major European policy think tank founded in 1983 (CEPS 2017a). With a budget of almost €8 million from a variety of sources (notably EU research projects amounting to 37 per cent recently), CEPS clearly is a leading European policy think tank of centrist, pro-integration orientation. Board and staff members include former government and commission officials (CEPS 2017b). Although the presence of pro and contra Eurobond publications suggests that CEPS was not a part of the Eurobond coalition as an organization, the presence of Eurobond proposals at CEPS suggests this was part of mainstream reflection.

Jones's own proposal from 2010 was published in the ISPI Policy Brief (of the Istituto per gli Studi di Politica Internazionale). Alongside his plan, the first outline for a European Debt Agency was offered by Belgian Prime Minister Yves Leterme (Bonds News 2010). Jones reports that he later came across a *Wall Street Journal* article by John Springford (2009) propagating a debt agency in a September 2009 opinion piece.[6] Springford is a

---

5 Earlier proposals exist, dating back to Boonstra (2005), for example. Compare Eijffinger (2011); Favero and Missale (2010). Eijffinger wrote a briefing note for the EP. Affiliations stated are Tilburg University and CEPR, a European "think net" of economists centred in London, and related to the progressive economic think tank based in Washington, DC. The European CEPR is financed by corporations, mostly banks. Eijffinger is also a board member of Tilburg's European Banking Center.

6 Springford is also mentioned in an *Economist* piece (2011) on support by Peer Steinbrück (Germany's former finance minister and later candidate for chancellor) for Eurobonds. Matthijs and McNamara credit Springford for launching the whole debate, but do not mention the CEPS publication by De Grauwe and Moesen (2009). It is quite likely that the debate was launched from different sides independently of each other.

British author who wrote at CentreForum, a London-based liberal think tank (now the Education Policy Institute), which counted the City of London, major banks, news, consulting and energy firms among its corporate partners. The board expressed a liberal yet cross-party orientation, with members belonging to advisory bodies of the Tory government and the previous Labour administration (CentreForum 2016). The organization was originally (1990s) related to the Liberal Party and turned into a non-aligned research and policy think tank in 2003.

In the proposals that Jones lists from the CEPS, the Belgian government, and the British think tank (CentreForum), it is interesting to note that they originate from countries burdened by high public debt and potential difficulties to emit national bonds (Italy, Belgium), from the European capital of financial markets (London), and from centrist European institutions that are embedded in mainstream pro-integration networks (CEPS). In any case, the Eurobond discourse coalition crossed party political lines, and at the same time brought to light divisions within major political parties and party families (like the European conservatives).

British Prime Minister David Cameron was reported to have urged French President Hollande to push for Eurobonds, while he clearly rejected the Tobin tax proposal (Bloomberg 2012). From a (British) financial market perspective, the stabilization of European financial markets by creating a common bond market was considered positive (see also below for the results of the Commission Consultation on Eurobonds), and the potential restriction of financial market activities through European taxation were considered negative. While Cameron led the European party alliance against an increasingly close union (Alliance of European Conservatives and Reformists, AECR), he thus was siding with Juncker and Southern European leaders (conservatives and socialists) against Angela Merkel and other conservative leaders on the Eurobond question back in 2012. In 2009/10, Eurobonds clearly were not synonymous with a genuine progressive (let alone left-wing) European integration perspective promoting fiscal solidarity. Rather, they were handled as a pragmatic approach to quell the financial crisis, needed to stabilize the major debtor countries and the whole Eurozone. The framing of Eurobonds as "stability" bonds in subsequent EU proposals underlines such a perspective.

The "blue bond" proposal by Delpla and von Weizsäcker (2010) dwarfed the other proposals mentioned so far. It distinguished between blue bonds (European sovereign bonds) as senior bonds to be served before any other government liabilities on the one hand, and red bonds, the remaining national level debt obtained at market rates, on the other hand. The policy brief was short, comprising only eight pages. But it was not the brilliance and clear structure of the proposal alone that made it quite popular. While Matthijs and McNamara (2015) refrain from discussing the background and linkages of the Eurobond proposals mentioned so far – Springford's CentreForum base referred to as a liberal think tank only, for example – Delpla and von Weizsäcker, and Bruegel, are introduced in greater detail. The "broad intellectual profile" of the authors – experience in private banking and the French Finance Ministry (Delpla), the World Bank and venture capital (von Weizsäcker) – are noted. "Their outsider views of what to do about the crisis were tempered by the insider position of Bruegel in the field of European economic policy making" (Matthijs and McNamara 2015, 237). It remains unclear, however, why this was an outsider view and what makes for Bruegel's insider position. The authors mention government and corporate backing, including from Germany's Deutsche Bank, but they are missing the German-French origins and the relevance of (new) Social Democracy for the early history of the highly influential think tank, which benefits from a unique position in the international economic policy discourse arena.

Bruegel has become a think tank that is highly regarded in the international media indeed, and enjoys a high-level US audience in particular. Bruegel was founded in 2005 after a German-French initiative to establish a European centre for international economics. The German government constituency was Social Democrat, closely aligned with Tony Blair's new Labour ideas, but also backed by funding from the French Central Bank, for example. Financing from major corporations (€50,000 each) and various EU member countries, including Germany (contribution varies by size), allows Bruegel to develop a European policy research position that maintains independence from the EU-level institutions, and thereby greater legitimacy than EU-funded organizations can obtain. It is clear, however, that Bruegel has become a major European voice in the EU policy debate that is closely related to the commission, despite financial independence, as evidenced by the flexicurity discourse,[7] for example.

---

7 The term was coined by Andre Sapir, a Belgian economist who wrote an influential Bruegel report on the topic of welfare reforms at the request of the European Commission in 2003. Sapir basically claims that a combination of liberal and Social Democratic welfare regimes can achieve a better balance of flexibility and social protection, a claim that has been strongly disputed in the meantime (Keune and Serrano 2014).

Bruegel is considered one of the most influential think tanks in general, and the most important European think tank in international economic policy, by insider evaluation reported in the U.S.-based think tank report published by James McGann (2017). The organization has been inspired by the example of the Washington-based Peterson Institute. The two organizations in the meantime share staff and have jointly organized projects. A review of American literature on the European financial crisis confirmed the relevance of Bruegel in the transatlantic community: most authors were referring to the Bruegel-based blue bond proposal if talking about Eurobonds (Plehwe 2013). Bruegel thus was home to the somewhat paradoxical alliance of transatlantic (financial capital) linkages and New Social Democratic ideas. What still fitted reasonably well with the German domestic power structure in 2009 when Christian Democrats governed with Social Democrats, did not fit so well in 2010 when Social Democrats were filling the opposition banks facing a right-wing Christian Democrat-Liberal coalition.

Delpla and von Weizsäcker obviously knew that they were fighting an uphill battle in Germany. They discussed likely objections from the neoliberal right wing, namely the legal status and the cost of Eurobonds for less indebted countries like Germany. They considered their proposal in line with the "no bailout" clause and other treaty requirements, because the limitation of Eurobonds of up to 60 per cent of public debt levels would not violate the requirements of the Maastricht Treaty "in economic substance" (Delpla and Weizsäcker 2011 6). The authors regarded only blue bond proposals that cover up to 100 per cent of public debt as violating the treaty clause. On the cost of Eurobonds, they suggested savings in general, due to the huge size of the market. They held it is likely that borrowing costs would even fall below current levels in Germany (7).

While other proposals floating in Brussels may have been easier to neglect, government authorities in Germany could hardly avoid the discussion of the blue bond proposal. Bruegel in a major way was officially set up and funded by the German economics and finance ministries. In 2010, when the blue bond proposal was written by the Social Democrat von Weizsäcker and his French colleague, it was impossible to avoid party political conflict over this proposal in Germany. The economics ministry – then under control of a neoliberal Free Democrat (first Brüderle until 2011, then Philip Rösler) – was facing rising pressure from the anti-Euro wing in its own party. The Bruegel proposal clearly added the German major opposition party (additionally backed by support from the trade unions) nominally to the transnational Eurobond discourse coalition, which made it difficult to maintain a united perspective of "national" interests regarding this question, although the Social Democratic party was certainly not united in its support for Eurobonds. In fact, the former Social Democratic party leader, Franz Müntefering, opposed his successor, Sigmar Gabriel, in May 2012 on the issue of Eurobonds. Gabriel was making no secret of his admiration for Francois Hollande and his initiative for Eurobonds, while Müntefering and the right wing opposed Eurobonds because there were alleged high costs for Germany (Medick 2012) (as calculated at the IFO Institute in 2011; compare Berg, Carstensen, and Sinn 2011, contradicting the claims made by Delpla and von Weizsäcker). The popular IFO calculation made Müntefering fear for the loss of Social Democratic voters, who might become easy prey for populist scaremongers.

Germany's mainstream Christian Democrats and Liberals nevertheless were under considerable pressure from abroad (including from the United States) and at home to pursue Eurobonds. At the same time they were also already under strong pressure from the right wing within their own parties in response to their support for the euro rescue operations.

The business wing of the Christian Democrats and the hardcore neoliberal wing of the Free Democrats "Liberaler Aufbruch" became a serious constraint for the Merkel government in conjunction with extra-party opposition against the financial umbrella. Already in 2005, 250 economics professors had launched a proclamation (Hamburger Appell) to put pressure on the Christian Democrats ahead of the upcoming federal elections. The group pursued a hardcore austerity line, raised moral hazard concerns, and objected to any demand-side policy measures (Truger 2013, 4). Two leading members of the German Bundesbank and the ECB, Axel Weber and Jürgen Stark, resigned in opposition to ECB purchases of government bonds of countries in trouble following the crisis (2).

Both the Hamburger Appell and the attacks on the European financial umbrellas, as well as the ECB rescue operations were backed by the Initiative for a New Social Market Economy (INSM) (Truger 2013). INSM is a neoliberal campaign operation financed by the German metal industries' business association with up to €8 million yearly since 2000 (compare Kinderman 2005, Speth 2004). Interestingly, the opposition did not talk much about Eurobonds, but focused on the steps already taken to erect financial umbrellas for the highly indebted states. With regard to the Eurobond debate, it is highly instructive to realize the criticism of the European financial mechanism first.

Intellectual Resources of the Anti-Eurobond Coalition

Much like the Eurobond discourse coalition drawing heavily on think tank output, Germany's Initiative for a New Social Market Economy relied on a think tank to oppose fiscal federalism and joint liability. INSM turned to the Centrum für Europäische Politik (CEP) in Freiburg to intellectually back up arguments against the bailout operation. In 2011, CEP authors published a study financed by INSM on the "demands on the restructuring of the euro-states: debt brakes and additional conditions." When Juncker and others were raising the stakes in the pragmatic Eurobond debate, the rigid austerity-minded opposition stepped up its own campaign for a more restrictive euro rescue campaign. This report unilaterally blamed irresponsible public finance as the cause of the financial crisis, complemented by economic structures that endanger credit-worthiness of corporations and states. While the neoliberal bottom line requires holding the public sector responsible, somewhat arcane language on problems with the "real economic structures" indicates recognition of additional private sector issues. The key consequences for the authors are nevertheless, first, restoration of sound public finance; second, economic reforms; third, solution for the "too big to fail" problem of financial organizations; and fourth, ensurance of credit practices in recognition of risks for the public sector in particular (Gerken, Roosebeke, and Voßwinkel 2011, 2).

According to the authors, the mechanism established by the stability and growth pact has failed. Since the European Union is incapable of securing the Maastricht criteria, a debt brake at the national level is recommended as an alternative. Debt brakes must be complemented by competitiveness-enhancing economic reforms, which lower trade deficits by lowering unit labour cost and bureaucratic constraints. Banks are to increase their net equity, and a European insolvency procedure is required to deal with insolvent financial institutes. Last but not least, credit supply needs to be more considerate of risks involved. Banks are also requested to price risks related to public bonds (ibid.)

It is clear from this study that the key question to be solved from this perspective is how to constitutionalize a rigid austerity regime and to cement "competitive nationalism/federalism." Interestingly, the EU is still to be in charge of insolvency procedures. The study mentions

Eurobonds once (Gerken, Roosebeke, and Voßwinkel 2011, 11). Common bonds are regarded as counterproductive since they encourage increasing debts, which is exactly the opposite of what the study aims to achieve through the instrument of a national debt brake. The two instruments are therefore considered incompatible and Eurobonds are rejected. The austerity extremism of this group of authors is best expressed by the demand that German lawmakers make the European umbrella payments conditional on implementation of *automatic* debt-reduction mechanisms at the national level, before asking for help (ex-ante conditionality known from IMF/World Bank discussions).

CEP has been a key resource of the ordo-liberal right wing in European policymaking since 2006. The think tank is funded by the Ordnungspolitik foundation (Stiftung Ordnungspolitik) headed by Lüder Gerken, who is also the head of CEP. The statement for the European Transparency Register claims donations of 1.5 million, without specifying the sources. Four individuals are listed with access to the EP premises (European Commission 2016).

Based in Freiburg, both the foundation and the think tank have close ties to the Walter Eucken Institute, which was the home of Germany's ordo-liberal orthodoxy, and also of Friedrich August von Hayek after his return from the United States. Gerken headed the Eucken Institute from 1991 to 2001. Gerken's CEP board includes (January 2017) former German president Roman Herzog (since deceased), former head of the Polish Central Bank and leading Polish neoliberal economist Leszek Balcerowicz, former EU Internal Market commissioner Frits Bolkestein, former president of the German Bundesbank, Hans Tietmeyer, and former head economist of the ECB, Jürgen Stark (CEP 2017b). Both Balcerowicz and Bolkestein are members of the Mont Pèlerin Society, and CEP is a member of the Stockholm network of neoliberal think tanks (like the British Institute of Economic Affairs, for example) across Europe.

In terms of services, the CEP offers policy briefs in basically all relevant fields of European legislation. About twelve experts work in different clusters (such as internal market, or transport). EU legislation is summarized and assessed from an economic perspective, specifically neoliberal (ordo-liberal) and with regard to existing (EU and German) legislation. CEP authors provide information on "options to influence the political process" (e.g., naming the lead directorate general) and signal the overall assessment of the proposal by assigning a traffic light value.

CEP authors were involved in many policy briefs on the euro crisis and in the externally funded study on the euro rescue operation discussed before. A search for the impact of the "debt brake" study for INSM yielded a very limited result, surprisingly. Only Hishow (2012) included a reference in a study on debt brake mechanisms conducted at the key advisory think tank of Germany's government, Stiftung Wirtschaft und Politik (SWP). The SWP study written to advise the German government is far more balanced than the CEP study, and rather critical of the pro-cyclical impact of debt brake versions.

The INSM/CEP study was apparently not meant to promote a media campaign. Likely it served the purpose of elite coordination in opposition to fiscal solidarity, joint liability, and Eurobonds (compare Schmidt 2002 on the distinction between public and elite coordination objectives). CEP information made available to the author in private communication suggested it would have been the task of the INSM to market the study to the media, which was apparently not done. CEP's own work is also directed mostly at a professional or expert audience, not the citizenry at large. We will describe the specialized public informed by CEP experts in relation to the CEP policy brief on the EU Commission Green Paper on the feasibility of introducing Stability Bonds (European Commission 2011). Green Papers of the commission of course are tools to increase the salience of issues, and can test the mood of European Council members and other stakeholders. This was certainly the case with the Green Paper on Stability Bonds.

European Stability Bond Green Paper: Opportunity to Watch the Transnational Coalitions

Following the original Eurobond proposals from Juncker and Tremonti, the Commission did not proceed to propose legislation. It is possible that the conflict lines within the conservative mainstream were also presenting an obstacle from within the Commission, where there must have been concerns about Council opposition from Germany in particular, at least. The European Parliament eventually pushed the Commission to present options in a decision on the financial, economic, and social crisis of 6 July 2011 (European Parliament 2011), which resulted in the Green Paper published four months later.

The Green Paper in turn presented three different options for the introduction of "stability bonds." The options differed in the degree to which common bonds replace national bonds, and with regard to the guarantee regime. Option one considered the complete replacement of national bonds in conjunction with joint liability. Option two distinguished between European and national (blue and red) bonds akin to the Bruegel proposal, and envisioned joint liability for the blue bonds. Option three foresaw liability for the European bond share according to the share a member state contributes, thence a limited liability for a limited amount European bond contingent. Obviously the different models are more and less compatible with the existing primary law. Options one and two would likely require treaty changes. Option three, however, would likely be less effective in r combating speculation attacks on national bonds of weak member states because the risk would still be relegated mostly to the national system of public finance.

The Green Paper was followed by a public consultation. Interestingly, public entities from six countries opposed the Green Paper, including Swedish, Danish, Finnish, German (and Bavarian), Austrian, Dutch, institutions. French and Czech institutions and the European Economic and Social Committee came out in favour. Among the business groups, thirteen came out in favour. Only Deutsche Bank, Germany's chamber of industry and commerce (Industrie und Handelstag), and the Austrian federal economic Chamber came out against the Eurobond proposals. An individual from Germany's chamber of crafts (Handwerkskammer) also opposed the proposal.

The spread of opinions is quite interesting. Most importantly, most business statements, including the principal European business association Business Europe, endorsed the Green Paper. Yet German business interests and the public anti-Eurobond coalition from Germany, Austria, the Netherlands, and Scandinavia obviously also are not representative of their countries as a whole. Germany's trade union federation, for example, endorsed the Eurobond proposal. The understanding of the social logic of austerity thinking needs complementary insight from the political logic of austerity-related battles in order to understand the reach and the limits of knowledge regimes and related institutions. If German austerity orthodoxy is taken for granted, there would be no need for dedicated efforts to reproduce an austerity-minded hegemonic constellation.

Feeding the Opposition in Germany and Elsewhere: CEP Policy Briefing

Just in time for the public consultation and discussion of the commission Green Paper, CEP published *Eurobonds* (Kullas and Hohmann 2012) to assess the Green Paper. The think tank has a regular format for such policy briefs, which give the reader the net result with the symbol for a traffic light: green for endorsement, yellow for mixed record, and red for no go. The Green Paper, unsurprisingly, was given the red light. The brief summary on the top offers a short summary of pros and cons. CEP saw no pros. The cons were summed up in two points: "(1) Eurobonds suspend market disciplining, thereby reducing budgetary discipline and the willingness of Member States to reform. The policy processes proposed by the Commission cannot compensate this. (2) Eurobonds of option 1 infringe the German Bundestag's budget responsibility which is protected by the Basic Law's guarantee of the permanence of basic principles" (Kullas and Hohmann 2012, 4).

Evidently the brief focused on the moral hazard concern and strongly objected to joint liability and complete replacement of national bonds by Eurobonds, pointing to German constitutional obstacles. European treaty concerns are listed in the detailed discussion, but evidently could not be presented as a game-killer. The European treaty obstacles are correctly considered less severe than the requirement of a two-thirds majority to change the German constitution. It makes sense for a transnational discourse coalition to focus on the German domestic veto position in such a case.

CEP policy briefs are published in German and in English. The responsible official in financial policy suggested that the English-language and German-language audiences were of roughly equal size. Briefs are mailed to people who signed up for the service if CEP staff consider them appropriate recipients. The distribution is tailored to experts in politics, business, media, and academic worlds. The Eurobond brief would be sent to the groups such as the Economic and Monetary Committee of the European Parliament and similar groups in the German parliament, for example. CEP clearly aims for an expert audience. CEP in fact has a framework contract with the EP Economic Committee to supply expertise regularly (personal communication of CEP official, 12 February 2015).

Even if individual studies and policy briefs do not seem to target the media, CEP officials are featured regularly in relevant media. Lüder von Gerken was cited several times late in 2011 (*Die Welt* 2011; *Berliner Morgenpost* 2011), when the threat by Standard & Poor to lower the ratings for Germany fuelled concerns about the euro rescue operation. Bert van Roosebeke is the CEP individual most frequently mentioned as chief witness for debt brakes and against Eurobonds. Germany's economic press (*Wirtschaftswoche, Handelsblatt*) reported the Eurobond critique of "economists," referring to CEP staff. By representing neoliberal perspectives as economic perspectives, the economic debate is represented in rather narrow ways. In any case, CEP staff play a major role in the collection and preparation of evidence and arguments feeding neoliberal perspectives in European policymaking. Authors are invited to discussions organized by political parties and to many other venues of the think tank circuit. While not representing specific interests directly, CEP is clearly involved in "deep lobbying," the expanded effort to influence internal and public discussions in policymaking. The think tank has four EP cardholders, as mentioned before, and travel to Brussels (or nearby Strasbourg) is frequent (personal communication of CEP official, February 12, 2015). The question of opening an office in Brussels (and Berlin) is on the agenda time and again. So far, funding appears to fall short of expanding operations. Still, if Bruegel and a few other mainstream European policy think tanks can be thought of as a centre of closer union advocacy, CEP is clearly at the centre of neoliberal counter-perspectives in favour of restrictions on integration. CEP has close ties to like-minded think tanks across Europe, such as Balcerowicz's FOR think tank in Poland, or the British Open Europe organization with offices in London, Brussels, and Berlin, for example. As part of the Stockholm network, CEP is a part of the major right-wing liberal networks that seek influence across the whole political spectrum, even if there are close ties to the conservative and liberal mainstream, as well as the new European right-wing faction of the Alliance of European Conservatives and Reformers (compare Plehwe and Schlögl 2014).

Bruegel contra CEP: How Relevant Are the Think Tanks in the Eurobond Battle?

Given the apparent strength of the pro-Eurobond coalition, the sudden defeat in Germany should come as a surprise. Again it is necessary to more fully review the battles that were fought to achieve success in Germany and elsewhere. Even the most powerful think tank has to back off if key constituencies are unhappy.[8] Germany's ministries

---

8 A recent example in the United States is telling. The Cato Institute had to change course when the Koch brothers did not feel they got enough bang for their bucks (Mayer 2012).

(economics and finance) threatened to cancel the financing of Bruegel in 2011 after its promotion of the blue bond proposal and the popularity of the Eurobond solution (private communication with Bruegel official, 13.2.2014). What normally would be the greatest success for a think tank in this case backfired for Bruegel. One major constituency became increasingly upset about the dynamics of a proposal. Unlike proposals of a few years earlier on the future orientation of the welfare state (promoting "flexicurity"), the Eurobond proposal became synonymous for a "wrong" European development (shared debt community threatening to undermine the stability of the euro). This needed to be avoided at all costs (quite literally: consider the higher expenses for the European stability mechanism and the extremely high social cost in the peripheral countries). While it is not clear if and how CEP played a role in the conflict with Bruegel, the expertise and perspective supplied by CEP was strongly opposed to the pragmatic austerity and integration line followed by the Eurobond coalition. The mobilization of CEP in favour of national debt-brake solutions by the Initiative Neue Soziale Marktwirtschaft likely mobilized government officials in German finance and economic ministries opposed to the Bruegel propositions. While CEP is not financed and supported by the German government, as Bruegel is, the conservative liberal coalition was forced to move closer to the INSM-CEP-led anti-Eurobond discourse coalition in order to defend its own pragmatic austerity line. However, the government's autonomy from the business wing of Christian Democrats and the anti-Euro wing of the Free Democrats needed to be defended as well. The majority of Social Democrat/Green governments in the German Bundesrat (the upper house), and the requirement of a two-thirds majority to pass the laws needed for the European Stability Mechanism and the domestic fiscal consolidation pact, forced the centre-right coalition to compromise with the centre-left parties. At this point, Social Democrats and Greens withdrew their demand for Eurobonds and received a commitment for a multi-billion investment program from the Conservative-Liberal coalition government. Because the opposition agreed with the government that this investment should not be financed by higher debt, a second compromise was reached on the financial transaction tax. This tax also met popular demand to make the financial sector pay for the crisis and lower the appetite for short-term speculation. A key aspect of the solution found in Germany is the focus on the domestic level. While the demand for Eurobonds would have addressed the needs of highly indebted states and social classes abroad, the Tobin tax (still not realized in 2017) and the investment program mostly benefit Germans. Social Democrats and Greens involved in crafting this compromise were thus clearly selling whatever internationalist inclinations they had as part of the Eurobond coalition out for national objectives. Since there are no plans for a generally pragmatic European austerity regime, the national consensus appears to favour pragmatic austerity at home and rigid austerity abroad, which is hardly a winning formula for European integration.

Peace was eventually made also between Bruegel and the conservative-liberal coalition in Germany. Angela Merkel's key economic advisor, Lars-Hendrik Röller, became a member of Bruegel's board in 2011, taking the place of the previous German board member Caio Koch-Weser, who served as state secretary in the finance ministry under Chancellor Gerhard Schröder. Evidently, think tank expertise can be independent from key constituencies only to a point. Even powerfully positioned think tanks (or rather the individuals therein) are only as strong as the discourse coalitions of which they are a part. The Freiburg-based CEP in this case was on the winning side, even if it was a much less prominent organization compared to Bruegel in this battle.

Conclusions

The battle over Eurobonds was clearly won by the opponents. This is the message Angela Merkel expressed in unusually draconian terms ("Only over my dead body"). This message that has been confirmed with the steadfast refusal of new debt policy options advanced by the Greek government in 2015. Although the Merkel coalition government was under strong pressure in 2013, Christian Democrats thrived in the federal elections, though the even stronger pro-austerity liberal coalition partner did not. Matthijs and McNamara (2015, 243) claim that "the thorny issue of the introduction of a common debt instrument has remained off the table in Germany, and Europe, since then. The whole debate over Eurobonds … demonstrated the strength of the German economics profession and the dominant view of the euro as an economic problem with mainly national economic solutions." So why did the staunchly anti-Eurobond Free Democratic Party lose? Why did the anti-Eurobond and anti-Euro party Alternative für Deutschland gain almost 5 per cent in federal elections and enter the European Parliament? Substantively, the European Stability Mechanism and quantitative easing by the ECB have yielded some of the Eurobond objectives.

Speculation against national bonds has been curtailed and bond spreads across the Eurozone are limited. Radical austerity voices continue to attack the departure from strictly national economic solutions to the euro problem exactly because Angela Merkel has been the architect of a more rigid, but still quite pragmatic austerity project. The winning formula found to appease the opposition both in Germany and abroad was an investment program and a subscription to the financial transaction tax – not exactly instruments loved by rigid austerity supporters, although the German government of Christian and Social Democrats has yet to deliver on the promise of the financial transaction tax, together with the other nine Eurozone members who officially endorsed the measure (European Council 2016). Since the Eurobond proposals themselves were not as radical a departure from the austerity agenda as sometimes thought, the defeat can hardly be explained by the strength of the German economics profession, although the mobilization of radical neoliberal austerity forces was quite important within and beyond the German debate. The German-based Glienicker group is suggested to offer additional evidence for the absence of the Eurobond idea in Germany, but the group includes Mr blue bond proposal Jacob von Weizsäcker, and the group's statement is adamant about "controlled transfer elements" as a part of a deeper euro-union, pace Matthijs and McNamara (2015, 242). It is crucial to not mistake exceedingly strong neoliberal forces among economists (and non-economists) as *pars pro toto* for the whole of the German profession. We rather need to still learn much more about the domestic and transnational networks that advance more or less pragmatic austerity perspectives, and we still need more symmetry indeed by searching for anti-austerity perspectives, which can also include Eurobonds. Think tank networks advancing and opposing austerity across Europe can be considered a promising source of information to identify transnational expert, consulting and lobby, or advocacy networks involved in the European economic and social policy struggles. Databases have been compiled and await collaborative research linked to the study of professions and economic ideas (Think Tank Network Research 2016).

Both pragmatic and restrictive austerity perspectives help to explain major dynamics of the contemporary transformation of neoliberal hegemonic constellations. A willingness to step up cross-national transfers, at least temporarily, to secure social stability (moderate fiscal federalism with or without Eurobonds) is confronted with an advocated need to maintain the present European treaty configuration of competitive federalism, which stipulates fiscal nationalism and national responsibility for social integration (Streeck 2013). German Social Democrats and Greens, nominally opposed to rigid austerity, have been won over by the Merkel doctrine of pragmatic austerity at home and rigid austerity abroad. As long as the forces who are nominally opposed to supply side economics are willing to sacrifice their anti-austerity soul on the altar of national unionism, there is little hope for a European public finance regime beyond permanent and intensified austerity.

REFERENCES

Alesina, Alberto, and Silvia Ardagna. 2010. "Large Changes in Fiscal Policy: Taxes versus Spending." In *Tax Policy and the Economy*, vol. 24, ed. Jeffrey R. Brown, 35–68. Cambridge, MA: National Bureau of Economic Research. http://dx.doi.org/10.1086/649828.

Alesina, Alberto, and Roberto Perotti. 1995. "Fiscal Expansions and Fiscal Adjustments in OECD Countries." *Economic Policy* 10 (21): 205–48. http://dx.doi.org/10.2307/1344590.

Baker, Tom. 1996. "On the Genealogy of Moral Hazard." *Texas Law Review* 75:237–92.

Berg, Tim Oliver, Kai Carstensen, and Hans-Werner Sinn. 2011. "Was kosten Eurobonds." *ifo Schnelldienst* 64 (17): 25–33. http://www.cesifo-group.de/DocDL/ifosd_2011_17_4.pdf.

Berliner Morgenpost. 2011. "Ökonom warnt vor Mega-Inflation in der Euro-Zone." 29 November.

Bieling, Hans-Jürgen. 2013. "Zum gesellschafts- und integrationspolitischen Charakter des europäischen Krisenkonstitutionalismus." *Forschungsjournal Soziale Bewegungen* 26 (1): 51–60. http://dx.doi.org/10.1515/fjsb-2013-0108.

Bloomberg. 2012. "Cameron Urges Hollande to Back Eurobonds Rejects Tobin Tax." 18 May. https://www.bloomberg.com/news/articles/2012-05-18/cameron-urges-hollande-to-back-eurobonds-rejects-tobin-tax.

Blyth, Mark. 2013. *Austerity: The History of a Dangerous Idea*. New York: Routledge.

Bonds News. 2010. "Belgian PM Leterme Proposes European Debt Agency." Reuters, 5 March. http://www.reuters.com/article/eurozone-greece-agency-idUSLDE6240FH20100305.

Carrigan, Mark. 2010. "How Right-wing Think-tanks Laid the Foundation for the Coalition's Agenda." Liberal Conspiracy. http://liberalconspiracy.org/2010/08/09/how-right-wing-think-tanks-laid-the-foundation-for-the-coalitions-agenda/.

CEP. 2017. "Kuratorium [Board of Trustees]." http://www.cep.eu/cep/ kuratorium/.

CEPS. 2017a. "About CEPS." https://www.ceps.eu/content/about-ceps.

CEPS. 2017b. "Staff." https://www.ceps.eu/staff.

Day, Alan J. 2000. "Think Tanks in Western Europe." In *Think Tanks & Civil Society: Catalysts for Ideas and Action*, ed. James G. McGann and R. Kent Weaver, 103–38. New Brunswick, NJ: Transaction Publishers.

De Grauwe, Paul, and Wim Moesen. 2009. "Gains for All: A Proposal for a Common Euro Bond." CEPS Commentary, 3 April.

Delpla, Jacques, and Jakob von Weizsäcker. 2011. "Eurobonds: The Blue Bond Concept and Its Implications." Bruegel policy contribution 2, Brussels.

Die Welt. 2011. "Ökonom warnt vor Mega-Inflation in der Euro-Zone." 29 November.

Dorgan, George. 2012. "The Euro Crisis: Details and Chronology and the German Perspective on It." SNBCHF.com. https://snbchf.com/eurocrisis/ 2012-ec/eurocrisis-chrononology/.

Economist. 2011. "Without the Free Lunch." 13 September.

Eijffinger, Sylvester C.W. 2011. "Briefing Note: Eurobonds – Concepts and Implications." Document requested by the European Parliament's Committee on Economic and Monetary Affairs. Brussels: European Parliament.

European Commission. 2011. "Green Paper on the Feasibility of Introducing Stability Bonds." 23.11.2011 COM(2011) 818 final. Brussels.

– 2016. "Stiftung Ordnungspolitik – Centrum für Europäische Politik." Transparency Register. http://ec.europa.eu/transparencyregister/public/ consultation/displaylobbyist.do?id=488753210783-18.

European Council. 2016. "Enhanced Cooperation in the Area of Financial Transaction Tax." Interinstitutional file: 2013/0045 (CNS). http://data. consilium.europa.eu/doc/document/ST-13608-2016-INIT/en/pdf.

Favero, Carlo A., and Allesandro Missale. 2010. "EU Public Debt Management and Eurobonds." In *Euro Area Governance: Ideas for Crisis Management Reform*, 111–36. Brussels: European Parliament.

Gerken, Lüder, Bert Van Roosebeke, and Jan S. Voßwinkel. 2011. *Anforderungen an die Sanierung der Euro-Staaten. Schuldenbremse plus Nebenbedingungen*. Freiburg: Centrum für europäische Politik.

Giavazzi, Francesco, and Marco Pagano. 1990. "Can Severe Fiscal Contractions Be Expansionary? Tales of Two Small European Countries." *NBER Macroeconomics Annual* 5:75–111. http://dx.doi.org/10.1086/654131.

Guajardo, Jaime, Daniel Leigh, and Andrea Pescatori. 2011. "Expansionary Austerity: New International Evidence." IMF Working Paper 11/15.

Hayek, Friedrich A. (1948) 1980. "The Economic Conditions of Interstate Federalism." In *Individualism and Economic Order*, ed. Friedrich A. Hayek, 255–72. Chicago: University of Chicago Press.

Hishow, Ognian N. 2012. *Schuldenbremsen in der EU: Das ultimative Instrument der Budgetpolitik*. Berlin: Stiftung Wissenschaft und Politik.

Jones, Erik. 2010. "A Eurobond Proposal to Promote Stability and Liquidity while Preventing Moral Hazard." ISPI Policy Brief 180. Milan.

– 2012. "The Eurobond: Proposals, Comments, and Speeches." http://www.jhubc.it/facultypages/ejones/eurobond.pdf.

Juncker, Jean-Claude, and Giolio Tremonti. 2010. "E-bonds Would End the Crisis." *Financial Times*, 5 December.

Keune, Maarten, and Amparo Serrano. 2014. *Deconstructing Flexicurity and Developing Alternative Approaches*. London: Routledge.

Kinderman, Daniel. 2005. "Pressure from Without, Subversion from Within: The Two-Pronged German Employer Offensive." *Comparative European Politics* 3 (4): 432–63. http://dx.doi.org/10.1057/palgrave.cep.6110064.

Kotz, Hans-Helmut. 2011. "EMU's Response to the North Atlantic Financial Crisis: Policymaking from Incompatible Views." In *Europe's Economic Crisis*, ed. Robert M. Solow and Daniel S. Hamilton, 29–44. Washington: Center for Transatlantic Relations and Curnot Centre.

Kotzias, Nikos. 2013. *Greece Colony of Debt: European Empire and German Primacy*. Athens: S. Patakis.

Krugman, Paul. 2014. "How the Case for Austerity Has Crumbled." *New York Review of Books* 61:7.

Kullas, Matthias, and Iris Hohmann. 2012. *Eurobonds*. CEP Policy Brief no. 2012-04. Freiburg: Centrum für europäische Politik.

Matthijs, Matthias, and Kathleen McNamara. 2015. "The Euro Crisis' Theory Effect: Northern Saints, Southern Sinners, and the Demise of the Eurobond." *Journal of European Integration* 37 (2): 229–45. http://dx.doi.org/10.1080/07036337.2014.990137.

Mayer, Jane. 2012. "The Kochs v. Cato: Winners and Losers." *New Yorker*, 27 June. http://www.newyorker.com/news/news-desk/the-kochs-v-cato-winners-and-losers.

McGann, James. 2017. "2016 Global Go to Think Tank Index Report." University of Pennsylvania. http://repository.upenn.edu/cgi/viewcontent.cgi?article=1011&context=think_tanks.

McNamara, Kathleen R. 1999. *The Currency of Ideas: Monetary Politics in the European Union*. Ithaca, NY: Cornell University Press.

Medick, Veit. 2012. "Müntefering warnt SPD vor Kurs à la Hollande." *Spiegel Online*, 23 May. http://www.spiegel.de/politik/deutschland/muentefering-a-834681.html.

Mirowski, Philip. 2013. *Never Let a Serious Crisis Go to Waste*. London: Verso

Plehwe, Dieter. 2010. "Brussels Think Tanks and Corporate PR." In *Bursting the Brussels Bubble: The Battle to Expose Corporate Lobbying at the Heart of the EU*, ed. Helen Burley, William Dinan, Kenneth Haar, Olivier Hoedeman, and Erik Wesselius, 53–61. Brussels: Alter-EU.

– 2013. "Europäische Krise oder europäische Dimension der Krisen? Amerikanische Perspektiven." *Das Argument: Zeitschrift für Philosophie und Sozialwissenschaften* 55:61–72.

Plehwe, Dieter, and Matthias Schlögl. 2014. "Europäische und zivilgesellschaftliche Hintergründe der euro(pa)skeptischen Partei Alternative für Deutschland (AfD)." WZB Discussion Paper SP III 2014–501r. Berlin. http://bibliothek.wzb.eu/pdf/2014/iii14-501r.pdf.

Scharpf, Fritz. 2010. "The Socio-economic Asymmetries of European Integration or Why the EU Cannot Be a 'Social Market Economy.'" *European Policy Analysis* 10. http://www.sieps.se/sites/default/files/2010_10epa.pdf.

Schmidt, Vivian A. 2002. *The Futures of European Capitalism*. Oxford: Oxford University Press. http://dx.doi.org/10.1093/0199253684.001.0001.

Sinclair, Timothy. 2000. "Deficit Discourse: The Social Construction of Fiscal Rectitude." In *Globalization and Its Critics: Perspectives from Political Economy*, ed. Randall D. Germain, 185–203. London: Macmillan and St Martin's. http://dx.doi.org/10.1007/978-1-137-07588-8_7.

Sorge, Arndt. 2010. "Financial Catastrophe and Its Implications for Socioeconomics." *Socio-economic Review* 9 (1): 1–18.

Speth, Rudolf. 2004. *Die politischen Strategien der Initiative Neue Soziale Marktwirtschaft*. Düsseldorf: Hans-Böckler-Stiftung.

Spiegel Online. 2012. "Merkel zur Schuldenpolitik: 'Keine Euro-Bonds, solange ich lebe.'" 26 June.

Springford, John. 2009. "A Bonding Exercise for the Euroland." *Wall Street Journal*, 7 September.

– 2012. "Europe Needs Service-Market Liberalization." *Wall Street Journal*, 20 September.

Straßheim, Holger. 2013. "Politische Expertise im Wandel. Zur diskursiven und institutionellen Einbettung epistemischer Autorität." In *Der moderne Staat: Zeitschrift für Public Policy, Recht und Management* 6, 65–86.

Streeck, Wolfgang. 2013. *Gekaufte Zeit: Die vertagte Krise des demokratischen Kapitalismus*. Berlin: Suhrkamp.

Truger, Achim. 2013. "Austerity in the Euro Area: The Sad State of Economic Policy in Germany and the EU." Institute for International Political Economy Berlin Working Paper 22.

Varoufakis, Yanis. 2013. "One Very Simple, but Radical, Idea: To Democratise Europe." https://yanisvaroufakis.eu/euro-crisis/modest-proposal/.

Verhofstadt, Guy. 2012. "Germany Knows Way to Solve Crisis." *Financial Times*, 29 February.

Wegmann, Milene. 2002. *Früher Neoliberalismus und europäische Integration. Interdependenz der nationalen, supranationalen und internationalen Ordnung von Wirtschaft und Gesellschaft (1932–1965)*. Baden Baden: Nomos.

Wolf, Martin. 2014. *The Shift and the Shocks: What We've Learned – and Have Still to Learn – from the Financial Crisis*. New York: Penguin.

10 Constructing Economic Policy Advice in an Age of Austerity

BRYAN M. EVANS

This chapter is concerned with the construction and relay of policy ideas within the neoliberal state. In this respect, it takes its cue from the well-worn adage to never let a crisis go to waste and the political conundrum presented by the Great Financial Crisis of 2007. That is to say, the crisis presented the most serious crack in the edifice of capitalism since the Great Depression of the 1930s. Unlike that earlier crisis, through which capitalism was reconstructed both in policy and political terms into a different variety of capitalism, the crisis of 2007 left neoliberalism essentially intact in policy terms, though much more seriously contested politically, albeit unevenly, as events in Greece, Spain, Portugal, Scotland, and the Jeremy Corbyn and Bernie Sanders phenomena suggest. While policy instruments and strategies have been subject to innovation, these have not reset the policy echo chamber within the state.

As the Great Financial Crisis (GFC) deepened and spread through 2007–8, alarmed governments and central banks mobilized an unprecedented intervention. The rapid and unexpected reanimation of the surviving "institutional legacy of Keynesianism" (Strange 2012, 121) caused one social democratic intellectual to state the "2008 crisis marks the end of the Reagan-Thatcher counter-revolution. Neoliberalism and monetarism are dead" (Collignon 2008, 8). Recent history has proven otherwise. Indeed, what was initially a crisis within the banking sector, a product of decades of financial deregulation, was reframed as a problem of public spending to be remedied through a program of "expansionary austerity." The result was a gattopardoesque[1] manoeuvre where

---

1 *Gattopardoesque* is a reference to Giuseppe Tomasi di Lampedusa's novel *Il Gattopardo* (The Leopard) set in mid-nineteenth-century Italy when Garibaldi's forces have

preserving the essence of the status quo requires some semblance of change (Tomasi di Lampedusa 1958), causing one observer to ask, "What remains of neoliberalism after the financial crisis? The answer must be virtually everything" (Crouch 2011, 179). Power is immanent in all relationships, and ideas serve to link structures to actors (Peters 1999, 71–2). This is particularly salient for the relationship of ideas to public policy and the state. Constitutionalizing austerity, as addressed by McBride in his chapter, is an outcome as well as a means for the reproduction of neoliberal policies within the state apparatus and further serves as a barrier to alternatives. This chapter is concerned with how constitutionalization of austerity is manufactured within the state.

The power of economics as a body of knowledge is its ability to structure a problem, in addition to its privileged position within the hierarchy of power more broadly. In this respect, a central consideration must be the political foundations of economic epistemology and how this intersects with the role of a specific policy community centred upon and through state institutions. The intersectionality of the economics profession, the structure of the policy advisory system within the state, the bureaucratic politics within the state apparatus, and the embedded role of neoliberal intellectual agents within the state are the subjects of this contribution. The resilience of "dead ideas" (Quiggin 2010) can thus be understood, in part, through the lens of epistemic power relationships and the institutional structures through which they are relayed. Specific features of policymaking praxis insulate the state policy function from non-neoliberal policy alternatives. These include an array of means by which alternatives are "crowded out" through a dense network of ideational relays including think tanks, advocacy coalitions, and policy entrepreneurs within or well-linked to the state.

It is key that the production and transfer of policy ideas take place within what are effectively "gated" policy communities and are increasingly privatized through the outsourcing of policy advice. What underpins the foregoing are the power resources of the dominant classes, and specifically the "pre-eminence" of the "class owning financial (and real estate) assets" (Serfati 2013, 154), and the success of their political

---

landed in Sicily and threaten to overthrow the island's feudal nobility. The central protagonist, the prince of Salina, must confront the political change that threatens old class privileges. The strategy chosen to preserve privilege is to break with tradition in symbolic ways in order to preserve the fundamental order of things. Thus, for "things to stay as they are, things will have to change."

project – neoliberalism – in restructuring class relations and the consequent redistribution of power. Woodward's discussion of tax havens in this volume is a blunt but direct reflection of the central political concern for this class with "protecting the gains made by capital in the last thirty years," and a central strategy in achieving this goal is through effective control of the state apparatus (Radice 2010, 38). Embedded neoliberalism, "constituted by historically specific institutions and social relations which structure people's everyday lives" (Cahill 2014, ix), is the result. Neoliberalism is embedded through three mechanisms: class relations, institutions, and ideology. All three inform the policy process in important ways. The privileged position of capital is further strengthened as other political actors, notably labour, are marginalized; state institutions are "integral to the implementation, reproduction and extension of neoliberalism"; and, ideologically, neoliberalism is the common sense of policy elites serving to frame collective problems and define solutions (81).

Of course, this is not to say there is totalizing policy coherence. Indeed, contradictions abound. A key illustration is provided by the United States. There the Federal Reserve embarked upon the most expansive (and expansionary) program of quantitative easing in history while the subnational state governments slashed away at public expenditures, eliminating public sector jobs and reducing entitlements and public services. In part this is a function of the paradoxes of multi-level governance where constitutional allocation of powers to different levels of government establish distinct areas of policy responsibility. Overlapping and corresponding to such divisions of authority are also variable political dynamics where localized elites and more reactionary political forces mobilize and win government power. In short, the Federal Reserve acts on behalf of the national, if not global, economy, while the more conservative state legislatures and governors serve more local interests. Consequently, the choices before each venue will be shaped by different objectives and political-economic calculations. An additional explanation, equally or more compelling, points to the limitations of the Obama administration's stimulus program. State and local governments were under extraordinary fiscal pressure after 2008 due to the housing foreclosures, which hit local property tax revenue particularly hard, and the recession took its toll on state finances (income taxes, sales taxes). Nearly all states are prohibited by their constitutions from running deficits for operating budgets and so, facing this legal block, they argued there were no alternatives to deep austerity.

The American Recovery and Reinvestment Act (ARRA), signed into law by President Obama in 2009, provided for only approximately one-third the budget gap experienced by states. Thus states were left with filling in the remaining two-thirds, and funding for the ARRA ended in 2012, thus leaving states and municipalities to find their own solutions (Pollin and Thompson 2011). The result is "fiscal purging," which deepens the "cumulative incapacitation of the state" (Peck 2015, 4). In this way we can see how the limitations of the fiscal stabilization intervention of 2009 were not only rather inadequate and feeble, in comparison to the monetary interventions of the Federal Reserve, but further eroded subnational state capacity in a process of normalization. The effect of embedded neoliberalism is observed in this instance where the demand to resuscitate finance was allocated greater priority than the need to sustain subnational public services and programs. Moreover, reactionary state governments seized the opportunity to attack public sector workers and unions specifically.

Explaining Neoliberal Resilience: The Ideational Foundations of Policy Advice

The financial crash of the 1930s created a crisis in economic orthodoxy and led to a revolution in economics. Yet the Great Financial Crisis of 2007–8 did not give rise to a similar rethink of the new orthodoxy in economics (Mirowski 2013, 2). For Keynes, the challenge to having his expansionary counter-cyclical ideas accepted in place of the prevailing orthodoxy of fiscal prudence and sound money was not the complexity of his ideas but rather "escaping from the old ones," which had the status of common sense (Keynes 1936, 4). And now, historically situated in the aftermath of the Great Financial Crisis of 2008, or at least its first phase, a similar challenge confounds us. Economists and their journalistic allies overwhelmingly frame the problem as too much public expenditure, too much public debt, greedy, self-interested unions, and unmotivated, overcompensated public sector workers. And despite the "no one saw it coming" crisis of 2008, the state elite, both elected and bureaucratic everywhere and across mainstream partisan identities, "regard economic theory as the sole source of wisdom about the manner in which a modern society should be governed" (Keen 2011, xv). This enduring intellectual legitimacy is a rather peculiar state of affairs.

Zombie ideas are those that, although "the evidence seems to have killed them, they keep on coming back" (Quiggin 2010, 1) and guide economic policy. Failure to recognize that expansionary austerity and the assortment of allied economic axioms of the past thirty or more years are not working is puzzling, given that other periods of economic crisis led to paradigm-shifting reconsiderations. The Great Depression of the 1930s set the stage for the ascent of Keynesianism to orthodoxy, and the 1970s crisis gave rise to neoliberalism. Paradoxically, the crisis and its aftermath are marked by economic volatility, an uneven though expanding resistance to neoliberalism, and, among policy elites, broad ideological stability. Neoliberalism is not questioned, but policy specificities respecting how to sustain the model have begun to differ. For example, European political leaders embarked upon massive public sector cuts while the American federal state, notwithstanding subnational state actions, withheld from an all-out assault upon its core workforce and programs (Karger 2014, 34). More pointed has been the International Monetary Fund's critique of destabilizing austerity policies, including a public acknowledgment that the policy prescription handed to Greece was "wrong" (Andreou 2014), but the core point of contention is not austerity in and of itself but rather the "pace" by which it is implemented (Beams 2012). And more recently, as the post-crisis global economy falters again, the IMF's call for "bold and ambitious" intervention, meaning for governments to ramp up spending, was criticized by Germany's finance minister as "economic alarmism" (Deutsche Welle 2014). But none of this questions the austerity program itself or seriously considers non-austerian alternatives. Consequently, notwithstanding the enormity of the 2007 crisis, there has not been a rethink of economic orthodoxy as there was in the wake of the Great Depression of the 1930s (Gamble 2013, 53).

Three specific features of neoliberal ideational resilience are: (1) the continuity of neoliberal ideas over time; (2) the hegemonic dominance of these ideas; and (3) their survival even in the face of their own failures (Schmidt and Thatcher 2013, 15). The ideational foundation for this continuity, dominance, and survival has been the "construction of political consent" constituting nothing less than "common sense" (Harvey 2005, 39). Through processes of bricolage (grafting of new ideas onto older ones), diffusion (relaying neoliberal ideas), and translation (adaptation of neoliberal ideas to new contexts), ideational continuity and hegemony are achieved (16).

Importantly, this context establishes the basis for policy agenda-setting within the state. That is, how and whether the state will intervene. In this process, certain concepts and narratives are formulated and used, while others are not. These then "frame" "what and who is taken into consideration in and excluded from policy deliberation" (Brock, Cornwall, and Gaventa 2001, 5). This "framing" is a significant source of neoliberal resiliency: "Neo-liberal ideational entrepreneurs use their ideas to 'frame' current problems" and "weave together policy prescriptions, policy programmes, and philosophical principles into a seemingly coherent account of what happened and why" (Schmidt and Thatcher 2013, 32). Policy framing thus requires policy actors to design an understanding or "story" that makes the issue/problem understandable and solvable. Moreover, framing will determine which policy actors are included in and will benefit from the process (Zito 2011). Such "programmatic ideas," which establish a course of action, are very effective in placing parameters around which alternative policy frameworks are acceptable as they "set the definitions, goals, objectives, and instruments" (Schmidt and Thatcher 2013, 20–1). In this respect, certain policy actors and ideas are privileged, while others are ignored to some greater or lesser extent. Policy framing thus places constraints on what is possible by establishing the normative boundaries determining which problems are identified and then the range of possible solutions limited to those that are within the range of acceptability. This may be understood as a form of culturally broad ideological insulation from alternative ideas. In this way policy becomes "rules bounded" as a consequence of the "internalization of the guiding assumptions of the prevailing economic paradigm" (Hay 2004, 503). Consequently, the prevailing orthodoxy is that economic growth and competitiveness are dependent upon a program of ongoing neoliberal reform.

Moreover, the crowding-out of alternatives has been achieved rather systematically in the "battle of ideas" though a dense network of ideational relays composed of think tanks, advocacy coalitions, and policy entrepreneurs who work to popularize their work to the mass public in the process of constructing a new common sense, as well as political elites (Schmidt and Thatcher 2013, 32). Policy entrepreneurs are key to understanding how policy ideas are disseminated and gain favour. Policy entrepreneurs mobilize ideas to "define problems in ways that both attract the attention of decision makers and indicate appropriate policy responses" (Mintrom and Vergari 1996, 422). Successful policy entrepreneurs are typically those able to network in and around government and who present the most uncontentious arguments (Mintrom 1997). To accomplish this they first must have access to decision makers.

The role of think tanks is specifically addressed in this volume by Plehwe. The Eurobonds case he presents illustrates how think tanks seek ideational influence through norms creation and the diffusion of policy ideas (Pautz 2012; Béland and Orenstein 2013). Influential think tanks are those that have money and resources. Less-resourced think tanks tend not to be as successful in the battle to shape policy (Béland 2009).

Advocacy coalitions composed of activists, experts, and elected officials share a particular belief or value system and demonstrate coordinated activity over time (Sabatier 1988). These coalitions shape their beliefs to fit with the dominant policymaking group possessing the greatest influence in the policy process (Sabatier and Weible 2002, 194–6). Implicit in the idea of advocacy coalitions is that, in order for ideas to have an impact, they must be part of a subsystem. Moreover, the advocacy coalition must be able to dominate its subsystem in order to influence policy, which means that ideas not shared by the dominant coalition are very unlikely to have any impact on policy.

Each of these ideational relays serves as a gatekeeper to the policy process. Policy ideas are powerful within the policy process; however, there are real limits to which ideas enter the process.

Framing is thus linked to argumentation, with its focus on discourse, and popularization as a powerful tool in the construction of a widely held neoliberal common sense. The ideas thus conveyed "are easy to understand and resonate with 'common sense' and with deep values and personal experience" (Schmidt and Thatcher 2013, 32). This characteristic makes such ideas easily communicated. But common sense can "be profoundly misleading, obfuscating or disguising [of] real problems under cultural prejudice" (Harvey 2005, 39). That is precisely the source of its power to structure popular understanding of social and political reality in such a way as to buttress resilience and inform a populist anti-politics.

The "argumentative turn" identified in critical policy studies acknowledges that policy work entails much more than a rational analysis of data and evidence but rather involves an active, strategic selection of ideas. State-employed policy analysts are not policy eunuchs but instead are central actors in the construction of meaning through discursive framing: "They scan a political environment as much as they locate facts, and they are involved with constructing senses of value even as they identify costs and benefits" (Fischer and Forester 1993, 2). This understanding is a powerful counterpoint to the orthodoxy of state policy analysts working as neutral rational technocrats in an open and accessible policy process where influence is seemingly disconnected from power (Noveck 2011).

This was not simply misfortune. The construction and provision of policy advice for government consumption by "ideological entrepreneurs," working both in and outside the state, is of central importance. These are the "prime movers for neo-liberal reform, offering a set of overarching philosophical ideas that inform their policy programmes and ideas" (Schmidt and Thatcher 2013, 23). This construction of meaning is the foundation of neoliberal resilience, as "policy makers customarily work within a framework of ideas and standards that specifies not only the goals of policy and the kind of instruments that can be used to attain them, but also the very nature of the problems they are meant to be addressing" (Hall 1993, 279). And so the neoliberal policy paradigm becomes normalized through internalization by "politicians, state managers and policy experts alike and may become institutionally embedded in norms, conventions and standard operating procedures" (Hay 2004, 504). Thus the cognitive framework used by policymakers that determines what is possible is constructed as thoroughly neoliberal.

Economic policy ideas do not necessarily become translated into public policy simply because they are grounded in solid research and evidence. For policy transfer and utilization to happen, policy ideas require a political vehicle, whether that is a party, a broad-based social movement, or links to powerful socio-economic interests (Gourevitch 1989, 87). The ascent of neoclassical ideas to a position where they became hegemonic in policy terms was made possible largely because economists, acting as ideational agents, mobilized these ideas and presented an alternative to the wobbling Keynesianism of the 1970s. Their adoption by electorally successful political parties searching for a theoretical model to replace the failing model provided that vehicle into the state.

As a strategic epistemic community, economists and the economics profession are accorded substantial legitimacy in the policy advisory process and thus play a critical role in the production of advice. They have "been at the forefront of the generation and promulgation of neoliberal ideas" as well as occupying a central role and function in the provision of policy advice (Schmidt and Thatcher 2013, 23–4). Their contribution requires some greater unpacking.

Economists and Economics: The Contestability of "Expert" Knowledge

Economics, more than any other social science, has been tremendously influential, through its policy prescriptions for the direction of economic development (Schneider and Kirchgässner 2009, 324). The role of economists in policy is that of "gatekeepers" influencing resource allocation (Markoff and Montecinos 1993, 52). In this role they serve as ideational agents, purveyors of a powerful tool to frame policy problems, as well as being responsible for the transfer of economic ideas into and within the "mind" of the state. It has been said that senior ranking state elites, "along with elected politicians and some types of intellectuals are the 'switchmen' of history; when they change their minds the destiny of nations takes a different course" (Pusey 1991, 2). The intellectuals referred to here are often economists serving as policy advisors to state elites who govern the direction of policy. In short, they are the conceptual framers of problems and designers of policy interventions.

Through the years of the Great Depression, and into the post-war era, a "generation of Keynesian trained economists and policy analysts came to the fore and populated a growing state apparatus and institutionalised a 'state ideology'" (Evans 2005, 25). However, even as that paradigm faded, economists remained in demand as policy actors in possession of "newer ideas of economic management" armed "with an impressive variety of complex and esoteric models" (Markoff and Montecinos 1993, 43). Economists, in this sense, are strategically located within the state policy advisory system, whether as external advisors or directly employed by the state. Their role in ushering in the "Silent Revolution" that made the Neoliberal Era is identical to that of a previous generation of Keynesian economists whose "extensive networks" served to transmit their economic ideas. Just as governments turned to fiscal policy as a key tool of macroeconomic management when Keynesian ideas dominated the economics profession, so did monetary policy became the new orthodoxy when those ideas came to prevail over the "profession" (Lindvall 2009, 710).

The widespread adoption of Keynesian approaches required significantly more robust policy capacity within the state to plan, design, and manage expanding public expenditures and the instruments and institutions of fiscal stabilization. Consequently, "technical economic advisors" were recruited to conduct analyses and translate them into applied policy. As this model faltered through the 1970s and 1980s, the demand for economists as policy advisors did not diminish as monetarist/supply-side methods came with "an impressive variety of complex and esoteric models of their own and require equally elaborate technical staffing" (Markoff and Montecinos 1993, 43). The number of economists working in government directly, and in the role of providing strategic advice in all policy domains, has contributed to a transformation in how state policy elites come to see and understand public problems and identify solutions. In other words, the "mind of the state" perceives the world through the filter of neoclassical economics.

The substantial influence of economists on policy is founded upon the claim that their domain of knowledge is genuinely scientific and presents an objective account of economic behaviour and dynamics. In short, it stakes out an intellectual TINA (there is no alternative). This claim is in turn based upon the scientization of economics, which refers to the application of empirical testing of theory, typically by mathematical methods. The technical expertise of economists is the foundation for their role in designing economic policy. Very often, economists understand their role as above sectional politics and see themselves rather in the service of "rationality," as theirs is a discipline "whose intellectual achievements are held to be in the refinement of beautifully abstract and highly mathematized models" (Markoff and Montecinos 1993, 51). Economists regard themselves as scientists whose interest is in producing knowledge. Whether that knowledge is of policy relevance is immaterial to them (Coats and Colander 1989, 2). Thus, scientization has served to depoliticize economic policy (Dyson and Marcussen 2009) and so contributes to insulating the prevailing orthodoxy from alternative models. More than this, scientized economics reduces the debate to one based on purely technical, and therefore apolitical, solutions that share the same assumption respecting macroeconomics. This depoliticization through scientization is not unique to the neoliberal state. Indeed, policy problems were framed by Keynesian economics as "technical questions to be solved by economic experts. Because the problems are understood as merely technical ones, they appear to be beyond the political sphere" (Wisman 1991, 118). What has changed, however, is that through the transition to neoliberalism, the architecture of power within the state, and the consequent effect on the policy process, has shifted significantly.

The assumption within economics is that it is not possible for scientized ideas to comingle with normative ones. As long ago as 1828, Jean-Baptiste Say argued that such issues as the distribution of wealth in society were political issues and not ones with which economics ought to be concerned. The focus of economics was on "production, distribution, and consumption" and marked by little interest in the role of political and economic power (Fontaine 1996, 387 and 388). Blyth dispels this claim with the observation that "all positive statements about the causal order of the economy necessarily imply value trade-offs and hence different patterns of distribution" (Blyth 2002, 11).

By way of illustration, six guiding ideas dominate contemporary neoclassical/liberal economics: (1) the Great Moderation: the belief that we have experienced unparalleled macroeconomic stability since 1985; (2) the Efficient Market Hypothesis: prices created in financial markets reflect the actual value of an investment; (3) Dynamic Stochastic General Equilibrium: the focus of economics should be on individual behaviour rather than on aggregates such as trade balances and debt; (4) Trickle-Down Economics: policies that benefit the wealthy will serve to everyone's benefit; (5) Privatization: private firms will be more effective than the public sector in providing any service/function; and (6) Austerity: the best response to the Great Financial Crisis, or any similar crisis, is for government to pursue a balanced budget policy and thereby desist from crowding out the private sector (Quiggin 2010, 2). These are hardly technocratic, apolitical nostrums. They establish a particular framing of the workings of the economy based on normative assumptions of cause and effect. In turn they limit the range of possible policy options available to decision-makers. And despite decades of economic policy based upon these ideas, the projected benefits have not materialized (Schneider and Kirchgässner 2009, 325). So ultimately, the policy preferences of the economist are less about science and evidence and more about deeply held values and beliefs respecting how the economic world works. The chief economic advisor to the British government during the period of post-war reconstruction noted that government economists are seriously challenged in their efforts to base their work on scientific evidence, as conflicting views about the interpretation of the same facts was a reality of policy advising. Ultimately, interpretation cannot be anything but normative, given the lack of agreement even over facts (Hall 1955, 126, 130, and 134). Fast forward to the years following the Great Financial Crisis, and mainstream economics is "dismissive" of any criticism, and the intellectual stubbornness of its adherents' work is akin to that of "zealots" rather than objective scientists (Keen 2011, 4). To this point Stiglitz wrote that "neoliberal market fundamentalism was always a political doctrine serving certain interests" (Stiglitz 2008).

The exogenization of politics from economics is analogous to the public administrative theory of the politics-administrative dichotomy. The dichotomy posits a sharp division of labour within the policy process. The elected political leadership have a mandate to decide on policy while the public service, as a neutral but technically competent instrument, would implement those directions. Applying this doctrine to economists whose function is to provide policy advice to government ministers would mean, in practice, that their role would be limited to preparing the analyses, while the political leadership would then formulate their policy response based on that analysis. The reality is that policy work is much more blurred than this mechanical division of labour imagines (Marris 1954, 759). The economist advisors frame the problem on the basis of their understanding of the economy, and this in turn establishes the range of acceptable policy interventions. But in addition, economic policy is rarely, if ever, determined by purely technical analysis. Economic policy is, by definition, laden with political factors, and who is going to get what, when, and how is not determined by mathematical formulations.

There is another dimension to the role of economic policy advisors, which speaks to a particular inability to understand themselves as "captured" by their own self-interest. A key theoretical perspective underlying orthodox economics is public choice. Here, all human behaviour is understood by the drive for utility maximization. But somehow economists fail to apply this motivation to their own role. Public sector workers are characterized as "rent seekers" by economists who adopt the analytical approach of public choice theory. But is this a case of the pot calling the kettle black (Peacock 1994, 191)? This notion of capture applies equally to economists who produce work for the consumption of government and business. Economists who cater to the knowledge needs of government and business will find that they are in demand for well-compensated consulting and other career-enhancing opportunities if they produce research conforming to what is deemed acceptable (Zingales 2014, 125). In short, the economists who work to produce policy and business advice have a serious disincentive not to challenge established centres of power. The privatization of policy advice has led to an expanding "consultocracy" (Hood and Jackson 1991), which is one aspect of what Wilks in this volume refers to as the "public services industry" – the commodification of public service functions through outsourcing. The policy "products" are seen to be of questionable quality and are designed expressly to reinforce government objectives rather than fully canvass the range of alternatives (Howlett and Migone 2014).

Contemporary neoclassical economic theory functions "mainly as a surrogate ideology for the market economy" (Keen 2011, 4) and economists are the principal carriers for this ideology. State elite and their advisors "play an important part in the process of governmental deci-sion-making, and therefore constitute a considerable force in the con-figuration of political power" (Miliband 1969, 107). The roles are hardly narrowly technocratic, and importantly they are not apolitical. Gram-scian theory, particularly the concept of organic intellectuals, is useful in understanding the explicitly political role of ideational agents – in this case, economists but also state elites – as a transmission belt of neolib-eral ideas. Gramsci's insights contribute to understanding neoliberal resiliency within the key institutions of the state. First, it refocuses the traditional preoccupation of public policy and administration with insti-tutions and "techniques" ("technocratism") by introducing the trans-formative potential of ideology to "reprogram" the state apparatus; and second, a Gramscian framework provides a means of understand-ing "how" the state "changes its mind" and becomes an instrument in driving a new political project. Ideational agents and state elites work in tandem in "consolidating specific accumulation regimes" (Blyth 2002, 6). Organic intellectuals provide leadership through their work as organizers of "social hegemony and state domination" (Gramsci 1971, 12–13). As with state elites, economists are not neutral actors but are instead an influential force in restructuring the state. And since 2008, despite their failures, neoliberal economists have only "consolidated their occupation of the glittering heights" (Mirowski 2013, 158).

The Political and Policy Architecture of the Neoliberal State

It is the most remarkable example of ideological sleight of hand that neoliberalism is presented as a force hostile to the state. The historical record demonstrates the opposite. The objective of neoliberalism has been to command the state in order to employ its capacities to drive neoliberal policies into all domains of economy and society (Lapavitsas 2014, 7). Policy innovation begins with the transfer of new ideas into the state's policy advisory system. To gain traction, these ideas "must first be held to be 'legitimate' to be taken seriously. And to gain that status, these ideas must align with the 'structural-economic relations rooted in the dynamics of capitalism and its power relations can be seen to set boundaries' on what is understood as legitimate" (Bradford 1999, 18). In addition, the institutional arrangements of the state work to process and filter policy ideas coming forward. Those that cross the threshold of legitimacy, move forward; those that do not are abandoned. Rather than diminish the state and its institutions, neoliberalism reconfigures the distribution of power within and between the state's component parts and its relationship to forces outside of the state such as capital, labour, and other civil society movements (Harvey 2005, 78). To enable this process, there is a specific architecture of power within the state. The neoliberal state has reordered the location of authoritative power within the state from where it had existed in the Keynesian welfare state, and this has been consequential in insulating the state policy advisory system from alternative ideas that challenge neoliberal orthodoxy.

Centralization of Power and Politicization of the State

The authoritarian tendency within neoliberalism derives from an understanding of democratic politics as problematic. The 1975 Report of the Trilateral Commission contended that the Western democracies were "overloaded with participants and demands" and as such were overwhelmed with an "excess of democracy" (Crozier, Huntington, and Watanuki 1975, 12). The post-war welfare state came to be equated with ungovernability, with the conclusion that mass democracy and welfare state policies, a politics where subordinate social actors had some influence over policy, was diagnosed as the root of the problem. This speaks to an apparent paradox at the heart of neoliberalism and, with respect to Thatcherism in Britain, that Gamble characterized as a contradiction where "a free economy was also understood by some to mean a state strong enough to intervene actively in all institutions of civil society to impose, nurture and stimulate the business values, attitudes and practices necessary to relaunch Britain as a successful capitalist economy" (Gamble 1988, 232). To formulate and implement such interventions requires a concentration of decision-making authority and policy capacity at the centre of the state. The "strong state" Gamble refers to is in practical terms a strategy to centralize greater power in the political executive (Savoie 1994, 187). This centralization of power is well documented and is a general phenomenon in the initiation of the neoliberal project. In New Zealand, a Cabinet Policy Committee was established in 1985 to review and coordinate all policy initiatives from across the government. In the United Kingdom, Thatcher disbanded the Central Policy Review Staff unit in 1983, which served all of Cabinet, and expanded the role of the Prime Minister's Policy Unit to better support the strategic goals of the government (Willetts 1987). Thatcher found this unit, in comparison to the CPRS, much more responsive to her policy needs as a "conviction" politician. She found that "a policy unit reporting directly to the prime minister, on the other hand, had her political agenda at the top of its priority" (Savoie 1994, 203). The paradox is that rather than depoliticization, we observe a movement to repoliticize the state by concentrating policymaking authority in specific strategic centres. Moreover, the political arm of government is strengthened, which is to say the policy capacity of the executive is increased dramatically, a phenomenon that has been termed the New Political Governance (Aucoin 2010). Given the political challenges inherent in the restructuring and marketization project, this is a necessary tactic in marshalling the political/managerial resources to overcome political and sectional opposition. In the 1980s, neoliberal governments seized "power over strategic decisions, especially expenditure budgets, [and they] became inexorably concentrated at the centre, that is, in the offices of the prime ministers and presidents, and in treasury or finance departments" (Aucoin 1996, 647). Resurrecting the politics-administrative dichotomy where state managers are concerned with implementation and where the governors are concerned with setting policy and priorities, became an important dimension of neoliberal governance (Rhodes 1994, 139). Such reforms communicate a clear and negative signal to the public service that their political masters possess little faith in the neutrality of the bureaucracy. The public policy expertise upon which governments rely is increasingly centred outside of the civil service. Public policy work becomes politicized as work that had been the purview of the public service is "turned over to ... partisan policy advisors, to think tanks and to lobby firms for advice" (Savoie 1993, 21–2).

Politicization is not to be conflated with partisanship, as party association is much less important than a sharing of values and an overall orientation of being "one of us," as Margaret Thatcher would query of senior public servants. That is, a key job qualification is the possession of a shared ideological conviction respecting the necessity for public sector restructuring (Peters and Pierre 2004, 2). With the centralization of decision-making at the apex of the administrative state, that is where the politics over policy choices is contested; public service advisors are either shunted aside or are recruited for their "political" fit. For Whitehall scholar Peter Hennessey, the expanding role of external policy advice has produced "an era when the Armani-clad minds in the penumbra of fad-and-fashion prone private think tanks can be preferred (especially if their advice comes gift-wrapped and suitably politically tinted) to that more sober, sometimes inconvenient fare served up by the tweed-clad minds in the career bureaucracy" (1997, 4–5).

These conjoined tendencies to the centralization of power and the politicization of the state are not intended to diminish the power of the state but rather reshape it. Leading transformation necessitates an enabled centre of government. As noted, a "strong state" is the necessary midwife to a different kind of state.

In Canada, as with most countries and especially those in the Westminster model, through the golden age of the Keynesian welfare state, so-called government line departments – departments responsible for program delivery and/or regulatory enforcement – provided key roles in conducting policy research and development. Policy proposals generally move "upward" through the line departments/ministries to cabinet committees for political consideration and decision. The sources informing policy proposals were varied: stakeholders, issues identified by frontline field offices, collaboratively developed with other departments or agencies, and politically directed by the executive. Policy advocacy for redistribution was robust and supported by influential cabinet ministers and knowledgeable senior state managers who were supported with public service–led policy analysis (Good 2013, 213). Given the policy activism of the public service, and the inherently political nature of all policy work, this role contradicts the doctrine of the politics-administrative dichotomy and was an area of significant concern for neoliberals.

The political arm of government has become more robust through centralization of power in the executive. Expanding numbers of political staff provide an alternative source of analysis and advice to ministers and thus contribute to shifting power and influence away from the line departments and towards the political arm of government (White 2001, 21). This expansion of capacity and the consequent shifting of power towards ministers' offices, together with the expansion of the role of the centre of government (finance ministry, executive leadership such as the Prime Minister's Office), are said to constitute the emergence of a "new political governance" (Aucoin 2010, 64). Finance departments in particular have taken on a commanding role in "gatekeeping," blocking policy innovation deemed out of step with economic policy objectives. Moreover, they have become the overarching policy designer for the entire government. The result is a significant shift in power within the state where the "most critical issues of policy direction, resources, and program design are being handled directly and exclusively by the central players ... the policy advice of deputy ministers is becoming guarded, provided in a complaint fashion to address predetermined priorities" (Good 2013, 215–16).

Depoliticizing Monetary Policy: The Case of Central Bank Independence

The scientization of economics provides one means to depoliticize economic policy. A second tactic, emerging in the 1980s, where governments began to release their direct control over monetary policy by providing their central banks with either substantially more autonomy within certain constraints or complete independence. The primary rationales put forward in support for central bank independence were: (1) the *prevailing theoretical perspective* in ascendant monetarist economics was that manipulation of monetary policy would not reduce unemployment and would contribute to inflationary pressures; and (2) *globalization*, as manifested by the deregulation of trade and investment barriers, with resulting free movement of capital, render expansionary monetary policies – which lead to currency devaluation within a single state – ineffective and instead contribute to inflation and declining productivity (Carruthers, Babb, and Halliday 2001, 98–9). The case of central bank independence presents an innovation that provides an institutional expression of the notion that monetary policy is of such a purely technical nature that its formulation must be kept beyond the reach of self-serving politicians and their captured state managers. In this sense, central bank independence is a technocratic patina that assumes that "politics is restricted to the realm of government and politicians ... a central bank which is independent of that realm is therefore regarded as apolitical" (Bowles and White 1994, 240). This important institutional innovation is further an expression of the process of constructing a specifically neoliberal state designed to provide a structured foundation for ruling class interests in the era of financialized capitalism (Lapavitsas 2014, 3).

Of course, to say that economic policy is apolitical is absurd. And that central banks, as paramount policymaking institution in their own right, are better able to manage the economy by being free of political interference challenges the very idea of democracy. The political nature of these institutions has been bluntly stated, and with respect to the Federal Reserve, the central bank of the United States: "The political agenda of Wall Street dominates Federal Reserve policy, and the Federal Reserve is the predominant force in formulating and implementing national economic policy" (Pollin and Luce 1998, 6). Indeed, the sector that has benefited most from the actions of the neoliberal state is that of finance (Lapavitsas 2014, 7). Notwithstanding, the argument that counter-cyclical expansionary fiscal and monetary policy is politically driven while the central bank's preoccupation with low inflation is not, the argument that it is necessary to insulate monetary policy from electoral and other political pressures speaks directly to the objective of privileging certain interests over others. Central bank independence is ultimately concerned with placing constraints on which social and economic interests economic policymakers serve. And banking and financial sector interests are the uncontested beneficiaries of monetary stability (Carruthers, Babb, and Halliday 2001, 102).

In the wake of the Great Financial Crisis, the decisions by central banks, supported by their allied institutions in the form of the International Monetary Fund and World Bank, gave priority, and necessarily so, to private banks and other financial institutions. This motivation of the action, covering the well-trodden terrain of "too big to fail" and saving global capitalism from itself, was more than just the revival on Keynesian-like market intervention. Its objective in political economy terms was nothing less than the restoration of a particular form of class power that had been consolidated through the previous three decades. The crisis of 2007–8 was exceptional only in its magnitude, but crises of this nature were not unknown. Drawing lessons from the experiences of the 1987–8 savings and loans crisis, and the 1997 collapse of hedge fund Long Term Capital Management, Harvey wrote, "Neoliberal states typically facilitate the diffusion of influence of financial institutions through deregulation, but then they also too often guarantee the integrity and solvency of financial institutions at no matter what cost. This commitment in part derives from reliance upon monetarism as the basis of state policy – the integrity and soundness of money is a central pinion of that policy" (Harvey 2005, 73). In these cases, the state intervened to inject billions of dollars to ensure state money remained stable.

While neoliberalism looks formally askance at the prospect of any form of state intervention in the economy, financialization was enabled by state intervention, and most significantly so by central banks, by "providing liquidity and their ability to influence interest rates" in support of private banks. In addition, the state has drawn on public resources, including tax revenue, to subsidize the sector and shift the cost of financial market failure onto the public sector (Lapavitsas 2014, 3 and 13). Given such an audacious and explicit defence of the finance capitalist class, with the resultant shifting of the cost for failures onto the state, public sector workers, and public services, the movement towards central bank autonomy is a rational political strategy of insulation. Central bank independence, in this context, is sufficiently insulated from political interference so it can pursue "unpopular monetary policies" such as increasing interest rates, which affect not only consumers but also governments, who then are forced to reduce public expenditures (Carruthers, Babb, and Halliday 2001, 118).

Conclusion

The resilience of neoliberal economic ideas in informing policy is at least in part a function of the structure of the state and its policy advisory system. The manifest depth of centralization of power in tandem with significant politicization (or should we say re-politicization) establishes a barrier that excludes competing ideas from entering the policy process within the state. The process is highly exclusionary, and this in turn reflects the class nature of the state. The organization of the state, that is its division into different institutions, structures each policy sector. This is turn reflects the uneven distribution in society at large. The financialization of the economy has given unprecedented power to finance ministries and central banks, which have emerged as preeminent policy designers. Bluntly, this is a structure of domination from which the state cannot escape (Ham and Hill 1984, 179). The neoliberal state is immensely more instrumental in class terms than was the Keynesian welfare state. But none of this would matter a great deal if not for the ideational agents. To link ideas to political institutions and processes requires agents, and to this end, the intellectuals, economists, and state managers provide ideational leadership as organizers of "social hegemony and state domination" (Gramsci 1971, 187). Their role is nothing less than pivotal in their unrelenting framing of policy problems through the lens of neoliberalism.

REFERENCES

Andreou, Alex. 2014. "Christine Lagarde Thinks the Troika Got It Wrong on Greece? If Only She Knew." *Guardian*, 24 February. http://www. theguardian.com/commentisfree/2014/feb/24/christine-lagarde-troika-wrong-on-greece.
Aucoin, Peter. 1995. "Politicians, Public Servants and Public Management: Getting Government Right." In *Governance in a Changing Environment*, ed.

B. Guy Peter and Donald Savoie, 113–37. Montreal and Kingston: McGill-Queen's University Press.

– 1996. "Political Science and Democratic Governance." *Canadian Journal of Political Science* 29 (4): 643–60. http://dx.doi.org/10.1017/S0008423900014414.

– 2010. "Canada." In *Partisan Appointees and Public Servants: An International Analysis of the Role of the Political Advisor*, ed. Chris Eichbaum and Richard Shaw, 64–93. Northhampton, MA: Edward Elgar. http://dx.doi.org/10.4337/9781849803298.00008.

Beams, Nick. 2012. "Conflicts Come to the Surface at IMF–World Bank Meeting." World Socialist Web Site. http://www.wsws.org/en/articles/2012/10/pers-o17.html.

Béland, Daniel. 2009. "Ideas, Institutions, and Policy Change." *Journal of European Public Policy* 16 (5): 701–18.

Béland, Daniel, and Mitchell A. Orenstein. 2013. "International Organizations as Policy Actors: An Ideational Approach." *Global Social Policy* 13 (2): 125–43.

Blyth, Mark. 2002. *Great Transformations*. New York: Cambridge University Press. http://dx.doi.org/10.1017/CBO9781139087230.

Bowles, Paul, and Gordon White. 1994. "Central Bank Independence: A Political Economy Approach." *Journal of Development Studies* 31 (2): 235–64. http://dx.doi.org/10.1080/00220389408422359.

Bradford, Neil. 1999. "The Policy Influence of Economic Ideas: Interests, Institutions and Innovation in Canada." *Studies in Political Economy* 59 (summer): 17–60. http://dx.doi.org/10.1080/19187033.1999.11675266.

Brock, Karen, Andrea Cornwall, and John Gaventa. 2001. "Power, Knowledge and Political Spaces in the Framing of Poverty Policy." Working Paper #143. Brighton: Institute of Development Studies.

Cahill, Damien. 2014. *The End of Laissez-Faire? On the Durability of Embedded Neoliberalism*. Cheltenham, UK: Edward Elgar.

Carruthers, Bruce, Sarah Babb, and Terence Halliday. 2001. "Institutionalizing Markets or the Market for Institutions? Central Banks, Bankruptcy Law, and the Globalization of Financial Markets." In *The Rise of Neoliberalism and Institutional Analysis*, ed. John Campbell and Ove Pedersen, 94–126. Princeton, NJ: Princeton University Press.

Coats, A.W., and David Colander. 1989. "An Introduction to the Spread of Economic Ideas." In *The Spread of Economic Ideas*, ed. David Colander and A.W. Coats, 1–22. Cambridge: Cambridge University Press.

Collignon, Stefan. 2008. "The Dawn of a New Era: Social Democracy after the Financial Crisis." *Social Europe* 4 (1): 9–13.

Crouch, Colin. 2011. *The Strange Non-Death of Neoliberalism*. Cambridge: Policy.

Crozier, Michel, Samuel P. Huntington, and Joji Watanuki. 1975. *The Crisis of Democracy: Report on the Governability of Democracies to the Trilateral Commission*. New York: New York University Press.

Deutsche Welle. 2014. "German Finance Minister Schauble Warns against Economic Alarmism." DW Akademie. http://www.dw.com/en/german-finance-minister-sch%C3%A4uble-warns-against-economic-alarmism/a-17988962.

Dyson, Kenneth, and Martin Marcussen. 2009. "Scientization of Central Banking: The Politics of Apoliticization." In *Central Banks in the Age of the Euro: Europeanization, Convergence and Power*, ed. Kenneth Dyson and Martin Marcussen, 373–90. Oxford: Oxford University Press.

Evans, Bryan. 2005. "How the State Changes Its Mind: A Gramscian Account of Ontario's Managerial Culture Change." *Philosophy of Management* 5 (2): 25–46. http://dx.doi.org/10.5840/pom20055220.

Fischer, Frank, and John Forester. 1993. "Editors' Introduction." In *The Argumentative Turn in Policy Analysis and Planning*, ed. Frank Fischer and John Forrester, 1–17. Durham, NC: Duke University Press. http://dx.doi.org/10.1215/9780822381815-001.

Fontaine, Philippe. 1996. "The French Economists and Politics, 1750–1850: The Science and Art of Political Economy." *Canadian Journal of Economics/Revue canadienne d'économique* 29 (2): 379–93. http://dx.doi.org/10.2307/136295.

Gamble, Andrew. 1988. *The Free Economy and the Strong State: The Politics of Thatcherism*. Durham, NC: Duke University Press. http://dx.doi.org/10.1007/978-1-349-19438-4.

– 2013. "Neoliberalism and Fiscal Conservatism." In *Resilient Neoliberalism in Europe's Political Economy*, ed. Vivien Schmidt and Mark Thatcher, 53–76. New York: Cambridge University Press. http://dx.doi.org/10.1017/CBO9781139857086.004.

Good, David. 2013. "The New Bureaucratic Politics of Redistribution." In *Inequality and the Fading of Redistributive Politics*, ed. Keith Banting and John Myles, 210–33. Vancouver: UBC Press.

Gourevitch, Peter. 1989. "Keynesian Politics: The Political Sources of Economic Policy Choices." In *The Political Power of Economic Ideas*, ed. Peter Hall, 87–106. Princeton, NJ: Princeton University Press.

Gramsci, Antonio. 1971. *Selections from the Prison Notebooks*. London: Lawrence and Wisehart.

Hall, Peter. 1993. "Policy Paradigms, Social Learning and the State: The Case of Economic Policy-Making in Britain." *Comparative Politics* 25 (3): 275–96. http://dx.doi.org/10.2307/422246.

Hall, Robert. 1955. "The Place of the Economist in Government." *Oxford Economics Papers*, n.s. 7 (2): 119–35.

Ham, Christopher, and Michael Hill. 1984. *The Policy Process in the Modern Capitalist State*. New York: St Martin's.

Harvey, David. 2005. *A Brief History of Neoliberalism*. Oxford: Oxford University Press.

Hay, Colin. 2004. "The Normalizing Role of Rationalist Assumptions in the Institutional Embedding of Neo-Liberalism." *Economy and Society* 33 (4): 500–27. http://dx.doi.org/10.1080/0308514042000285260.

Hennessey, Peter. 1997. "The Essence of Public Service." In *The John L. Manion Lecture Series*, 1–5. Ottawa: Canadian Centre for Management Development.

Hood, C., and M. Jackson. 1991. *Administrative Argument*. Aldershot, UK: Dartmouth.

Howlett, M., and A. Migone. 2014. "Making the Invisible Public Service Visible? Exploring Data on the Supply of Policy Management Consultancies in Canada." *Canadian Public Administration* 57 (2): 183–216. http://dx.doi.org/10.1111/capa.12065.

Karger, Howard. 2014. "The Bitter Pill: Austerity, Debt, and the Attack on Europe's Welfare States." *Journal of Sociology and Social Welfare* 41 (2): 33–53.

Keen, Steve. 2011. *Debunking Economics*. London: Zed Books.

Keynes, John M. 1936. *The General Theory of Employment, Interest and Money*. London: Macmillan.

Lapavitsas, Costas. 2014. *State and Finance in Financialised Capitalism*. London: Centre for Labour and Social Studies.

Lindvall, Johannes. 2009. "The Real but Limited Influence of Expert Ideas." *World Politics* 61 (4): 703–30. http://dx.doi.org/10.1017/S0043887109990104.

Markoff, John, and Veronica Montecinos. 1993. "The Ubiquitous Rise of Economists." *Journal of Public Policy* 13 (1): 37–68. http://dx.doi.org/10.1017/S0143814X00000933.

Marris, R.L. 1954. "The Position of Economics and Economists in the Government Machine." *Economic Journal (London)* 64 (256): 759–83. http://dx.doi.org/10.2307/2228043.

Miliband, Ralph. 1969. *The State in Capitalist Society*. London: Quartet Books.

Mintrom, M. 1997. "Policy Entrepreneurs and the Diffusion of Innovation." *American Journal of Political Science* 41 (3): 738–70. http://dx.doi.org/10.2307/2111674.

Mintrom, M., and S. Vergari. 1996. "Advocacy Coalitions, Policy Entrepreneurs, and Policy Change." *Policy Studies Journal: The Journal of the Policy Studies Organization* 24 (3): 420–34. http://dx.doi.org/10.1111/j.1541-0072.1996.tb01638.x.

Mirowski, Philip. 2013. *Never Let a Serious Crisis Go to Waste: How Neoliberalism Survived the Financial Meltdown*. London: Verso.

Noveck, B. 2011. "The Single Point of Failure." In *Open Government: Collaboration, Transparency, and Participation in Practice*, ed. Daniel Lathrop and Laurel Ruma, 49–70. Sebastopol, CA: O'Reilly Media.

Pautz, H. 2012. *Think-Tanks, Social Democracy and Social Policy*. New York: Palgrave Macmillan. http://dx.doi.org/10.1057/9780230368545.

Peacock, Alan. 1994. "The Utility Maximizing Government Economic Advisor: A Comment." *Public Choice* 80 (1–2): 191–7. http://dx.doi.org/10.1007/BF01047955.

Peck, Jamie. 2015. *Austerity Urbanism: The Neoliberal Crisis of American Cities*. New York: Rosa Luxemburg Stiftung.

Peters, B. Guy. 1999. *Institutional Theory in Political Science: The New Institutionalism*. London: Continuum.

Peters, B. Guy, and Jon Pierre. 2004. "Politicization of the Civil Service: Concepts, Causes, Consequences." In *Politicization of the Civil Service in Comparative Perspective: The Quest for Control*, ed. B. Guy Peters and Jon Pierre, 1–13. London: Routledge.

Pollin, Robert, and Stephanie Luce. 1998. *The Living Wage: Building a Fair Economy*. New York: New.

Pollin, Robert, and Jeffrey Thompson. 2011. "Fighting Austerity and Reclaiming a Future for State and Local Governments." *New Labour Forum* 30 (3): 22–30.

Pusey, Michael. 1991. *Economic Rationalism in Canberra: A Nation-Building State Changes Its Mind*. New York: Cambridge University Press.

Quiggin, John. 2010. *Zombie Economics: How Dead Ideas Still Walk among Us*. Princeton, NJ: Princeton University Press.

Radice, Hugo. 2010. "Confronting the Crisis: A Class Analysis." In *Socialist Register: The Crisis This Time*, ed. Leo Panitch, Greg Albo, and Vivek Chibber, 21–43. London: Merlin.

Rhodes, R.A.W. 1994. "The Hollowing Out of the State: The Changing Nature of the Public Service in Britain." *Political Quarterly* 65 (2): 138–51. http://dx.doi.org/10.1111/j.1467-923X.1994.tb00441.x.

Sabatier, P.A. 1988. "An Advocacy Coalition Framework of Policy Change and the Role of Policy-Oriented Learning Therein." *Policy Sciences* 21 (2–3): 129–68. http://dx.doi.org/10.1007/BF00136406.

Sabatier, P.A., and C. Weible. 2002. "The Advocacy Coalition Framework: Innovations and Clarifications." In *Theories of the Policy Process*, ed. P.A. Sabatier, 189–220. Boulder, CO: Westview.

Savoie, Donald. 1993. *Globalization and Governance*. Ottawa: Canadian Centre for Management Development.

– 1994. *Thatcher, Reagan, Mulroney: Search of a New Bureaucracy*. Toronto: University of Toronto Press.

Schmidt, Vivien, and Mark Thatcher. 2013. "Theorizing Ideational Continuity: The Resilience of Neo-Liberal Ideas in Europe." In *Resilient Neoliberalism in Europe's Political Economy*, ed. Vivien Schmidt and Mark Thatcher, 1–50. New York: Cambridge University Press. http://dx.doi.org/10.1017/CBO9781139857086.002.

Schneider, Friedrich, and Gebhard Kirchgässner. 2009. "Financial and World Economic Crisis: What Did Economists Contribute?" *Public Choice* 140 (3–4).

Stiglitz, Joseph. 2008. "The End of Neoliberalism." *Project Syndicate*. https://www.project-syndicate.org/commentary/the-end-of-neo-liberalism?barrier= accessreg.

Strange, Gerard. 2012. "Understanding the Fundamentals of Capital, the Crisis and the Alternatives: Marx's Legacy beyond Revolutionary Marxism." *British Journal of Politics and International Relations* 15 (1): 107–24. http://dx.doi.org/10.1111/j.1467-856X.2012.00542.x.

Tomasi di Lampedusa, Giuseppe. 1958. *Il Gattopardo*. Milan: Casa editrice Feltrinelli.

White, Graham. 2001. "Adapting the Westminster Model: Provincial and Territorial Cabinets in Canada." *Public Money & Management* 21 (2): 17–24. http://dx.doi.org/10.1111/1467-9302.00255.

Willetts, David. 1987. "The Role of the Prime Minister's Policy Unit." *Public Administration* 65 (4): 443–54. http://dx.doi.org/10.1111/j.1467-9299.1987.tb00674.x.

Wisman, Jon. 1991. "The Scope and Goals of Economic Science." In *Economics and Hermeneutics*, ed. Don Lavoie, 113–33. London: Routledge.

Zingales, Luigi. 2014. "Preventing Economists' Capture." In *Preventing Regulatory Capture*, ed. Daniel Carpenter and David Moss, 124–51. New York: Cambridge University Press.

Zito, Anthony. 2011. "Policy Framing." In *The International Encyclopedia of Political Science*, ed. Bertrand Badie, Derk Berg-Schlosser, and Leonardo Morlino, 1924–8. Thousand Oaks, CA: Sage Publications. http://dx.doi.org/10.4135/9781412959636.n445.

11 Tax Havens in an Austere World: The Clash of New Ideas and Existing Interests

RICHARD WOODWARD

Aside from fleeting interest in some particularly egregious scandals, tax havens rarely pervaded the public consciousness prior to the global financial crisis of 2007–8. Likewise, some notable exceptions notwithstanding (see, for example, Hampton 1996; Palan 2003; Sharman 2006), tax havens and offshore finance were seldom the subject of serious scholarly study. Indeed the academic community and the public at large appeared to regard tax havens as some kind of "exotic sideshow" (Shaxson 2011, 7) remote from everyday life and unrelated to broader developments in the global economy. In fact, as a spate of recent literature has demonstrated (Palan, Murphy, and Chavagneux 2010; Shaxson 2011; vanFossen 2012; Brooks 2013; Eccleston 2013; Gravelle 2013; Findley, Nielson, and Sharman 2014; Urry 2014; Deneault 2015; Zucman 2015), nothing could be further from the truth. During recent decades tax havens have become integral parts of the global economic landscape whose existence is indispensable to the overarching economic strategies of major economic actors and central to many of the most pressing conundrums of global governance (Wojcik 2013), including underdevelopment, prudential regulation, money laundering, and, the main theme of this chapter, tax evasion and avoidance.

The global financial crisis hammered home the truth about tax havens. Although they were not directly incriminated in the causes of the crisis, it is widely held that tax havens hastened its arrival through regulations that allowed and encouraged the build-up of debt and secretive financial structures that prevented financiers from accurately assessing the creditworthiness of their counterparties, thus intensifying the initial credit crunch (OECD 2009; IMF 2009). Against this background it is unsurprising that tax havens have been a key focus of post-crisis efforts to reform the international financial architecture; however, two other factors generated extra momentum. First, whereas tax policy and administration were previously treated as technical matters whose discussion was dominated by lawyers, accountants, and government revenue officials, the post-crisis environment lent oxygen to civil society organizations campaigning for curbs on tax havens as part of a broader package of measures to promote "tax justice." By gleefully and imaginatively seizing upon some of the most blatant examples of tax avoidance and evasion by corporations and high-net-worth individuals and juxtaposing this with the austerity inflicted upon the majority of citizens, the tax justice campaigns have alerted governments and public opinion to the distributional consequences of these seemingly technical discussions. As well as stoking considerable public discontent, these campaigns have advanced the case for enhancing tax transparency, pointing out that it would make it difficult, or at least potentially embarrassing, for corporations and rich individuals to sidestep their tax obligations, an innovation that would obviate, or at the very least alleviate, the need for austerity. Second, for governments looking to stanch bloodletting on their public balance sheets, a crackdown on tax shirkers was fiscally and electorally appealing. By its very nature, a precise measure of the "tax gap" arising from tax avoidance and evasion remains elusive. Nevertheless, Zucman (2014, 140) estimates that governments lose $190 billion in tax revenue annually from undeclared offshore assets, while Citizens for Tax Justice (2014, 7) believe the United States alone loses $110 billion each year to corporate tax avoidance.

The combination of gaping deficits, public anger, and an increasingly animated campaign agitating for international tax transparency created a climate conducive to a crackdown on territories thought to be facilitating tax avoidance and evasion. Desperately casting around for policies that would give the impression that they were mounting an effective response to the crisis, the G20 latched onto and gave fresh impetus to the Organisation for Economic Cooperation and Development's (OECD's) seemingly moribund international tax transparency project. At its London Summit in April 2009, the G20 (2009) proclaimed that "the era of banking secrecy is over," pledged to take "action against non-cooperative jurisdictions," and stood "ready to deploy sanctions to protect our public finances and financial systems." The gradual strengthening of the OECD's project, as well as further tax transparency initiatives aimed at individual tax evasion (such as the unilateral US Foreign Account Tax Compliance Act [FATCA] [2010] and the

European Union's Directive on Administrative Cooperation in the field of taxation), and latterly corporations (e.g., the G20/OECD's Base Erosion and Profit Shifting [BEPS] scheme [2013] and the EU's Tax Transparency Package [2015]) give the outward appearance of a determined effort to constrict tax haven activities. Nonetheless, the authors cited in the opening paragraph and the civil society groups monitoring this issue have heaped scorn on the weaknesses of these initiatives. Indeed, despite protests from many tax havens, the empirical evidence suggests overwhelmingly that they continue to prosper (Boston Consulting Group 2014; Johannesen and Zucman 2014).

As the burgeoning post-crisis literature on tax havens and global tax governance avers, the reasons why meaningful reform of the international tax regime is proceeding slowly, despite ostensibly propitious circumstances, are complex. Virtually all of this writing points to the fact that fresh ideas to inject greater transparency into international tax affairs have struggled to gain traction, because they have run headlong into entrenched interests, not least the transnational tax-planning industry and their clients. This chapter takes a slightly different tack, arguing, perhaps counterintuitively, that a systematic campaign to eradicate tax havens is not in the interests of many leading states. In particular it suggests that the preference of elites for austerity rather than a genuine clampdown on tax havens is because the latter have become crucial elements of their overarching economic strategy. Indeed many states have aggressively promoted themselves as tax havens, writing laws with the express purpose of soliciting non-resident business. Although most commonly associated with small states, this "commercialisation" (Palan 2002) of state sovereignty is widely used by OECD states to siphon off rent surpluses that would otherwise accrue to their competitors. Since the 1950s, offshore finance and tax havens have developed in a haphazard manner, often as states have sought to advance their own interests or manage the instabilities and contradictions of the international economy. However, with each response, tax havens and the instruments they supply have progressively become intrinsic to the strategies and interests of key economic actors. The closure or a significant tapering of tax havens would endanger those economic strategies. Thus when faced with a choice between clamping down on tax havens and imposing austerity, leading states have invariably plumped for the latter. The choice of austerity represents the latest stage in the entrenchment of tax havens in state economic strategies, because the successful delivery of austerity is critically dependent on the instruments they supply.

The Rise of Offshore Financial Centres and Tax Havens

Popular conceptualizations of offshore, "special territorial or juridical enclaves characterised by a reduction in regulations" (Palan 1998, 626), conjure images of idyllic island settings whose physical detachment from the mainland provides sanctuary from the tentacles of "onshore" authorities. This view is somewhat misleading. While significant financial activities do occur in islands dotted around the Pacific and the Caribbean, many of the world's biggest offshore centres are located, in a physical sense, "onshore," most notably in London and New York. Increasingly therefore, most commentators argue the significance of offshore lies in its juridical rather than its physical properties. *Offshore* refers to the set of legal rules under which a transaction takes place, rules that may be very different from those prevailing in the physical location in which the transaction occurred (Palan 2003).

Tax havens are one of the most conspicuous manifestations of this offshore world (Urry 2014). The definition of a tax haven remains contested, but there is some agreement that they are jurisdictions that specialize in financial transactions for non-resident investors whom they attract by offering indulgent fiscal, regulatory, and legal frameworks. These inducements are complemented by a cloak of secrecy that camouflages these transactions, thus enabling them to circumvent tax and regulatory obligations in their country of residence (see Sharman 2006, 21; Hines 2010; Slemrod 2010). For example, although tax havens typically apply no or very low rates of taxation to investment income received by non-residents, alone these generous tax rates are not conducive to non-resident investors fleeing their tax obligations. This is because most countries tax investment income of their residents on a worldwide basis. This system relies on taxpayers declaring income earned overseas to their local revenue authorities. Taxpayers "have an economic incentive to under-report their true income. Because of this the enforcement of resident taxation relies on the intense exchange of information between tax authorities" (Rixen 2008, 61). Unfortunately the intensity and effectiveness of these exchanges are undermined by the failure of many tax havens to collect and share the necessary information. Although they have been weakened by the recent slew of international initiatives aimed at boosting transparency, for individuals the main attraction of tax havens was strict banking secrecy laws that made it a heavily punishable offence to reveal information about the owners of assets, except in criminal cases and structures such as trusts and foundations that conceal the real beneficiaries of assets. For corporations the principal attraction was the ability to set up a network of anonymous "shell" companies that cleave their "real" geographic activity and revenue from their profits. Using accounting tricks such as transfer pricing, multinational corporations are able to artificially shift their profits to tax haven jurisdictions and their losses (which can be used to reduce tax liabilities) to high-tax countries.

The contested definition of tax havens and their secrecy means the precise value of assets stockpiled offshore is unknown. Nevertheless, conservative estimates suggest that personal financial wealth held in tax havens grew from $11 billion in 1968 to $7.6 trillion in 2013 (Zucman 2014, 139). These figures, however, exclude financial assets hidden in trusts and non-financial assets such as yachts, works of art, and real estate. Transparency International's (2015) revelations that £122 billion of property in England and Wales is held by companies operating in tax haven jurisdictions gives credence to Henry's (2012) calculations that $21 trillion to $32 trillion of private wealth is held in tax havens. Figures from the Bank for International Settlements and the International Monetary Fund suggest that around half of banks' cross-border assets and liabilities and a third of foreign direct investment are routed offshore (Palan, Murphy, and Chavagneux 2010, 51) while 85 per cent of banking and bond issuance originates in the offshore Euromarkets (Lane and Milesi-Ferretti 2010). In short, "the offshore system is not just a colourful outgrowth of the global economy, but instead lies right at its centre" (Shaxson 2011, 9).

The centrality of tax havens to the contemporary global economy is far from accidental. While states have periodically checked the development of offshore for the most part, to paraphrase Polanyi, the road to offshore financial markets was opened and kept open by an enormous increase in continuous, centrally organized and controlled state interventionism. Many of the initial post-war developments in the rise of tax havens and offshore reflected unplanned responses (and non-responses) by states to specific developments, but the world soon witnessed the rise of "interests ... seeking to strengthen the institutional machinery that makes possible offshored worlds" (Urry 2014, 14) and the steady embedding of tax havens and offshore finance into the strategies of major economic actors. Indeed, by the mid-1980s, virtually all OECD countries had transformed themselves into tax havens and have subsequently subjugated their economic policies to the needs of tax haven interests.

The first tax havens appeared in the late nineteenth century, with several more, most notably Switzerland, Austria, and Liechtenstein, developing in the interwar period (Palan, Murphy, and Chavagneux 2010; see also Picciotto 1992). The placing of tax havens and offshore finance at the centre of the global economy gathered pace in the 1950s with the establishment of the Euromarkets. Scholars still debate the exact order of events and the constellation of ideas, interests, and institutions that gave rise to the Euromarkets (see, for example, Burn 1999, 2006; Helleiner 1994). Nevertheless, there is some agreement that the process commenced when banks in the City of London started accepting US dollar deposits from non-residents that were unrelated to trade or commerce. These banks then began lending to non-residents in dollars, effectively putting control over dollar credit at one remove from the American regulators. This practice was boosted by limits imposed by the United Kingdom on the use of sterling in response to periodic balance of payments crises. These restrictions endangered those City institutions whose core business was international lending to finance trade between third parties, and many responded by using dollars to finance them. Instead of intervening to restrict this innovation, which offered a way to circumvent the capital controls imposed under the Bretton Woods system, the Bank of England, sensing an opportunity to restore the City's international role by substituting a sterling empire for a dollar empire, chose to ignore it, arguing that even though they took place in London, financial transactions between non-residents in a foreign currency were not subject to UK regulation (Burn 1999; Kane 1983).

During the 1960s, the Euromarkets expanded briskly as persistent US deficits ensured a constant outflow of dollars and US investors flocked to London to escape regulatory oversight. Unenamoured about these developments the US government attempted to stifle the use of the Euromarkets, most notably through the Interest Equalisation Tax of 1963, a levy on foreign securities designed to deter US banks from exporting capital. This move backfired when US financial institutions scrambled to invest in the UK before the new regulations took effect. Thereafter the US softened its stance and was often a subtle supporter of the Euromarkets. Burn (2006) demonstrates that powerful banking interests in New York neutered proposals that would have subdued the budding offshore environment. Furthermore, successive US governments came to understand that the Euromarkets provided another means of preserving the dollar's pre-eminence as the international reserve currency, providing it with the "exorbitant privilege" of issuing debts denominated its own currency (Eichengreen 2010). As Douglas Dillon, US Under Secretary of State commented, Eurodollars provided "a good way of convincing foreigners to keep their deposits in dollars" (quoted in Helleiner 1996, 21) and allowed the US to shift the burdens of adjustment onto other countries. Various tax concessions were introduced to encourage US firms and banks to invest offshore as a method of entrenching US power. Underpinned by the interests of leading states and private financial actors assets invested in the Euromarkets grew from a value of $200 million in 1959 to over $1 billion in 1970.

Whereas the emergence of the Euromarkets was almost a historical accident, subsequent phases in the development of offshore financial centres and tax havens were more deliberate. One important aspect was the reinvigoration of a web of tax havens and offshore financial centres in small dependent territories, most notably those of the United Kingdom. In places such as the Channel Islands this process was driven principally by private financial institutions that set up in these locations to serve a wealthy clientele (Hampton 1996), but elsewhere, such as in the Isle of Man or the Cayman Islands (Freyer and Morriss 2013; Deneault 2015), efforts to establish offshore finance were purposefully steered by public authorities. The Bank of England, for example, foresaw the advantages of a network of havens that would funnel capital to the City of London. This strategy has been extraordinarily successful, with Foot (2009) reporting that the British Crown dependencies channelled $332.5 billion to the City in the second quarter of 2009. As well as being important booking centres for Euromarket transactions, the United Kingdom's network of offshore dependencies were also important in repairing the competitiveness of British banks. Euromarket rules that had allowed transactions between non-residents put UK banks at a disadvantage, but the development of offshore centres in Crown dependencies allowed them to create subsidiaries that would make them "non-resident" for the purpose of City transactions.

During the economic upheavals of the 1970s and 1980s, the Euromarkets started to become critical to global economic management. Spiro (1999) reveals how the United States exploited the Euromarkets to recycle OPEC wealth resulting from the oil crisis in a manner that underwrote the expansion of US private and government debt. The offshore world also dovetailed with prevailing ideas and economic interests. As low-tax, low-regulation environments, tax havens and offshore financial centres were lionized by apostles of the free market creed. Leading states began to aggressively tout themselves as tax havens, offering inducements for non-resident corporations and individuals to invest on the basis that these activities would be camouflaged from overseas tax authorities. Indeed by the 1990s many were asserting that the United States was the world's largest tax haven (Palan and Abbott 1996; Mitchell 2001). Policies designed to tempt non-residents to park their assets in the United States dated to the 1920s, but these were ramped up by a Reagan administration desperate to control the steepling deficits resulting from its economic and military program. In addition to introducing a raft of new exemptions for foreign-owned capital, the United States also moved closer to the United Kingdom's Euromarket model, introducing the International Banking Facility, which allowed US-based financial institutions to offer deposit and loan facilities to non-residents outside normal regulatory controls. US banks could now do from New York what they had previously done in London and the wider network of offshore centres, making the United States a magnet for inward investment. Furthermore, a string of US states including Delaware, Nevada, and Wyoming reinforced their own provision of tax haven services. The United States also became shrewder in its calls for greater transparency in international tax matters. The US government recognized that existing tax treaties enabled it to increase tax revenues by seeking information about the assets its citizens had squirrelled away overseas. However, if it did so it would also be obliged to tell its treaty partners about their residents with assets stationed in the United States, which could stimulate capital outflows as these investors fled to jurisdictions that continued to promise secrecy. To forestall this, the United States invented the Qualified Intermediary (QI) program, which gave responsibility for reporting not to treaty partners (governments) but to foreign banks, who were asked only to reveal details about US citizens. In a forerunner of FATCA, the QI program represented a classic mercantilist strategy whereby the United States sought to maximize its own tax revenues by demanding information from foreign banks about its citizens but refused to reciprocate with those seeking information about their own citizens with investments in the United States (Eccleston and Gray 2014).

By the late 1980s, the use of tax havens had become hard-wired into the economic strategies of leading states, many of whom started to believe their own rhetoric about the hyper-mobility of capital and concerns that investment would flee if they did not deliver a tax-friendly investment environment. As Richard Brooks's (2013) analysis of the United Kingdom has demonstrated, the result has been the craven capitulation of government to firms of lawyers and accountants peddling legislation that will allow them to design tax-avoidance schemes for their clients. While it is often assumed that lawyers and accountants engage in a cat-and-mouse game with governments, with the former looking to sneak around tightly written tax laws drafted by the latter, the reality is that the cat and the mouse conspire, and the government's mission is "unashamedly to adjust the framework of tax legislation to suit large businesses" (28). Inversions, the relocation of a corporation's headquarters to a foreign location while retaining its material operations at home, are merely the latest newsworthy issue in this regard.

The Financial Crisis: The Clash of New Ideas with Existing Ideas and Interests

Today there is a rich and vibrant movement campaigning against tax havens as part of a wider battle to promote "tax justice." For example, the Financial Transparency Coalition (2014), an alliance of civil society organizations, governments, and independent academic and professional experts urging an end to financial secrecy, now boasts over 150 members. In addition to the emergence of associations and organizations devoted specifically to these questions such as the Tax Justice Network and Global Financial Integrity, the issue of tax avoidance and evasion has been mainstreamed into the agendas of high-profile organizations such as Oxfam, Christian Aid, and Transparency International. A coruscating series of reports from non-governmental organizations and international organizations, in addition to sleuthing from journalistic organisations, most notably the International Consortium of Investigative Journalists (ICIJ) through high-profile stories like "Luxleaks" (ICIJ 2014b) (which revealed that PwC had negotiated 548 sweetheart deals with the Luxembourg government for 340 multinational companies) and "Swissleaks" (ICIJ 2015) (which highlighted HSBC's role in assisting clients to engage in a spectrum of illegal behaviour, including tax evasion) have kept the issue in the spotlight. This contrasts sharply with the situation a decade earlier where discussions of tax issues were dominated by pro-market civil society organizations lobbying for lower taxes and, despite some ephemeral interest (see Oxfam 2000), ignored by groups pushing for social justice. Indeed as its brief official history attests, when it was launched in 2003 the ideas of the Tax Justice Network garnered little enthusiasm, even among what might be regarded as natural allies such as trades unions (Tax Justice Network 2014a). Over the next few years, the ideas of tax justice advocates slowly seeped into mainstream policy debates, but it was unquestionably the financial crisis that oxygenated these ideas and catalyzed the movement (Eccleston 2013).

Prior to the financial crisis, tax justice activists had taken issue with the orthodoxy that lower taxes on the rich and corporations, including the effective tax cuts resulting from these actors engaging in tax avoidance and evasion, would be an incentive to take risk and leave more spare capital to be invested to raise economic growth and productivity. First, they pointed out that much of this capital is tied up in offshore financial assets and never finds its way into productive investment. For example, many states create inducements for multinationals to send money overseas by allowing them to defer paying taxes on profits attributed to foreign entities. Unsurprisingly many multinational corporations choose to reinvest this money offshore rather than repatriate it. In 2013, the offshore reinvested earnings of large capitalized US companies amounted to $2.119 trillion (Audit Analytics 2014). Paradoxically Citizens for Tax Justice (2014) reckon that almost half of this offshore money resides in international banking facilities hosted by US banks. Second, they pointed out that the use of tax havens to avoid or evade taxes abrogated the social contract upon which the prosperity of rich individuals and success of corporations depended. These actors are the principal beneficiaries of public goods paid for out of general taxation, not least the range of coercive state instruments that ultimately protect private property rights, but their use of tax havens means they are able to shirk making a full contribution to this collective pot. Tax justice advocates promoted a miasma of reforms to make tax arrangements more progressive at the domestic level, such as raising taxes on income and capital gains, the introduction of inheritance taxes, and changes to remove incentives for corporations to shift profits offshore. Nevertheless, for these modifications to achieve any real impact they would have to be complemented by efforts to enhance the enforcement of tax law through promoting greater tax transparency.

Ideas connected with the notion of tax justice gained purchase in the context of austerity. Indeed tax justice campaigns cleverly exploited the austerity debate to further their agenda. The fiendish intricacy of transnational tax-planning strategies and the esoteric rules underpinning it had helped to ensure that such matters were presented as purely technical problems best resolved by experts in the cloistered surroundings of remote international organizations. The onset of the austerity agenda, however, enabled champions for tax justice to expose the expressly distributional and hence political effects of these discussions. According to the US Public Interest Research Group, for example, in 2013 the United States forfeited $184 billion in federal and state revenue as the result of tax avoidance and evasion by corporations and individuals. Each individual taxpayer would need to pay an extra $1259 in taxes to make up this shortfall (U.S. PIRG 2014; see also Gravelle 2013; Citizens for Tax Justice 2014). In other words, tax justice campaigners sought to propagate a simple message to the average citizen, that the exploitation of tax havens by rich individuals and corporations is intensifying the austerity they are suffering. Likewise, they have sold the idea of a clampdown on tax havens as a seductive alternative to austerity. In the United Kingdom, for example, the Tax Justice Network made a mockery of the then Conservative-Liberal coalition government's "we're all in this together" slogan by indicating that recouping the £18.5 billion in tax revenue lost through tax haven activities annually (Murphy 2008) would more than cover the cumulative £83 billion cuts by 2014/15 announced by Chancellor George Osborne in his 2010 spending review. Whereas the government has attempted to present the austerity as a burden falling predominantly on the shirkers (see Joy and Shields, this volume), the tax justice activists stress that tax shirkers are a primary cause of austerity.

In other words, unlike areas covered by some of the other chapters in this volume, campaigns for tax justice were advocating an alternative to austerity. Although they paint a mixed picture, surveys of public opinion in OECD countries indicate that attitudes towards tax avoidance and evasion have hardened. The weight of these arguments also appeared, given the commitments already made by G20 and OECD countries to promote tax transparency, to be leaning on an open door. However, the efforts of the G20/OECD have been almost unanimously derided as a damp squib (see Shaxson 2011; Brooks 2013; Eccleston 2013). Particular opprobrium was heaped upon the weakness of the G20/OECD standard, which rested on voluntary exchange of information. In order to avoid the stigma of blacklisting, the G20/OECD requested that all countries sign a minimum of twelve Tax Information Exchange Agreements (TIEAs) outlining the protocols under which they would agree, upon request, to the exchange tax information with their counterparts abroad. Unfortunately TIEAs were designed in such a way that in order to request information about the assets of residents held overseas, tax authorities would need to supply their overseas counterparts with precisely the kinds of details that tax-haven secrecy is designed to obfuscate. Consequently, as one frustrated tax inspector explained, "You already have to have pretty much all of the information you're after to get the last piece. It's a catch-22" (quoted in *Economist* 2013). Furthermore, many tax havens signed the bare minimum number of TIEAs required, assiduously avoiding autographing agreements with major economies in which the majority of investors resided. The "creeping futility" (Meinzer 2012) of the G20/OECD's tax transparency regime generated a groundswell of support for stronger standards to counter tax avoidance and evasion based on the automatic exchange of information – a position endorsed by the G20 finance ministers in April 2013. By the end of 2015, ninety-seven territories had made commitments to implement the new Standard for Automatic Exchange of Financial Information in Tax Matters before 2018 (OECD 2015). In parallel the OECD launched its BEPS program at the behest of the G20 to overhaul the patchwork of existing tax agreements whose contradictions and imperfections facilitate the ease with which corporations can apportion taxable profits to fiscally lenient jurisdictions far from where their real business activities occur. The final package was endorsed by the G20 (2015) in November 2015, with implementation to commence immediately. These schemes have received a more enthusiastic reception from advocates of tax justice, who nonetheless argue they still possess loopholes that will be systematically exploited by tax planners (see Tax Justice Network 2014b).

Explaining Resistance to Tax Transparency

The failure to develop a more robust international tax transparency regime is normally ascribed to three interrelated factors. First, the ideas of those advocating tax transparency as an alternative to austerity have not gone unopposed. Groups agitating for tax justice have amassed most of the column inches, but they are out-muscled and outnumbered by organizations promoting financial privacy and low taxes that possess the additional advantages of bountiful funding and privileged access to political and administrative elites. For example, ICIJ (2013, 150) reports that the Centre for Freedom and Prosperity, a right-leaning think tank, has met with over 175 offices on Capitol Hill to brief them about the benefits of tax competition and tax havens. Second, should more radical ideas leach into the G20/OECD agenda, they will be swiftly defanged by lobbying from a determined coalition of tax-planning interests that have been systematically organized into the process. For instance, after a consultation dominated by the transnational tax-planning industry it was supposed to tackle, the OECD announced that it would be narrowing the scope of the BEPS campaign and dropping critical reporting requirements that have been at the heart of many profit-shifting scandals (Oxfam 2014). As one representative of a US law firm described it, the "game plan" of US corporations "is to be positive but hope as little as possible happens" (quoted in Gapper 2014). Likewise, fears about a revolving door between the guardians of the international tax regime and the vested interests of the transnational tax planners were heightened in May 2014, when Andrew Hickman, formerly of KPMG, was appointed to head the OECD's Transfer Pricing Unit. As ICIJ (2014b) noted in the aftermath of the Luxleaks scandal, "The Big 4 accountants shuttle back and forth between the accounting industry and government so often … that it undermines authorities' efforts to police the industry and enforce tax laws." Third, opportunities for more fundamental change are frittered away in the process of reconciling the interests of the growing roster and diversity of states enrolled in the G20/OECD initiatives. Superficially it appears that all states have an interest in promoting international tax cooperation and information exchange, because this will facilitate the ease with which they can impose levies on the overseas earnings of their residents and boost revenues. Recall, however, that to remain attractive to mobile capital, many major states have made being a tax haven a centrepiece of their economic strategies. Thus, many states have adopted a Janus-faced position from which they argue for transparency and international cooperation to ensure they can tax their own citizens' offshore income but simultaneously maintain tax systems that attract foreign investors by shielding them from the privations of their resident tax authorities. The remainder of this chapter argues that the onset of austerity exacerbates this tension by making states more reliant on tax haven strategies, potentially sounding the death knell for more progressive ideas connected with tax transparency.

In the era of internationally mobile capital, governments have faced a difficult balancing act. On the one hand, to bolster their legitimacy at the domestic level, governments often make lavish public expenditure promises while, on the other, they need to maintain strict control over public finances to retain the confidence of international investors. Post-financial-crisis austerity represents a sharpening of this dilemma, but happily the embrace of offshore finance and tax haven strategies offers a number of ways of squaring this circle.

As previously described, one way in which this can be achieved is for states to become tax havens by offering the kinds of inducements previously described to non-resident investors. As well as directly easing the financial position, especially where residents earn more abroad on their foreign assets than foreigners on domestic assets, such "offshore" borrowing has the additional benefit of being cheaper because, among other things, of the lighter regulatory environment. Unquestionably the United States provides the most successful example among leading states of this strategy in action. Figures from the US Department of Commerce (2014) show that foreigners own $30.38 trillion of US assets, while assets held overseas by US residents amounted to $24.93 trillion, a $5.4 trillion gap that is helping to hold down the current account deficit. Since the financial crisis, the United States has exploited its preponderant position in the global economy to enhance its reputation as a safe haven for non-resident investors, most notoriously through FATCA. FATCA requires foreign financial institutions (FFIs) to disclose to the Internal Revenue Service the identities and personal information related to the assets of US account holders. Any FFI that fails to meet these reporting standards will be subjected to a 30 per cent withholding tax on payments related to US source income. Crucially the majority of the Intergovernmental Agreements (IGAs) that provide FATCA's legal underpinnings have been negotiated on a non-reciprocal basis. In other words, the United States is practising precisely the strategy previously outlined whereby it simultaneously seeks to extract revenues from its own citizens whilst protecting foreign investors in the United States from investigations by tax inspectors in their country of residence. Under these provisions, which came into force for new customers in July 2014 and for existing account holders in 2016, the United States is likely to thrive as a tax haven (Eccleston and Gray 2014). Moreover, the United States appears to be backsliding on its commitment to automatic, reciprocal information exchange at the OECD (Cobham 2014), leaving "a vortex-shaped hole in global financial transparency" (Shaxson 2015).

The proliferation of private finance initiatives is a second way in which states are exploiting offshore to finesse their delivery of austerity. The basic principle of private finance initiatives is that private companies borrow money to build and own infrastructure. This expenditure is then recovered through charging fees for the provision of that service over a fixed period. In short, as Whiteside (this volume) puts it, policymakers committed to fiscal consolidation have "reconceptualized public infrastructure as untapped revenue streams." Importantly, because this money is being borrowed by companies, the resulting debt does not appear on the government's balance sheet. In this way governments are able to meet pledges to invest in public services without unduly alarming the international financial markets. A vast literature argues that states have deliberately stacked the deck to make private financial deals a profitable and attractive proposition (see Whiteside, this volume), but the deal is sweetened further by the financial alchemy afforded by tax havens and offshore financial centres. For example, the earnings of private finance initiative (PFI) companies ultimately derive from government-backed income capping the risks associated with the project, which should lower borrowing costs. In practice, the interest rates on PFI borrowing are invariably higher, indeed often substantially higher (see, for example, Whitfield 2013), than the rates on government gilts. Handily these higher borrowing costs generate tax-deductible interest expenses for PFI companies who, in some extreme cases, have incurred up-front losses that will wipe out potential tax bills for years to come (Brooks 2013). Furthermore, the guaranteed income arising from PFI projects made these companies ideal products to sell on secondary markets. Recognizing that the PFI process could be accelerated if the builders and investors behind the initial scheme could sell up and move on to the next project. Finance ministries have encouraged this with tax breaks and incentives. As a consequence many PFI companies and the income they generate now reside in secretive tax havens beyond the reach of the taxman.

A third way offshore is central to the delivery of austerity is as a mechanism for expanding the stock of private debt. Even austerity's devotees recognize that it is a self-defeating strategy. Rapid fiscal consolidation, combined with private sector deleveraging, runs the risk of dragging countries back into recession, curtailing tax receipts and amplifying pressure on public expenditure (Delong and Summers 2012). With wages stagnating (see Peters, this volume) and inequality mounting, proponents of austerity envisage this gap in aggregate demand being offset by private borrowing. In the United Kingdom, for instance, the Office for Budget Responsibility (2014) forecasts that household debt will soar by £566 billion by 2019 (see Lee, this volume). Since the crisis, many financial institutions have been more concerned to repair their balance sheets than extend lending facilities to the private sector. Such risk aversion has been heightened by the introduction of tougher capital adequacy requirements and stress tests designed to inhibit the ability of financial intermediaries to expand and leverage their balance sheets. This raises the question of where the additional lending needed to deliver a private sector–driven economic recovery will come from. As well as providing a cheap source of wholesale finance, offshore financial centres and tax havens are helping to open the private lending spigot in three main ways. First, tax havens have played a central role in mopping up the toxic assets left by the 2007–8 financial crisis. The Cayman Islands was the domicile of choice for fund managers investing in the bad assets of US banks. Second, although most tax haven jurisdictions now meet international standards, lighter offshore regulatory regimes will allow financial institutions to set up structures that permit them to take "off-balance sheet" risks far in excess of, and hidden from, those mandated by national and international authorities. Recall that the near-collapse of the British high street bank Northern Rock was prompted by the failure of Granite, an offshore securitization vehicle located in Jersey, designed to allow the parent bank to sell on its mortgage book. Although Granite was ultimately controlled by Northern Rock, it was a separate legal entity, meaning that Northern Rock was not obliged to find additional capital to cover its extra liabilities. Financial institutions still maintain thousands of these offshore entities that bolster their capacity to take and (mis)manage risk. Finally, some governments are encouraging private borrowing by underwriting the risks. For example, having had their fingers burnt by the housing bubble, many financial institutions now require prospective customers to put down large deposits before granting a mortgage. Despite the financial crash, house prices remain high relative to incomes in many countries. Consequently the need for a large deposit effectively excludes many prospective borrowers. Since 2013, the UK government has sought to overcome this through a succession of schemes devised to enable borrowers to buy homes with deposits as small as 5 per cent. In exchange for their willingness to make 95 per cent mortgages available, the lenders get an effective guarantee from the government that protects them against losses in the event of the property being repossessed. Interestingly, however, the instrument that makes this initiative possible is a protected cell company (a corporate structure in which a single legal entity comprises several cells with separate assets and liabilities) in Guernsey, which provides the insurance to the lenders and is the channel for the guarantee from the UK government (Gorringe 2012).

Conclusion

Since the financial crisis there has been significant progress in the quest to promote greater tax transparency. In 2008 it would have been quixotic to suggest that five years later states that had long maintained strict financial secrecy would consent to a new international norm centred on the idea of the automatic exchange of information for individuals. If the current proposals for automatic exchange of information are implemented as planned, then the G20 will have fulfilled its promise to end the era of bank secrecy, making it much more difficult for individuals to engage in outright tax evasion. Likewise, if the BEPS initiative is successfully implemented, it may signal the end, or at least the reduction, of possibilities for corporate tax avoidance. The key word here, however, is *if*. This chapter has suggested that offshore financial centres and tax havens are central to the economic strategies of a host of powerful actors, not least many of the leading states in the OECD and G20. Intuitively the onset of the austerity and the desire for fiscal consolidation should have strengthened the case against tax havens. However, this chapter has sought to argue that austerity has further sensitized states to their dependence on offshore financial centres and tax havens, indeed that the successful delivery of the austerity agenda is heavily reliant upon them. Therefore this chapter predicts that while the rhetorical commitment to tax transparency will remain, this is unlikely to result in comprehensive deals that will prompt the demise of tax havens.

REFERENCES

Audit Analytics. 2014. "Overseas Earnings of Russell 1000 Tops $2 Trillion in 2013." http://www.auditanalytics.com/blog/overseas-earnings-of-russell-1000-tops-2-trillion-in-2013/.
Boston Consulting Group. 2014. "Global Wealth 2014: Riding a Wave of Growth." https://www.bcgperspectives.com/content/articles/financial_institutions_business_unit_strategy_global_wealth_2014_riding_wave_growth/.
Brooks, Richard. 2013. *The Great Tax Robbery: How Britain Became a Tax Haven for Fat Cats and Big Business*. Oxford: Oneworld.
Burn, Gary. 1999. "The State, the City and the Euromarkets." *Review of International Political Economy* 6 (2): 225–61. http://dx.doi.org/10.1080/096922999347290.

– 2006. *The Re-emergence of Global Finance*. Basingstoke, UK: Palgrave. http://dx.doi.org/10.1057/9780230501591.

Citizens for Tax Justice. 2014. *Offshore Shell Games: The Use of Offshore Tax Havens by Fortune 500 Companies*. http://ctj.org/pdf/offshoreshell2014.pdf.

Cobham, Alex. 2014. "Has the United States U-Turned on Tax Information Exchange?" Center for Global Development. http://www.cgdev.org/blog/has-united-states-u-turned-tax-information-exchange.

Delong, Bradford J., and Larry H. Summers. 2012. "Fiscal Policy in a Depressed Economy." *Brookings Papers on Economic Activity* 44 (1): 233–97. http://dx.doi.org/10.1353/eca.2012.0000.

Deneault, Alain. 2015. *Canada: A New Tax Haven; How the Country That Shaped Caribbean Tax Havens Is Becoming One Itself*. Vancouver: Talon Books.

Eccleston, Richard. 2013. *The Dynamics of Global Economic Governance: The Financial Crisis, the OECD, and the Politics of International Tax Cooperation*. Cheltenham, UK: Edward Elgar. http://dx.doi.org/10.4337/9781849805988.

Eccleston, Richard, and Felicity Gray. 2014. "Foreign Accounts Tax Compliance Act and American Leadership in the Campaign against International Tax Evasion: Revolution or False Dawn?" *Global Policy* 5 (3): 321–33. http://dx.doi.org/10.1111/1758-5899.12122.

Economist. 2013. "Special Report: Offshore Finance." 14 February.

Eichengreen, Barry. 2010. *Exorbitant Privilege: The Rise and Fall of the Dollar and the Future of the International Monetary System*. Oxford: Oxford University Press.

Financial Transparency Coalition. 2014. "Overview: Peter Caruana Rocks the Boat." http://www.financialtransparency.org/about/overview/.

Findley, Michael G., Daniel L. Nielson, and Jason C. Sharman. 2014. *Global Shell Games: Experiments in Transnational Relations, Crime, and Terrorism*. Cambridge: Cambridge University Press.

Foot, M. 2009. *Final Report of the Independent Review of British Offshore Financial Centres*. London: HM Treasury.

Freyer, Anthony, and Andrew P. Morriss. 2013. "Creating Cayman as an Offshore Financial Centre: Structure and Strategy since 1960." *Arizona State Law Journal* 45:1297–397.

Gapper, John. 2014. "Defensive Play in the World Cup of Corporate Taxation." *Financial Times*, 27 June.

Gorringe, Jason. 2012. "Guernsey Is Europe's Captive Domicile of Choice." Tax-News, 22 March. http://www.tax-news.com/news/Guernsey_Is_Europes_Captive_Domicile_Of_Choice____54549.html.

Gravelle, Jane G. 2013. *Tax Havens: International Tax Avoidance and Evasion*. http://fas.org/sgp/crs/misc/R40623.pdf.

G20. 2009. "Global Plan for Recovery and Reform." http://www.g20.utoronto.
ca/2009/2009communique0402.html.
– 2015. "G20 Leaders' Communique." http://www.g20.utoronto.ca/2015/
151116-communique.html.
Hampton, Mark. 1996. *The Offshore Interface: Tax Havens in the Global Economy.*
Basingstoke, UK: Macmillan. http://dx.doi.org/10.1007/978-1-349-25131-5.
Helleiner, Eric. 1994. *States and the Re-emergence of Global Finance: From Bretton
Woods to the 1990s.* Ithaca, NY: Cornell University Press.
Henry, James S. 2012. *The Price of Offshore Revisited: New Estimates for "Missing"
Global Private Wealth, Income, Inequality, and Lost Taxes.* http://www.
taxjustice.net/cms/upload/pdf/Price_of_Offshore_Revisited_120722.pdf.
Hines, James R., Jr. 2010. "Treasure Islands." *Journal of Economic Perspectives* 24
(4): 103–26. http://dx.doi.org/10.1257/jep.24.4.103.
International Consortium of Investigative Journalists (ICIJ). 2013. *Secrecy for
Sale: Inside the Global Offshore Money Maze.* http://www.icij.org/offshore/
secret-files-expose-offshores-global-impact.
– 2014a. "Big Four Audit Firms Play Big Role in Offshore Murk." https://
www.icij.org/project/luxembourg-leaks/big-4-audit-firms-play-big-role-
offshore-murk.
– 2014b. "Leaked Documents Expose Global Companies' Secret Tax Deals in
Luxembourg." http://www.icij.org/project/luxembourg-leaks/leaked-
documents-expose-global-companies-secret-tax-deals-luxembourg.
– 2015. "Swiss Leaks: Murky Cash Sheltered by Bank Secrecy." http://www.
icij.org/project/swiss-leaks.
International Monetary Fund (IMF). 2009. "Debt Bias and Other Distortions:
Crisis Related Issues in Tax Policy." https://www.imf.org/external/np/
pp/eng/2009/061209.pdf.
Johannesen, Niels, and Gabriel Zucman. 2014. "The End of Bank Secrecy? An
Evaluation of the G20 Tax Haven Crackdown." *American Economic Journal:
Economic Policy* 6 (1): 65–91. http://dx.doi.org/10.1257/pol.6.1.65.
Kane, Daniel R. 1983. *The Eurodollar Market and the Years of Crisis.* London:
Croon Helm.
Lane, Philip R., and Gian Maria Milesi-Ferretti. 2010. "The History of Tax
Havens: Cross Border Investment in Small International Financial Centres."
IMF Working Paper WP/10/38.
Meinzer, Markus. 2012. *The Creeping Futility of the Global Forum's Peer Reviews.*
http://www.taxjustice.net/cms/upload/GlobalForum2012-TJN-
Briefing.pdf.
Mitchell, Daniel J. 2001. "Don't Scapegoat Tax Havens." http://www.heritage.
org/taxes/commentary/dont-scapegoat-tax-havens.

Murphy, Richard. 2008. "The Direct Cost of Tax Havens to the UK." Tax Research. http://www.taxresearch.org.uk/Documents/TaxHavenCostTRLLP.pdf.

OECD. 2009. "Responding to the Global Financial and Economic Crisis: The Tax Dimension, 2nd Meeting of the SEE Working Group on Tax Policy Analysis 16–19 June 2009, Dubrovnik." http://www.oecd.org/globalrelations/43215230.pdf.

– 2015. "AEOI: Status of Commitments." http://www.oecd.org/tax/transparency/AEOI-commitments.pdf.

Office for Budget Responsibility. 2014. *Office for Budget Responsibility: Economic and Fiscal Outlook*. London: HMSO.

Oxfam. 2000. *Tax Havens: Releasing the Hidden Billions for Poverty Eradication.* http://oxfamilibrary.openrepository.com/oxfam/handle/10546/114611.

– 2014. *Business among Friends: Why Corporate Tax Dodgers Are Not Yet Losing Sleep over Global Tax Reform.* 185 Oxfam briefing paper. http://www.oxfam.org/sites/www.oxfam.org/files/bp185-business-among-friends- corporate-tax-reform-120514-en_0.pdf.

Palan, Ronen. 1998. "Trying to Have Your Cake and Eating It: How and Why the State System Has Created Offshore." *International Studies Quarterly* 42 (4): 625–43. http://dx.doi.org/10.1111/0020-8833.00100.

– 2002. "Tax Havens and the Commercialisation of State Sovereignty." *International Organization* 56 (1): 151–76. http://dx.doi.org/10.1162/002081802753485160.

– 2003. *The Offshore World: Sovereign Markets, Virtual Places and Nomad Millionaires*. Ithaca, NY: Cornell University Press.

Palan, Ronen, and Jason P. Abbott. 1996. *State Strategies in the Global Political Economy*. London: Continuum.

Palan, Ronen, Richard Murphy, and Christian Chavagneux. 2010. *Tax Havens: How Globalization Really Works*. Ithaca, NY: Cornell University Press.

Picciotto, Sol. 1992. *International Business Taxation: A Study in the Internationalization of Business Regulation.* Cambridge: Cambridge University Press.

Rixen, Thomas. 2008. *The Political Economy of International Tax Governance.* Basingstoke, UK: Palgrave. http://dx.doi.org/10.1057/9780230582651.

Sharman, Jason C. 2006. *Havens in a Storm: The Struggle for Global Tax Regulation*. Ithaca, NY: Cornell University Press.

Shaxson, Nicholas. 2011. *Treasure Islands: Tax Havens and the Men Who Stole the World*. London: Bodley Head.

– 2015. "Loophole USA: The Vortex-Shaped Hole in Global Financial Transparency." http://www.taxjustice.net/2015/01/26/loophole-usa- vortex-shaped-hole-global-financial-transparency-2/.

Slemrod, Joel. 2010. "Location, (Real) Location, (Tax) Location: An Essay on Mobility's Place in Optimal Taxation." *National Tax Journal* 63 (4, Part 2): 843–64. http://dx.doi.org/10.17310/ntj.2010.4S.02.

Spiro, David E. 1999. *The Hidden Hand of American Hegemony: Petrodollar Recycling and International Markets.* Ithaca, NY: Cornell University Press.

Tax Justice Network. 2014a. "An Informal History of TJN and the Tax Justice Movement." http://www.taxjustice.net/5828-2/.

– 2014b. "TJN Responds to New OECD Report on Automatic Information Exchange." News release, 13 February. http://www.taxjustice. net/2014/02/13/press-release-tjn-responds-new-oecd-report-automatic-information-exchange/.

Transparency International. 2015. *Corruption on Your Doorstep: How Corrupt Capital Is Used to Buy Property in the UK.* http://www.transparency.org.uk/ publications/corruption-on-your-doorstep/.

U.S. PIRG. 2014. *Picking Up the Tab 2014.* http://www.uspirg.org/sites/pirg/ files/reports/Picking%20Up%20the%20Tab%20vUS_web.pdf.

Urry, John. 2014. *Offshoring.* Cambridge: Polity.

US Department of Commerce. 2014. "U.S. Net International Investment Position: End of Second Quarter 2014." http://www.bea.gov/ newsreleases/international/intinv/intinvnewsrelease.htm.

vanFossen, Anthony. 2012. *Tax Havens and Sovereignty in the Pacific Islands.* Brisbane: University of Queensland Press.

Whitfield, Dexter. 2013. "Fingers in the PFI." *Red Pepper* 188:16–18.

Wojcik, Dariusz. 2013. "Where Governance Fails: Advanced Business Services and the Offshore World." *Progress in Human Geography* 37 (3): 330–47. http://dx.doi.org/10.1177/0309132512460904.

Zucman, Gabriel. 2014. "Taxing across Borders: Tracking Personal Wealth and Corporate Profits." *Journal of Economic Perspectives* 28 (4): 121–48. http:// dx.doi.org/10.1257/jep.28.4.121.

– 2015. *The Hidden Wealth of Nations: The Scourge of Tax Havens.* Chicago: University of Chicago Press. http://dx.doi.org/10.7208/ chicago/9780226245560.001.0001.

12 Profiting off Austerity: Private Finance for Public Infrastructure

HEATHER WHITESIDE

Austerity budgets aim to reduce government debt and deficit, a task accomplishable equally by raising revenue (through assets, taxation, and growth) and/or cutting government expenditures (targeting services, operations, jobs, and programs). The resurgence of austerity today is unique to its context – the 2008 global financial crisis and its aftermath – but is also part of a longer historical trend. Mark Blyth (2013a, 2013b) has traced the "love of parsimony over prodigality" in economic thought back to Adam Smith and finds examples of fiscal austerity over the past century. Similarly, austerity policies adopted since 2010 repackage and re-employ pre-existing (pre–2008 crisis) neoclassical strategies first aimed at resolving stagflation in the 1970s through tight fiscal and monetary policy, and later renamed "expansionary fiscal consolidation" in the 1990s, which was said to stimulate growth by improving the long-run expectations of investors and consumers (Blyth 2013c). Thus the widespread use of fiscal austerity today follows decades of neoliberal spending restraint.

In light of this longer historical context, Streeck (2014) argues that for states long since starved of funds but with services, operations, and infrastructure costs to cover (even after significant episodes of privatization), the tax state has been transformed into a debt state – one that is heavily reliant upon credit accessed through financial markets for its financing. While useful for its parsimony, this description is too blunt to capture the nuance of fiscal policy transformation witnessed over the neoliberal period. Rather than a full-fledged switch to a debt state, in countries like Canada and the United States we see that debt and private financing now tend to fund capital expenditures, whereas services and operations are still mostly covered by taxation – albeit in the context of dwindling receipts through balanced budget legislation, spending control, regressive taxation, and protracted low growth/recession. In other words, austerity is not necessarily applied evenly to all budgetary elements. Expenditures on services, programs, and employees (benefits, pensions, jobs) face the axe of fiscal restraint, but those that draw on the market for financing, and are therefore of benefit to investors, often escape unscathed. In a related development, privately financed public works projects may even be cast as a source of stimulus and seen as a revenue stream to be tapped into, in order to balance the books.

By converting public infrastructure into a monetized asset, or one where anticipated revenue streams are bought and sold in financial markets by private investors, the financialization of public sector budgets adds a new dimension to austerity politics.[1] No longer is the austerity story principally one of cuts and market-oriented state restructuring; it has also come to feature revenue-generating schemes that rely upon global financial markets. With public infrastructure exposed to the decision-making logics of private finance, considerations of creditworthiness, risk, and public indebtedness come to greatly constrain or otherwise influence fiscal policy. The use of private financing for public infrastructure and the austerity agenda are therefore mutually reinforcing and co-constitutive developments. Describing a separate but related process, Harvey (1989) calls this a "two way relationship of reciprocity and domination": the dynamics of capital accumulation shape and are shaped by state governance strategies.

Privately financed public infrastructure is doubly profitable for capital. First, the projects themselves – physical infrastructure projects like bridges, highways, and water treatment facilities – generate stable and predictable revenue from user fees or state-provided payments, with most projects enjoying monopoly privileges and captive demand. Second, as a financial asset, infrastructure funds are known to bring in high returns for low risk, and, once financialized, the terms and conditions of infrastructure debt can be manipulated on secondary markets by private partners to produce even higher rates of return.

---

1 Epstein (2005, 3), following Krippner (2005), defines *financialization* as "the increasing role of financial motives, financial markets, financial actors and financial institutions in the operation of the domestic and international economies." Here we focus on how the austerity context augments the role and influence of private finance vis-à-vis public sector budgets and infrastructure.

The themes of how austerity can be profitable and for whom will be examined in two sections. The first looks at the recurrent phenomenon of fiscal austerity over the past few decades. It argues that while spending restraint has been a relatively consistent feature of the neoliberal era, budgetary imbalances have been dealt with by using different fiscal strategies over the years. With previous episodes of austerity, budget cuts often reduced or eliminated infrastructure spending, but more recently public infrastructure has come to be regarded as an untapped source of revenue for the state and, through financialization, a new asset class for finance capital. The second section details the ways in which beneficiaries of austerity are profiting: policymakers bent on fiscal consolidation and capital looking for new, reliable, and profitable investment sites. Examples of why these arrangements are less than desirable for other social groups appear throughout the chapter, with a focus on Canada and the United States in particular.

Recurrent Austerity

The neoliberal period has witnessed a series of financial and economic crises but never yet one as widespread, deep, and pervasive as the 2007/8 global financial crisis, nor one centred on the core countries of the current order, hitting Wall Street and the City of London particularly hard. For a short time it even appeared as though this crisis might engender a shift away from neoliberalism; the 2009–10 period even featured a return of quasi-Keynesian discourse and policy. But "crisis" can be a slippery concept, subject to interpretation and manipulation. Within a few short years, after stimulus and bailout packages had been enacted, most OECD countries were in search of "exit strategies" and sought an "unwinding of extraordinary circumstances," and the banking sector crisis was effectively transmuted into public sector profligacy in need of familiar neoliberal fiscal austerity. In their description of the alchemy of austerity, Clarke and Newman (2012) call this manipulation of the concept of crisis "shape changing" and suggest it has been the product of intensive ideological manoeuvring.

Clarke and Newman (2012) describe the significance of austerity today as being rooted in its enabling of greater market-oriented restructuring of the welfare state. We might also add that there has been a longer historical interrelation between neoliberal restructuring and austerity: the neoliberal era has been largely an age of austerity, and this has allowed for pre-existing rhetoric, policy prescriptions, and economic logics to be exhumed in 2010 and beyond (on "expansionary fiscal consolidation" in the 1990s, see Alesina and Perotti 1995; Alesina et al. 1998; Alesina and Ardagna 1998; Giavazzi and Pagano 1990; on "expansionary austerity" today, see Guajardo, Leigh, and Pescatori 2011). It is even commonplace now to see examples of austerity "success" stories from the 1980s and 1990s being used to justify fiscal restraint today. Detailed below, shape-changing over the years has therefore encompassed selective borrowing of results and rationale, inherited legacies of earlier forays into austerity, and variety in the forms of policies and measures used to balance the budget.

In a review of twenty-four OECD countries from 1978 to 2007, Guichard et al. (2007) find that there were eighty-five episodes of fiscal consolidation.[2] In Australia, for example, these episodes ran 1979–80, 1986–8, 1994–9, and 2002–3; and in the United Kingdom 1979–82, 1988, 1994–9 (ibid.). More broadly, Pierson describes the 1990s as a period of intense pressure within the global North to pursue austerity (2001, 411). In neoliberal pioneers like the United Kingdom, fiscal restraint and state cutbacks were quite rapid; in Canada, on the other hand, earlier use of austerity measures has been described as being *relatively* cautious and targeted throughout the 1980s and 1990s (434). Austerity policies at this time included transforming universal into selective programs, tightening eligibility requirements to qualify for some benefits such as unemployment insurance, imposing ceilings on program costs, and forcing programs to be self-financing or subject to "clawbacks" over a certain benefit level (Houle 1990). Reforms and restraint varied over time, by policy area and jurisdiction (Banting 1987), tempered by how much popular support a given program enjoyed. In contrast to austerity in the 1980s, which featured incremental erosion of the social safety net rather than outright dismantling, by the mid-1990s deficit reduction was clearly prioritized. Federal funding to the provinces dropped, provinces cut their budgets accordingly, social programs were redesigned to fit with the reality and vision of austerity, and social assistance recipients bore the full brunt of fiscal restraint (McBride and Whiteside 2011).

Spending on Canadian public infrastructure also switched from federal to municipal governments over the 1980s and 1990s (a topic returned

---

2 An *episode* is defined by Guichard et al. (2007) as starting when the cyclically adjusted primary balance improves by at least 1 per cent of GDP the following year, and ending if the balance improves by less than 0.2 per cent of GDP in one year.

to in the final section of the chapter), leading to a 2004 estimate that the deficiency in the addition, maintenance, and replacement of public infrastructure stock had reached $125 billion, or six to ten times the size of annual investment (TD Economics 2004), a figure matched in an earlier study that pegged the infrastructure gap at $125 billion and warned it could reach $400 billion by 2020 (Mirza and Haider 2003). Decades of neoliberal austerity and public sector spending control meant that by the mid-2000s, most of Canada's public infrastructure was built during the Keynesian era in the 1950s–1970s (Mirza 2007, 5–6).

With public debt as a percentage of GDP lowered from 117 per cent in 1986 to 25 per cent in 2007, Ireland has recently become an often-used example of how austerity can lead to robust growth, given its 1990s/2000s "Celtic tiger" economic turnaround (Kinsella 2011, 16). However, isolating austerity as *the* principal factor encouraging growth and reducing debt is a less straightforward exercise than the expansionary fiscal consolidation school might admit. Instead, Kinsella (16–18) shows that the Celtic tiger economy can be related to a host of other historically contingent factors. This includes growth in the international economy, fiscal transfers from the EU, the opening up of a single market, a 14 per cent increase in the average industrial wage between 1986 and 1989 and similar public sector wage increases, an income tax amnesty in 1988, and a well-timed currency devaluation in August 1986. In a similar vein, Dellepiane and Hardiman (2012, 13) argue that Ireland's "success" with austerity was not the result of greater investor confidence, as the expansionary fiscal consolidation literature suggests, but rather currency devaluation (which is now impossible with the euro) and growth in the global economy, which produced demand for Irish exports (absent following the economic stagnation experienced with the onset of the 2009 great recession – a phenomenon aggravated by austerity, according to Wolf 2013).

Dellepiane and Hardiman (2012) raise an additional and related concern with the economics of austerity: the need to consider "politics in time" when analysing the results of fiscal consolidation. As they describe, the treatment of austerity through formal mathematical modelling breaks down country experiences into multiple discrete episodes so that changes in a state's fiscal condition may be examined from one period to the next. This approach is problematic, given that it ignores the highly varied ways in which countries went from large deficits in the 1980s to balanced budgets by the early 2000s. There is in fact a range of possible reasons for balanced budgets, such as economic growth, increased demand (domestic and international), tax increases, and fiscal restraint. In Canada, austerity in the 1990s was disproportionately titled in favour of cuts to public spending rather than raising revenue through higher taxes. Posner and Sommerfeld (2013, 152) calculate the composition of austerity measures to be 87 per cent spending cuts and 13 per cent revenue increases. Compare this to Britain, where fiscal consolidation under the Conservatives (1980s–1997) occurred mainly through revenue measures (taxation), not restraint (spending cuts); under Labour, austerity took the form of spending and cost control (Dellepiane and Hardiman 2012, 13).

Austerity, Risk, and Restructuring

Austerity today is a clear example of what Hacker (2008) calls the "neoliberal risk shift," where some groups in society benefit but most are left worse off. A technical definition of austerity budgeting would have it refer narrowly to reductions made in the cyclically adjusted fiscal deficit; but seen from a wider perspective, changes in fiscal policy greatly influence both state and society. Austerity is, as Peck (2013, 4) suggests, a strategy of redistribution that pushes "the costs, risks, and burdens of economic failure onto subordinate classes, social groups and branches of government." In the United States, for example, we see the stark impact of scalar downloading where "austerity urbanism" involves foisting the costs of a global banking and financial crisis and national deregulation onto municipalities and local authorities, who are in no position to shoulder these burdens and costs (Peck 2012). By 2012, roughly 300 municipalities were thought to be in some form of default on their debt obligations (ibid.). Municipal bankruptcies, the theft of workers' savings (pensions), and greater social disparities are the inevitable result, given the overarching neoliberal context.

The most high-profile case of municipal fiscal distress leading to deep austerity and state restructuring today is Detroit. A brief examination of its bankruptcy saga reveals that cuts to vertical intergovernmental transfers create significant problems for the municipal budget (austerity-induced risk downloading), opportunities for neoliberal structural reform can be created through financial crises and fiscal imbalance, and bondholders' rights are often protected at the expense of taxpayers (public service recipients) and employees (public sector workers).

In his report for FY 2003–4, Detroit's auditor general (2003) projects a deficit from 2004 to 2008, linking it to revenue decline and expenditure increase. Detroit's main sources of revenue are municipal income tax, property tax, utility taxes, taxes and fees associated with gambling, and state revenue sharing. By 2003–4, all sources are flat or declining, and by FY 2004–5 the city's General Fund is in deficit by $155 million; the fiscal imbalance only gets worse over time when the city floats bonds to (temporarily) balance the budget, beginning in 2003. The reasons for this decline in revenue relate to both structural and proximate causes. The former includes aspects such as population decline, economic stagnation and secular job loss, and lower property values; and the latter to fairly recent policy choices such as competitive income tax reductions by the city and cuts to state revenue sharing. The Michigan Municipal League (Minghine 2014) calculates that between 2003 and 2014, Detroit loses over $732,000 that it should have received through state revenue sharing. This loss is significant in its own right and because it affects key expenditure items in the budget: public sector wage settlements, pension plans, and health benefit agreements. These commitments were made in part on the basis of expected revenue that did not materialize as the result of changes in state government fiscal policy (lower taxes and fewer intergovernmental transfers).

In FY 2005–6, the tipping point in Detroit's municipal finances, $1.44 billion of new debt is issued in the form of city pension Certificates of Participation (COPs) to fund its two retirement systems and at this time a thirty-year repayment schedule is negotiated involving swaps to make COPs more attractive for investors. In the process the city switches from a fixed interest rate to a variable one: it stands to benefit if interest rates rise, it will owe more to investors if interest rates drop. In that same year the city also issues $250 million in bonds to yet again stabilize the budget. After the onset of the global financial crisis in late 2007, in November 2008 the US Federal Reserve begins quantitative easing. Short-term interest rates drop to near zero, meaning Detroit owes an additional $1.14 billion through COPs-related swaps commitments. The city issues more bonds and pledges casino tax revenue to cover future debt payments. By 2012 Detroit's finances are such that it exchanges fiscal oversight for financial assistance from the state. By July 2013 the city had $18 billion in outstanding debt and was forced to file bankruptcy.

Along with cuts to public sector jobs, pensions, and other forms of spending, the sale/lease of public assets is likely to become a major facet of austerity-induced neoliberal restructuring. Emergency management plans released in February 2014 call for monetizing revenue streams from the District Water and Sewerage Department, public lighting, city parking garages, parking meters and lots. Monetization involves converting a city's assets into legal tender through long-term leases or outright sales (leases sell the income from specific city operations or assets for a specified period of time), which is therefore a novel combination of privatization and financialization. However, these plans are nothing new – in 2009 Detroit's mayor proposed "unlocking the value of the city's assets" through the monetization of the Detroit-Windsor tunnel, city parking meters and lots, and public lighting. And well before the fiscal crisis these assets were targeted for privatization. In the city auditor general's FY 2003–4 report, leasing meters, parking lots, lighting and water and sewage assets were each proposed, and that report furthermore refers to an earlier 1998 plan to privatize those assets.

Extreme cases like Detroit may lead to greater privatization of the already lean American night-watchman state, with the role of public infrastructure provider now being shed from the short list of activities justifiable by laissez-faire doctrine, but elsewhere many social obligations remain, even decades after the shift away from Keynesian demand management. "Structural functionalism" (Doern, Maslove, and Prince 2013), or the widespread expectation that governments of all stripes and levels will continue to address fundamentals such as employment and effective demand, must therefore coexist with fiscal austerity. Where new spending is verboten or direct expenditures are being cut, the tax system becomes a key way to address social need and economic fundamentals (see Block and Maslove 1994). By redistributing wealth in society through exemptions, deductions, credits, preferential tax rates, and the like, "tax expenditures" can take on such roles, albeit in often invisible ways and with their own distinct repercussions. As Harder (2003, 62) describes it, "In enabling market provision, tax expenditures not only represent public spending but also redistribute foregone public revenues in the service of private profit."

Foregone tax revenue is often concomitant with an expansion of market-dependence for citizens (for their services) and the state (for its financing). Despite the heavy reliance on municipal bonds in the United States for public infrastructure financing, these bonds are tax exempt – exempt from federal tax in all instances and exempt from state tax when the bondholder lives in that state. A major part of their appeal to creditors is this tax exempt status, but it simultaneously represents foregone revenue for already cash-strapped states, making municipal bonds a significant, but hidden tax expenditure (see Cormier 2014). Further, whereas the rights of bondholders are sacrosanct (illustrated most recently with Detroit's "emergency management" strategies), taxpayers are granted no such rights to claims on city wealth or assets in tough times. The financialization of city budgets therefore redistributes rights to the detriment of citizens and benefit of creditors (Hackworth 2007). In Streeck's (2014) words, creditors become a "second constituency."

Financial market dependence has been encouraged over the years by restraints on revenue and spending. Within the context of balanced budget legislation in particular, the municipal bond market becomes an "essential element of the politics of circumvention" (Sbragia 1996, 10). Savage (1988) describes four techniques that governments have used to evade constitutional limits on borrowing, each of which deepens financial market dependence: issuing state agency revenue bonds; borrowing through public corporations, commissions, and authorities; delegating state operations to local governments and agencies; and lease-purchase agreements. For all of these reasons, Sbragia (1996, 10–11) argues that, despite finance capital gaining significant structural power over the state in the neoliberal era, financialization has been encouraged by states and municipalities seeking to use private finance to advance their own economic and political interests.

New debtor categories are created along the way. Following a series of public sector debt defaults, in the late nineteenth century American municipalities began to switch from general obligations bonds, where debt is backed by the full faith and credit of government (supported principally by property taxes), to revenue bonds where earnings from the operation of that infrastructure is pledged to retire the debt. This not only avoided balanced budget legislation but also shifted debt from taxpayers to ratepayers and service users, making revenue bonds a popular option for user fee–based infrastructure such as highways, ports, and water and sewer projects. Thus where infrastructure-related services can be priced, debt has been individualized; where it is impractical or impossible to price consumption, as with sidewalks and city streets, a collective bearing of debt has been maintained, and most of these public works are financed through general taxation (Pagano and Perry 2008).

Infrastructure property assets are now being sold or revenue streams are being monetized as a way to enhance state finances, and investments in public infrastructure are being pursued in order to generate revenue, far beyond the historical use of tolls and user fees to recoup capital expenses incurred by the state (see O'Neill 2013). The city of

Chicago is something of a pioneer in this respect. It has entered into three major infrastructure monetization deals since 2005 as a way to generate revenue and (temporarily) stave off fiscal crisis: the ninety-nine-year, $1.83 billion 2005 Chicago Skyway toll road; the ninety-nine-year, $563 million 2006 lease of downtown parking garages; and the seventy-five-year, $1.15 billion 2009 lease on public parking meters. Each of these deals is linked to austerity in a unique way: each has been structured by the city so that a large amount of the total revenue is received upfront from the private partner, with this money used to pay down the municipal debt/deficit (DiNapoli 2013).

Entering into long-run P3 deals for short-term budget relief has (temporarily) improved Chicago's credit rating but is not a sustainable strategy to address structural deficit. Further, hasty deals like the parking meter P3 that took only three days to negotiate have been flagged as being of particularly poor value for money. In January 2009 Chicago's Inspector General's Office launched an investigation into the arrangement, later that year reporting that the parking system would have been worth $2.13 billion over seventy-five years – therefore the city underpriced its asset by 46 per cent (Hoffman 2009, 3).

Private Finance for Public Infrastructure

Historically, funds for public capital expenditures (infrastructure and equipment) have been relatively plentiful in the United States. When the post-war pipeline of federal funding for infrastructure dried up in concert with the abandonment of Keynesianism in the 1970s, state and municipal governments replaced federal support with gas taxes and other user fees, and enjoyed access to the thriving municipal bond market (worth roughly $380 billion) that could be drawn on for public infrastructure projects (Sagalyn 1990; Thornton 2007). Savings were also generated through the use of municipal bonds, with an interest rate spread of 2 to 4 per cent in favour of public rather than private financing (NCPPP 2012, 7). As a result, by the end of the 1980s, state and local governments were responsible for 90 per cent of all public works spending in the United States (Leighland 1995, 142).

The availability of public financing for public infrastructure has been eroded in many US jurisdictions since 2008 through austerity and fiscal imbalance (Davidson and Ward 2014; Peck 2013). In 2012, forty-two states had budgetary shortfalls, totalling $103 billion, and forty-six states cut services or cancelled projects as a way to address spending imbalances (NCPPP 2012, 5). Cuts such as these are occurring within the pre-existing context of a chronic and now growing infrastructure spending gap. The National Surface Transportation Policy and Revenue Study Commission calculated in 2008 that $86 billion is needed each year to pay for infrastructure maintenance and construction, and that fuel taxes – which are not indexed to inflation and are unlikely to increase in a tax-averse climate – along with other sources of traditional public funding for infrastructure are/will be inadequate to address infrastructure needs (see Page et al. 2008). This has opened up space for the use of private financing through various P3 schemes as a mechanism to access private funds to pay down public debt and to build public infrastructure without incurring upfront capital costs.

Distinguishing features of the P3 model include lengthy (multi-decade) lease-based bundled contracts and complex risk-sharing arrangements. Many P3s transfer financial risks through private financing, exposing public infrastructure and services to the vagaries of volatile capital markets, and pushing up the cost of capital through the higher interest rates paid by private debtors. One would assume that higher costs in the midst of austerity would discourage P3 use; however, privately financed P3s also offer politicians and policymakers a "build now, pay later" opportunity to achieve off-book financing and/or gain access to funds otherwise prohibited under balanced budget legislation or other forms of spending control. When episodes of austerity and budget constraint coincide with the need for infrastructure spending, conditions encourage private financing to meet public sector obligations.

Private financing for P3 projects is typically split between debt and equity. An equity stake involves fundamental ownership rights over the P3's private partner (a firm, consortium, or special project vehicle), entitling asset holders to revenue after costs are met and debt obligations are paid (Hellowell and Vicchi 2012, 7). Debt during the construction phase of a project is often secured through private commercial banks, with bond financing used for the operational phase. Stakeholder investors (equity holders) are typically engineering, procurement, construction, operations, and maintenance firms; project investors (debt holders) are usually pension funds, sovereign wealth funds, infrastructure funds, and banks (public investment banks and private commercial banks) (Waterston 2012). Infrastructure funds raise money on capital markets through collateralization: bundled savings that seek safe yet high returns on investment (often a site of investment by pension funds) (Sclar 2009).

Following the subprime crisis–induced restructuring of global finance, major players on Wall Street (e.g., Goldman Sachs, Morgan Stanley, the Carlyle Group, and Citigroup) began moving into infrastructure assets, with an estimated $250 billion amassed in infrastructure investment funds in 2007–8 alone (Anderson 2008). More broadly, a 2007 estimate pegged the wealth contained within the world's top thirty infrastructure funds at upwards of $500 billion – although it is almost certainly higher now (Thornton 2007). As Mark Weisdorf, head of JP Morgan's infrastructure investments put it, "Ten to 20 years from now infrastructure investments could be larger than real estate" (quoted in ibid.). As natural monopolies (a status often augmented by non-competition clauses), P3 projects are low-risk assets with captive customers, and governments are the ultimate guarantor over the long run.

Increasingly sophisticated, private financing is not merely a substitute for public funds. It is now an avenue of profit making of (potentially) greater significance than what is typically offered as "justification" for privatization – relating to operational efficiencies, design enhancements, and project cost control (Murphy 2008; Vining and Boardman 2008). The reorganization of debt through "financial engineering" can significantly reduce private investors' costs and improve revenue earnings for private partners. Mechanisms such as debt swaps and sweeps that switch from short-term to longer-term liability, change the nature of interest rate payments, restructure dividend payouts and debt-repayment schedules, allow for new dimensions of profit-making beyond revenue earned from the infrastructure itself (e.g., tolls, user fees) (Ashton, Doussard, and Weber 2012). Mark Florian, head of North American infrastructure banking at Goldman Sachs, summarizes the eagerness of investors: "There's a lot of value trapped in public assets" (Thornton 2007). Accessing that value, of course, requires supportive state policies.

Legislative support for private finance in the United States includes the granting of tax-exempt status for private activity bonds to counter the attractiveness of municipal bonds. Within water and wastewater infrastructure financing, the 2013 federal Sustainable Water Act and Water Infrastructure Now Public Private Partnership Act lift taxes on private activity bonds, which is believed will "encourage billions of dollars of private investment in water supply and wastewater systems around the country" (Colombini 2013b). For transportation projects, the federal government's 2005 Transportation Infrastructure Finance and Innovation Act (TIFIA) provides additional P3 encouragement for states seeking to strike P3 deals: direct loans with flexible terms amounting to upwards of one-third of total project costs, loan support and guarantees for institutional investors funding infrastructure projects, and lines of credit for the first ten years of a project's operations. Some industry insiders consider the TIFIA "possibly the most advantageous mezzanine financing available anywhere for PPP in the transport sector" (*P3 Bulletin* 2006). The TIFIA exists alongside a $15 billion exemption for private activity bonds used towards highway and intermodal freight facilities (ibid.). Changes in legislation relating to private activity bonds and P3 support more generally are the result of lobbying and policy promotion by groups such as the Urban Land Institute, the National Council for P3s, and the Performance-Based Building Coalition. There is, however, no counterpart to private activity bonds or TIFIA for social infrastructure, inherently limiting P3 use in areas like public schools and courthouses, although this is likely to be a target of future lobbying efforts (Colombini 2013a).

From the perspective of capital, public infrastructure is both profitable and unique, given its high barriers to entry, monopoly characteristics, long concession periods (leases are often ninety-nine years in length), large scale of investment, inelastic demand, low operating costs, and stable/predictable cash flows (Newell and Peng 2008). Further, public infrastructure is also now seen as a new asset class for finance capital, and one that is a particularly attractive investment, given its low risk. As *Businessweek* puts it, "Infrastructure is ultra-low-risk because competition is limited by a host of forces that make it difficult to build, say, a rival toll road. With captive customers, the cash flows are virtually guaranteed. The only major variables are the initial prices paid, the amount of debt used for financing, and the pace and magnitude of toll hikes – easy things for Wall Street to model" (Thornton 2007).

The financialization of public sector budgets and infrastructure through global financial market–reliant P3 deals are therefore a way to satisfy pressures from private finance and from legislated austerity. But this drive is not innocuous, and financialization changes the nature of public infrastructure. O'Neill (2013) summarizes the three principal implications of financialization of infrastructure: services need to be commercialized in order to generate competitive returns for private investors (displacing other concerns); infrastructure design must be made to conform to the characteristics of a financial instrument (e.g., ownership, management, regulatory environment, and material performance); and risks must be controlled in a manner consistent with private property rights and commercial/investor interests.

The financialization of public infrastructure is far from an American phenomenon. As previously mentioned, Canadian municipal-level infrastructure equally faces a chronic and growing backlog, and in 2013 the Canadian Federation of Municipalities identified the need for infrastructure spending and federal cost-sharing for public works as being at the top of their agenda. Roughly 25 per cent of the municipal infrastructure gap comes from the need to renew or improve water and wastewater infrastructure, nearly 35 per cent relates to transportation and transit infrastructure, and approximately 8 per cent to waste management (Mirza 2007, 15).

The long-run worsening of the municipal infrastructure gap can be attributed to a number of factors, including responsibility downloading, tax cuts, and balanced budget legislation imposed from above, but it is due primarily to the neoliberal era withdrawal of the federal government from public capital investment and the ownership of public capital stock. As Mackenzie (2013, 7–8) shows, in 1955 the federal government owned 44 per cent of the Canadian public capital stock, the provinces owned 34 per cent, and local governments owned 22 per cent; by 2011 this federal–municipal relationship had reversed: the federal government's share dropped to 13 per cent, municipalities owned 52 per cent, and the provincial ownership portion was almost identical at 35 per cent.

TD Economics (2004) and Deloitte (2004) recommend greater use of the P3 model to address the infrastructure gap, since it is uniquely able to leverage private financing for the delivery of public infrastructure and services. This rationale is in part ideological (i.e., the perception that public debt is a sign of mismanagement) and in part practical, given the presence of balanced budget legislation or other forms of spending control. P3s are therefore presented as a way to deliver new infrastructure at a time of fiscal austerity. This stance is contradictory, given the higher long-run costs and risks associated with private finance and the financialization of public infrastructure. Prior to 2007, government borrowers in Canada were able to secure interest rates that were, on average, 2 per cent lower than those charged to private borrowers, but between 2007 and 2009 this increased to an average of 3 or 4 per cent – making P3s nearly 70 per cent more expensive than publicly funded infrastructure (when measured in present value terms) (Mackenzie 2009, 2).

P3 schemes are not only more expensive, they are also risky. Securing profit for the private partner requires transforming public infrastructure into a tradable financial product by selling performance outcomes and transferring failure risks to the investor, which is, as O'Neill (2009) describes it, derivatization not through the sale of an asset but through the buying and selling of risk itself. P3s inscribe risk onto and into infrastructure through, for example, the creation of fee structures and insertion of financial instruments, in order to buy and sell risk.

In Canada, private financing for P3 infrastructure deals often relies upon "mini-perm" finance structures. Mini-perm financing refers to when the tenure of a project's senior debt is much shorter than the duration of the P3 project agreement (Hellowell and Vicchi 2012). Refinancing will typically be required within the first five to seven years of a thirty-year (or greater) contract. The underlying assumption with this arrangement is that P3 projects can and will be refinanced periodically at projected rates. As Mackenzie (2009) argues, that builds in the questionable expectation that credit-fuelled bubbles will continue indefinitely. Should trouble emerge with refinancing attempts, mini-perms create problems for operational projects: public infrastructure and services in areas vital to the public interest. Refinancing guarantees are being offered by Canadian public partners. Essentially this means taxpayers will repay lenders if the private partner cannot obtain refinancing, and/or, depending on the terms of the project agreement, the state may also compensate partners if refinancing generates less favourable results (see Hellowell and Vicchi 2012).

Amid austerity-induced cuts to services, employment, and benefits in other parts of the public sector, key P3 infrastructure-spending commitments have nonetheless been made by federal and provincial governments (for more detail, see Whiteside 2014). Examples include the 2007 $33-billion Building Canada Plan federal government initiative and its $47-billion new Building Canada Plan introduced in Budget 2013. A significant role has been carved out for P3s in recent infrastructure spending schemes. The federal government created P3 Canada in 2007 to "develop the Canadian market for public-private partnerships" at the municipal level in particular (municipalities and other jurisdictions will be able to access technical and financial support only if a project uses the P3 model), and P3 Canada received funding commitments from the federal government of $2.8 billion per annum for 2011–13 (*P3 Canada* 2009). The P3 Canada Fund was renewed once more in Budget 2013 with a $1.25 billion commitment "to continue supporting innovative ways to build infrastructure projects faster and provide better value for Canadian taxpayers through public-private partnerships" (described in chapter 3.3, "The New Building Canada Plan"). Contrast this with federal Budget 2010 and its efforts to save $17.6 billion over five years through government department spending cuts and freezes to some operating budgets; and likewise Budget 2012, which introduced cuts totalling $5.2 billion, targeting the federal public service in particular through the elimination of roughly 19,000 jobs.

Conclusion

Peck (2013) argues that austerity has to be continually "pushed" discursively, given that it is not self-evidently desirable or necessary. However, the appeal of austerity must also be understood within the neoliberal context outlined by Blyth (2013a): there is now a generation of economists and policymakers for whom Keynesianism is but "a footnote" in textbooks and in practice. The relegation of alternative economic paradigms (even those as prominent historically as Keynesianism) to literal or figurative footnote status suggests a myopia in orthodox economics today and helps explain the "common sense" appeal to austerity. Taming government growth and trimming back the public sector is now, as it was in the past, the target and implication of fiscal consolidation. Ultimately austerity is less about achieving economic growth than it is about shifting blame for economic conditions from market actors to government departments, and displacing the burdens of adjustment from capital to labour.

However, as this chapter has shown, austerity budgeting entails not only cuts to expenditures, it can also mean generating revenue through asset monetization, sales, and financialization. After decades of neoliberal market-oriented state restructuring, public infrastructure remains a principal asset held by the state. This provides the opportunity for fiscal conservatives and austerians to benefit from its sale and monetization, with creditors (investment funds, banks, wealthy individuals) all too eager to profit from the low-risk, high-return nature of public works through infrastructure bonds and investment in P3 deals. The opportunity to profit from austerity emerged in part through current day austerity budgeting, and, from a longer historical perspective, through the infrastructure gap produced by bouts of fiscal restraint over the past three decades. Thus the forms, phases, and implications of austerity change over time.

Writing a year before the global financial crisis hit, Broadway (2006, 375) argued that "the study of redistributive intergovernmental transfers remains a lively research area." This statement ought to be truer now than ever – austerity has meant shifts to risk and responsibility that will set the tone for state-society relations, public policy, and claims on social wealth for years to come. Themes of "framing" and "manufacturing" can be identified in the current phase of fiscal consolidation. The frame created by austerity circumscribes policy choices and opens avenues for the financialization of public sector budgets, especially capital expense portions of state spending. Similarly, the austerity imperative is manufactured by today's circumstances and those of yesterday. Whereas the global financial crisis has since been transformed into an opportunity for greater market-oriented reforms, previous episodes of spending restraint are also a source of justification for state indebtedness to finance capital.

REFERENCES

Alesina, A., and S. Ardagna. 1998. "Expansionary Fiscal Contractions in Europe: New Evidence." European Central Bank working paper no. 675.
Alesina, A., and R. Perotti. 1995. "Fiscal Expansions and Adjustments in OECD Countries." *Economic Policy* 21:205–48.
Alesina, A., R. Perotti, J. Tavares, Maurice Obstfeld, and Barry Eichengreen. 1998. "The Political Economy of Fiscal Adjustments." *Brookings Papers on Economic Activity* 1998 (1): 197–266. http://dx.doi.org/10.2307/2534672.
Anderson, J. 2008. "Cities Debate Privatizing Public Infrastructure." *New York Times*, 27 August. http://www.nytimes.com/2008/08/27/business/27fund.html?pagewanted=all&_r=0
Ashton, P., M. Doussard, and R. Weber. 2012. "The Financial Engineering of Infrastructure Privatization." *Journal of the American Planning Association* 78 (3): 300–12. http://dx.doi.org/10.1080/01944363.2012.715540.
Auditor General, Detroit. 2003. *Budget Analysis*. Accessed 7 January 2015. http://www.detroitmi.gov/CityCouncil/LegislativeAgencies/AuditorGeneral/BudgetAnalysis/20032004BudgetAnalysis/tabid/2784/Default.aspx.
Banting, Keith G. 1987. *The Welfare State and Canadian Federalism*. 2nd ed. Montreal and Kingston: McGill-Queen's University Press.
Block, S., and A. Maslove. 1994. "Ontario Tax Expenditures." In *Taxes as Instruments of Public Policy*, ed. A. Maslove. Toronto: University of Toronto Press.
Blyth, M. 2013a. *Austerity: The History of a Dangerous Idea*. Oxford: Oxford University Press.

– 2013b. "Power & Prejudice: The Politics of Austerity." New Left Project. 14 August. http://www.newleftproject.org/index.php/site/article_comments/power_prejudice_the_politics_of_austerity_part_1.

– 2013c. "Why Austerity Is a Dangerous Idea." *Time*, 18 April. http://ideas. time.com/2013/04/18/why-austerity-is-a-dangerous-idea/.

Broadway, R. 2006. "Intergovernmental Redistributive Transfers: Efficiency and Equity." In *Handbook of Fiscal Federalism*, ed. E. Ahmad and G. Brosio, 355–80. Cheltenham, UK: Edward Elgar.

Clarke, J., and J. Newman. 2012. "The Alchemy of Austerity." *Critical Social Policy* 32 (3): 299–319. http://dx.doi.org/10.1177/0261018312444405.

Colombini, D. 2013a. "Socially Acceptable." *P3 Bulletin*, 1 June. http://www. p3bulletin.com/features/view/1136.

– 2013b. "Water Goal." *P3 Bulletin*, 27 November. http://www.p3bulletin. com/features/view/1161.

Cormier, C. 2014. "Servicing Bondholders and Defaulting on Basic Public Services: How the Current Recession Is Leading US State and Local Governments to Forsake Social Protection for Their Residents." *Studies in Political Economy* 93 (1): 53–80. http://dx.doi.org/10.1080/19187033.2014.11 674964.

Davidson, M., and K. Ward. 2014. "'Picking Up the Pieces': Austerity Urbanism, California and Fiscal Crisis." *Cambridge Journal of Regions, Economy and Society* 7 (1): 81–97. http://dx.doi.org/10.1093/cjres/rst030.

Dellepiane, S., and N. Hardiman. 2012. "Fiscal Politics in Time: Pathways to Fiscal Consolidation, 1980–2012." UCD Geary Institute Discussion Papers. December. http://www.ucd.ie/geary/static/publications/workingpapers/gearywp201228.pdf.

Deloitte. 2004. *An Opportunity to Meet Transportation Infrastructure Needs.* Accessed 2015. http://www.deloitte.com/view/en_ca/ca/3be51060261fb11 0VgnVCM100000ba42f00aRCRD.htm.

DiNapoli, T.P. 2013. "Private Financing of Public Infrastructure: Risks and Options for New York State." June.

Doern, B.D., A.M. Maslove, and M.J. Prince. 2013. *Canadian Public Budgeting in the Age of Crises.* Montreal and Kingston: McGill-Queen's University Press.

Epstein, G. 2005. "Introduction: Financialization and the World Economy." In *Financialization and the World Economy*, ed. G. Epstein, 3–16. Cheltenham, Northampton: Edward Elgar. https://www.peri.umass.edu/media/k2/attachments/chapter1.pdf.

Giavazzi, F., and M. Pagano. 1990. "Can Severe Fiscal Contractions Be Expansionary? Tales of Two Small European Countries." National Bureau of Economic Research. http://www.nber.org/papers/w3372.

Guajardo, J., D. Leigh, and A. Pescatori. 2011. *Expansionary Austerity: New International Evidence*. IMF Working Paper, July. http://www.imf.org/external/pubs/ft/wp/2011/wp11158.pdf.

Guichard, S., M. Kennedy, E. Wurzel, and C. Andre. 2007. "What Promotes Fiscal Consolidation: OECD Country Experiences." OECD Economics Department Working Papers, no. 553, OECD Publishing. http://www.oecd-ilibrary.org/economics/what-promotes-fiscal-consolidation_180833424370;jsessionid=qpwr802st2hc.x-oecd-live-02.

Hacker, J. 2008. *The Great Risk Shift*. Oxford: Oxford University Press.

Hackworth, J. 2007. *The Neoliberal City*. Ithaca, NY: Cornell University Press.

Harder, L. 2003. "Tax Expenditures: The Social Policy of Globalization?" In *Global Turbulence: Social Activists' and State Responses to Globalization*, ed. M.G. Cohen and S. McBride, 59–71. Aldershot, UK: Ashgate.

Harvey, D. 1989. "From Managerialism to Entrepreneurialism: The Transformation in Urban Governance in Late Capitalism." *Geografiska Annaler. Series B, Human Geography* 71 (1): 3–17. http://dx.doi.org/10.2307/490503.

Hellowell, M., and V. Vicchi. 2012. "The Credit Crunch in Infrastructure Finance: Assessing the Economic Advantage of Recent Policy Actions." Paper given at the PPPs for Economic Advantage Conference, Copenhagen, 26 August.

Hoffman, D.H. 2009. *Report of Inspector General's Findings and Recommendations: An Analysis of the Lease of the City's Parking Meters*. Office of the Inspector General, City of Chicago, 2 June. http://chicagoinspectorgeneral.org/wp-content/uploads/2011/03/Parking-Meter-Report.pdf.

Houle, François. 1990. "Economic Renewal and Social Policy." In *Canadian Politics: An Introduction to the Discipline*, ed. Alain-G. Gagnon and James P. Bickerton, 424–55. Peterborough, ON: Broadview.

Kinsella, S. 2011. "Is Ireland Really the Role Model for Austerity?" UCD Geary Institute Discussion Papers. September.

Krippner, G. 2005. "The Financialization of the American Economy." *Socio-economic Review* 3 (2): 173–208. http://dx.doi.org/10.1093/SER/mwi008.

Leighland, J. 1995. "Public Infrastructure and Special Purpose Governments: Who Pays and How?" In *Building the Public City: The Politics, Governance, and Finance of Public Infrastructure*, ed. D. Perry, 139–54. Thousand Oaks, CA: Sage.

Mackenzie, H. 2009. *Bad Before, Worse Now*. Toronto: Hugh Mackenzie and Associates.

– 2013. "Canada's Infrastructure Gap: Where It Came From and Why It Will Cost so Much to Close." Alternative Federal Budget Technical

Paper. Canadian Centre for Policy Alternatives. January. https://
www.policyalternatives.ca/sites/default/files/uploads/publications/
National%20Office/2013/01/Canada%27s%20Infrastructure%20Gap_0.pdf.

McBride, S., and H. Whiteside. 2011. "Austerity for Whom?" *Socialist Studies* 7
(1–2): 42–64.

Minghine, A. 2014. *The Great Revenue Sharing Heist*. Michigan Municipal
League. http://www.mml.org/advocacy/great-revenue-sharing-heist.html.

Mirza, S. 2007. *Danger Ahead: The Coming Collapse of Canada's Municipal
Infrastructure*. Ottawa: Federation of Canadian Municipalities.

Mirza, S., and M. Haider. 2003. *The State of Infrastructure in Canada: Implications
for Infrastructure Planning and Policy*. Report prepared for Infrastructure
Canada Research and Analysis.

Murphy, T. 2008. "The Case for Public-Private Partnerships in Infrastructure."
Canadian Public Administration 51 (1): 99–126. http://dx.doi.org/10.1111/
j.1754-7121.2008.00006.x.

National Council for Public-Private Partnerships (NCPPP). 2012. *Testing
Tradition: Assessing the Added Value of Public-Private Partnerships*. Arlington,
VA: National Council for Public-Private Partnerships. http://www.ncppp.
org/wp-content/uploads/2013/03/WhitePaper2012-FinalWeb.pdf.

Newell, G., and H.W. Peng. 2008. "The Role of U.S. Infrastructure in
Investment Portfolios." *Journal of Real Estate Portfolio Management* 4 (1):
21–33.

O'Neill, P.M. 2009. "Infrastructure Investment and the Management of Risk."
In *Managing Financial Risks*, ed. G.L. Clark, A.D. Dixon, and A.H.B. Monk,
168–88. Oxford: Oxford University Press. http://dx.doi.org/10.1093/acprof
:oso/9780199557431.003.0008.

– 2013. "The Financialisation of Infrastructure: The Role of Categorisation and
Property Relations." *Cambridge Journal of Regions, Economy and Society* 6 (3):
441–54. http://dx.doi.org/10.1093/cjres/rst017.

Pagano, M.A., and D. Perry. 2008. "Financing Infrastructure in the 21st
Century City." *Public Works Management & Policy* 13 (1): 22–38. http://
dx.doi.org/10.1177/1087724X08321015.

Page, S.N., W. Ankner, C. Jones, and R. Fetterman. 2008. "The Risks and
Rewards of Private Equity in Infrastructure." *Public Works Management &
Policy* 13 (2): 100–13. http://dx.doi.org/10.1177/1087724X08326311.

Peck, J. 2012. "Austerity Urbanism." *City* 16 (6): 626–55. http://dx.doi.org/10.
1080/13604813.2012.734071.

– 2013. "Pushing Austerity: State Failure, Municipal Bankruptcy and the
Crises of Fiscal Federalism in the USA." *Cambridge Journal of Regions,
Economy and Society* 7 (1): 17–44.

Pierson, P. 2001. "Coping with Permanent Austerity: Welfare State Restructuring in Affluent Democracies." In *The New Politics of The Welfare State*, ed. P. Pierson, 410–55. Oxford: Oxford University Press. http://dx.doi.org/10.1093/0198297564.003.0014.

Posner, P.L., and M. Sommerfeld. 2013. "The Politics of Fiscal Austerity: Democracies and Hard Choices." *OECD Journal on Budgeting* 13 (1): 141–74. http://dx.doi.org/10.1787/budget-13-5k3w6lk42l33.

PPP Canada. 2009. *Annual Report 2008–2009*. http://www.p3canada.ca/~/media/english/annual-reports/files/2008-2009%20annual%20report.pdf.

P3 Bulletin. 2006. "American Dreams." 5 November. http://www.p3bulletin.com/reports/view/11.

Sagalyn, L.B. 1990. "Explaining the Improbable Local Redevelopment in the Wake of Federal Cutbacks." *Journal of the American Planning Association* 56 (4): 429–41. http://dx.doi.org/10.1080/01944369008975447.

Savage, J. 1988. *Balanced Budgets and American Politics*. Ithaca, NY: Cornell University Press.

Sbragia, A.M. 1996. *Debt Wish: Entrepreneurial Cities, U.S. Federalism, and Economic Development*. Pittsburgh: University of Pittsburgh Press.

Sclar, E. 2009. "The Political-Economics of Private Infrastructure Finance: The New Sub Prime." Paper presented to the Annual Meeting, Association of Collegiate Schools of Planning, Crystal City, VA, 1 October.

Streeck, W. 2014. *Buying Time: The Delayed Crisis of Democratic Capitalism*. London: Verso.

TD Economics. 2004. *Mind the Gap: Finding Money to Upgrade Canada's Aging Public Infrastructure*. Toronto: TD Bank Financial Group.

Thornton, E. 2007. "Road to Riches." BloombergBusinessweek, 7 May. http://www.businessweek.com/stories/2007-05-06/roads-to-riches.

Vining, A., and A.E. Boardman. 2008. "Public-Private Partnerships in Canada: Theory and Evidence." *Canadian Public Administration* 51 (1): 9–44. http://dx.doi.org/10.1111/j.1754-7121.2008.00003.x.

Waterston, L. 2012. "The Future of PPP Financing." Presentation to EPEC Private Sector Forum, Financing Future Infrastructure, 6 June. http://www.eib.org/epec/resources/presentations/psf-06062012-presentation-smbc.pdf.

Whiteside, H. 2014. "P3s and the Value for Money Illusion: Orchestrating Future Austerity?" In *Orchestrating Austerity*, ed. D. Baines and S. McBride, 162–74. Halifax: Fernwood.

Wolf, M. 2013. "Austerity in the Eurozone and the UK: Kill or Cure?" *Financial Times*, 23 May. http://blogs.ft.com/martin-wolf-exchange/2013/05/23/austerity-in-the-eurozone-and-the-uk-kill-or-cure/?

13 Austerity and Outsourcing in Britain's New Corporate State

STEPHEN WILKS

Introduction

After 2010, austerity in Britain became a central, and at times a dominant, discourse. The 2015 general election virtually revolved around debates on the scale and implications of austerity, with the three big parties (Conservative, Labour, and the Liberal-Democrats) competing over their tax and spending plans and their ability to achieve a balanced budget. Only the smaller and the nationalist parties resisted the debt reduction imperative. But austerity should not be seen simply as a driver of public policy, far less as an exercise in fiscal retrenchment, but as an expression of deeper-seated structural and institutional transformations in the United Kingdom. Austerity has been employed with great ingenuity to consolidate a transformation in the nature of the British state and to bolster the neoliberal forces that have created what I have termed the "new corporate state" (Wilks 2013, 70). The chapter reviews the impact of austerity and the rise of the public services industry as a preamble to an analysis of how companies have exploited the profitable potential of austerity. It then explores the implications of institutional change in three areas: the emergence of the new corporate state in the United Kingdom; the inadequate accountability of companies that deliver public services; and the impact on the practical operation and constitutional position of the British civil service.

The new corporate state rests on a reconfiguration of British elites since the triumph of Thatcherism in the early 1990s. This has involved a decline in the old "establishment" elites and in the central civil service and the trade unions. New elites have come to the fore, including a careerist party/political elite and a corporate elite of leading managers of large companies and financial institutions. These newly powerful elites have crafted a new political settlement that rests on market rhetoric but is structurally biased towards the interests of large corporations. The austerity discourse has been embraced within the political and corporate elites to reinforce the new settlement. In turn the contours of austerity have been defined and imposed in line with the values and principles of the new corporate state, specifically involving managerial values, market tests, tolerance of inequality, rejection of public solutions, and pursuit of a smaller state. Austerity has been employed to cut public spending by transferring governmental activities to the private sector and boosting the profitability and value of corporations. Austerity appears as a systemic force reinforcing institutional change and, in a dismal paradox, rewarding the very people who precipitated the financial crisis. This may not be a very novel argument (for an exemplary deployment, see Crouch 2011), but the chapter goes on to examine implications of the new political settlement and presents a more novel discussion of the resilience of the new corporate state, the accountability of the public services industry, and the constitutional implications of rampant outsourcing.

Austerity and Public Spending

Austerity has come to frame British governance and public life in a way that is dominant and remorseless. It grew, of course, out of the 2008 financial crisis, although counter-cyclical spending meant that it did not begin to bite into public services until 2010. It is in the nature of crises that they can shock policies and institutions into new paths, and it was not inevitable that austerity would reinforce existing trends; there was a brief moment during which social democratic alternatives were seriously visualized. But with the creation of the Coalition Government in 2010, the crisis worked perversely to intensify pro-business and pro-market policies and to undermine forces of resistance. In particular the crisis legitimized austerity and was used to justify a meta-policy of cutting public spending. In turn this legitimized and justified the resort to outsourcing and to redefinition of the role of the civil service.

Before exploring the reasons for the shift to outsourcing of public services, we should consider the contours of austerity and the dimensions of the public services industry, which was poised to shape an agenda requiring the comprehensive contracting out of public services. The origins of austerity and the dimensions of the United Kingdom's acute fiscal crisis have been extensively debated, and something of a statistical fog tends to descend. All the figures in this section are therefore drawn from the authoritative Office for Budget Responsibility (OBR) Report published in September 2014. For 2007–8 the government was already planning a deficit of 2.6 per cent of GDP. Total UK borrowing was not high by international or historical standards (see Lee chapter in this volume), but the Labour government was tolerating a structural budget deficit that allowed accusations of fiscal mismanagement to undermine their opposition to Coalition fiscal consolidation. By 2009–10 the deficit had quadrupled to reach £157 billion or 11 per cent of GDP and was still at £115 billion by 2012–13. Over the same five years public sector borrowing grew from 37 per cent of GDP to 74 per cent (Riley and Chote 2014, 2). The response from the new Coalition Government, in the June 2010 Budget, was to emphasize strict austerity, planning to eliminate the deficit by 2015. Chancellor Osborne adopted an uncompromising stance, which the Coalition consistently maintained and was perpetuated by Osborne, who continued as chancellor in the majority Conservative government after the 2015 election.

By 2014 only about 40 per cent of the budget deficit had been eliminated. Clearly the Coalition missed its target to achieve fiscal balance before the 2015 general election, but the assault on public spending continues. The 2015–16 budgets and spending plans do not anticipate eliminating the deficit until 2019–20 (see Riley and Chote 2014, 125; and IFS, 2016), so that the austerity imperative, already in its seventh year, will continue for another three years with its associated cuts in public spending and public sector pay freezes.

Expressed in terms of public spending in the 2014 plans, the pattern measured against GDP looked as in table 13.1.

As these numbers indicate, the main burden for closing the deficit falls on public spending. Receipts from taxation make only a minor contribution, mainly from a rise in the rate of VAT (Value Added Tax, a regressive sales tax). Corporation tax receipts fall over the period. The implications for spending are captured in the following quote: "With relatively small contributions from tax increases and capital spending cuts, the vast majority of the savings required to eliminate the pre-crisis deficit and to accommodate higher spending on welfare, debt interest and other … spending are projected to come from cuts in RDEL [resource departmental expenditure limits] – the day-to-day running costs of public services, primarily public sector pay and procurement" (Riley and Chote 2014, 126).

Table 13.1. Trends in Public Spending

Year	Public spending as % of GDP
2007–8	40.6
2008–9	44.1
2009–10	47.0
2010–11	44.9
2011–12	44.8
2018–19	37.8

Source: Riley and Chote (2014, 88 and 121)

The distribution of actual and planned cuts is, however, very variable. Three areas have been protected: overseas development (trivial); education (substantial) and the National Health Service (huge). The NHS is actually scheduled for growth to allow for inflation. This leaves all other expenditure programs in an extraordinarily vulnerable situation. The OBR remarked that in real terms "total RDEL spending in 2018–19 would be 22% down on 2010–11 and for the unprotected departments down 45%" (Riley and Chote 2014, 119). As I have argued elsewhere, cuts on this scale are beyond the ability of the civil service to manage without radical system change (Wilks 2010). The scale and intensity of fiscal austerity is captured by final quotes from the OBR: "From its peak in 2009–10, the improvement in the budget balance is forecast to total 11.2 percent of GDP by 2018–19. That would be one of the largest budget reductions among advanced economies in the post-war period," which "implies that by 2018–19 public services spending would fall to its lowest share of national income at least since 1948 … probably the lowest share since 1938" (Riley and Chote 2014, 119 and 128). Thus the politics of austerity translate in the United Kingdom into an onslaught on public spending and revolutionary cuts in the majority of public services.

This bleak picture has ominous implications for all public servants, and for those who depend on public services, but it may not be such bad news for private sector companies. Austerity is as much an opportunity as a threat for the private sector, and to understand why this is the case we have to appreciate that austerity policies are being implemented by a state apparatus that is in flux. The Institute for Government captures the institutional transformation: "The past 30 years have seen a dramatic shift in the way British public services are provided. Government is now rarely the sole provider of publicly-funded services. In education, employment, health – indeed, almost every area – private, public and voluntary organisations compete for the right to provide our services ... Today, roughly £1 in every £3 that government spends on public services goes to independent providers." The institute goes on to emphasize the uncertainties of this huge ideological experiment in prosaic but potentially terrifying terms: "The impact of this vast shift is, in truth, not well understood" (IfG 2013, 4).

The Public Services Industry as an Alternative Civil Service

The new providers of public services are predominantly private sector companies that have grown at a remarkable rate to form a distinct new industrial sector, known as the public services industry (PSI). The scale of this new industry was revealed in the Julius Report commissioned by the Department for Business to explore ways in which the industry could be supported. The Julius Report revealed that in 2007–8 the PSI had revenue of £79 billion; it employed over 1,200,000 people and accounted for about 6 per cent of GDP (BERR 2008, ii). Since then it has grown to about £100 billion and it has received increased attention, often for the wrong reasons. The National Audit Office (NAO) prepares reports for the independent, cross-party, Parliamentary Public Accounts Committee (PAC), which has undertaken a series of investigations into performance and value for money (NAO 2013; PAC 2014). The ability of the civil service to work with the PSI has been explored by the Parliamentary Public Administration Select Committee (PASC 2011); and the major reformist think tank, the Institute for Government, has placed study of commissioning and public-private partnerships at the centre of its research efforts (IfG 2013). These studies are responding to the government's frequently reiterated determination to downsize the civil service (and local government) by increased outsourcing. This determination was presented in the *Open Public Services* White Paper (Open Public Services and Cabinet office 2011) and has been implemented through annual iterations of the Civil Service Reform Plan, which affirms that "the Civil Service will need to do less centrally and commission more from outside" (Cabinet Office 2012, 7). Currently, therefore, the standard mode of delivering public services has become either partnership with the private sector, or outright delegation of service provision to companies, in each case managed through contractual arrangements. This revolutionary but badly understood, and barely examined transition from an "administrative state" to a "corporate state" is the central preoccupation of this chapter.

The rise of the public services industry has been charted elsewhere (Wilks 2013, 132–44). Drawing on that analysis, we can briefly review the more familiar reasons for its creation, before turning to some of the underemphasized reasons that bear more directly on the influence of austerity. It is tempting to argue that the rise of the PSI is simply an expression of the ideological shift to neoliberalism. It certainly appears as the logical extension of the ideas underpinning the New Public Management; the ideas of market disciplines, competition and private sector management that have driven reform of the civil service since the early 1990s. But an ideological explanation is deceptive in two respects. First, this is not party-political ideology. Outsourcing originated with the Thatcher governments in the late 1980s, but it became bipartisan and flourished under New Labour. It is more persuasive to see outsourcing as part of a new hegemony, part of the shift towards the market state so ably analysed by Blyth (2002). Second, outsourcing has a complex relationship with neoliberalism. Neoliberalism celebrates the market, but there has been what Crouch (2011, 49) terms a "corporate takeover of the market." Corporations have not only been able to exploit market power, their colonization of government has allowed them to design the very markets in which they operate. Neoliberalism has opened the door to what can be termed "regulatory capitalism" in which the regulations are more influenced by corporate imperatives than by the public interest, with the result that the markets are far removed from the ideal free markets of neoliberal myth. We return to this point in the concluding comments on "constitutionalizing" corporate power.

The PSI is therefore an expression of the neoliberal hegemonic shift, which also finds expression in a systematic critique of bureaucracy and disdain for the state and public service. Again, this is a familiar and depressing dimension of contemporary politics. The expressions of political dissatisfaction with the civil service and direct ministerial criticism of civil servants have become ubiquitous. Tony Blair famously referred to "scars on my back" in attempting civil service reform (1999), whilst David Cameron, in his 2011 speech to the Conservative Party conference, "announced the government's intention to take on "bureaucrats in government departments," whom he described as *"enemies of enterprise"* (PASC 2011, 12). The *Open Public Services* White Paper gave substance to that intention, alleging that "too many public services are still run according to the maxim 'the man in Whitehall really does know best'" (Open Cabinet Services and Cabinet Office 2011, 7). The PASC brought together much of this dissatisfaction with the rather world-weary thought that "the need for frequent civil service reform programmes … can be attributed to failure to consider what the civil service is for, … and what it can reasonably be expected to deliver" (PASC 2011, 10), and it called for a systematic civil service reform plan. What we have seen is the collapse of the traditional Whitehall model and the inchoate, tendentious attempts to replace it with a new model that, in the form of outsourcing and the public services industry, has been termed "the alternative civil service" (Wilks 2014b).

Rather paradoxically, the imperative to cut public spending also favours the growth of the PSI. As noted above, the austerity agenda in the United Kingdom is concentrated on massive cuts in public spending, which generate huge incentives to pursue value for money. There is no comprehensive study that establishes clearly that private provision of public services creates better value for money than public provision, but there are some clear examples of success. The received wisdom, broadly endorsed by the NAO and reformist think tanks, is that outsourcing will produce real savings, especially in simple services and where there is also a private market for services such as catering.

The familiar explanations for the growth of outsourcing and the rise of the huge public services industry therefore rest on ideology and a critique of the traditional civil service. This is combined with the view that fiscal crisis requires bold, innovative, and entrepreneurial measures that can be provided by private sector companies. What is less often considered, in popular and academic accounts, is the role of the companies themselves in shaping the dominant discourse. The public services industry is large and diverse, stretching from small care home operators to the huge global outsourcing specialists such as Serco and G4S. But the critical competitive advantage for all these companies is their ability to win government contracts. It is hardly surprising, therefore, if they make strenuous efforts to encourage government to outsource as much as possible, and to do so on terms advantageous for the companies terms. This could be visualized as "lobbying," but that is a wholly inadequate description; instead the industry's political campaign is far more systematic and effective, and the leading companies have organized to effect structural change in the institutions of the British state.

The pressures for outsourcing draw support from the City and the financial services industry. Outsourcing creates a range of substantial and lucrative profit opportunities from bond and share markets to contract finance and transactional banking. The City had, and has regained, huge economic influence through the mobilization of ideas as well as wealth. Financial services providers had already established great political influence within government and proved a valuable ally in opening doors for the PSI. A perceptive critical research group note, "Explaining why the 'politics of austerity' took this form ... [targeting the public sector] after the great crisis depends on recognising the importance of the *new* politics of the City state ... the striking development of recent decades has been the reconfiguration of the institutional mechanisms that convert ... financial muscle into influence over policy" (Erturk et al. 2011, 19). The City had become a cornerstone of the new corporate state and lent its weight to the outsourcing bandwagon.

The political campaign by the PSI has been a campaign of ideas comparable to the combination of ideas that Blyth analyses to explain the dis-embedding of liberalism in the United States (Blyth 2002). It deploys arguments about public choice theory; the failure of the state; the critical importance of competition; managerial competence, corporate efficiency, and sound finance. The ideas have been mobilized in alliance with politicians working as a politico-corporate elite, and the industry has been able to mobilize the corporate elite, including accountants, the financial services industry, and crucially, management consultants. As discussed below, the corporate elite has colonized the civil service and has moved the debate about reform of the state away from concerns about how the civil service can "deliver," to how best the civil service can "commission" the private sector. We come back to the civil service below, but first let's consider how austerity has accelerated the turn to outsourcing and has consolidated the institutional transformation to the new corporate state.

The PSI and the Exploitation of Austerity

The major PSI companies are organized into the Business Services Association, which articulates the industry's policy preferences. Since 2003 the companies have also been organized through the Public Services Strategy Board of the Confederation of British Industry (CBI). The CBI link gives them greater legitimacy and greater political purchase, since the CBI is extremely influential and has outstanding contacts at every level of government. In 2014 the Public Services Strategy Board (PSSB) included eighteen senior executives of the biggest outsourcing companies, including G4S, Serco, Atos, and Capita (the chair was Ruby McGregor-Smith, CEO of MITIE Group). As the financial crisis unfolded in 2009–10 the PSSB resumed its campaign to capture a greater share of public spending by crafting a persuasive austerity discourse.

The proposition from the PSSB was bold and unapologetic: "Our message is clear: a tight spending environment is precisely the right time to look again at how public services operate and where providers from outside the public sector can help deliver better value for money. That means promoting new models for running public services" (PSSB 2010, 2).

The seductive prospect offered by the industry was to sustain service levels whilst cutting costs quite dramatically. A 2009 budget submission suggested that moving to private sector public service providers could generate £130 billion in savings over a five-year period. The industry argued for a greater share of spending but also a changed relationship with Whitehall, which would be based on "strategic commissioning," contracts awarded to achieve "outcomes" rather than outputs, and new long-term partnerships between the civil service and outsourcing companies.

The campaign was launched in April 2010. In May came the general election, which ushered in the Conservative-dominated Coalition Government. The PSI could hardly have dreamed of a better outcome. The chancellor's stress on spending reductions was matched by the Cabinet Office's enthusiasm for outsourcing. The Cabinet Office minister, Francis Maude, proved both an outspoken critic of the civil service and a great enthusiast for engaging with the PSI. Consideration of private provision became the norm, in local government even more than at the national level, with public agencies and the NHS also ramping up their outsourcing. The outcome in a headline was "State Gripped by Biggest Wave of Outsourcing since 1980s" (*Financial Times*, 17 July 2012).

The industry maintained its siren song. A 2012 report from the PSSB drew on research conducted by Oxford Economics to establish an order of magnitude for the savings that the private sector was delivering. The consultancy identified average savings of 11 per cent, and the report set the scene: "Balancing the budget by the end of 2016–17 will require significant reductions in public spending … Central department budgets will be on average 8% below their current levels in real terms in 2014–15. The situation in local government is tough too: councils face a cut of 28% in the central government grant." What then was the answer? Obvious really: "Open up the provision of services to competition" (PSSB 2012b, 5) which means, of course, more outsourcing. In the foreword to the report, the newly appointed and robustly pro-market

director-general of the CBI observed, "This report sets out a compelling case for the government to go further and faster in opening up
public services markets. By applying a 'best provider' approach the
government could realise average efficiency savings from productivity improvement of 11% or more across billions of pounds worth of
expenditure on public services which the CBI believes could conceiv-
ably be opened up more to independent providers." Government, he
insisted, will have "to metamorphose from a direct provider to a market
manager" (John Cridland, PSSB 2012b, 4). The report put numbers on
the savings. Calculating that £278 billion in public services were capable of being delivered by the private sector meant that annual savings
of £22.6 billion could be achieved. This provided an enticing prospect
for hard-pressed ministers.

It seems that the CBI was pushing at an open door. Earlier in 2012 the
government had published its *Open Public Services* White Paper and the
Civil Service Reform Plan, both of which implemented the CBI's agenda,
but there were some ominous portents. Some drawbacks of outsourcing
had become apparent through a series of contractual failings that aroused
considerable media attention. A care home operator, Southern Cross,
went bankrupt, creating uncertainty and distress for thousands of elderly
residents whose care was funded by local government. The real drama
came with the failure of G4S to fulfil its contractual obligation to provide over 10,000 security guards for the 2012 Olympic Games. To avert
disaster, the government drafted in the army, but it was a public relations disaster for G4S, which had to pay compensation, lost contracts, and
also parted company with its CEO, Nick Buckles, who had been forced
to accept a Parliamentary Committee's contention that the episode had
been "a humiliating shambles." The PSSB responded with a policy paper
underlining the need to build trust in public services markets (PSSB
2012a), including the development of policies to deal with corporate failure. Later scandals have embraced Serco as well as G4S, both engaged
in fraudulent misrepresentation of delivery targets, but the outsourcing
locomotive was not derailed; instead, much of the blame was bizarrely
shifted to the civil service, accused of incompetent commissioning. In further rounds of civil service transformation it is envisaged that officials
will be creating markets for public services, commissioning within those
markets, and undertaking market studies. The IfG (2013, 6) visualizes this
new role as "market stewardship," and we come back to it below.

The public services industry thus emerges as an agent and ben-
eficiary of the dismantling of the state apparatus in favour of hybrid

modes of public service delivery, outsourcing, and complete privatization. These radical transformations are gradually being recognized in the academic literature and are finding their way into textbooks (for instance, Hughes 2012; Alford and O'Flynn 2012). Surprisingly though, and with some limited exceptions, such as the Green Party and the formidable former chair of the Public Accounts Committee (Margaret Hodge), there has been very little critical comment (for a further exception, see Derbyshire 2014). Yet transformations of this magnitude demand serious and critical debate. This chapter goes on to examine three areas where debate is imperative.

Austerity, the Rise of the New Corporate State (and the Decline of the Welfare State)

The transformations in the delivery of public services were underway before the recession. But whilst austerity did not create new institutions, it emerged from and reinforced the new, neoliberal-inspired political settlement. The new corporate state operates within a culture of business dominance and respect for managerialism, and it rests on a deployment of corporate power that finds expression in models of partnership working between companies and the agencies of the state. This is not a "market state" of the type outlined by Bobbitt (2012), but it is a state defined by its relationship to markets. These markets are structured by regulation created by government in dialogue with business, or often self-regulation by business itself.

Various terms have been used to capture the shifts in the nature of the state and the role of the corporations in governance. The companies have been termed "parastatals" (Derbyshire 2014, 43) engaged in "shadow government" (Stanger 2009, 13), and there is a venerable legacy of discussions of "the contract state" or the "hybrid state" (Kettl 1993; Donahue and Nye 2002). Interestingly, most of these studies are from the United States, and the direction of travel of reform implies a steady "Americanization" of the British state. This could involve the effective dismantling of the permanent civil service, the depoliticization of regulation and service delivery, and the dismantling of the welfare state. Many would argue that these trends are already well established, but the settlement is still fragile, and the new corporate state may come under challenge. It is in this context that austerity exerts its influence. It can be used as an effective weapon to divert criticism.

Criticisms of the transformations intrinsic to the new corporate state are multiple, but let's consider four. First is public concern. Polls show a consistently sceptical public attitude to the operation of public services by private companies (Wilks 2013, 144), which has been reinforced by recent contractual failures. Thus, a recent YouGov survey indicated, "The advocates of the market system have won the basic argument ... However, it is clear that there are also widespread concerns about the way government and private companies behave" (Kellner 2013, 16). Second is an increased incidence of policy failures, which seem to be arising from a combination of business overconfidence and ministerial incompetence, compounded by their refusal to take advice from a civil service that is itself suffering from poor morale. Policy failure is a rich topic that has generated a new term: *omnishambles* was applied to a series of blunders in George Osborne's 2012 budget and also to failures in managing railway franchises; the failed attempts to privatize the national forests; the collapse of private consortia modernizing the London Underground; and the breakdowns in border control and tracking of immigrants, to cite only a sample (see King and Crewe 2014).

A third area of vulnerability lies in the NHS, which is simultaneously the biggest plum for those who would expand outsourcing, and by far the most precious institution to the mass of the British public. Support for the NHS is a national religion, to criticize it is political sacrilege, and it was a key issue in the 2015 general election. And yet the NHS is already party to considerable outsourcing, estimated by the NAO to amount to £50 billion or 40 per cent of its spend (NAO 2013, 6). Current legislation in the form of the Health and Social Care Act 2012 is designed to create markets and has imposed a new competition regulator called Monitor to enforce competition. Health markets are therefore being created, but the pressures of austerity within the Service are intense, with predictions of a financial crisis across the NHS. There is a groundswell of academic, trade union, and medical concern about privatization through contracting out, and failures in NHS delivery could discredit outsourcing. Finally, a fourth source of criticism lies in the inequality debate. Clearly there is a growing academic debate, both globally and nationally, symbolized by the extraordinary attention devoted to Picketty's work (Picketty 2014). The public debate about inequality in the United Kingdom has intensified and affects outsourcing in numerous ways. There is, for instance, unequal access to public services, which is prone to increase when private sector operators become involved and market dynamics come into play. Then there is the differential effect of cuts in public services, which clearly have greater impact on the poor, the disadvantaged, and those with ill health and handicaps. This feeds into a post-recession critique of excessive remuneration, which has been popularized by, among others, work from the High Pay Centre (e.g., Wilks 2014a). This discontent about inequality has gained increasing political traction and was articulated during the general election, especially by the Green Party (although it ought to be natural territory for the Labour Party). It could explode to threaten the elite consensus underpinning the new corporate state, which is a consensus built on financial reward legitimized by wealth creation.

Austerity has been employed to provide a compelling response to criticisms and threats to the new corporate state. As a discourse or series of ideological weapons, it can be used to justify radical changes in the apparatus of the state; it gives credibility to criticism of the alleged privileges enjoyed by the public sector; it enhances promises of additional value for money from the private sector; it explains policy failures; it provides a climate of "harsh reality" to rationalize growing inequality; and, in terms of neoliberal economic policy, it provides a platform of "sound finance" on which to pursue the absolute imperative of renewed economic growth. In the early days of the Coalition, ministers were derided for asserting that "we are all in this together" (a claim made additionally ridiculous by the wealth enjoyed by the millionaires who formed a majority of the Coalition Cabinet). Nowadays the refrain is TINA, the phrase popularized by Margaret Thatcher to the effect that "there is no alternative."

This interpretation of the importance of austerity in sustaining the new political settlement appeared to find confirmation in the May 2015 general election campaign. Instead of concessions and electoral promises of more generous spending programs, TINA, dressed in the harsh colours of austerity, dominated the manifestos of the major parties. Each party remained committed to further expenditure cuts and promised a balanced budget by the end of the next Parliament. The Conservatives were most extreme, with promises to reduce taxation and to run a surplus, which means that their expenditure cuts would be swinging, estimated by the Institute for Fiscal Studies (IFS) to be a further 18 per cent, giving spending reductions to "unprotected" departments of 33 per cent between 2010 and 2011 and 2018–19. But, as the independent IFS notes, "All four parties' plans imply further austerity over the next parliament" (IFS 2015, 2–3). To a dismal extent this debate about fiscal rectitude and promises to "finish the job" featured as one of the key themes of the campaign. Indeed, the surprise victory of the Conservatives ensured that the austerity policy would be sustained and the reappointment of George Osborne as chancellor reinforced the spending cuts and the austerity narrative.

The Responsibility of the Public Services Industry

The PSI is a corporate success story. It has grown rapidly and it has avoided the impact of spending cuts by increasing its share of public spending quite dramatically. The *Financial Times* noted that "the value of government contracts handed to the private sector has doubled in four years to £20 bn, as the coalition has sought big cuts in the cost of delivering public services" (Stacey 2013). The industry includes a huge range of companies, some quite specialist, some large multinationals (often foreign owned), some mixing public and private business, and some focused almost exclusively on the public sector. Solid data are hard to come by but profit levels and share prices indicate high levels of sustained profitability. What the companies have in common is that they all operate under British company law and, for the quoted companies, under UK requirements of corporate governance.

British companies have a fiduciary duty to maximize returns for their shareholders. If the company is quoted on the London Stock Exchange, it is obliged to conform to certain requirements about its governing board and to publish details of its corporate governance and operations, including board remuneration. In practice, in a familiar feature of Anglo-American stock market capitalism, companies pursue "shareholder value," which involves short-term maximization of profits and, for quoted companies, strategy skewed to raising the share price. These strategies are congenial to the senior managers, who in practice control major quoted companies, because they enhance their huge remuneration packages and share options (the High Pay Centre put the average remuneration of a FTSE 100 CEO at £4.3 million by 2012).

The companies in the PSI are therefore driven by the same incentives that drive all corporations in the United Kingdom but their strategic goals and lack of any additional framework of accountability generates an almost visceral scepticism about their suitability for the provision of public services. This scepticism is reflected in the opinion polls referred to above, but, for the purposes of this discussion, it is interesting to speculate on whether we are seeing a qualitative change. It is possible that the structure of public services delivery has actually been transformed. In the past a powerful and resource-rich government contracted at arm's length with deferential private sector companies for a range of specific service components. Now we are reaching a position where a weak and austerity-obsessed government is operating in partnership with assertive monopoly providers of public services who are providing entire services. It is government that has become deferential. Ministers applaud private sector solutions, civil servants are cowed and out of their depth in dealing with well-resourced corporate bidders, and government itself has been colonized by the private sector (a point returned to below).

Naturally there is criticism of creeping privatization and of the failures of contracting out. The companies respond with programs of corporate social responsibility and protestations of ethical codes and caring corporate cultures. But all of these corporate initiatives are entirely voluntary, they are not regulated, they appear to have minimal impact on front-line service delivery, and they are arguably a diversion from more effective modes of accountability (see Wilks 2013, 207). There is insufficient space to review the evidence for failure, deception, and outright fraud in private sector service delivery, but we can note the following:

- There is evidence of undue influence in the winning of contracts (see Gosling 2008 and campaigns from various public sector unions; on the revolving door, see Wilks 2015).
- There is evidence that companies "game" the system to submit deceptively low bids and to exploit inadequately specified performance targets (IfG 2013, 27).
- The civil service has poor commissioning skills, and the companies have been able to negotiate favourable contracts with unanticipated (by government) profit opportunities (IfG 2013, 34; NAO 2014).
- There is an oligopoly of provision in several key service areas, which precludes real competition.
- There are examples of companies "walking away" from unprofitable contracts, requiring government to increase subsidy or to fund alternative provision (the paradox of residual service responsibility).

More recently, cases of outright fraud have soured trust in the whole outsourcing process. Two of the largest outsourcing companies, G4S and Serco, had been engaged in systematic overcharging on government contracts and were the subject of fraud investigations. They have been profusely apologetic and, along with two other companies, Capita and Atos, were investigated by the NAO and the Public Accounts Committee (see NAO 2014). Their senior board members appeared before the committee to present embarrassing pictures of contrition. The chairman of Serco referred to "the particular issues that have arisen this year that sadden me, shock me and which I am deeply sorry about" (PAC 2014, Ev7, Q43).

The PAC report on the four contractors was modest but does begin to define an agenda for reform. It had harsh words for government: "Government is clearly failing to manage performance across the board." And it defined some of the dilemmas: "The contracting out of services has led to the evolution of private-owned public monopolies, who largely, or in some cases wholly, rely on taxpayer's money for their income. The state is then constrained in finding alternatives where a big private company fails" (PAC 2014, 3).

As part of their recommendations the PAC called for more transparency from companies, including "information on corporate social responsibility, including the company's approach to taxation" (which they studiously avoid); and that the companies should be "expected to behave with the same standards of honesty, integrity and fairness that apply to the public sector itself" (PAC 2014, 7 and 11). This is an important perspective: should companies that are delivering public services, funded by public money, be operated according to a more accountable business model?

The question of suitable business models for public service delivery is a potentially important area for debate, and we can briefly consider three aspects of the agenda through the issues of voluntary change, contractual obligations, and reform of company law. For voluntary change, it is clear that companies would be willing to accept measures of greater accountability, to protect their reputations and to strengthen their ability to win contracts. They told the PAC that they would be happy to operate under principles of open book accounting (which would allow government to appraise operational performance and profitability) and would accept greater transparency. Serco even went so far as to offer a seat on the board of its UK operating company to a representative of government. As regards contractual obligations, again it would be relatively easy for government to insert standard clauses into contracts requiring companies to meet certain behavioural standards, such as paying "a living wage" or even sharing windfall profits. Such standard provisions could extend into mechanisms of accountability such as ensuring access for the NAO, securing reports from third party auditors, or requiring company managers to report to, and to appear before, parliamentary committees. Interestingly, the NAO has begun to press for personal accountability from senior corporate executives (NAO 2014, para 18).

Finally, there is the question of company law reform. If, as argued above, there has been a radical institutional transformation in the operation of the British state; if the public services industry has emerged as an "alternative civil service," then we need an equally radical transformation in the nature of the companies that undertake public functions. A whole raft of reforms are possible, some of which have been debated for decades but take on a new salience in the context of a contract state. Thus we could consider legislation to create more socially responsible corporate governance (here the German model is suggestive); we could consider imposing social obligations through stakeholder rights; and we could consider alternative partnerships or public interest legal forms through expanding the role of Community Interest Companies. One creative set of proposals has been advanced by Colin Mayer. He presents an excoriating critique of the shareholder value imperative, and asks, "Why should I trust an organization that is owned and controlled by anonymous, opportunistic, self-interested wealth seekers?" (Mayer 2013, 244). His solution is to create "trust firms," which are corporations controlled by a board of trustees who are the guardians of the corporation's values and principles. Such corporations would remain market orientated but would define and consistently pursue a set of values, which could include public service, impartiality, and fairness, the sort of values that are incorporated in the widely used "Standards of Public Life" (see Mayer 2013, 201 and 247). Such moral corporations could win the sort of trust from the public and from government that is unlikely to be earned by conventional shareholder value companies.

Constitutional Implications for the Civil Service

The reciprocal of the rise of the public services industry is, of course, the decline of the civil service. Outright privatization shifts services from government to the private sector. Outsourcing, in contrast, is a hybrid mode of service delivery that requires continuing partnership between the public and private sectors. In the new corporate state that partnership has brought a qualitative change, with the dominant partner moving from the traditional civil service to the private sector companies. This is a transition that is still plastic and ill-defined, but it involves government being unable to deliver certain services without private sector cooperation; and it also involves the wholesale delegation of policymaking. These are big arguments that deserve more extended treatment and have been explored elsewhere (Wilks 2013, 100–5). Here we can simply pick out a couple of illustrations of change before considering the constitutional implications of the new partnership in public service delivery.

For apologists the central civil service has been "modernized." An alternative view is that it has been colonized. It has been colonized by managers and managerialism. The argument is easily validated simply by examining the annual Civil Service Reform Plans. They are replete with managerial ideas and reforms. A recent plan, for instance, has the fatuous requirement that any person appointed as a permanent secretary should have taken a business school leadership course (Cabinet Office 2014). More to the point, the managerial obsession simply opens the door to business influence. Two quick examples.

First, every department in Whitehall now has a "board" modelled on the boards of plcs, which will be chaired by the minister and will have non-executive directors (NEDs) who are almost all senior executives from the private sector. The lead NED will be involved in the appointment of the permanent secretary and will have the right to recommend his or her removal in the event of under-performance. The lead NED for the Cabinet Office, and coordinator of the NED initiative, was none other than Lord John Browne, the former CEO of BP, who had an extraordinarily influential role within government. As a second example, the imposition of austerity across Whitehall was led by the Cabinet Office, by Francis Maude, the minister, and by the Efficiency and Reform Group. The permanent secretary of the Cabinet Office, also referred to as the chief operating officer (COO) of that group was initially Ian Watmore. The bulk of his career had been outside the civil service, including managing director of Accenture UK from 2000 to 2004. Watmore left the civil service in 2012 to be replaced by Stephen Kelly, former CEO of a quoted software company, Micro-Focus. In turn Mr Kelly left in 2014 to become CEO of the Sage Group. He was succeeded by John Manzoni, who took on an enlarged and spectacular role as the first "CEO of the civil service." He was not the titular head of the Civil Service (that remained Sir Jeremy Haywood, Cabinet secretary) but he was the lead executive in a number of areas including major projects and austerity. Mr Manzoni had also been recruited from the private sector. He was CEO of Talisman, the Canadian oil and gas group, but before that he was with BP and sat on its main board from 2003 to 2007. His former boss, Lord Browne, was on the appointment panel (Mason and Dudman, 2014). These two examples of business influence being injected into Whitehall at the highest level are part of a wider syndrome of managerialization of the civil service.

There is something demeaning in the way that private sector corporate governance has been introduced into Whitehall (see Wilks 2007), and something tragically appropriate about the imposition of austerity on Whitehall by leading exponents of business management. Austerity empowers managerial reform and is turning the screw very painfully on the civil service itself. In addition to pay freezes and reduced pension entitlements, cuts in civil service posts are at the centre of the austerity drive. There will be cuts of 22 per cent in staff numbers since spring 2010 when there were 490,000 civil servants. By spring 2015 there were 405,000 and the Coalition was planning to get the numbers down to 380,000 (see IfG 2014). Let's now turn to the constitutional implications of the transformation in the status and role of the civil service.

The Whitehall model may be dead in practice, but it is very much alive in constitutional convention. The mechanisms of political accountability still include an independent, impartial civil service, together with the doctrine of ministerial responsibility (the principle that the minister is responsible for the activities of her department) and the principle of departmental accountability to Parliament and parliamentary committees. These principles have become threadbare and are increasingly flouted (especially ministerial responsibility) but they have not been replaced. So where does this leave the public services industry? Four areas seem intensely problematic for the constitutional accountability of public services operated by the PSI.

First, the classic Weberian definition of the state was that it enjoyed a monopoly of legitimate violence. That has changed. The state has now delegated some deployment of violence to private sector corporations. This is familiar in private security, but it also applies to the operation of prisons, support for the police, and deportation of illegal immigrants (where controversial deaths have occurred). The legal position of private sector employees who exert violence under state contract is unclear, as is the ethical code of expectations under which they operate. This dimension of outsourcing may have affected the high levels of public unease displayed in the surveys quoted above, and it raises the question of whether exceptional safeguards should be imposed by the state when sanctioned violence against individuals is involved.

Second, the chain of democratic accountability is broken by extensive outsourcing. The principle of ministerial accountability becomes unworkable when those delivering public services are not government employees, when their work is defined in a legal contract, and when their companies have no obligation to answer to ministers or to Parliament. There must be a suspicion that this distancing of ministers (and officials) from delivery is not entirely unwelcome. For ministers a tactic of blame avoidance is congenial. The companies themselves can be blamed for service failure, and ministers can avoid embarrassment unless things go catastrophically wrong. But for processes of democratic accountability this is bad news, service delivery becomes depoliticized, and cynicism about government increases. This seems an obvious constitutional issue but it is simply not being debated. A recent House of Lords investigation into the accountability of the civil service ignored the issue entirely (House of Lords 2013), although the PASC did begin to think about some of the issues and called for "a new Haldane model" for accountability for service delivery (PASC 2011, 29).

Third, in recent years the status and responsibilities of the British civil service have been formalized with a civil service code and standards for ethical behaviour and expectation of integrity and fairness in the operation of government. Yet at the same time implementation of many services has been transferred to private sector companies, and employees who have no such framework of ethical behaviour. The PAC affirms that firms "are expected to behave with the same standards of honesty, integrity and fairness that apply to the public sector itself" (PAC 2014, 11), but there is no constitutional framework to require them to conform. At the altruistic end of the spectrum, ideals of public service that condition the behaviour of many public servants will not come into play. At the formal end of the spectrum, the legal liability of those operating services funded by the taxpayer becomes ambiguous. In all cases the ethical standards that might be thought to be relevant to the relations between a citizen and a representative of government dissolve into a strictly commercial transaction, political rights become contractual rights, citizenship dissolves into market relations, and constitutional rights evaporate.

Fourth, when outsourcing begins to apply to whole services, then delegation moves beyond "delivery" to embrace "policy." In areas such as training, transport, energy, offender management, or social housing, government is no longer able to define policy options and pursue them, it is obliged to work with non-governmental suppliers and to choose whatever policy options they are willing to cooperate with. Democratic choice becomes market feasibility, government itself is to some extent privatized. As the Institute for Government expresses this shift, "Government must urgently professionalise its approach ... embracing what we call a 'market stewardship' approach ... adjusting the rules of the game in an attempt to steer the system ... to achieve their high-level aims" (IfG 2013, 6).

As we saw above, this is exactly what the CBI wants. John Cridland exhorted government "to metamorphose from a direct provider to a market manager." For many people, and arguably all democrats, this is a deeply depressing thought, and a prospect that austerity is bringing closer. Indeed, why bother with a Constitution at all if government is simply there to manage the market?

Conclusion

Austerity in the United Kingdom has embraced fiscal consolidation and structural and institutional reform of the public sector but, as argued above, it has also been mobilized to bolster the power of the corporate elite and to consolidate the creation of the new corporate state. The commitment to austerity involved a strategy of persuasion and ideational initiatives as part of a concerted campaign waged by business associations and companies in financial services and the public services industry. It has been depressingly successful and has shifted the impact, and partially the blame, for the financial crisis from finance to the public sector. It has been manifest in the harshest program of public service reductions for at least half a century, which has involved remorseless commodification of public services and transformational reform of the British civil service.

Austerity as a principle of public life has been sustained, despite its economic illiteracy. Paul Krugman (2015) has bemoaned the delusional endorsement of austerity by British political parties, pointing out that "the doctrine that ruled the world in 2010 has more or less vanished from the scene. Except in Britain." In explanation he cites business interests: he asks, "Why does big business love austerity?" simply because "scare talk about debt and deficits is often used as a cover for a very different agenda, namely an attempt to reduce the overall size of government." Krugman's analysis seems all too accurate. Like Krugman, and like Lee (see chapter 6), this chapter sees austerity in Britain as a matter of conscious political choice. And like McBride (see chapter 8), we can also see moves to "constitutionalize" austerity through a range of institutional changes. Both the Conservative and Labour parties included in their 2015 election manifestos proposals for formal rules for "budget responsibility" whilst the forces opposing the austerity imperative have been weakened by the reduction in the capacity of the state and the growth of the public services industry. The scale and the importance of the institutional transformations that accompany the growth of the new corporate state are only gradually being appreciated.

REFERENCES

Alford, John, and Janine O'Flynn. 2012. *Rethinking Public Service Delivery: Managing with External Providers*. Basingstoke, UK: Palgrave Macmillan.
Business Enterprise and Regulatory Reform, Department of (BERR). 2008. *Public Services Industry Review, Department for Business Enterprise and Regulatory Reform*. London: BERR.
Blair, Tony. 1999. "Speech." *Guardian*, 7 July.
Blyth, Mark. 2002. *Great Transformations: Economic Ideas and Institutional Change in the Twentieth Century*. Cambridge: Cambridge University Press. http://dx.doi.org/10.1017/CBO9781139087230.
Bobbitt, Philip. 2012. *The Shield of Achilles: War, Peace and the Course of History*. London: Penguin.
Cabinet Office. 2012. *The Civil Service Reform Plan*. London: Cabinet Office.
– 2014. *Civil Service Reform Plan Progress Report*. London: Cabinet Office.
Crouch, Colin. 2011. *The Strange Non-Death of Neoliberalism*. Cambridge: Polity.
Derbyshire, Jonathan. 2014. "A Contract Too Far." *Prospect*, February, 42–4.
Donahue, John, and Joseph Nye, eds. 2002. *Market-Based Governance: Supply Side, Demand Side, Upside and Downside*. Washington, DC: Brookings Institution.
Erturk, Ismail, Julie Froud, Sukhdev Johal, Adam Leaver, Michael Moran, and Karel Williams. 2011. "City State against National Settlement: UK Economic Policy and Politics after the Financial Crisis." CRESC Working Paper 101.
Gosling, Paul. 2008. *The Rise of the "Public Services Industry."* London: UNISON.
House of Lords. 2013. *The Accountability of Civil Servants*, Sixth Report, 2012–13. London: House of Lords Constitutional Committee.
Hughes, Owen. 2012. *Public Management & Administration*. 4th ed. Houndmills, UK: Palgrave Macmillan. http://dx.doi.org/10.1007/978-1-137-00305-8.

Institute for Government (IfG). 2013. *Making Public Service Markets Work: Professionalising Government's Approach to Commissioning and Market Stewardship*. London: Institute for Government.

– 2014. "Whitehall Monitor 2014." http://www.instituteforgovernment.org. uk/our-work/whitehall-monitor.

Institute for Fiscal Studies (IFS). 2015. *Post-Election Austerity: Parties' Plans Compared*. London: Institute for Fiscal Studies.

– 2016. "Boxed In by His Own Rule, Mr Osborne Has to Pull Off a Precarious Balancing Act." News release, 8 February. http://www.ifs.org.uk/publications/8161.

Kellner, Peter. 2013. "Report: Cross-Country Attitudes to Ownership and Competition." In YouGov, *Public Opinion and the Evolving State*, 12–16. http://cdn.yougov.com/cumulus_uploads/document/aw7tbwnya9/YouGov-Cambridge_2013_Report.pdf.

Kettl, Donald. 1993. *Sharing Power: Public Governance and Private Markets*. Washington, DC: Brookings Institution.

King, Anthony, and Ivor Crewe. 2014. *The Blunders of Our Governments*. London: Oneworld.

Krugman, Paul. 2015. "The Austerity Delusion." *Guardian*, 29 April.

Mason, Rowena, and Jane Dudman. 2014. "Whitehall Accused of 'Love-in with Business' over New CEO." *Guardian*, 3 October.

Mayer, Colin. 2013. *Firm Commitment: Why the Corporation Is Failing Us and How to Restore Trust in It*. Oxford: Oxford University Press.

National Audit Office (NAO). 2013. *Memorandum on the Role of Major Contractors in the Delivery of Public Services; and the Cabinet Office's Progress in Improving How the Government Manages Its Relationship with Its Strategic Suppliers*. London: Stationery Office.

– 2014. *Transforming Government's Contract Management*. London: Stationery Office.

Open Public Services and Cabinet Office. 2011. *Open Public Services White Paper*. London: Stationery Office.

Public Account Committee (PAC). 2014. *Contracting Out Public Services to the Private Sector. Public Accounts Committee, HC777*. London: TSO.

Public Administration Select Committee (PASC). 2011. *Change in Government: The Agenda for Leadership*. Public Administration Select Committee, HC714. London: Stationery Office.

Picketty, Thomas. 2014. *Capital in the Twenty-First Century*. Harvard University Press. http://dx.doi.org/10.4159/9780674369542.

Public Services Strategy Board (PSSB). 2010. *Creative Ideas for Challenging Times: A CBI Public Services Board 2009 Campaign Review*. London: Confederation of British Industry.

– 2012a. *Licence to Operate: Winning Trust in Public Service Markets*. London: Confederation of British Industry.

– 2012b. *Open Access: Delivering Quality and Value in Our Public Services*. London: Confederation of British Industry.

Riley, John, and Robert Chote, Office for Budge Responsibility. 2014. *Crisis and Consolidation in the Public Finances*. Office for Budget Responsibility. http://budgetresponsibility.org.uk/docs/dlm_uploads/WorkingPaper7a.pdf.

Stacey, Kiran. 2013. "Public Contract Suppliers under Fire." *Financial Times*, 1 February.

Stanger, Allison. 2009. *One Nation under Contract: The Outsourcing of American Power and the Future of Foreign Policy*. New Haven, CT: Yale University Press.

Wilks, Stephen. 2007. "Boardization and Corporate Governance in the UK as a Response to Depoliticization and Failing Accountability." *Public Policy and Administration* 22 (4): 443–60.

– 2010. "Cutback Management in the United Kingdom: Challenges of Fiscal Consolidation for the Administrative System." *Korean Journal of Policy Studies* 25 (1): 85–108.

– 2013. *The Political Power of the Business Corporation*. Cheltenham, UK: Edward Elgar. http://dx.doi.org/10.4337/9781849807326.

– 2014a. *Cheques and the City*. London: High Pay Centre. http://highpaycentre.org/files/Cheques_and_the_city.pdf.

– 2014b. "The Public Service Industry: A Constitutional Blasphemy and a Democratic Perversion." LSE. http://blogs.lse.ac.uk/politicsandpolicy/the-alternative-civil-service-a-constitutional-heresy/.

– 2015. *The Revolving Door, and the Corporate Colonisation of UK Politics*. London: High Pay Centre.

14 Austerity and the Non-profit Sector: The Case of Social Impact Bonds

MEGHAN JOY AND JOHN SHIELDS

Introduction

We position the non-profit sector as a prime location to understand the societal effects of neoliberalism and austerity. Long ignored in the public policy literature, the non-profit sector has become a subtheme in policy studies as neoliberal governments have used the sector to transfer the social responsibility to care to the community, family, and individual. In particular, the non-profit sector is front and centre in the most recent austerity rhetoric in the wake of the 2008 financial crisis that blends neoliberalism and philanthropic localism, serving to reinforce and enhance the role allotted to the non-profit sector under neoliberalism. Non-profit organizations are situated as efficient and innovative service delivery agents, best equipped to deal with local social problems. The sector is made to compete, sometimes directly with for-profit entities, in a market for predefined social service contracts. The neoliberal state continues to govern from a distance through competitive procurement and a new emphasis on measured outcomes.

While there is an appeal to the collective and claims to enhance civil society by empowering local service delivery, non-profit organizations, who are the organized voice of civil society, are handcuffed. An increasingly marketized, professionalized, and bureaucratized sector acts less and less as a voice for the community and more as simply a cheap delivery arm of the state. The non-profit sector is used to responsibilize community, family, and individuals to take on a greater portion of caring work, particularly the work that serves marginalized and vulnerable individuals forgotten by the private market.

Innovations in social financing have created an opportunity for the private sector to profit from those that the market had left behind. Social Impact Bonds (SIBs) are a financial product and policy tool used to pool private investment to support social service projects with the attendant promise of a profit if the project meets outcome targets. Moreover, SIBs are being employed by the neoliberal state to reshape the social welfare mix (see Johansson, Arvidson, and Johansson 2015). SIBs open up greater space for the private sector to shape actual social policy and programing and to further marketize the delivery of social and human services provided largely through non-profit actors. In addition, those private interests funding SIBs are positioned to place program performance evaluation on purely business-oriented footings and away from public and community-based foundations.

In this chapter, we conduct a critical analysis of SIBs to understand welfare state reconfiguration and the shifting roles of the non-profit and private sectors in social provision in a context of austerity. We begin with a discussion on the impact of neoliberalism on the health and societal role of the non-profit sector. We then move to focus on SIBs as a case to explore the further marketization of the non-profit sector in an austerity context and outline the challenges and contradictions that this new policy tool poses.

Austerity, Neoliberalism, and the Non-profit Sector

The recession caused by the financial crisis of 2008 harmed the financial health of the non-profit sector within the OECD as government funding support dried up, charitable donations declined, and the need for social services expanded. A survey of the sector in Canada revealed that a quarter of non-profit organizations reported that the economic crisis put their organization at serious risk, and almost half said that the crisis made it difficult for them to fulfil their missions (Laforest 2013, 12). The situation in the United States and the United Kingdom was no better (Casey 2013; Taylor 2013). The economic crisis and the austerity response by government aggravated an already difficult financial situation and reduced the non-profit sector's capacity to respond to increased societal need.

The response of governments to the 2008 crisis in much of the OEDC was to follow the path of an austerity agenda. This was certainly the case with the national government in Canada, even though the economic downturn was milder than elsewhere (Fowler 2013, 7). The austerity response represents a continuation of neoliberal restructuring that has been evident since at least the 1980s. In fact, the adoption of austerity has been used by governments to expand and deepen this neoliberal agenda (Baines and McBride 2014). Particularly vulnerable to budget cuts and reconfiguration in this austerity period has been the state's role in social reproduction (see Cohen, this volume).

The role of the non-profit sector in advancing the neoliberal restructuring of society and in weakening the welfare state has been under-examined academically and in the public consciousness. Interestingly, while Esping-Andersen's (1990) typology of welfare states does not identify the use of the non-profit sector as a factor in diminishing the scope and scale of different welfare state regimes, it has played an important role, particularly in Anglo-American democracies (Hardill and Baines 2011, 2). The active use of non-profit organizations financed and regulated by the state to provide public social, human, and health services is a core feature of liberal Anglo-American welfare states that has been used to limit the scale and scope of social policy.

All modern welfare states, to various degrees, provide for the welfare of their citizens through a system of mixed social provision. The social mix consists of welfare provided by the state, the market, the non-profit sector, and informally through the unpaid labour of family members, particularly women. These elements of welfare provision exist in every OECD country, but their mix varies. However, attention to the importance of the mixed welfare system has been largely neglected (Powell 2007, 8–9, 2; Henriksen, Smith, and Zimmer 2015). Neoliberal restructuring, which has been given further impetus through austerity measures, has involved the rebalancing of the components of the welfare mix, with a much weaker level of public provision as a result. This has been most visible in the United Kingdom with the Coalition Government's promotion of the Big Society policy, which significantly cut public social provision with an expectation that the more profitable portion of social reproduction would be transferred to the new public service industry (see Wilks, this volume), while non-profit organizations, local government, philanthropy, volunteering, and family would care for those who cannot afford private provision. The Big Society policy also cut funding to non-profit service providers, promoting alternative sources of funding (like SIBs) and pushing the sector to become more entrepreneurial (Szreter and Ishkanian 2012, 12).

The importance of the welfare mix lies not only in the proportions allocated to the different providers, but such reconfigurations often involve shifting the operating principles of how social welfare is designed and delivered. For instance, "a transfer from state to informal (read: female) care leads to increasing gender inequality, and ignores entitlement (citizenship), as there are no 'rights' to informal care. In short, it is more than 'mere rearranging of furniture in the drawing room'" (Powell 2007, 4–5). Moreover, only an organization with the capacity of the state can "ensure that welfare benefits and services are fairly distributed to all citizens. A large role for the commercial, voluntary [/non-profit] and informal sectors is associated with [heightened] inequality" (4–5). The shift in the balance away from state-centred welfare is important, not just because it means more use of markets but also because the strategies of how welfare is provided are affected, including the turn to such things as charging for services, contracting out, the use of vouchers, and the creation of competitive markets for delivery (10, 5). Neoliberal approaches to welfare support are, of course, very much in favour of the more commercial, voluntary, and informally based measures over the more active use of the state. Neoliberalism's claim is that the state needs to shrink because of "state failure" and the highly contestable proclamation that markets, non-profit, and informal institutions and arrangements are more efficient and effective than those driven by the logic of statist approaches (5–10).

With the economic crisis of 2008, non-profits have been encouraged to take this as an opportunity to reinvent and reposition their organizations. As Casey notes. "Organizations are being exhorted to restructure, explore mergers, cut costs, intensify fundraising, strengthen communication – and simply understand better how to do more with less" (2013, 47). The state's retreat from social provision is presented as a positive development by neoliberalism, because it opens up space for non-profits to innovate and take advantage of opportunities in an area marked by abundance (McIsaac, Park, and Toupin 2013, 8–9). Neoliberalism subscribes to the position that the big state crowds out the non-profit sector. Consequently, shrinking the state allows the non-profit sector, and civil society and the family more generally, to fill the space left from state retreat. Neoliberalism casts the relationship between the state and the non-profit sector as opposing forces; for one to grow and prosper, the other must shrink and be diminished (Taylor 2013, 86). In reality, however, the relationship between the state and the non-profit sector is dynamic and symbiotic. Financial support to non-profit service providers by the state during the Keynesian period enabled the state and the non-profit sector to expand in tandem. The non-profit sector was a partner, albeit a junior one, with government charged with enlarging the social policy realm (Evans, Richmond, and Shields 2005).

Cuts to the welfare state brought on by the austerity agenda harms non-profit sector financing, causing a contraction not only of the state but of the non-profit sector as well, contrary to neoliberal assumptions (Shields 2014). Neoliberal approaches have placed the non-profit sector in a role where they become an agent that can be used to hollow out the welfare state and to marketize and diminish the public social policy sphere. Large government cuts to social programs and to funding of the non-profits that deliver them (80 to 90 per cent of such funding comes from government sources in Canada) is undermining the capacity of the sector to address growing societal needs. The social policy world is shrinking, leaving non-profit actors with diminished resources to cope with expanding needs, especially for the most disadvantaged (Baines et al. 2014).

Neoliberalism advocates for a "voluntary/non-profit policy turn" as part of an effort to shift the balance of welfare provision away from state responsibility (Milligan and Conradson 2011, 1). Such a remixing of welfare provision is also intended to recast the relationship between the state and individuals, supposedly empowering individuals to do more for themselves and become less dependent on government (see McBride and Mitrea, this volume). Neoliberalism has drawn an analogy to the customer/consumer and the difference between the market counter and the supermarket. Rather than being passive customers who wait to get goods brought to them for purchase at the store counter, in the supermarket they become empowered consumers who engender cost savings by retrieving purchasable items for themselves, which improves the shopping experience and reduces the costs of items (Hardill and Baines 2011, 158). In a parallel way, neoliberalism proposes to restructure the welfare state to make individuals and society more responsible for their own well-being. In doing so, social risk is transferred away from state responsibility and downloaded onto individuals, families, and the limited resources of local communities, including non-profits. This also means the moral sphere of the state as a place where some measure of social fairness can be achieved is reduced (Milbourne 2013, 223–4). The general idea is that an excessively generous welfare state, or as Margret Thatcher framed it, the "nanny state," has taken responsibility away from individuals and made them too soft and less able to care for themselves, resulting in an over-extended state with diminished capacity and excessive tax burdens.

Neoliberalism, in contrast, supports "the heroic, autonomous individual and their liberty to act economically and socially as they see fit" (Szreter and Ishkanian 2012, 10). The rhetoric is about empowering individuals and communities to be responsible for their own interests and support. This hyperbole "diverts attention away from government and towards the responsibility of others during a[n austerity] programme of deep cuts to the public sector" (10). If the state is to do less, then we as individuals and communities will need to do more for ourselves and others. This neoliberal discourse has come to be labelled "responsibilization" (Kelly and Caputo 2012). It involves the promotion of a "culture of personal responsibility" and a laissez-faire approach to the notion of "empowering citizens" as individuals (Butcher 2013, 180–1) and as civil society actors, but within a restrictive community sphere.

It is not just individuals who neoliberalism argues have become too dependent on government, but also many non-profit service-providing organizations (Taylor 2013, 85–6). In the case of the Big Society, Prime Minister Cameron asserted that those non-profit providers whose budgets comprised 70 per cent or more from government sources have become dependent and need to be subject to government funding cuts and the expectation that they must raise funding from other sources (Hardill and Baines 2011, 157). While other neoliberal governments, in Canada and elsewhere, have not been as explicit about non-profit reliance on government funding, they have been actively engaged in measures that have compelled non-profits to partner, seek alternative funding sources, and explore social financing (like SIBs) and social enterprise endeavours to replace state financing. The additional benefit, according to neoliberal proponents, is that it promotes non-profit funding "independence" (Bridge, Murtagh, and O'Neill 2014).

Under neoliberalism, the idea of civic engagement through individual acts of giving, volunteering, and social involvement has been strongly encouraged, but at the same time significantly narrowed. Taxes for social redistribution have been reduced, particularly for corporate investors and higher income earners, with the hopes that these elites will support the poor through philanthropy and corporate social responsibility. This leaves it up to the rich to determine which causes are worthy of support (Szreter and Ishkanian 2012, 13). Furthermore, "Philanthropy is associated with altruism towards people who are perceived as outsiders" (Hardill and Baines 2011, 6). This is an elitist "good works model," in contrast to a broad societal understanding of and commitment to addressing structures of oppression and a more organic grassroots approach involving mutualism, community self-organizing, advocacy, and agency. Neoliberalism pitches the community liberated from big government as a space that is opened up to exercise responsibility and promote opportunity, entrepreneurial innovation, and individual civic involvement; moreover, compassionate conservatism through the workings of philanthropy is claimed to foster inclusion (152).

Neoliberalism's "commitment to privatization and to embedding the values and mechanisms of the market into public services [and society more generally] will increasingly define the space occupied by volunteers and volunteering" (Rochester, Paine, and Howlett 2012, xiv) within the community sector. Volunteering is being pushed from the top down rather than being an organic community-based initiative. This is driven by "the need to fill gaps left by the shrinking state. Volunteering is seen not as a complement to state action [as it was in the Keynesian era] but as part of the mix of resources needed to replace it" (xiv). Particularly valued are professional volunteers for larger service-centred non-profit organizations and the unpaid labour of women in the home and the more informal spheres of civil society (Hardill and Baines 2011, 165). Moreover, "the expectations that volunteers and volunteer-involving organizations will be ready and able to replace the shrinking state in many areas of activity are challenging at best and unrealistic at worst" (Rochester, Paine, and Howlett 2012, xv). Neoliberalism itself has become dependent on the low-waged work of non-profit care workers and unpaid volunteers, of whom 70 per cent or more comprise women, to make up for the vacuum in social supports left by the retreating state (Hardill and Baines 2011, 147–8).

While there has been a rhetoric of neoliberal governments to turn away from the big state towards community with the framework of austerity, responsibilization and government devolution, the reality is that unless non-profit organizations adopt the goals and orientations of the government, they come to be marginalized within current policy and government support frameworks (Milbourne 2013, 19). Even with reduced government funding, non-profit service organizations remain heavily reliant on government financing, and few would survive without it. Government funding has been contract-based, performance-oriented, and strictly regulated through accountability measures and the imposition of New Public Management (NPM) governance systems (Richmond and Shields 2004). This means that local non-profit organizations often have their operating autonomy limited, and "community action is being subsumed into government purposes" (Milbourne 2013,

19). The use of contracts and performance-based contracting is part of a larger trend towards the enhanced regulation and bureaucratization of non-profits by the state (Smith 2013, 28).

The organizational environment of the non-profit sector increasingly has come to be driven to conform to the dominant culture and practices of NPM and the market. NPM's imposing of a business-oriented managerial culture has embedded ideas of control and the "right to manage" into the non-profit sector, compromising its flexibility and community-based orientation. Government funding and accountability measures represent coercive pressures to conform. Foucauldian notions of governmentality, where non-profit service providers are directed and guided along neoliberal paths of action, are very much in evidence (Milbourne 2013, 25, 34).

Rather than working in true partnership with the non-profit sector, neoliberal governments use the sector, narrowing its role to a cheap source of social services. The sector's role as a community voice has come to be negated as the culture of market-based values is imposed on non-profit providers (Evans and Shields 2014). As demonstrated in the case of austerity, "governments turn to non-governmental institutions to pick up the social deficits created by economic recession and the state's retreat from social provision responsibilities" (Joy and Shields 2013, 40). SIBs are an important innovation for helping to understand these developments.

Understanding and Locating SIBs

SIBs are a financial product used to pool capital to support social service projects and provide investors a return, depending on the project results. To engage in an SIB project, government first identifies a social policy field where it is looking to cut costs and a population group targeted for its dependency on that social policy area. This is likely in a field where there are large service providers already operating with a measurable and scalable delivery approach (Azemati et al. n.d., 26). An independent project intermediary is contracted to manage the SIB project and prepare the bond instrument, which includes establishing the desired project results, costs, savings, and the rate of return to investors (Third Sector 2011). The intermediary issues the bond to one or more private investors, who offer immediate capital to support the service project. These funds are then used by the intermediary to subcontract with one or more service agencies. Service providers receive an immediate payment to deliver programs over several years in areas such as social housing, criminal justice, education, childcare, and health care (Palandjian and Hughes 2014). If the project achieves the result targets, the government funds the intermediary to pay investors the agreed rate of return. The SIB model requires intensive and ongoing program evaluation, as results must be attributed to the project intervention, thus an independent evaluator may be hired. SIBs create a market for care and illustrate a new trend towards financialization and a greater role for the financial sector in social reproduction (see Peters, this volume).

The impetus for the increasing popularity of SIBs has been national government enthusiasm, particularly in the United Kingdom and the United States, which builds on trends towards payment-by-results in service provision (Cave 2014). SIBs were first developed by a New Zealand economist in 1988 and since 2008 have been touted by powerful foundations, think tanks, and consulting firms with privileged policy access to US and UK governments (ibid.). The national government in the United Kingdom has taken a direct role in facilitating impact investment and SIB experimentation through the Social Outcomes Fund and Centre in the UK Cabinet Office; Big Society Capital, an impact investment bank that supports project intermediaries; a social stock exchange; and a tax relief program for SIB investors (see ibid.; UK Cabinet Office 2013, 8; McHugh et al. 2013, 247–8). The world's first SIB project was introduced in the United Kingdom in 2010 as part of an austerity agenda in the field of youth criminal justice and illustrates the model in action. The UK Ministry of Justice contracted project intermediary Social Finance to obtain funds from seventeen investors and to subcontract with four non-profit organizations to deliver services to 3000 short-term male offenders to reduce recidivism in the Peterborough Prison over six years (Social Finance 2011, 7). Over a period of eight years, the investors will receive a financial return of 7.5–13 per cent, depending on the outcome per year if Peterborough has a rate of reoffending that is 7.5 per cent below that of a comparator group (Social Finance 2011, 7). However, despite interim results in Peterborough indicating a modest reduction in reconviction from 41.6 to 39.2 per cent, the Ministry of Justice cancelled the program in 2014 in favour of a wider policy shift to privatize probation services (Travis 2013; Barker 2014).

Cave (2014) suggests that the rapid adoption of SIBs in the United States after 2010 illustrates a transnational policy transfer managed by a network of powerful actors from the private and public sectors.

318 The Austerity State

President Obama's 2014 budget included close to $500 million to support the development of SIBs, an investment that encompassed $185 million to extend pilot projects across the federal government and $300 million to incentivize state and local governments to develop SIB pilots, to be administered by the Federal Treasury Department (Shah and Costa 2013; Greenblatt and Donovan n.d., 19). The most publicized SIB project is in New York City, also in the area of recidivism, which has received $10 million in funding from Goldman Sachs (Chen 2012). Canada's national government has also shown interest in developing SIBs, most recently in the area of employment, which it uploaded from the provincial governments (Curry 2013). A wide range of jurisdictions have indicated interest in SIB experimentation, though complex SIB structures have dampened a more complete expansion.

Austerity, Neoliberalism, and SIBs

Mounting interest at all levels of government in SIBs as a policy tool is a product of a post-2008 economic recession context of government austerity and a narrative that government can no longer afford costly social programs, thus other societal actors must take on responsibility to care (Arena et al. 2016). The underlying logic is that big government and its universal welfare systems are hierarchical, bureaucratic, and risk averse, and have failed to tackle the intractable social problems of vulnerable individuals. The most recent recession has brought an end to "big government," and society can no longer look to the state to solve its problems. The austerity narrative of crisis is reframed in a positive light as scarcity breeds innovation, the development of new partnerships, and opportunities to cut waste. Non-profit and private partners are supposedly freed to pick up the care deficit left by the state.

SIBs have appeal at both ends of the political spectrum, which has been fundamental to their growing popularity. The promise of support for preventive care by community-oriented non-profit organizations holds potential attraction for those politically to the left. For the political right, the use of competitive market-based mechanisms is enticing. Those at the centre of the political spectrum are likely to support trends towards partnership and network development between government, non-profit, and private sector actors.

So-called partners are not created equal in the new state-created markets for care. SIBs serve primarily to empower markets and narrow the nature of partnerships and the role of participating policy actors from the public and non-profit sectors. SIBs extend neoliberal restructuring, legitimated through the language of partnership and community building, and represent a deeply value-driven shift in the role of various societal actors to provide care.

SIBs are a continuation of earlier waves of neoliberal reform that encourage the public sector to operate more like a business, with many similarities to earlier versions of NPM and its associated focus on subsidiarity, alternative service delivery, value for money, and customer service (Joy and Shields 2013). SIBs are situated as a tool to reconcile the failures of earlier waves of neoliberal restructuring and to further push NPM-style reform in the public sector. A 2010 report by consulting firm KPMG critiques government in the United Kingdom for failing to link financial consequences to performance outcomes through its alternative service delivery mechanism, positioning a transition to SIBs as a way to reconcile this omission (Downey, Kirby, and Sherlock 2010, 6–7). The supporting rhetoric is that there has been a failure to produce adequate results through public care systems and grant-based funding to the non-profit sector because investments are not linked directly to outcomes. Project intermediaries are assigned the task of seeking out local service approaches that have outcomes that are proven to prevent costly institutional responses and that can be "scaled up." This bottom-up, program-based, and collaborative service design is framed in opposition to a hierarchical, technocratic, and siloed government-led approach to social policy.

A transition to SIBs would reform the public sector's social policy role, though in practice it is unlikely to reduce government administration and budgets (NUPGE 2014, 5–6). The bureaucracy would need to be retrained in market definition, program evaluation, and payment-by-results contracting, or these skill sets would need to be contracted out at an additional cost to government (Preston 2012, F1; Liebman 2011, 68). The KPMG report cites a complementary "divestment" of civil servants to the private and non-profit sectors as a further benefit of the SIB tool, though there is no mention of the costly legal battles that will ensue with public sector unions (Downey, Kirby, and Sherlock 2010, 13). Additional costs include the ongoing services of lawyers, accountants, and program evaluators.

SIB reliance on program evaluation presents a multitude of challenges, beginning with the acquisition of population data that are costly to retain. Evaluation experts clarify that SIB projects should be undertaken using social experimentation methods in which all participants are randomly selected and are matched with an identical control group (Fox and Albertson 2011, 404–5). More accurately attributing results requires a SIB project with a sample population size of at least 200 persons per year (Kramer 2012b). To cover these added costs and to make the transition to SIBs worthwhile, contracts should be worth at least $20 million and should thus be sizeable in scale and impact (Azemati et al. n.d., 27; Kramer 2012b). This challenges the framing that SIBs are about supporting small community-oriented projects. SIBs illustrate a valorization of economic modelling in public policy, a trend that has depoliticized questions of access and redistribution (see Evans, this volume). Measuring results remains highly problematic and politically directed. Who is selected to define a favourable outcome becomes part of the politics of measurement.

Critics warn that SIBs are a "wolf in sheep's clothing," because of the rhetoric around supporting community which serves to mask marketization (McHugh et al. 2013, 247). SIBs empower governments to create new welfare markets where private and non-profit agencies compete to deliver in highly lucrative social service sectors where there has previously been a significant public presence, such as in hospitals and prisons. Though lauded as pragmatic, the reorientation towards results shifts the focus away from which sector is delivering the service, and in effect quells the difference between the private and non-profit sectors, as they are both market actors competing for a contract (NCVO 2011). SIBs thus continue the trend of transforming non-profit organizations into efficient and innovative market actors. SIBs provide capital for non-profit organizations desperate for operating funds after decades of neoliberal restructuring that has included funding cuts, shifts to program-based and away from core funding, and heavy reporting requirements. Social finance is positioned as a saviour for the sector, as it provides experience with social ventures that will build their market reputation. SIBs thus support the most market-oriented non-profits, whereas those who resist encroaching marketization risk evisceration. Non-profits that have adapted over the last few decades to decreases in public and private funding as well as shifts away from core funding through mergers and more entrepreneurial endeavours are primed as SIB partners.

Partnerships are lauded as the saviour of public services in an austerity context. SIBs are supposed to present an alternative to service privatization because public dollars are used to maintain social service funding through partnerships (NCVO 2011). It is politically difficult to cut social services, thus SIBs provide a way to legitimate these cuts and to encourage a greater financial, policy, and delivery role for the private sector in social welfare provision. Government acts as a catalyst for new partnerships, the project intermediary "steers" the policy process, the service agencies "row," and private funders invest and profit. SIBs thus extend the neoliberal trend of alternative service delivery, as now policy design and funding are outsourced to the project intermediary and private sector respectively. The SIB partnership model is, in theory, neutral and technocratic. It is assumed that each partner will play its prescribed role, ignoring the differential political, economic, and social power of the players.

For private investors, SIBs are a particularly risky financial tool, because repayment is not guaranteed but depends on results. SIB investors are risk averse and will invest money only when there is confidence of a substantive and secure financial return. Deloitte and MaRS (2014, 9) illustrate that in the Canadian case, potential investors would prefer to receive a capital guarantee on their investment as well as a market rate of return of between 5% and 15%. While the intention is that SIBs will be supported financially by the business sector, research illustrates that philanthropic trusts are more likely to fund SIB initiatives and that government will have to take on more risk through tax credits and capital guarantees if it wants private sector investment (Azemati et al. n.d., 31; Deloitte and MaRS 2014, 8). Government still has to fund results, and this public money must be budgeted, either through borrowing or by diverting funds from other programs. Consistent with the public private partnership model brought in during the neoliberal area, it is likely that government will end up spending more money, because borrowing is based on private sector interest rates and the additional transaction costs associated with partnerships, such as the lawyers needed to draw up contracts (Kramer 2012a) (also see Whiteside, this volume).

Given the risk they are asked to assume, private investors are likely to want a say in how service projects are run and in choosing service providers. Sinclair et al. (2014, 9) clarify that this involvement in the steering process could include seats on project management tables, taking over a project that is not meeting outcome requirements, or cancelling the project by pulling funds. SIBs therefore offer private actors further access to policy design and delivery decisions in lucrative service areas. There is potential for collusion between project intermediaries and private funders, which will require public oversight and regulation (McHugh et al. 2013, 251). If a service delivery project does work and has the potential to create profit, the question is who will "own" the service approach – the public, non-profit, or private sector. There is also the possibility that secondary markets would be created in which bonds are revised and resold while government regulation lags (252) (also see Peters, this volume).

SIBs are coming to be cast as creative social investments. SIBs are about investing in vulnerable, and more importantly, costly individuals by providing them with skills to operate "successfully" in the political economy. A successful outcome is then a responsible citizen (economic contributor) who does not unfairly burden society by making demands on public institutions and programs. However, unlike the third way social investment state where it was the state investing through non-profit procurement (Jenson 2010), with SIBs the state creates the infrastructure for the private sector to invest through non-profit delivery. The private sector does not just provide charity but can, through SIBs, invest in people and save society money by producing positive social outcomes. In doing so, the private sector is able to make money on individual vulnerability. Presenting SIBs as social investment engines serves as a legitimation cover for what is actually the privatization of social welfare. The state's role is minimized and hollowed out; it is left to create the infrastructure, control, and monitoring of SIBs (though increasingly even this is contracted off to a third party), thus facilitating profit-making on social investment initiatives.

The SIB model is promoted as empowering non-profit organizations to take on a greater role in service delivery. However, SIBs require large organizations with significant scale to generate savings, and if there is not a non-profit agency of that scale in the service area, there very well might be a private sector actor interested in the project. In a bidding process, non-profit organizations are at a competitive disadvantage, compared to the private sector, because they have less access to immediate capital, human resources, and credit history to prepare a successful bid (NCVO 2011; Hayes 2012). While SIB funding is provided upfront, it remains tied to projects and there is no support to facilitate a project bid. It is also unclear whether funding can be used to support core operating costs for a service agency, as well as to develop the capacity to design outcome measures with service clients. SIB proponents rarely consider the risk that projects present to participating non-profits who do not have exclusive control over results, and a poor outcome could ruin their reputation and very survival (NCVO 2011). It remains a question as to whether non-profit partners truly have independence over service delivery design, given the powerful role of the project intermediary and private funder. SIB monitoring, or the demand for evaluation and outcome controls, is likely to be just as burdensome as pre-existing reporting requirements brought in during the neoliberal period (Sinclair et al. 2014, 5).

SIBs are designed in theory to require partnerships between multiple non-profit service providers who service different dimensions of an individual's problem. However, in an article about the challenges of SIBs for small agencies, Hayes (2012) clarifies that government often prefers to negotiate with a single larger agency than multiple smaller agencies. Larger agencies are also more likely to have a "proven" delivery approach, as they have greater capacity to conduct research and to have staff specialized in policy work, reporting, service bidding, and contract negotiation (ibid.). Smaller agencies may thus have to enhance their collaboration, using scarce resources, or merge with larger agencies (ibid.). The underlying assumption that the non-profit sector is inherently collaborative ignores the reality of competitive bidding in a neoliberal climate. Palandjian and Hughes (2014) clarify that the SIB process extends competition between potential service providers, project intermediaries, and even investors, complicating the assumption of collaboration. Furthermore, markets are secretive about sharing information on such things as service approaches, staff salaries, and projects costs, reducing potential learnings as well as transparency and accountability in public expenditure (ibid.). Sinclair et al. (2014, 10) claim that there is a dearth of evidence illustrating that the SIB tool will actually encourage innovative service approaches and increase the number of service providers. The requirement for scale could further concentrate and reduce the number of service providers, as smaller agencies meeting niche needs are less likely to bid for a SIB contract. SIBs encourage social welfare delivery by large, bureaucratic, hierarchical, and unelected private and non-profit agencies. This is especially undemocratic, because the SIB tool is likely to decrease the state's capacity to regulate and monitor projects.

SIBs represent more than a new instrument added to the government's social policy toolkit. They represent a substantive and deeply ideological policy change that Sinclair et al. (2014, 7) term a "boundary shift." SIBs chip away at entrenched ideas about the public nature of social policy, specifically public accountability and the protection of user rights, as provision is motivated by profit triggered by quantitative outcomes measures (8). The issue here is not the focus on outcomes per se, but who has the power to define a good outcome in a model where a neoliberal government, the private sector, and an unelected project intermediary have significant control. The question is whether the outcome will be defined in participation with non-profits, communities, and citizen care-users. The introduction of private actors holding the purse strings could shift the direction of accountability for social welfare to private actors rather than the needs and rights of service users and the public at large (8). The value of social services moves further away from considerations of equity and towards profit.

SIBs encourage the commodification and dehumanization of service users who, rather than having intrinsic value, become market units used as a means to profit (Sinclair et al. 2014, 9–10). SIB rhetoric puts a positive spin on this as vulnerable service users are reframed from a dependent cost burden to a business opportunity. The pressure placed on service users involved in SIB interventions is likely considerable and could enhance their vulnerability, though qualitative research on the well-being of participants has not been undertaken. Vulnerable populations could be further left behind with SIBs, as there is an incentive to focus on those service types and groups most likely to succeed (NCVO 2011). Strict results frameworks could also reduce the capacity for participating agencies to meet unpredictable community needs as they arise.

SIBs narrow the societal role of the non-profit sector, which is framed as an efficient service delivery agent rather than a meaningful policy voice that engages government in a democratic conversation about the diverse and intersecting needs of community and the values and norms that inform policy. This represents a continuation of a neoliberal trend to reduce the alternative voice of the non-profit sector, which stigmatizes this key function as "special interest" undeserving of public funds. The very structure of SIBs reduces the direct policy relationship between the non-profit sector and government as delivery agencies work with the project intermediary (NUPGE 2014, 12; Evans and Shields 2014). Furthermore, non-profit engagement with service clients may become increasingly technocratic, and the community development and empowerment component of non-profit work is potentially lost (Sinclair et al. 2014, 9). Sinclair et al. (7) also remind us of the important role played by non-profit staff in providing intimate care and supporting their clients, which is crucial to achieving socially desirable results. The competitive nature of the SIB model may enhance the precarity of non-profit staff, as the reduction of benefits and salaries could make for a more competitive bid. Hence, SIBs can be seen as a policy "innovation" emerging out of the austerity period that reinforces the neoliberal restructuring of the welfare state and the non-profit sector.

Conclusion

SIBs risk weakening the potential for government to encourage and support social innovation, because they narrow the societal role of the non-profit sector to a low-priced service delivery agent. The non-profit sector has a unique approach to service delivery, simultaneously ensuring that social policies are informed by local needs and wants. Non-profits provide a representative voice for the community to improve public policy. The local knowledge and community trust fostered through engagement and advocacy is what makes the non-profit sector innovative, and it is this function that risks disappearing when the sector becomes more bureaucratic, technocratic, market-driven, and focused only on service-oriented crisis response. Small local non-profits are especially close to their communities, and these agencies are most at risk with SIBs. SIBs represent a continuation of a neoliberal trend towards defunding and silencing small, niche, grassroots, and critical policy-oriented non-profit organizations. Social innovation requires government to respect the diversity of the sector and to expand its understanding of non-profit work. This requires stable and long-term funding that supports unique projects tailored to local needs, core administration, and community engagement and organizing.

A marketized non-profit sector is being positioned under neoliberalism to be a major player in the reconfiguration of the mixed welfare system. SIBs can deepen the non-profit marketization path and further diminish the state's role in social provision. The austerity agenda has been used to further justify the need for state fiscal restraint, promote individual and community responsibilization, and advance the value of social entrepreneurship, as in the case of SIBs. It is wishful thinking, however, to believe that at a time when the state under austerity is cutting social spending and financial support for non-profit service providers as well as downloading responsibility onto lower orders of government and communities, that complex social policy problems are going to be effectively addressed through entrepreneurial social innovations like SIBs. A failure by the state to comprehensively tackle the intersecting structures of oppression at the root of complex social problems through social reproduction risks contributing to greater economic volatility in the future (see Cohen, this volume).

REFERENCES

Arena, M., I. Bengo, M. Calderini, and V. Chiodo. 2016. "Social Impact Bonds: Blockbuster or Flash in a Pan?" *International Journal of Public Administration*, 28 January. http://dx.doi.org/10.1080/01900692.2015.1057852.

Azemati, H., M. Belinsky, R. Gillette, J. Liebman, A. Sellman, and A. Wyse. n.d. "Social Impact Bonds: Lessons Learned so Far." *Federal Reserve Bank of San Francisco Community Development Investment Review*, 23–33.

Baines, D., J. Campey, I. Cunningham, and J. Shields. 2014. "Not Profiting from Precarity: The Work of Nonprofit Service Delivery and the Creation of Precariousness." *Just Labour: A Canadian Journal of Work and Society* 22:74–93.

Baines, D., and S. McBride, eds. 2014. *Orchestrating Austerity: Impacts and Resistance*. Halifax: Fernwood.

Barker, M. 2014. "A Prisoner Rehabilitation Programme in Peterborough Seemed to Be Working: Now It's Been Cut." *Independent*, 28 April. http://www.independent.co.uk/voices/a-prisoner-rehabilitation-programme-in-peterborough-seemed-to-be-working-now-its-been-cut-9298882.html.

Bridge, S., B. Murtagh, and K. O'Neill. 2014. *Understanding the Social Economy and the Third Sector*. Houndmills, UK: Palgrave Macmillan.

Butcher, J. 2013. "The National Compact: Civilizing the Relationship between Government and the Not-for-Profit Sector in Australia." In *Government–Nonprofit Relations in Times of Recession*, ed. Rachel Laforest, 165–88. Montreal and Kingston: McGill-Queen's University Press.

Casey, J. 2013. "Impact of the Economic Crisis on the Nonprofit Sector in the United States." In *Government–Nonprofit Relations in Times of Recession*, ed. Rachel Laforest, 41–60. Montreal and Kingston: McGill-Queen's University Press.

Cave, J. 2014. "'From Concept to Execution': The Role of Policy Networks in the Transfer of Social Impact Bonds from the United Kingdom to the United States." MA thesis, University of Oxford.

Chen, D.W. 2012. "Goldman to Invest in City Jail Program, Profiting if Recidivism Falls Sharply." *New York Times*, 12 August.

Curry, B. 2013. "Tories Launch 'Social Financing' Programs to Boost Literacy and Job Skills." *Globe and Mail*, 3 October. http://www.theglobeandmail.com/news/politics/tories-launch-social-financingprograms/article14696232/.

Deloitte and MaRS Centre for Impact Investing. 2014. *Social Impact Bonds in Canada: Investor Insights*. Deloitte and MaRS.

Downey, A., P. Kirby, and N. Sherlock. 2010. *Payment for Success: How to Shift Power from Whitehall to Public Service Customers*. KPMG LLP.

Esping-Andersen, G. 1990. *The Three Worlds of Welfare Capitalism*. Cambridge: Polity.

Evans, B., T. Richmond, and J. Shields. 2005. "Structuring Neoliberal Governance: The Nonprofit Sector, Emerging New Modes of Control and the Marketization of Service Delivery." *Policy and Society* 24 (1): 73–97. http://dx.doi.org/10.1016/S1449-4035(05)70050-3.

Evans, B., and J. Shields. 2014. "Nonprofit Engagement with Provincial Policy Officials: The Case of Policy Voice in Canadian Immigrant Settlement Services." *Policy and Society* 33 (2): 117–27. http://dx.doi.org/10.1016/j.polsoc.2014.05.002.

Fowler, T. 2013. "From Crisis to Austerity: An Introduction." In *From Crisis to Austerity: Neoliberalism, Organized Labour and the Canadian State*, ed. T. Fowler, 7–21. Ottawa: Red Quill Books.

Fox, C., and K. Albertson. 2011. "Payment by Results and Social Impact Bonds in the Criminal Justice Sector: New Challenges for the Concept of Evidence-Based Policy?" *Criminology & Criminal Justice* 11 (5): 395–413. http://dx.doi.org/10.1177/1748895811415580.

Greenblatt, J., and A. Donovan. n.d. "The Promise of Pay for Success." *Community Development Investment Review*, Federal Reserve Bank of San Francisco, 19–22.

Hardill, I., and S. Baines. 2011. *Enterprising Care? Unpaid Voluntary Action in the 21st Century*. Bristol: Polity. http://dx.doi.org/10.1332/policypress/9781847427212.001.0001.

Hayes, S. 2012. "Social Impact Bonds and Small Organizations: Solution or Nemesis?" *Guardian*, 25 February. http://www.guardian.co.uk/voluntary-sector-network/2012/feb/15/social-impact-bonds-small-organisations?newsfeed=true.

Henriksen, L.S., R.S. Smith, and A. Zimmer. 2015. "Welfare Mix and Hybridity: Flexible Adjustments to Changed Environments. Introduction to the Special Issue." *Voluntas* 26 (5): 1591–600. http://dx.doi.org/10.1007/s11266-015-9622-y.

Jenson, J. 2010. "Diffusing Ideas for after Neoliberalism: The Social Investment Perspective in Europe and Latin America." *Global Social Policy* 10 (1): 59–84. http://dx.doi.org/10.1177/1468018109354813.

Johansson, H., M. Arvidson, and S. Johansson. 2015. "Welfare Mix as a Contested Terrain: Political Positions on Government–Non-Profit Relations at National and Local Levels in a Social Democratic Welfare State." *Voluntas* 26 (5): 1601–19. http://dx.doi.org/10.1007/s11266-015-9580-4.

Joy, M., and J. Shields. 2013. "Social Impact Bonds: The Next Phase of Third Sector Marketization?" *Canadian Journal of Nonprofit and Social Economy Research/Revue canadienne de recherche sur les OBSL et l'économie sociale* 4 (2): 39–55.

Kelly, K., and T. Caputo. 2012. *Community: A Contemporary Analysis of Policies, Programs, and Practices*. Toronto: University of Toronto Press.

Kramer, S. 2012a. "Social Impact Bonds: Approach with Caution (Part One)." SocialFinance.ca. http://socialfinance.ca/2012/11/22/social-impact-bonds-approach-with-caution-part-one/.
– 2012b. "Social Impact Bonds: Approach with Caution (Part Two)." SocialFinance.ca. http://socialfinance.ca/2012/11/23/social-impact-bonds-approach-with-caution-part-two/.
Laforest, R. 2013. "Muddling Through Government-Nonprofit Relations in Canada." In *Government–Nonprofit Relations in Times of Recession*, ed. Rachel Laforest, 9–17. Montreal and Kingston: McGill-Queen's University Press.
Liebman, J.B. 2011. "Testing Pay-for-Success Bonds." *Public Management* 40 (3): 66–8.
McHugh, N., S. Sinclair, M. Roy, L. Huckfield, and C. Donaldson. 2013. "Social Impact Bonds: A Wolf in Sheep's Clothing?" *Journal of Poverty and Social Justice: Research, Policy, Practice* 21 (3): 247–57. http://dx.doi.org/10.1332/20 4674313X13812372137921.
McIsaac, E., S. Park, and L. Toupin. 2013. *Human Capital Renewal in the Nonprofit Sector: Framing the Strategy.* Toronto: Mowat.
Milbourne, L. 2013. *Voluntary Sector in Transition: Hard Times or New Opportunities?* Bristol: Polity. http://dx.doi.org/10.1332/policypress/9781847427236.001.0001.
Milligan, C., and D. Conradson. 2011. "Contemporary Landscapes of Welfare: The 'Voluntary' Turn?" In *Landscapes of Voluntarism: New Spaces of Health, Welfare and Governance*, ed. Christine Milligan and David Conradson, 1–14. Bristol: Polity.
National Council for Voluntary Organizations (NCVO). 2011. "Payment by Results." Discussion paper.
National Union of Public and General Employees. 2014. *Privatization by Stealth: The Truth about Social Impact Bonds.* NUPGE.
Palandjian, T., and J. Hughes. 2014. "A Strong Field Framework for SIBs." *Stanford Social Innovation Review*, 2 July. https://ssir.org/articles/entry/a_strong_field_framework_for_sibs.
Powell, M. 2007. "The Mixed Economy of Welfare and the Social Division of Welfare." In *Understanding the Mixed Economy of Welfare*, ed. Martin Powell, 1–21. Bristol, UK: Polity.
Preston, C. 2012. "Getting Back More Than a Warm Feeling." *New York Times*, 9 November.
Richmond, T., and J. Shields. 2004. "NGO Restructuring: Constraints and Consequences." *Canadian Review of Social Policy* 53:53–67.
Rochester, C., A.E. Paine, and S. Howlett. 2012. *Volunteering and Society in the 21st Century.* New York: Palgrave Macmillan.

Shah, S., and K. Costa. 2013. "White House Budget Drives Pay for Success and Social Impact Bonds Forward." Centre for American Progress. http://www. americanprogress.org/issues/economy/news/2013/04/23/61163/white-house-budget-drives-pay-for-success-and-social-impact-bonds-forward/.

Shields, J. 2014. "Constructing and 'Liberating' Temporariness in the Canadian Nonprofit Sector: Neoliberalism and Nonprofit Service Providers." In *Liberating Temporariness? Migration, Work and Citizenship in an Age of Insecurity*, ed. Robert Latham, Valerie Preston, and Leah Vosko, 255–81. Montreal and Kingston: McGill-Queen's University Press.

Sinclair, S., N. McHugh, L. Huckfield, M. Roy, and C. Donaldson. 2014. "Social Impact Bonds: Shifting the Boundaries of Citizenship." *Social Policy Review 26: Analysis and Debate in Social Policy.* http://dx.doi.org/10.1332/policypress/9781447315568.003.0007.

Smith, S.R. 2013. "The New Reality of the Government–Nonprofit Relationship in the United States." In *Government–Nonprofit Relations in Times of Recession*, ed. Rachel Laforest, 19–40. Montreal and Kingston: McGill-Queen's University Press.

Social Finance. 2011. *Reducing Reoffending among Short Sentenced Male Offenders from Peterborough Prison.* London: Social Finance.

Szreter, S., and A. Ishkanian. 2012. "Introduction: What Is Big Society? Contemporary Social Policy in a Historical and Comparative Perspective." In *The Big Society Debate: A New Agenda for Social Welfare?* ed. Armine Iskanian and Simon Szreter, 1–24. Cheltenham, UK: Edward Elgar. http://dx.doi.org/10.4337/9781781002087.00007.

Taylor, M. 2013. "England's Big Society: Can the Voluntary Sector Manage without the State?" In *Government–Nonprofit Relations in Times of Recession*, ed. Rachel Laforest, 79–95. Montreal and Kingston: McGill-Queen's University Press.

Third Sector. 2011. "Analysis: Can Social Impact Bonds Help to Create a Better Society?" Third Sector, 1 November. http://www.thirdsector.co.uk/analysis-social-impact-bonds-help-create-better-society/finance/article/1101352.

Travis, A. 2013. "Pilot Schemes to Cut Reoffending Show Mixed Results." *Guardian*, 13 June. http://www.theguardian.com/society/2013/jun/13/pilot-schemes-reoffending-results.

United Kingdom Cabinet Office. 2013, May. *Achieving Social Impact at Scale: Case Studies of Seven Pioneering Co-mingling Social Investment Funds.* London: Cabinet Office.

15 Conclusion

STEPHEN MCBRIDE AND BRYAN M. EVANS

This book has dealt with the resilience of neoliberalism in the face of a deep and prolonged crisis for which it bears the primary responsibility. Austerity has played a crucial role in consolidating and even re-energizing neoliberalism. The staying power of an ideology and capital accumulation strategy that produced such a crisis that, in its early stages at least, threatened to bring down the entire capitalist system, is on the face of it surprising. Most of the contributors to the book make some reference to this puzzle and pay some attention to what might explain neoliberalism's survival as a guide to action for policymakers and as a set of norms that, with some exceptions, has not been seriously challenged in the political process.

The depth of the ongoing financial and economic crisis that started in 2007/8 cannot be doubted. However, so far it has failed to trigger a crisis of the hegemonic ideology or of the institutions and policies that have inflicted austerity on populations that had no part in creating the crisis. In this concluding chapter we briefly review a number of interpretations or explanations for this phenomenon.

The crisis itself was endogenous to the neoliberal economic model and system of governance in place for several decades since the demise of the Keynesian era. It was not the result of outside pressures. Nor was it the result of social conflict in which well-organized adversaries of the system were able to undermine it and create a crisis. Forces with such capacity did not exist in the neoliberal period prior to the crisis. Labour had weakened as an organizational force. And the political arm of the labour movement had either disappeared or become marginalized, as with the communist parties of Western Europe, or had been thoroughly neoliberalized and integrated into the system of rule, as with most social democratic parties. Indeed, the ideological and policy makeover of the "old" Left, both communist and social democratic, in the pre-2007 crisis years, left it incapable of effectively responding to the depth of the crisis once it arrived. The largest Western European communist parties, those of France and Italy, were by the mid-1980s in serious decline. The Italian communist party, which at its height in the mid-1970s boasted two million members and could attract one-third of the vote, disappeared entirely into the fold of the ideologically ambiguous Democratic Party. Similarly, the French communist party, once capable of attracting a reliable one-fifth of the electorate, now struggled to win 4–6 per cent of the popular vote prior to joining the Left Front. And for social democrats, as governing parties in many countries, whether they held a clear single party majority, as in the United Kingdom, Spain, and Portugal, or were senior or junior members in coalition governments, their nearly universal embrace of neoliberalism in the guise of Third Way policy and the adoption of labour market flexibilization policies and privatization alienated large swathes of their working-class electorate. When the crisis emerged, social democrats simply did not know how to respond differently from governments of the centre-Right. The pre-crisis decline in social democrat vote shares turned into a complete implosion of their electoral fortunes, in several cases, notably Ireland, Greece, and the Netherlands. In many other instances, including Sweden, Finland, Germany, Spain, Austria, Denmark, and France, these parties have seen their electoral base fragment to the nationalist Right and radical Left, thus leaving them in electoral quagmires and being forced into "grand coalitions" with parties of the centre-Right.

One result was that in the aftermath of the crisis, although alternative ideas of what to do about it were in good supply, none of them was connected to a social or organizational base capable of challenging the status quo. Established elites enjoyed a significant advantage in defining the crisis and how to respond to it.

Even so, immediately after the financial crash it did seem possible that it would spread from the sphere of the economy into the realm of ideology and politics. This was reflected in early talk of the return to Keynesianism as governments engaged in stimulus spending, and takeovers and bailouts of industries and financial institutions in order to avert a complete economic collapse. To some degree fiscal measures, and monetary ones such as quantitative easing aimed at stimulating the economy, did represent a policy departure. But in most cases the fiscal measures, except for tax cuts in some cases, proved temporary and were replaced by fiscal consolidation in which spending cuts loomed large as a means to reduce government deficits and debt. These debts had been incurred largely by bailing out financial interests and as a result of the recession that the crisis caused. Monetary policies such as quantitative easing lasted longer in some jurisdictions. But the nature of that instrument, essentially placing public money into the hands of private banks in the hopes that through their lending to investors, benefits from investment would eventually trickle down and have a stimulative effect, seems a curious method if the aim were really Keynesian-style employment creation. Rather, as several contributors point out, it seems a measure designed to rescue finance from the consequences of its own actions, and austerity is then demanded to ensure that the public debt created by taking on bad debts from the private sector can be serviced. It carries the danger that instead of stimulating the real economy it will create asset price inflation and bubbles in the way that preceded the economic collapse in 2007.

Accompanying these measures are ones of structural reform of the public sector and further flexibilization of the labour market. Such measures not only target constituencies that had nothing to do with causing the crisis but also replicate long-standing neoliberal assaults on the state and on labour. And as noted above, social democrats in government became associated with these efforts in many cases. For all of these reasons the contributions to the book have taken the view that neoliberal restoration by way of austerity has been the ideological and political outcome of the crisis, at least to date.

In looking at the intractability of neoliberalism and austerity, a number of lines of interpretation or explanation are developed in different parts of the book. They are outlined here as subjects for further research, or at least research that is not fully developed here, but that is fruitful to explore.

Ideas and Institutions

It is well documented that austerity is an old and familiar idea towards which elites quickly gravitate in times of trouble. Blyth (2013, 98–9) gives the most coherent account in which elite concerns about the state are depicted as part of liberalism from its very beginning. The state was necessary for the development and protection of the capitalist system, but as it became more open to democratic pressures (Macpherson 1965) it potentially represented a threat to it. Austerity addresses concerns about the state by imposing limits on its actions, through fiscally constraining it in the name of balanced budgets, and especially on its capacity to raise debt to finance its activities. Moreover, according to Blyth (2013, 115) the general narrative of austerity speaks to "parsimony, frugality, morality, and a pathological fear of the consequences of government debt [that] lie deep within early liberalism's fossil record from its very inception." This may be an overstatement. Obviously elements of capital have been willing, over the years, to own public debt through lending to governments. The real issue is whether the state has the capacity and willingness to service its debt (Streek 2014, 76–8), and how prioritizing this might be guaranteed.

For several decades neoliberal political parties and associated interests have prevailed in the battle of ideas on these points. The efforts of well-funded private sector think tanks and an associated reduction in the state's independent policy analysis and development capacity have been central to this process. However, especially in times of crisis, there is no guarantee that such predominance in ideas, and at the polls, will continue. The ideas of austerity therefore need to be bolstered by institutions that render them an automatic response to fiscal imbalances, and this has led to intensified efforts to institutionalize or constitutionalize core principles, even as the intellectual case for austerity has been weakened, and culpability of neoliberalism for the crisis became discernible.

Promoters of austerity emphasize that government debt and deficits undermine investor confidence and that, as a result, investment declines, leading to recession. Getting fiscal affairs back into balance and instigating a downward trend in the public debt to GDP ratio restores investor confidence. Investment follows, leading to economic growth and job creation. In this scenario, the crisis is caused by a bloated public sector financed by debt, and the solution – fiscal consolidation – lies in getting it under control, through austerity measures. Several of the contributions in the book demonstrate that the "austerian" analysis is entirely ahistorical, ignores the deeper roots of the crisis, and really rests upon a triumph of discourse that consists of shifting the blame for the crisis from the reckless behaviour of an under-regulated private sector to public or sovereign debt, for which the public authorities are responsible. In fact, as Ian Gough (2011, 53–8) has pointed out, all the drivers of increased post-crisis public debt – costs of saving the banking and financial system, costs of the fiscal stimulus necessary to avert mass unemployment, increased social spending to offset the results of the recession, and the impact of the recession on tax revenues – are the result of a crisis triggered by the private sector.

Given its inaccurate account of the crisis, it is unsurprising that states following austerity policies have generally not performed well. Blyth (2013) painstakingly reviews the evidence. Typically, austerity does not lead to better fiscal health, because public spending cuts increase unemployment, which places yet more fiscal pressure on government programs. Nor does austerity unleash economic growth. Polychroniou (2014) points out that all the European countries under supervision of the Troika (the IMF, European Commission, and European Central Bank) experienced deterioration in employment levels and debt ratios as a result of imposed austerity policies (see also Greer 2014).

As a result, the intellectual case for austerity lacks credibility. Widely cited studies sought to demonstrate that once the public debt to GDP ratio exceeded 90 per cent of GDP, growth would decline rapidly (Reinhart and Rogoff 2010a, 2010b). But recalculations of their data showed no such effect (Herndon, Ash and Pollin 2013). Similarly, the case for "expansionary fiscal contraction" has been effectively debunked (Guajardo, Leigh, and Pescatori 2011; Blyth 2013). Heterodox economists (Quiggin 2010; Stanford 2008) had long criticized the claims of orthodox economists about the impact of austerity. They have been joined by eminent mainstream figures (Krugman 2013; Stiglitz 2011). From time to time austerity proponents such as the IMF have acknowledged the settings of austerity policies are unhelpful to economic growth – too much austerity, too fast, based on miscalculations of the multiplier effect of spending cuts (Blanchard and Leigh 2013; Blanchard 2012). Still, notwithstanding its empirical record and the shallowness of its theoretical foundation, austerity remains ensconced as the crisis policy of choice and is a candidate for constitutionalization and hence removal from effective debate. Clearly this does not involve the constitutionalization of "best practices" but rather of vested interests.

Some make the argument that these are the interests of finance capital (Konzelmann 2012). Thus the imposition of draconian austerity measures by the Troika on the peripheral countries of Europe is linked to the need to protect the Eurozone's integrity as well as that of the private bankers exposed to both public and private debt. Others emphasize the more general interests of capital rather than those of a specific sector.

Wolfgang Streek (2014, 79–86) has developed the idea that states are increasingly accountable to two constituencies or "peoples," often with divergent interests. These are the *Staatsvolk* (the nationally based general citizenry), and the *marktvolk* (investors with global interests who are the state's creditors). The emergence of finance "marks a new stage in the relationship between capitalism and democracy, in which capital exercises its political influence not only indirectly (by investing or not investing in national economies) but also directly (by financing or not financing the state itself)" (Streek 2014, 84). Austerity can then be viewed as functional for these interests because it involves fiscal rectitude, affecting the general citizenry, and, through balanced budgets and restraining public debt to manageable levels, builds the confidence of financial creditors that their interests will be prioritized by the state.

A complementary view is that austerity may benefit one or other fraction of capital in a particular context, but the common resort to it across time and place, and the desire to render it an automatic, normal, and constitutionalized response to economic crises, and perhaps a governing principle at all times, is because it is in the general interests of capital.

Viewed in class terms, the unemployment that results from austerity, the declining social wage, reduced public sector, structural reform of the labour market, and heightened insecurity with which working-class individuals are confronted all weaken labour – a potential threat to the interests of capital. Similarly, limits on budget deficits and debt curb any interventionist proclivities that may exist among states, themselves a potential limit on capital's freedom to operate in accordance with its own interests. In terms of capital's general interests, austerity policies are political stabilizers that may defuse challenges to its hegemony that might emerge, either from labour or from the state. Of course, as national election outcomes in 2015 and 2016 in Greece, Spain, Portugal, and Ireland, and the altogether unlikely ascent of Jeremy Corbyn and Bernie Sanders suggest, the austerian state can reanimate social and political forces, of the Left, which challenge four decades of neoliberal restructuring.

REFERENCES

Blanchard, Olivier. 2012. "Driving the Global Economy with the Brakes On." iMF Direct, 24 January. http://blog-imfdirect.imf.org/2012/01/24/driving-the-global-economy-with-the-brakes-on/.

Blanchard, Olivier, and Daniel Leigh. 2013. *Growth Forecast Errors and Fiscal Multipliers*. IMF Working Paper no. 1. http://dx.doi.org/10.5089/9781475576443.001.

Blyth, M. 2013. *Austerity: The History of a Dangerous Idea*. Oxford: Oxford University Press.

Gough, I. 2011. "From Financial Crisis to Fiscal Crisis." In *Social Policy in Challenging Times: Economic Crisis and Welfare Systems*, ed. K. Farnsworth and Z. Irving, 49–64. Bristol: Policy. http://dx.doi.org/10.1332/policypress/9781847428288.003.0003.

Greer, Scott. 2014. "Structural Adjustment Comes to Europe: Lessons for the Eurozone from the Conditionality Debates." *Global Social Policy* 14 (1): 51–71. http://dx.doi.org/10.1177/1468018113511473.

Guajardo, J., D. Leigh, and A. Pescatori. 2011. *Expansionary Austerity: New International Evidence*. IMF Working Paper. http://www.imf.org/external/pubs/ft/wp/2011/wp11158.pdf.

Herndon, Thomas, Michael Ash, and Robert Pollin. 2013. *Does High Public Debt Consistently Stifle Economic Growth: A Critique of Reinhart and Rogoff*. Working Paper 322. Amherst: University of Massachusetts, Political Economy Research Institute.

Konzelmann, Suzanne. 2012. *The Economics of Austerity*. Working Paper 434. Cambridge: Centre for Business Research, University of Cambridge.

Krugman, Paul. 2013. *End This Depression Now!* New York: W.W. Norton.

Macpherson, C.B. 1965. *The Real World of Democracy*. Toronto: CBC Publications.

Polychroniou, C.J. 2014. "The Greek 'Success Story' of a Crushing Economy and a Failed State." Truthout, 19 January. http://www.truth-out.org/news/item/21265-the-greek-success-story-of-a-crushing-economy-and-a-failed-state.

Quiggin, John. 2010. *Zombie Economics: How Dead Ideas Still Walk among Us*. Princeton: Princeton University Press.

Reinhart, C.M., and K.S. Rogoff. 2010a. "Growth in a Time of Debt." *American Economic Review* 100 (May): 573–8.

– 2010b. *Growth in a Time of Debt*. Working Paper 15639, National Bureau of Economic Research. http://dx.doi.org/10.3386/w15639.

Stanford, Jim. 2008. *Economics for Everyone*. Halifax: Fernwood.

Stiglitz, Joseph E. 2011. "Rethinking Macroeconomics: What Went Wrong and How to Fix It." *Global Policy* 2 (2): 165–75. http://dx.doi.org/10.1111/j.1758-5899.2011.00095.x.

Streek, Wolfgang. 2014. *Buying Time: The Delayed Crisis of Democratic Capitalism*. London: Verso.

Contributors

Marjorie Griffin Cohen is an economist and professor emerita of Political Science and Gender, Sexuality and Women's Studies at Simon Fraser University. She has written extensively on political economy and public policy, with special emphasis on the Canadian economy, women, labour, electricity deregulation, energy, climate change and labour, and international trade agreements. Her most recent books are *Climate Change and Gender in Rich Countries: Work, Public Policy and Action* (2017) and *Public Policy for Women* (2009).

Bryan M. Evans is a professor in the Department of Politics and Public Administration at Ryerson University. His research interests focus on the political and public administrative impact of neoliberalization and the political economy of Canada's provinces. Recent publications include "Alternatives to the Low-Waged Economy: Living Wage Movements in Canada and the United States," *Austerity, Urbanism, and the Social Economy – Alternate Routes: A Journal of Critical Social Research* 28 (2017); and "Policy Dialogue and Engagement between Non-Government Organizations and Government: A Survey of Processes and Instruments of Canadian Policy Workers" (with Adam Wellstead), in *Policy Work in Canada*, edited by Michael Howlett, Adam Wellstead, and Jonathan Craft (University of Toronto Press, 2017).

John Hogan is a research fellow in the College of Business, Dublin Institute of Technology, and chair of the Comparative Public Policy Section of the Mid-west Political Science Association. He researches public policy, lobbying regulations, and elite formation. He has worked with various governments on regulating lobbying. He is published widely and is co-editor, with Michael Howlett, of *Policy Paradigms in Theory and Practice*.

Meghan Joy is an assistant professor in the Department of Political Science at Concordia University. Her recent publications include *Toronto's Governance Crisis: A Global City under Pressure* (with Ronald K. Vogel) and *Social Impact Bonds: The Next Phase of Third Sector Marketization?* (with John Shields).

Simon Lee is senior lecturer in politics at the School of Law and Politics, University of Hull. He is the author of *The State of England: The Nation We're In* (forthcoming), and co-editor (with Matt Beech) of *The Conservative-Liberal Coalition: Examining the Cameron-Clegg Government* (2015).

Stephen McBride is professor of political science and Canada Research Chair in Public Policy and Globalization at McMaster University, where he is also a member of the Institute of Globalization and the Human Condition and an associate member of the School of Labour Studies. Recent publications include *After '08: Social Policy and the Global Financial Crisis* (co-edited with R. Mahon and G. Boychuk).

Sorin Mitrea is a comparative public policy PhD candidate at McMaster University. His research explores how the cognitive elements of policy interact with their material effects to shape the behaviour and subjectivity of workers. He approaches cognition at the intersection of political economy and labour market policy in Canada. His most recent publication is *ASEAN at 50: The Global Political Economy's Contribution to Durability* (2017), with Richard Stubbs.

Brendan K. O'Rourke works at the Dublin Institute of Technology, where he focuses on learning in the area of discourses of the economy, in particular examining narratives of neoliberalism, enterprise, and economists' communication with non-experts. He has been published in journals such the *Journal of Multicultural Discourses*, *Politics*, and *On the Horizon*.

John Peters is an associate professor of labour studies at Laurentian University, Sudbury, Canada. He is the author of *Boom, Bust, and Crisis: Labour, Corporate Power, and Politics in Canada* (2012).

Dieter Plehwe is a scientist and senior fellow, WZB Berlin Social Science Center, Department of Inequality and Social Policy. He has recently co-edited *Liberalism and the Welfare State: Economists and Arguments for the Welfare State* (2017). He also serves on the editorial team of *Critical Policy Studies*.

John Shields is a professor in the Department of Politics and Public Administration at Ryerson University. His recent publications include *Immigrant Experiences in North America: Understanding Settlement and Integration* (2015), edited with Harald Bauder, and he was a core researcher and author of *The Precarity Penalty: The Impact of Employment Precarity on Individuals, Households and Communities – and What to Do about It* (2015).

Gary Teeple, professor of sociology, teaches in the Department of Sociology and Anthropology at Simon Fraser University, and is former director of the Labour Studies Program. His publications include *Relations of Global Power: Neo-liberal Order and Disorder* (2011) (co-edited with S. McBride); *The Riddle of Human Rights* (2004); *Globalization and the Decline of Social Reform* (1995/2000); *Marx's Critique of Politics, 1842–47* (1984); and (editor) *Capitalism and the National Question in Canada* (1972).

Heather Whiteside is assistant professor of political science at the University of Waterloo and fellow at the Balsillie School of International Affairs. Her research and publications centre on the political economy of privatization, financialization, and fiscal austerity. She has published articles in journals such as *Economic Geography, Studies in Political Economy*, and *Health Sociology Review*, and her books include *About Canada: Public-Private Partnerships* (2016), and *Purchase for Profit: Public-Private Partnerships and Canada's Public Health Care System* (2015).

Stephen Wilks is professor of politics, University of Exeter, United Kingdom. Among his many publications is *The Political Power of the Business Corporation* (2013).

Richard Woodward is senior lecturer in the School of Strategy and Leadership at Coventry University. His research is concerned with international organizations (especially the OECD), tax havens, and offshore financial centres. He is author of *The Organisation for Economic Co-operation and Development* (2009) and (with Michael Davies) *International Organisations: A Companion* (2014).